Day by Day with Jesus

Day by Day with Jesus

with

by

JESUS

365 Meditations on the Gospels

John Killinger

DAY BY DAY WITH JESUS

Copyright © 1994 by Abingdon Press

This book is printed on recycled, acid-free paper.

Library of Congress Cataloging-in-Publication Data

Killinger, John.
   Day by day with Jesus/John Killinger.—[New ed., rev. and enl.]
     p.   cm.
   Rev. and enl. ed. of: A devotional guide to the Gospels. 1984.
   ISBN 0-687-12186-8 (pbk.: alk. paper)
   1. Bible. N.T. Gospels—Meditations.   2. Devotional calendars.
I. Killinger, John.   Devotional guide to the Gospels.   II. Title:
Day by day with Jesus.
BS2555.4.K54   1994
226'.06—dc20
                                   93-44082
                                      CIP

94 95 96 97 98 99 00 01 02 03—10 9 8 7 6 5 4 3 2 1

MANUFACTURED IN THE UNITED STATES OF AMERICA

This book is affectionately dedicated to
RALPH LANGLEY
churchman, preacher, and wonderful friend,
whose enthusiasm for its publication
has made the work doubly worthwhile.

INTRODUCTION

A FEW YEARS AGO, I asked a group of people, all college graduates, to name the most influential books or documents ever written. After some discussion, they produced the following list: The Code of Hammurabi, the Bible, the *Dialogues* of Plato, the Bhagavad-Gita, the Koran, the *Analects* of Confucius, Calvin's *Institutes,* the Book of Common Prayer, Darwin's *Origin of the Species,* and Karl Marx's *Das Kapital.* Then, asked to select from this list the most important book of all, they voted unanimously for the Bible—despite the fact that one of them was a Buddhist and two claimed to be agnostic.

If the Bible is the most important book ever written, then the four Gospels at the beginning of the New Testament are surely the most significant and influential part of the Bible, for in them the biblical story reaches its natural climax, fulfilling the plans and promises of God. The Gospel writers, sensitive to the themes and issues of the Old Testament period, gathered them up and wove them together as the adoring story of the long-awaited Messiah. The epistles, important as they are, could not have come into being without the events and teachings recorded in the Gospels.

Within the pages of the Gospels, Christ comes alive. They are the narratives, the tableaux, the stories of his earthly existence. They contain almost everything we know of his sayings, the way he thought, his manner of being in the world. The faith of the early Christians, and the entire history of the church in all the ages, would be unimaginable apart from the information chronicled in them.

Now, almost twenty centuries after the birth of Christ, we may respond to the Gospels by reading them in one of two ways, historically or devotionally.

Of the thousands of books about the Gospels, most are of the historical-critical variety. They examine everything in the Gospels with an eye to discovering its probable origins and its relation to other manuscripts, themes, and philosophies in the ancient world. They usually attempt to remain dispassionate and uninvolved in the polemical aspects of what they are studying. Their primary interest is in establishing an interpretation of the biblical materials that is technically accurate.

When we read the Gospels devotionally, on the other hand, our aim is to listen to them with the heart and the soul, so that our lives are touched and shaped by them. We put ourselves in the way of being completely transformed by them, as we are drawn into the magical web of their claim on our world views and imaginations.

It is in this manner that the Gospels were generally read in the Middle Ages, which produced so many great mystics and followers of the Way. It is in this manner also that they were approached by most of the noted reformers of the church in the sixteenth century, and by the single-minded men and women who established important new traditions of faith in the seventeenth and eighteenth centuries.

In this book of readings on the Gospel texts, I have attempted to bring together the best efforts of the scholars, who often provide indispensable insights into the accurate meaning of individual passages, with the general intention of the devotionalists, so that the daily study of the Gospels not only will provide you with a correct understanding of their contents but also will eventually lead you to actual companionship with the Christ who stands at their center.

By doing this, I have hoped to honor the aim of the Gospel writers themselves, whose concern was both historical and devotional. They wanted to present the narratives and traditions about Christ in such a way that his story would be carefully preserved for future generations; and they also wished to accomplish this so adroitly and ingenuously that the power of God's Spirit would leap almost automatically off the pages of their manuscripts to ensnare and compel the sympathies of their readers.

It is admittedly a risky enterprise to read the Gospels not only for their content but also for what might happen to one while reading. Yet this is precisely what the writers of the Gospels wished. They were not pedants or academics, spinning out idle theses for acceptance in the great universities. They were men caught up by a vision, commanded by a presence, and their immediate desire was to place their readers within the very force fields where they themselves had come to live.

If the sense of adventure appeals to you, and you are willing to read the Gospels in this manner, I have a suggestion to offer about how you might read this book. Approach the reading as if it were an act of prayer, or at least a prelude to prayer. Come with a feeling for the risk you are taking. Regard the risk as something you are desirous of offering to God.

Turn in your Bible to the suggested reading for the day. Read it reverently and thoughtfully, letting its words and images scroll through your mind with freshness and novelty, as if you had never heard or seen them before. Interact with what you read; be startled, amazed, comforted, rebuked, enticed, excited by it. If you feel the impulse to pray about it, do so, right then and there, without waiting. Let your spirit respond symbiotically to God's.

Then, when you have completed your reading of the passage and have interacted and prayed, read the interpretation in this book. See if there is anything in it that you missed in your own reading of the text. If there is, think about that.

Finally, when you feel that your mind and heart have encompassed everything of present significance in the two readings, the one in the Gospel and the one in this book, quietly and prayerfully read the short prayer at the end of the reading in the book. Make it your own prayer, if you can, or let it be the springboard to offering a little prayer of your own.

Remain in an attitude of quiet meditation for a few moments, letting the spirit of the Gospel continue to wash over and around you. Think about Christ. Imagine that he is there with you.

As I said, it is a risky business. If you read in this way, you will find yourself entering a new relationship with Christ, no matter what your old relationship happened to be. Like a genie released from a bottle, he will rise from the pages of the Gospels to transform you and the way you view reality.

It is inevitable, for there was never a time when it was not so.

JOHN KILLINGER

Day by Day with Jesus

THE ROYAL LINE OF DESCENT

*A*n account of the genealogy of Jesus the Messiah, the son of David, the son of Abraham." Matthew's Gospel was directed especially to the Jews. Therefore, he stressed Jesus' relationship to Abraham, the father of the Jews, and to David, the greatest king of the Jews, instead of to Adam, the first man. His book was to be about the Messiah, the long-awaited Savior of Israel, and he wanted his readers to know that Jesus bore an impeccable pedigree.

In our fast-paced, impersonal society, a genealogy may seem a boring note on which to begin. Not so for the Jewish Christians of Matthew's day! To them it would have been sheer poetry, fully as beautiful as the opening verses of the Gospel of John, which seem more majestic to us.

I grew up in the South, where folks used to sit on their porches after dark and discuss family histories. There was never anything trite or dull about such talk to them, even if they had heard it all before. And we can be sure there was nothing trite or dull about this list of names to the Jewish Christians. They knew stories about each person named. History to them was a web, a ladder, a series of interconnecting events, and now it led directly from Abraham to Jesus.

Read over the names in the list. Pronounce them lingeringly, lovingly, the way an early Christian would have: *Boaz, Rehoboam, Jehoshaphat, Hezekiah, Eleazar.* They *are* poetry, aren't they? The poetry of God's plan of redemption.

PRAYER

O God, you are at work in all generations. But we are creatures of a brief span, and often fail to see your plan as it unfolds through history. Teach us how to submit our years to you, that they may be woven with grace and beauty into the pattern of eternity. Through Jesus the Messiah, who was descended from Abraham and all these ancient people. Amen.

THE PRESENCE OF GOD IN THE WORLD

*T*he heavens and the earth, according to the book of Genesis, were created by the Spirit of God. The Spirit moved over the face of the dark waters and brought forth the sun and the stars and the world. So

Matthew, who was preparing to tell the story of the new creation in Jesus the Messiah, wished to emphasize the role of the Spirit in his life. The Spirit, not the earthly father of Jesus, was responsible for his existence.

The prophet Isaiah had promised long ago that a young woman would conceive and bear a special child. His name would be called Emmanuel, or God-with-us.

God had been present in the first creation. The author of Genesis pictures the divine Creator walking in the garden in the cool of the evening and speaking with the first man and woman. Now, in the new creation, says Matthew, God is to be present in a different way, through the child born to Mary. The Messiah, the bearer of God's Spirit, is to be tempted, to suffer, and to die like one of us. It is a form of intimacy with the divine for which, as the apostle Paul had already put it, the whole creation groaned until now. God will be in Christ, making the world God's own again.

PRAYER

God, it is exciting to think of your Spirit at work in the world where I live, helping to bring about a new creation out of the old one. I want to be a part of the new creation. I want my family and friends to be part of it. Help me to submit my entire being to your Spirit, so that my life flows with your purpose and not against it, through Jesus, who has shown us your Spirit. Amen.

Day 3   *Matthew 2:1-2*

WHAT IS THE SECRET OF WISDOM?

*O*f all the miracles associated with Jesus' birth, none seems more miraculous than the arrival of these strangers. Because there were three gifts, we have traditionally assumed there were three visitors. But this is only an assumption. There may have been several more.

Matthew's purpose in telling about them was to indicate the worldwide significance of the birth of the Messiah. These travelers symbolized the eventual homage of all nations before the Son of God. They brought gifts usually associated with royalty. And for good reason—Jesus was destined to rule over all.

What could induce men like these to leave their homes and travel to distant lands? They said they had seen the star and knew that the prophecy concerning Jesus' birth in Bethlehem was being fulfilled. That is amazing, when you think about it. The whole beings of these men appear to have been open to receive the messages of God in the universe around them.

How different from the way most of us live! We are so preoccupied with matters of daily existence—with maintaining our households or making our livings or watching TV—that we rarely take time to watch and listen to the universe we live in. How many messengers we probably miss—and how impoverished our lives are as a result.

PRAYER

O God, I have eyes, but I am so insensitive that I have learned to live without seeing. Teach me to have a sense of wonder again, as I did when I was a child. Let me look at everything as if for the first time, and marvel not at *what* things are, but *that* they are. Through Jesus, who is the greatest object of wonder, amen.

Day 4   *Matthew 2:3-18*

CHRIST AND THE BEAST

*H*ere is a part of the Christmas story we are prone to omit—the part about terror and cruelty and evil. But it ought to be there, every Christmas, for it is an inseparable part of life in this world.

The book of Revelation ends with the struggle between Christ and the Great Beast, the symbol of evil; and there is where the Gospel must really begin, as Matthew saw it. Herod, like most tyrants, felt extremely insecure. Although he probably didn't believe God was ready to send the Messiah to Israel, he did worry that a popular figure might topple his precarious throne. So he lashed out demonically at the news of Jesus' birth, and had all the male children under two years of age in the town of Bethlehem slain. Wails of agony must have gone up from their parents.

What a tangled skein life is. How impossible it is to separate the wheat from the tares, the good from the bad. As the apostle Paul said, we can't even do it in our own lives; we often do evil when we want to do good. Can we hope that it will be any better with groups, institutions, and nations?

This is why, in many liturgical traditions, a prayer of confession is set right at the heart of Christian worship. Our only hope is in the righteousness of God, for we cannot claim any righteousness ourselves. We admit our mixed motives, impure thoughts, and failure to love our neighbors.

15

It is the least we can do, for however much we belong to Christ, we are still troubled by the beast within.

PRAYER

O God, I long to be pure and honest and to deal lovingly with all persons, but I am too weak and unwise to fulfill the longing. Life is too complicated, and I often make mistakes. Help me not to despair, but to rely more on you. And enable me to accept in others the weakness I find so deeply embedded in my own nature. Through Jesus, whose coming helped us to deal more hopefully with evil, amen.

Day 5   *Matthew 2:19-23*

THE IMPORTANCE OF DREAMS

*M*ore dreams! First there was Joseph's dream of the angel, telling him that God's Spirit was the father of the child Mary carried. Then there was the one warning him to take Mary and the child into Egypt. Now there are these additional dreams, in which he is advised to return to Israel and settle in Galilee.

Would you follow the advice you received in a dream? Probably not. We belong to a culture that puts great emphasis on rationality. We have even developed rational explanations for dreams, so that we don't have to pay much attention to them.

But this may well be a mistake. If it is true that we reason better with our whole selves, not merely with our minds, then the messages that come through the unconscious may be of real importance.

Could it be that God uses our subconscious minds to implant suggestions in us that our tougher conscious minds would reject? Perhaps our lives would be richer and more exciting if only we learned to trust our impulses from the unconscious more than we presently do.

When I have a hard decision to make, I pray as I fall asleep, "Speak to me in my dreams, O God," for I know I am more likely to hear there than in my busy waking life.

PRAYER

Sometimes, dear God, you come to us in conscious modes; other times you come when the mind is relaxed and not on its guard. Help me to be so open to the possibility of hearing your voice that I may hear it in any way it comes to me. Through Jesus, who always heard, amen.

THE NECESSITY OF REPENTANCE

S ome scholars believe that John the Baptist was reared in or near the Essene community of Qumran, on the Dead Sea. The Essenes placed great emphasis on simple, righteous living and on ritual lustration, or baptism.

Wherever John came from, his message and actions were an appropriate prelude to the ministry of Jesus, for what they called for most was a radical reordering of priorities, a total conversion of life-style. They became the background against which Matthew would shortly set the Sermon on the Mount, with its teachings of a transformed ethic for the new creation. We cannot begin to understand these teachings if we forget this. Only the person who has submitted to John's demand for repentance and cleansing can hope to meet the challenge of Jesus' way of living in the realm of God.

Already the word is laid down for the Pharisees and Sadducees, the people who think their religious affiliation will give them an advantage in entering the divine realm. Tradition and heritage are only excess baggage in the day of the Lord. God can raise up new children for the realm out of the very stones that crowd the riverbanks. Christ's arrival will be a judgment on the falsely religious; they will be cut down like trees that do not bear fruit and burned like the useless chaff that is winnowed from the wheat.

PRAYER

God, help me to hear this stringent demand for personal conversion and righteousness, that I may soon be able to consider the ethical teachings of Jesus when I read them. Let me depend on no artificial standards of worthiness as I come before you for judgment, but rely wholly on your saving grace. Through Jesus, who baptizes the world with fire, amen.

THE SIGN OF THE NEW CREATION

W hen the earth was created, God's Spirit hovered over the face of the waters. Now, in the new creation, the Spirit is identified with baptism, the ritual entry into the realm of God. This is why Jesus himself came to John to be baptized. John demurred because he stood in the presence of the One who was God's Spirit in the flesh. But Jesus insisted.

Human pride might prevent our doing what Jesus did. We like to be begged, cajoled, and complimented into joining a movement. But Jesus did not wait. He knew that a new age was coming into being. He came directly to the fiery prophet to be baptized with all the others.

It was an important moment in human history, as was testified by the descent of the dove and the voice out of heaven, saying, "This is my Son, the Beloved."

The full meaning of this event strikes us only as we compare it with the story of Adam in the garden and God's disappointment in his failure to obey. Jesus' humility in accepting baptism "to fulfill all righteousness" was a sign of his willing obedience, and God was pleased. The new creation would not be hindered by the new Adam.

PRAYER

Human beings baptize with water, O God, and you baptize with the Holy Spirit. I need both. Without the water, I hold myself apart from others in the realm; without the Spirit, the water has no real effect. Fill me now with your Spirit, that I may be ready to meet the radical demands of the new age. Through Jesus, who has led the way as my Lord, amen.

Day 8   *Matthew 4:1-11*

HOW THE COMMONWEALTH COMES

*M*atthew wrote his Gospel primarily as a catechism for teaching the Christian community what it needed to know. He must, therefore, have regarded prayer and fasting as very significant, to have placed this selection at the beginning of Jesus' public ministry.

We can only conclude that if prayer and fasting were so essential in Jesus' life, they must also be essential in ours today. But how many of us behave as if they were? We give them so little attention in our daily existence.

What would our lives be like if they were built around prayer and fasting?

First, we would live with a new awareness of the presence of God in all our affairs.

18

Second, the anxieties and fears that cripple us in our attempts to live full and meaningful lives would blow away like chaff from the wheat.

Third, we would perceive the world as gift instead of punishment. What has been wilderness to us would become a paradise where we have everything we truly need.

We tend to associate prayer with miracles—with making things happen outside ourselves. But the greatest miracle prayer ever works is the transformation of the self so that it recognizes the blessings of God that lie around us all the time.

In other words, prayer reveals God's realm to us.

PRAYER

O God, I have eyes to see, but am often blind to the miracles around me. I have ears to hear, but I usually talk so much that I cannot perceive what others are saying. Teach me quietness and wonder, so that the glory of life can enter my senses and I can feel the abundance of your grace, which is always present to me. Through Christ, who learned obedience by praying and fasting, amen.

Day 9   *Matthew 4:12-25*

DOING GOD'S WILL IN GALILEE

*R*eligion makes some of us headstrong. If God is with us, we think, then we ought to assume the most prominent positions as quickly as possible.

But here is our Lord doing exactly the opposite. Leaving Judea, the region around Jerusalem, he preached and taught in the remote area of Galilee—the equivalent of a bright young seminary graduate's going to pastor a church in rural Nebraska. He even called two sets of brothers who were Galilean fishermen to become his most intimate followers. Together they traveled the countryside, interpreting the scriptures in synagogues as they went—in the country churches of their day!

Surely there is a lesson in this for us about working faithfully wherever God wants us to work. We are never required to serve in highly visible positions—only to apply ourselves cheerfully and faithfully wherever we are.

Ironically, the greatest movements often begin in the least conspicuous places. The crowds that gathered around Jesus in Galilee soon spread his fame abroad, and people began coming from as far away as Jerusalem to hear his teachings and find healing for their infirmities.

PRAYER

Dear God, I suspect that Jesus' time of prayer and fasting in the desert prepared him for serving in inconspicuous places. I pray that my own seasons of devotion will leave me as filled with peace and contentment as he was, that I too may glorify you in humility and readiness to serve the poor. Amen.

Day 10   *Matthew 5:1-12*

ONE GREATER THAN MOSES

*M*atthew wrote his Gospel for people whose whole religious life had once centered in the Torah, the Law brought down from the mount by Moses. It was, therefore, important that they see Jesus as the Moses of the new creation, the one whose teachings from the mount would establish a realm greater than the kingdom of Israel. Hence this "sermon," put together with editorial license from sayings of Jesus that probably occurred in many settings during his ministry.

It begins by defining who are the members of God's new realm—the humble, the heavyhearted, the gentle, the righteous, the merciful, the pure in heart, the peacemakers, the persecuted, the maligned. At a stroke, Jesus sets these over against all the self-righteous people who regarded themselves as the cream of the godly society.

The Law of Moses had been subject to misinterpretation. The Pharisees had followed it scrupulously, but had missed the point of it. There would be no missing the point of the new law. Jesus made it plain that no law could supplant true devotion to God—even prostitutes and tax collectors could be numbered among the blessed ones.

The Messiah was ushering in a new era!

PRAYER

God, I need to remember that it is possible to be blessed and happy even when I am not well off. I would rather be one of your "little ones" than to be wealthy or famous, for your realm is forever. Amen.

YOU ARE SALT AND LIGHT

You are the salt of the earth. . . . *You* are the light of the world" (italics added). Read this passage with the right emphasis. Jesus was setting his disciples over against the old Israel, over against Judaism, over against Mosaic religion.

He wanted them to see that it was *they*, not the priests and keepers of the old Law, for whom the world was waiting. *They,* not the scribes and Pharisees, would be heralds of the new realm. *They,* not the old rabbis, would bring spice and light to the people of the earth.

If we dare read ourselves into the *you,* then the words commit us to action. If we are salt, then we must season. If we are light, then we must shine. Salt that does not season is thrown out, and light that does not illumine is useless.

Let your light shine, Jesus said, so that it provides illumination to everyone and so that those who see your good works will recognize the glory of God in you.

This is no theology of good works Jesus was recommending, but a theology of the glory of God. We bring seasoning and light to the world, not that the world may praise us, but that it may see and fall down before the presence of God in our midst. Salt is lost in the flavoring of food; we do not praise the salt but the taste of the food. Light is overlooked when it reveals the contents of a room; we do not praise the light but the room itself.

So it is with us. The joy of our calling is to help people discover the glory of God!

PRAYER

Being salt and light is a problem for me, O God. I am so inclined to seek attention for myself. I want to have *my* flavor brought out and *my* qualities illuminated. Help me to discover how rich life is when it is devoted to helping others to see you instead of me, so that they praise your name instead of mine. Through Jesus, who always reminded us that what he did was through your presence and not his own power, amen.

JESUS' TEACHINGS AS FULFILLMENT

*H*ere is the teacher of righteousness at his most inclusive! Think of the battles of grace versus works that had already swept through

Christendom when Matthew wrote his Gospel. Paul had had conflict after conflict with the Judaizers, Jewish Christians who insisted on the primacy of legalism in their newly founded religion. The question was by no means settled.

How does Matthew resolve it? By grouping Jesus' teachings into a remarkable *both . . . and* combination.

No, you cannot work for the realm. Jesus says that God *gives* the realm—to the humble, the mourners, the gentle, those who long for righteousness—to all those who are described in Matthew 5:3-12.

But of those to whom much is given, much is expected. Now that you are given the heavenly realm, you must go beyond the dry righteousness of the scribes and Pharisees, and fulfill the law in love.

Jesus didn't come to do away with the law. The law was never our problem. The human will is our problem. When the will is bad, we can find ways of getting around any law or statute. Jesus came to tell us that God gives us the realm without regard to the law, but that, once we know this, we should desire to go far beyond the law, obeying the highest impulses of the human soul. Only in that way can we reveal God's perfect way to the world, and be real salt and light in the world.

PRAYER

O God, I have accepted the gift of your realm without really considering how I should live in it. I know that I have obscured for others the true meaning of discipleship. Forgive me and transform me, O holy One. Help me to live with the law not as a requirement to be met but as a guideline to go beyond. Through Jesus, who fulfilled everything, amen.

Day 13   *Matthew 5:21-26*

GOING BEYOND THE "MURDER" COMMANDMENT

*E*very Jew knew the injunction against murder. It had stood for centuries as a cornerstone of the Law of Moses. It was one of the Ten Commandments (Deut. 5:17). Righteous Jews not only didn't kill other human beings, but also they abstained from fellowship with anyone who did.

We can imagine what a point of pride this must have been for many of the people in Jesus' audience. "I am a good person," they may have thought to themselves. "I am not like the murdering, thieving rogues one finds along the highways."

But Jesus punctured their balloons.

If you have even been angry with a brother or sister, he said, you have offended God. If you have spoken an insult or said something hurtful, you are as guilty in God's eyes as if you had stabbed someone in the heart.

Here is what Jesus meant about our righteousness exceeding the righteousness of the scribes and Pharisees (Matt. 5:20). Their righteousness is based on a callous understanding of the law as mere requirement. The righteousness of those in the realm of God has nothing to do with ticking off mere requirements. It has to do with a new spirit, with a transformed heart, in which the slightest injury to another is felt as sensitively as if it were an act of murder.

Understanding this, we shouldn't even pretend to come before God in worship while harboring resentments against other persons in our lives. We should rush out immediately to make restitution to them, and live in that transcendent attitude characterizing the realm of God, and then come to honor God.

PRAYER

How this thought indicts me, O God. I rarely live in that wonderful mood of love wherein I instantly forgive all my enemies and think kindly of all people. Cleanse my heart, O heavenly Spirit, and restore a right attitude within me. Let me share generously the love and mercy you have shown to me with every person I know. Through Jesus, who even loved and forgave his enemies, amen.

Day 14   *Matthew 5:27-30*

GOING BEYOND THE "ADULTERY" COMMANDMENT

*I*n yesterday's reading, Jesus used the relationship of anger to murder as an illustration of the true meaning of God's law. Here he uses the relationship of lust to adultery. The point is that God is so unspeakably holy and righteous that human beings can never take any great pride in their moral achievements, for none of us is completely without stain or guilt.

Then Matthew throws in that fanatical-sounding bit about tearing out one's eye or cutting off one's hand if it offends. What did Jesus mean by those harsh sayings?

We would probably be surprised to know how many people have taken these words literally. Psychologists often write about cases of patients who gouged out their eyes or inflicted bodily wounds on themselves because of guilt feelings induced by religious beliefs. To their credit, they have taken the Messiah's words seriously. And the truth is that Jesus spoke in such demanding, apocalyptic terms on many occasions.

But it is entirely possible in this instance that Matthew or one of his editors allowed a saying of Jesus from another context to intrude upon the subject matter here—namely, how inadequate is our understanding of the divine law. The saying is about purity and integrity. But it would seem to fit more appropriately in a discourse about zeal or single-mindedness, not in one about what it means truly to fulfill all righteousness.

In any case, we are reminded again that holy living is serious business and that the Pharisees, though they were serious, were only being petty.

PRAYER

When I am totally honest, O God, I have to admit that I have never been able to live without the kind of desire that Jesus said is as bad in your eyes as adultery. Help me to be so caught up with your presence in my life—the presence that Christ's Spirit has brought—that I am no longer a slave to my lower impulses, for I do want to enter your realm. In Jesus' name, amen.

Day 15   *Matthew 5:31-32*

GOING BEYOND THE "DIVORCE"
COMMANDMENT

*F*ew families these days do not have to reckon with this "hard" saying of Jesus. The current national divorce rate is approximately one out of every two marriages. Most churches have special classes or seminars for persons who have gone through the trauma of divorce. Some churches even have public rituals for divorced couples that allow them to confess the failure of their marriages and receive the loving support of other Christians.

In general, Christians no longer take the hard line against divorce that once represented the mind of the church. Even many Roman Catholic priests privately take a softer position on the issue than the official view of their church would actually permit. Most of us have come to believe that there are instances where divorce is not only justified by circumstances but is in reality more humane than forcing couples to live together all their lives. Beside this more liberal view, the older, more inflexible position reminds us of the intolerant attitude of the scribes and Pharisees in Jesus' day.

In the end, each person must decide what the real intention of Jesus' remarks was. But, taken in context with the other sayings about the law, it clearly underlines his contention that it is all but impossible to live guiltlessly before the law of God. Instead of pursuing such an impossible course, therefore, we should learn to live with such an awareness of the divine presence that we desire always to glorify God and not to satisfy mere personal needs and ambitions.

PRAYER

O God, I am a sinful person, and I live in the midst of sinful people. We have all sought our own ways so long that we no longer know how to go about pleasing you. Teach me to love you so dearly that I may make all my moral decisions in the light of that love, and forgive me if I still err. Through Christ, who understood the meaning of true righteousness, amen.

Day 16   *Matthew 5:33-37*

GOING BEYOND THE "OATHS" COMMANDMENT

At first glance, this illustration seems anticlimactic after the powerful issues of murder, adultery, and divorce. What is taking an oath falsely in comparison with such explosive matters?

The fact that we should even ask such a question condemns us for having a lax attitude toward truth and falsehood. We live in a culture where integrity in speech is stretched, bent, and broken so many times every day, in so many ways, that we have all but become insensitive to it. We *expect* politicians, manufacturers, and salespersons to lie to us. Some people even think their ministers and teachers will lie to them, either intentionally or unintentionally.

What Jesus is saying is similar to what he said about the other ethical issues—namely, that God is not fooled by our pretensions at goodness. There is no point in swearing elaborate or dramatic oaths to back up our words. In the Spirit of God, we should speak simply and quietly, and not let ourselves get carried away in a noisy, worldly manner. Otherwise, we put ourselves at risk of being like all the liars and braggarts who live under the spirit of evil.

PRAYER

O God, I fear for myself, for I live in a world where few words are honest and trustworthy. Help me to think and speak chastely, knowing that you are always with me and that you respond to the intentions of my heart, not to the volume or rapidity of my speech. Through Jesus, whose every word was true, amen.

Day 17   *Matthew 5:38-42*

GOING BEYOND THE LAW OF RETALIATION

*T*he "law of retaliation": an eye for an eye, a tooth for a tooth, a limb for a limb, a life for a life. It was hard, simple justice, and the Law of Moses had taken no exception to it. In fact, it had spelled it out with great care.

Whoever killed another person was to be put to death. Anyone who injured another person in a quarrel, though not fatally, should compensate that person for loss of time. If a participant in a fight injured a pregnant woman, causing her to miscarry, he must pay whatever the husband demanded. If any further harm occurred to the woman, it was to be repaid "life for life, eye for eye, tooth for tooth, hand for hand, foot for foot, burn for burn, wound for wound, stripe for stripe" (Exod. 21:24; see Exod. 21:12-27).

Jesus, in the face of this powerful tradition, posed a startling alternative: Those who live in the Spirit of God, expecting to enter the heavenly realm, are not to exact their pound of flesh. On the contrary, they are to bend over backward to accommodate those who have something against them. If someone strikes them on one cheek, they are to turn the other. If someone requires them to go a mile, they are to go not one, but two.

The scandal of this latter proposal must have struck ancient Christians at once. It was a law in the Roman Empire that a soldier could compel an ordinary citizen to carry his baggage from one milepost to another. Most people, naturally, hated being under such an obligation, and automatically despised any soldier who enforced it. Yet Jesus said they should not only fulfill the obligation of the law but go beyond it as well.

Here again was the spirit of the realm of God. It would not be based on merely meeting requirements, but on having a new heart, a new attitude about everything.

PRAYER

Dear God, I have not yet learned to live as cheerfully and positively as Christ asked. Please be patient with me, and help me this day to live out of the overflow of your love. Through Christ, who carried my burden when he didn't have to, amen.

Day 18   *Matthew 5:43-48*

WHO ARE WE SUPPOSED TO LOVE?

*H*ere is the crux of what Jesus was trying to say about fulfilling the law of God's realm. God's law is not like humanity's laws. It is not a mere codification, an arrangement whereby certain parties engage to behave in a specified way in order to complete a contract. No, it is much more than that. It involves having a new heart, seeing things differently, reacting to everything in love.

The old law that was given for humanity's weakness, said Jesus, was designed to enable people to love their friends and dislike their enemies. But God isn't like that at all. God even loves those who dislike God.

That is what Pastor Martin Niemoeller discovered in Nazi Germany. He was amazed. "I have learned," he said, "that God is not the enemy of my enemies. God is not even the enemy of God's enemies."

In the realm of God, all the inhabitants learn to love as God loves. In that way, they become "perfect" as God is "perfect"—not in a limited way, as meeting a set standard, but perfect in the sense of being fulfilled. God, who is love, created us to be lovers too. Only when we realize this and give up our need for mere laws and regulations will our lives become truly full.

I am enthralled, O God, by the thought of living in this new manner. How happy I would be if I could only attain it. How happy the world would be if everyone could attain it. Please help me not to be discouraged because we have so far to go. If Jesus could go to the cross and not be dismayed, then surely I can continue to try to live as he said. For his name's sake, amen.

Day 19   *Matthew 6:1-6*

A DEPTH OF HONEST PIETY

*I*n the preceding passage, Jesus said that true righteousness lies not in fulfilling the demands of the law but in going beyond them. Now he warns against mere superficial piety—practicing our religion in order to be seen by others. When we give gifts to the poor, we are to do it quietly—so quietly, in fact, that one hand doesn't know what the other is doing.

When we pray, we are to do it without ostentation—even in a small room with the door shut. Nor are we to seek virtue through extremely long prayers as though God sold divine favor by the yard. We are to pray simply and economically, as the manifestation of a sincere and devoted spirit.

A friend of mine, who leads a wonderful Christian life, says candidly that he rarely prays for very long at a time. He quotes an old farmer he knew who said, "There's no use in hanging around the bank after your check's been cashed."

Jesus' point is that if our lives are fully attuned to God's Spirit, and we have a sense of living in the new realm, there is never a time when we are far from praying. We need not pretend before others that we are religious, for we are caught up in something else that is far better—genuine spirituality.

PRAYER

When I am with you, O God, I feel like being honest about everything. Please help me to remember that you are always with me, so that I am able to live simply and honestly all the time, wherever I am, totally without pretension. Through Jesus, who was always what he appeared to be, amen.

A MODEL FOR PRAYING

*P*ursuant to what he said earlier about not praying long, pretentious prayers (Matt. 6:1-6), Jesus now provides a beautiful example of how complete and effective a brief prayer can be. In approximately sixty words, he covers almost everything that is essential for us to pray about.

Notice the structure of the prayer. It begins by praising God. Then the first petition, which sets the tone of the entire prayer, is for the coming of the kingdom or realm of God. This is in keeping with everything that has been said thus far in the Sermon on the Mount—when life is predicated on the arrival of God's realm, our perspectives on everything else are transformed.

The only part of the prayer devoted to "things" is a request for daily bread—for the very simplest form of sustenance. How different this is from a lot of praying we hear around us, that asks for new cars, bigger houses, and increased salaries. Again, if our vision is really focused on the coming of God's realm, we will not be concerned about more mundane things. Our hearts will simply be somewhere else.

Finally, there are petitions for forgiveness and for not being subjected to having our faith sorely tested. This latter item would have been of particular interest to members of the early Christian fellowship, who often had to pay an enormous price for confessing belief in Jesus as the Messiah.

The prayer for forgiveness probably led Matthew to append the saying about forgiveness in verses 14 and 15. Jesus always taught that true forgiveness is interrelated—that we can't have ours unless we give others theirs.

PRAYER

O God, I am condemned by this brief prayer Jesus told us to pray. To pray it, my whole life must be sincerely dedicated to you—must, in fact, be a prayer. Maybe I am more wordy when I pray because my relationship to you is not as complete as it should be. Forgive me, for I think I am at peace with all others, and let me glorify your name through honest religion in days ahead. Amen.

THE HEART AND ITS TREASURE

*W*e cannot help being impressed, after all these passages on the topic of sincerity in religion, with how important the subject must have been to Jesus. But the reason is simple. He lived among some of the most aggressively religious folk in the history of the world. One group of them, the Pharisees, even gave their name for all time to persons who are excessively scrupulous about the smallest details of their religion or morality.

Can you think of religious groups today that behave the way the Pharisees did then? What would Jesus say to them?

The whole intention of religious faith, he says in this passage, is not to impress others with our apparent commitment, but to establish ourselves fully in the spiritual realm of God. If we only desire to have others think well of us, then we will probably succeed in building an earthly reputation. But if we are truly concerned about God's realm and what it means for the redemption of the earth, then we will be laying up heavenly treasures that are not subject to the vicissitudes and decay of things with worldly value.

As our bodies receive their vision from the eye, so our spiritual lives receive their light from the way we look at things. If we are shortsighted and concerned only about how others perceive our righteousness, then we shall be full of darkness. But if we see things truly, as God sees them, then we shall be filled with light.

PRAYER

I do long to see things clearly and truly, dear God. Help me so to conform myself to you and your ways that I shall live each day in the light, and glorify you forever and ever. Through Jesus, who cared nothing for treasures on earth, amen.

HAVING TRUE PEACE

*S*halom, the Hebrew word for fullness and peace, was frequently heard among the Jews. But Jesus struck at the irony of a religion in which so many people spoke of *shalom* and so few people actually possessed it. Most Jews, he observed, were like the Gentiles—they clamored for food and clothing and security as if they were the most important things in life. True *shalom* had not become part of their life-style.

None of us, said Jesus, can worship both God and worldly possessions. If we care about mere things—if we pile them up in order to have plenty tomorrow—they inevitably interfere with our giving full attention to God.

How this cuts across the grain with us, just as it did in Matthew's day! We must prefer the theology occasionally found in the Old Testament that says that possessions are a sign of God's favor. But the New Testament seems to have a bias in favor of being poor—not because there is any special virtue in poverty itself, but because the poor are freer to respond to the radical demands of God's realm.

God's wayfarers in the world—that is how the New Testament pictures the disciples of Jesus. People like Peter and John, who, when accosted by the crippled beggar in Acts 3, had no silver or gold coins to give but gave him instead the healing power that sprang from their dedication and purity of heart.

Peter and John had *shalom—really* had it—because they had left everything to follow Jesus. When will we learn there is no other way to have *shalom?*

PRAYER

Dear God, I am really uncomfortable with one foot in the boat and the other on shore. I don't know why I try to live this way; it is really agony. I guess I am afraid to leave the land. But I see the inadequacy of this position and ask for faith to commit myself entirely to the boat. Help me to launch out into the deep. Through Jesus, who will be in the boat with me, amen.

Day 23   *Matthew 7:1-12*

HOW TO LIVE IN THE WORLD

*I*n these verses, Jesus turns to practical advice for Christians who must go on living in the world.

First, he speaks about how we are to look upon others who live and think differently from us. It is easy to get upset with them and complain about their way of seeing or behaving. But, given the fact that we are all unrighteous in God's eyes, who is really in a position to judge?

31

Second, he admonishes us to be discreet in how we try to give what we have to others. Some people will be ready to receive our love and testimony about the heavenly realm. But others will be like dogs in the street, which turn and snap at those who try to befriend them; or they will be like rough swine that trample on anything of value thrown before them.

Third, he reminds us that we are not alone in facing the world, for God is always there to hear us when we pray. Just as a parent watches out for a child, so also God is watching over us and will respond to our cries for help.

Finally, Jesus sums up how we are to behave toward others in the world: In simplest terms, we should do everything for them that we would like them to do for us. This, said Jesus, is what all the law and the prophets come down to. They are not a vast, complicated compendium of rules and regulations for binding our spirits and making us feel guilty. They are guidelines to help us interact more equitably and happily with others. And if we have the Spirit of God in our hearts, we will do it without stopping to recall chapter and verse from the law.

PRAYER

O God, I would like to be a "natural" Christian, who doesn't have to stop and think about what I'm supposed to do before I go ahead and do it. I would like to be so caught up in the spirit of Christ that I just automatically think and do the right thing. Please help me to become more like this every day. Through Jesus, who understood your will perfectly, amen.

Day 24   *Matthew 7:13-23*

BEING CAREFUL ABOUT WHO WE FOLLOW

*C*ontinuing his "worldly advice" for Christians, Jesus warns about the importance of care and vigilance in living as members of God's realm. Contrary to our tendency to feel buoyant and expansive about the ease of following Christ's way, he cautions that the way is actually narrow and difficult, so that few who set out in it finally reach their destination.

Part of the problem is the many unprincipled, opportunistic leaders who easily take advantage of our eagerness and gullibility. Lacking real spiritual depth, they are nonetheless adroit at manufacturing the appearance of religious knowledge and devotion. They include pastors who are inwardly unsure of their own faith and evangelists who preach only for materialistic rewards and teachers who manipulate and abuse the truth for their own advantage. These "false prophets," as Jesus called them, not only lead the ignorant and undiscerning astray, but also cause even the wise and thoughtful to wonder whether the message of Christ is fundamentally and irrevocably true.

The real test of any follower, leader, and disciple, said Jesus, is not in the outward manifestations of faith—whether he or she calls publicly on the name of God—but in the quiet and consistent way in which the follower seeks and does the will of the divine. Many Christians will probably die under the illusion that they are among the elect of God, only to discover that they have missed the mark altogether.

PRAYER

I am frightened by this warning, O God. Is it possible that I too have been misled in my thinking and beliefs, and will be among the disappointed in the afterlife, learning that we were never really members of your realm? Help me to live more soberly and thoughtfully, and not to presume upon your grace. Through Jesus, who faced everything with great realism, amen.

Day 25   *Matthew 7:24-28*

MINDING HOW YOU BUILD

When Hurricane Andrew cut its devastating path through southern Florida in 1992, it severely tested the standards of building construction. Authorities who investigated the scenes of misery and destruction laid the blame for much of the property loss on contractors who had taken short and easy routes to the erection of houses. Houses that had been built properly, they said, with all the joists and beams secured in the recommended fashion, generally suffered little damage. While they sometimes lost shingles, almost never did their roofs blow away or walls collapse.

Jesus, who may have grown up as a carpenter's son in Nazareth, understood the principles of home construction. It is fitting that the conclusion of the Sermon on the Mount, which is a summary of teachings about living as God wants us to live, should be drawn from such plain, down-to-earth experience. The wise person, he said, will establish his or her home on a trustworthy foundation. Then, when life becomes difficult or when the soul stands before the judgment of eternity, that person's inner being will emerge safe and intact.

It was no wonder that the crowds of people who heard Jesus speak were amazed at his teachings. They were not the carefully hedged and footnoted sayings of a young rabbi, always deferential to older scholars and teachers. They were the strong, incisive, no-nonsense statements of one who obviously knew both life and God and was able to relate them in ways that were immediately relevant for everybody. People knew instinctively that he spoke with divine authority.

PRAYER

Dear God, I know why people thought Jesus had authority, and did not speak empty things he had borrowed from others. It was because his life was real and because he spoke to the depths in their own hearts. I can sense his authority too, all these centuries later. Enable me to hear all that he has said and to apply it to my life. For his name's sake, amen.

Day 26   *Matthew 8:1-4*

THE POWER TO HEAL

*A*fter the section on Jesus' teachings, Matthew now turns to reports of Jesus' healing power. The very first story, of the healing of a leper, continues the theme we touched on earlier, that Jesus is greater than Moses, who gave the Torah.

The Torah, in Leviticus 13 and 14, gave very specific instructions about persons having leprosy. At the very first sign of an itching sore, the inflicted were to present themselves to the priest. If he verified that they had contracted leprosy, then they must go outside the community and live alone until they either died or were cured of the dread disease. In the event of a miraculous cure, the healed person was to present himself or herself to the priest, who would determine whether the person was indeed relieved of the disease. If the priest decided that the person was cured, he would kill a bird, dip a living bird in its blood, sprinkle some blood on the cured person, and release the living bird to fly away as he pronounced the person well.

Moses' memory was sacred among the Jews because he was the giver of the law. But here was one who could do more than give a law about a person with leprosy—he could heal the person. Jesus reached out and touched a man, says Matthew, and immediately the man was cleansed of his disease.

Finally, as if to emphasize again that he had come to fulfill the law, not to destroy it, Jesus told the man to go to the priest and make an offering of the two birds as Moses had commanded.

PRAYER

I am awed, O God, by the power of this man Jesus, who could touch a leper and make him whole again. I am also awed by his self-control in telling the man to go and show himself to the priest and fulfill the Torah. He must really have been in touch with himself to do that—and in touch with you. Help me to enter into this mystery, too. In the name of the Healer, amen.

Day 27   *Matthew 8:5-17*

MORE HEALINGS

*H*ere we have more stories of healings—two more, to be precise: the servant of the Roman centurion and Peter's mother-in-law. And then all those nameless ones who were brought with demons and illnesses.

Why, out of the hundreds of stories Matthew must have known, did he choose these two in particular?

The centurion probably represented the non-Jewish world, much as the narrative of the magi had symbolized it in the birth episode. Even though his Gospel was intended primarily for Jewish Christians, because he was at such pains to point out how Jesus fulfilled the Old Testament prophecies, Matthew obviously wanted to say something here to include all the non-Jews who had become Christians.

"Many will come from east and west," said Jesus, "and will eat with Abraham and Isaac and Jacob in the kingdom of heaven, while the heirs of the kingdom will be thrown into the outer darkness" (vv. 11-12).

As for Peter's mother-in-law, well, Peter had become something very special in the history of the church, and this little domestic touch would have meant much to the early Christians. This story is not entirely unlike the first. After all, Peter was an outsider to the Pharisees, too—one of the little folks, the people of the land, who were practically illiterate on important religious questions. And a mother-in-law would have enjoyed almost as little status as a servant. She was, in effect, a nobody. But even the nobodies are included in the gifts brought by Jesus.

PRAYER

No one could be more of an outsider to the faith of Israel than I am, O God. I'm not of the first century; I don't speak the language; I don't know the traditions. Yet you have opened your commonwealth to me. Why, dear God? It is a wonder too deep to contemplate. I can only marvel and live in constant thankfulness. In the name of the one who extended your power to nobodies, amen.

Day 28   *Matthew 8:18-22*

SAYINGS FOR DISCIPLES

*T*hese two sayings, involving would-be disciples, are interesting for their emphasis on the radical demands that Jesus laid upon those who would follow him.

First is the scribe who was awed at Jesus' teachings and vowed to follow him wherever he went. He did not know what he was saying, apparently, and Jesus apprised him: "Foxes have holes, and birds of the air have nests; but the Son of Man has nowhere to lay his head" (v. 20). Two suggestions leap from this saying—one, of the restless, itinerant nature of Jesus' ministry, and the other, of the stature of the man. "Son of Man" is one of several messianic titles found in the scriptures. Albright and Mann, in the Anchor Bible translation, render this title "The Man," insisting that it means "Representative Man" as in the book of Daniel. Either way, Jesus identifies himself with the end time of history and as a cosmic figure who should lack a specific residence. Persons wishing to follow him were thus reminded that it was no little movement they would become attached to, and that it was not one from which they could turn back whenever they desired.

Second was the follower who wished to come with Jesus after delaying to bury his father (Jewish law required burial within twenty-four hours). "Follow me," said Jesus, "and let the dead bury their own dead" (v. 22). What is the meaning of this apparently harsh answer? Would a day have made that much difference? Perhaps Jesus was underlining the demand for obedience among his disciples. Or perhaps he was emphasizing the difference between the old, the era of the Torah, and the new, the era of the Messiah, in which case he was saying in effect, "When you follow me, you are entering a completely new age; let those who belong to the old age take care of their own." Whatever the meaning, it is clear that the emphasis was on total commitment to the Messiah.

PRAYER

God, I have trouble with the tone of these verses. There is a streak of willfulness in me that doesn't want to surrender to you. Help me to deal with this willfulness, and to do it in such a way that I become a more faithful servant. Through Jesus, who both assures and frightens me, amen.

Day 29   *Matthew 8:23-27*

THE LORD OF THE WINDS AND SEA

*M*atthew now narrates three separate incidents depicting the extraordinary power of Jesus: the calming of the sea (8:23-27), the casting out of demons from two Gadarene demoniacs (8:28-34), and the forgiving and healing of a paralytic (9:1-8).

One of the remarkable things about the narrative of the storm, when we think about it, is that the cry for help came from disciples, some of whom were fishermen, men of the sea. For years, the sea had been their second home. They had surely ridden out many storms, for storms were prone to arise quickly on the Sea of Galilee. Why this sudden evidence of fear and distrust in their own ability to survive? We can only surmise that the storm's fury was greater than any they had seen before, and that in the height of the churning clouds and the depth of the troughs opening in the water they were genuinely afraid they would perish.

Jesus was the center of *shalom* through all of this. The violence of the storm did not even awaken him. The men had to shake him and cry out to him that they were on the verge of perishing. Turning his face toward them (Mark records that he had been sleeping on a pillow), he asked why they had so little faith. Then he stood and transferred the calm that was in him to the sea itself, and to the winds, so that everything became still.

"What sort of man is this," marveled the experienced seamen, "that even the winds and the sea obey him?" (v. 27).

37

Lord, does this story suggest that you are more the master of my situation—my home, my context, my business—than I am, just as you were master of the fishermen's sea? If it does, then maybe I had better rethink the matter of who is in charge here. Amen.

Day 30   *Matthew 8:28-34*

LORD OVER DEMONS

*W*hat have you to do with us, Son of God?" cried the demons. "Have you come here to torment us before the time?" (v. 29). Matthew surely used this story to emphasize that Jesus was recognized as the Messiah even by the evil spirits that inhabited people. In Enoch, a Jewish apocalypse, demons are said to have power until the day of judgment. Here, in Matthew, they realize that Jesus is the bringer of that day of judgment, though the final catastrophic day has not arrived.

The passage also indicates again the universal character of Jesus' messiahship, for he is in Gentile, not Jewish, country (hence the herd of pigs), and these particular demons inhabit two men who are not Jewish.

In Mark's Gospel (5:1-20) there is only one demoniac, and when Jesus has used his power to exorcise the demons, the man becomes the focus of attention for the townspeople who come out to see the effects of the miracle. But Matthew, who possibly has combined the Marcan account with another in Mark 1:23-28, so that there are two possessed men instead of one, has the crowds come out to see Jesus, not the cured demoniacs. It is a subtle change, perhaps, but an important one. The identity of the Messiah is what is important in all of these stories, not what is done in the stories. He is the Lord of the new creation, and that is the theme that matters to Matthew.

Mark makes it plain why the men begged him to leave their part of the country: They were afraid. Unaccustomed to witnessing such displays of power, they asked Jesus to go away. They preferred to keep matters the way they were.

PRAYER

Lord, I would probably have been right in there with those townspeople, if I had been there, asking you to move on to some other territory. Like them, I usually prefer the status quo I know to a new state of affairs

I don't know. Enable me to move beyond this, and to be ready for anything new you introduce into my life, for you are the master of all that is new and wonderful. Amen.

Day 31   *Matthew 9:1-8*

THE AUTHORITY TO FORGIVE AND THE POWER TO HEAL

*T*his story goes beyond the preceding miracle stories in Matthew because it raises the question of Jesus' authority to forgive sins. Mark's account of the same story (2:1-12) makes the problem more explicit: Only God can forgive sins. Jesus was accused of blasphemy, therefore, because he was exercising the divine right to forgive.

This would have been a ticklish issue for the Jews, for whom the matter of forgiveness was institutionalized into a system of priests and sacrifices. Jesus was flying in the face of the entire system by telling the paralytic that he was forgiven. But Matthew apparently set the story here for two reasons: to indicate the growing conflict between Jesus and the scribes (and by implication the Pharisees) and to further enhance the picture he has already drawn of Jesus as the leader greater than Moses, who was able to deliver the law but unable to exercise the priestly function of absolving guilt.

The healing miracle, which to human flesh would seem to require more power than forgiving sin, was performed in the story as a sign of authority, which the people could understand. And, while we do not know the reaction of the scribes to this, the crowds, as is often the case in Matthew's Gospel, respond as though electrified, glorifying God for having sent such authority among them in the flesh.

PRAYER

O God, I confess that I am like the crowds in this story: I react much more excitedly to signs and wonders than to the mystery of forgiveness, which is much less visible. Sharpen my perception that I may look more keenly to matters of the soul, which often are more important than the physical functions of the body. Through Jesus, who recognized at once that this paralytic needed forgiveness more than locomotion, amen.

A KINGDOM OF SINNERS

*M*ost scholars do not believe that the Matthew mentioned here was actually the author of this Gospel, but the story is told with the probable intention of linking the name of the disciple to the Gospel.

Tax collectors were held in disdain by religious Jews not so much because they worked for the occupying power as because they handled money with pagan inscriptions and drawings on it. The sinners referred to, moreover, were probably unobservant Jews, not grossly disreputable people. Both the tax collectors and the sinners were apparently friends of Matthew who gathered at his home with Jesus and the other disciples after Matthew decided to give up his office to be a follower of Jesus.

The Pharisees, who were among the thirty or forty persons who probably stood around the room in Matthew's home, mumbled to the disciples their amazement that this famous rabbi was eating with unobservant persons. Jesus, as happens several times in the Gospel, overhears remarks not intended for him and answers them. He cites Hosea 6:6—"I desire mercy, not sacrifice"—and says he came to call sinners, or nonobservers, not the traditionally righteous people.

We must remember that Judaism was very strong toward the end of the first century, when this Gospel was written, despite the overthrow of Jerusalem in A.D. 70, and that there was much wrangling between the Christians and the Judaizers. This narrative would have been a strong document in struggles such as that between Paul and the Judaizers in the Galatian churches.

Again, as promised by John the Baptist, it is a case of God's raising up new children of Abraham from the stones along the river of baptism.

PRAYER

I have the same problem as the Pharisees, O God. I keep expecting you in the old familiar places, behaving in traditional ways. Therefore, I do not watch for you to break out in new places, doing new things. Forgive my shortsightedness and help me to be alert to your presence. Through Jesus, whose freshness and authority seem to have lain at least partly in his ability always to see clearly, amen.

THE PRESENCE OF THE BRIDEGROOM

*T*his passage is easily linked to the preceding one because it has to do with nonobservance. John the Baptist's disciples ask Jesus why it is that they fast as the Pharisees do, while Jesus' disciples do not. The specific references of the passage may have been intended by the author as a rejection by Jesus of identification with the Essenes or other practitioners of cultic righteousness.

The ground for the rejection would be the fact that Jesus is someone special. He is the bridegroom and center of a celebration. He is the one greater than Moses. He is the Messiah, the Lord of the new creation.

There is apparently a reference to the death of the Messiah—the bridegroom will be taken away from the wedding guests, and then the guests shall fast again as others do. But for the moment they are enjoying a foretaste of the ultimate wedding, the end of all things in God's new era.

In that final time, Jesus seems to indicate, the Torah or law of Moses will be left behind. To try to graft the new realm onto it would be like putting a new, unshrunken patch on an old garment that has been washed many times, or putting powerful new wine into old skins that no longer have the flexibility to endure much expansion. Therefore, observances such as calendrical fasting (as opposed to fasting for self-discipline) are matters of mere fussiness among the followers of Jesus, and hardly worth attention.

As Jesus said to the Pharisees in Matthew's house, God desires mercy, not sacrifice—which is far more demanding than the old system of laws and regulations.

PRAYER

God, there is something comfortable about a rule or a law. It helps us to know where we stand. And there is something unsettling about Jesus' way of saying we are now beyond that and are ruled by a spirit, not a regulation. It sort of takes my breath. I hope I am ready for this. Give me the faith to live in the new era. Through Jesus, the bridegroom, amen.

JESUS AND THE CROWDS

*H*ere and in the following verses, Matthew gives us an impressionistic picture of the busy ministry of Jesus. Everywhere he turned there were people to be helped—people from all levels of society, including even the president of the local synagogue. And each time Jesus performed a miracle of healing or resuscitation, his reputation grew that much more, so that ever-greater crowds pressed at his elbow.

The enormous needs of the people may symbolize the sense of decay and hopelessness that had fallen upon Israel since the days of Moses. Then, the nation was young and vigorous and filled with hope. Now, it was suffering under foreign domination, and its towns and cities were populated by masses of people who were poor, ill, and in despair.

Now we can imagine the thrill of expectancy that spread among the masses as they heard the news of these miracles and began to believe that Jesus was indeed the long-promised Messiah, who had come to inaugurate the new age of God's presence in the land.

Imagine what it would do to the feelings of doom and despair in our own time to hear that the Savior of the world is showing up and performing miracles in New York and London and Rome and Hong Kong. And yet he is, if we accept the reports of the faithful.

PRAYER

What a difference it makes in my own life, O God, to believe that your power is still at work in Christ to mend lives, heal bodies, and alter destinies. I implore you that the confidence of this may continue daily in my mind, that I may react to each day's needs out of an overflow of faith and happiness. Through Christ, the hope of everybody's world, amen.

DEALING WITH THE DEMONS

*T*he people of Jesus' day had no sophisticated understanding of illness or mental disorders. Being largely naive and uneducated, they accepted the common belief that afflicted persons were inhabited by demons or bad spirits. This diagnosis always seemed to be borne out especially by people suffering from schizophrenia, epilepsy, and other forms of illness that produced symptoms of radical discomfort or disorientation, as in the case of the demoniac who had not spoken for a long time.

Thus Jesus' power, which was seen to be extraordinary in his ability to heal the two blind men in verses 27-30, was viewed with even greater astonishment when he was able to cure the man whose silence and behavior had marked him for years as antisocial and deranged. Clearly Jesus had power not only over infirmities but also over demons themselves.

The question naturally followed: Whence came this power? The common people, most of them poor and eager to welcome the Messiah, thought it was given by God. But the Pharisees, whose ideology and place in society were threatened by the Messiah's appearance, were only too quick to accept the notion that it was from the devil himself. "By the ruler of the demons he casts out the demons" (v. 34).

PRAYER

I hate to think, dear God, how skeptical I am and which group I would probably have sided with about the origin of Jesus' power. It makes me wonder how many times I fail to see your presence at work in the world today because I am so ready to dismiss or condemn the miracles performed around me. I don't want to be naive. But neither do I wish to be like the Pharisees. Teach me to see clearly because of my engagement with your realm. Through Christ, who is able to make the blind see and the deaf hear, amen.

Day 36   *Matthew 9:35–10:4*

JESUS AND HIS HELPERS

*E*verywhere Jesus went, teaching and preaching and healing, it was the same. Vast crowds of people thronged around him, many with illnesses and infirmities, others hungering to hear about God's coming rule on the earth. Jesus' heart went out to them, for they were "harassed and helpless, like sheep without a shepherd" (v. 36).

What would Jesus think today if he were to visit the center of almost any major city in the United States? Surely he would look at the crowds of poor, homeless individuals carrying their meager belongings in sacks; the many distraught, unhappy office workers and store clerks; the frustrated, hurrying, overworked professionals from the big office buildings—and feel the same way he felt among the people of his own time.

He would say, as he did then, "There are so many of them, and there is so much to do! We need help to deal with all of them. Pray, then, that God will send us more good-hearted folk to assist with the work."

Matthew records the names of the twelve men who became his most intimate followers and assistants in that day. He doesn't tell us much about them, except that they seemed to be a rather diverse lot, and included one of the despised tax collectors. Apparently all but one of them, Judas Iscariot, remained faithful to their calling and helped to found the Christian church in all the world. That is an excellent percentage, as any C.E.O. would readily testify.

PRAYER

I cannot look around me at the suffering in the world today, O God, without feeling the weight of Christ's calling to help with his work. If there was need in his day, there is much more today. Grant that I may not be overwhelmed by its enormity, but may resolutely put myself and all that I have at your disposal, for the sake of Christ and all his little ones. Amen.

Day 37   *Matthew 10:5-15*

BASIC INSTRUCTIONS

*I*n the beginning, at least, Jesus' followers were not empowered to work miracles. They were preachers. Wherever they went, they were to declare the news: "The kingdom of heaven has come near" (v. 7). In elaborating on this news, they no doubt described what they had seen: how Jesus had healed the sick, given sight to the blind and hearing to the deaf, and even raised the dead. The nearness of God's realm was predicated on the presence of the Messiah himself, and they had been living in the Messiah's company.

It is interesting that Jesus instructed them to carry their news only to the Israelites and not to the Gentiles. Later, the news would be shared with the Gentiles as well. But for the moment it was important that the "lost sheep" of the house of Israel hear that the Messiah had come.

The preachers were to travel lightly, depending on the hospitality of Jewish homes wherever they went to provide all their necessities. This betokened not only the urgency of their travels but also the sense of goodness and fellowship their news should engender. The ministry had not yet been institutionalized. It was still an expression of the divine movement in the world.

If people did not receive the good news of God's realm, the preachers were to shake the dust from their feet and leave for other places. A wise pastor I know once said that this should have been formalized as one of the sacraments of the church, so that religious workers today would feel justified in moving on from difficult and resistant situations.

PRAYER

I wish, dear God, that all your called ones still had the sense of urgency that was shared by these first preachers. Unfortunately, most preachers today—in fact, most Christians today—are more concerned about salaries, housing arrangements, and working conditions than about the crowds of poor and needy people and the wonderful news we have for them. Forgive all of us, I pray, and rekindle in us the original sense of mission. Through Christ, who must be ashamed of us, amen.

Day 38   *Matthew 10:16-31*

THE HARDSHIPS TO BE ENDURED

*T*he dangers Christ described for the preachers he sent out probably most characterized those faced by the disciples after his death, when the lines became more fiercely drawn between Christians and other Jews. They certainly find resonance in the book of Acts, which depicts the hardships of early missionary preachers when they came up against violent opposition to their activities.

Jesus obviously knew how divisive adherence to his teachings could be, for he said that even brothers would betray one another to death, and fathers their children. This is hard to imagine in our time, when most families are models of tolerance and understanding. But there are still places in the world where families and tribes expel members who adopt new and different ways or marry outside prescribed boundaries.

The picture Jesus paints is one of fear on the part of those who reject the Christian message—fear that the traditions will be broken, fear that life will change, fear that Beelzebub, the master of devils, is behind it all. The important thing, he says, is that the one bearing the message of Christ need not be afraid, but know that God will take care of him or her and provide the words to be spoken in a time of crisis. What can one's earthly enemies do? he asks. Only kill the body. But the power of God can destroy both the body and the soul.

Of all the birds and animals sold for sacrifice at the Temple in Jerusalem, sparrows were the smallest and cheapest. They were so cheap, in fact, that two could be purchased for the smallest coin. Yet God keeps an eye on every one of them, said Jesus. How much more can we expect that God will watch over us, who are the divine messengers! Why, God keeps track of every hair on our heads. So we mustn't be afraid when we are engaged in doing the work of the gospel. God is observing everything that happens!

PRAYER

I have often heard these verses quoted, O God, to prove your gentleness and love. Now I see that they refer to a special situation, when we are encountering hostility for the sake of the gospel. Forgive me for becoming so complacent that I had forgotten the ongoing conflict between good and evil in my time, and help me to reenlist in the struggle, which will end only when the Son of Man returns to earth and all creation will be transformed into your glorious realm. Through Christ, whose courage at the end should be a model for my own, amen.

Day 39   *Matthew 10:32-42*

FINDING LIFE BY LOSING IT

*J*esus was utterly realistic about the effect his coming with the new realm would have on many people. Ironically, the Prince of Peace would introduce conflict and rage in many quarters. Just as new wine tears up old wineskins that are too inflexible to expand, so also the new era of God's rulership puts stress on many lives, traditions, and institutions that are simply unable to accommodate it. It was true in Jesus' time, and it is still true in our own.

Think how many church councils have been thrown into conflict by the insistence of a member or members that they reform themselves along more Christlike, self-denying lines. And if it happens in churches, how much more is it likely to happen in a school, a community, or a secular organization?

Yet, said Jesus, we must never shy away from conflict for the sake of peace and tranquility. It is in risking everything that we discover the very meaning of life itself. As we have seen from the very beginning of Matthew's Gospel, God's realm is the most important thing on the entire human agenda, and we should never shrink from giving it everything we have.

The final verses of this passage contain a very beautiful thought—that all of those who welcome God's messengers, even by being kind or extending a cup of water when they are thirsty, will be somehow included in the benefits of the realm. There is tenderness and gentleness in this thought. These friends of the friends of God will share in the blessedness of the life to come.

PRAYER

I blush to think, dear God, how often I have failed to speak out against error, misguidedness, or evil because I did not want to hurt anyone's feelings. I must have forgotten how deep and serious is the conflict we are engaged in. Forgive me, I pray, and make me willing to contend earnestly for the faith. Through Christ, who gave his life, amen.

Day 40   *Matthew 11:1-19*

JESUS AND JOHN THE BAPTIST

*I*t was natural for John to raise the question, wasn't it? He was alone and in prison, probably treated with incredible harshness, miles away from the countryside and riverbanks he loved. A person can become desperately uncertain about things in a situation like that.

"Go and tell John," said Jesus, "what you hear and see: the blind receive their sight, the lame walk, the lepers are cleansed, the deaf hear, the dead are raised, and the poor have good news brought to them" (vv. 4-5).

It was a definitive answer. What more was there to say? The heavenly realm and its Lord were obviously there.

Afterward, Jesus mused on the rough old prophet. Surely no mother's son on earth was greater than John. Yet, said Jesus, in the realm of God, everyone is as great as John—the realm is an equalizer.

The times were violent, the way the weather is when a cold front and a warm front collide; and John, tough as he was, had gotten caught in the violence. Jesus himself would be crucified, but he was up to it. Is it possible that he was even a rough man, as John was? The satire in his language in verses 7-10 may indicate that he was.

People are funny, Jesus was thinking. John came as a temperate figure, eating little and refusing strong drink, and people said he was crazy. Jesus came as the opposite, eating and drinking with unobservant Jews, and the very same people said he was a glutton and a drunkard. Yet God's purpose was being worked out in both of them.

It is amazing how many ways God works.

PRAYER

God, this is such a human passage. I can almost hear Jesus laughing with joy as he told those men to go tell John what they saw. He had such utter confidence in it all. And that reverie about John—he really cared about John, the way someone cares about another who has done a good job. And that reflection on people, too—Jesus was no fool. He knew the price of things, didn't he? I can follow more joyfully for this passage, dear God. Thanks.

Day 41   *Matthew 11:20-30*

GOD AND THE SIMPLE FOLK

*A*h, the disappointment breaks through here for the towns that had already proven inhospitable to the work of God's realm. Even Capernaum, which had been Jesus' headquarters, had rejected the new creation. They had all written their own judgments, for the chief strategist of the new age was disappointed.

There is a touch of sadness and irony in his thanksgiving. God has indeed begun the new creation in the simple folk—the untutored people of the land, who don't stand very high in anybody's social register. They have rallied to the new realm.

Let them flock to him—the hard-working poor, the little people of the land—and he will give them relief. Let them join him in the yoke—they will find him gentle and humble-hearted like themselves. Together, they will usher in the new age.

The sophisticated townspeople and the religious leaders are too pre-occupied with other things to care about the new age, but God will build it yet from the little stones along the riverbank!

PRAYER

God, I have always liked country folk. They don't take things for granted the way city people do. They are affected by the rain, the smell of the earth, the movement of birds. There is an openness and honesty about them, bred by the land they work on. They are more in touch with themselves than are city dwellers. And they are still working for God's realm. God bless the peasants and the farmers. Through Jesus, who found them receptive, amen.

Day 42 *Matthew 12:1-14*

LORD OF THE SABBATH

*A*s is often the case in Matthew's Gospel, the spirit and thrust of the new creation are set over against those of the old. Under the Torah, which was the chief religious expression of the old order, some people had fallen into a way of life characterized by mere legal nit-picking; among the thirty-nine varieties of work that their excessive legalism forbade on the sabbath was the plucking of grain. But the spirit of God's reign shatters this narrow philosophy the way new wine shatters old wineskins.

First, Jesus reminds the Pharisees that David himself had once set a precedent for eating food forbidden by religious scruples when the scruples are transcended by the fact of simple hunger. Then he cites Numbers 28:9-10 and throws the discussion into another key: The priests in the Temple profane the sabbath by performing their duties on the holy day, and they are guiltless in doing so; and, as he himself is the Lord of the new creation, his disciples are as free to do whatever he permits them as the priests of the old order!

Then, in the synagogue, where there is a man with a withered hand, Jesus is taunted by some persons over whether it is permissible to heal on the sabbath. Jesus reminds them that their laws permit the rescue of animals on the sabbath and asks whether a person isn't of more value than an animal.

It is no wonder that the Pharisees go away angry and seek ways to destroy Jesus. His whole tone and temper are different from theirs. His disregard for legalism is only a handy excuse; the fact is, they cannot bear the new order he represents.

49

God, how clearly Jesus saw what the true priorities in life are, and how easily we confuse them. We are always setting into motion systems that run away from us and begin to oppress people—in government, in education, in business, in human relations. Help us to see when this happens and to be willing to terminate or modify them for the good of those affected by them. Through the One whose courage led to a cross, amen.

Day 43   *Matthew 12:15-21*

THE SECRET OF JESUS

*W*hen the time comes that you are well known to all people, said the poet Rainer Maria Rilke, then it is time to take another name—any name—so that God can call you in the night.

Here, in fulfillment of a prophecy in Isaiah, Matthew indicates the becoming modesty of Jesus as his fame grew throughout Israel. To be sure, there was an external reason for his asking those he healed not to tell anyone—the opposition of the Pharisees was growing, and he did not wish to provoke a final encounter before his hour had come (cf. John 12:27; 13:1). But the quiet manner that Isaiah had predicted for the Messiah accords well with the injunctions in Matthew 6 against making any display of piety or good works. Jesus was not letting his left hand know what his right had done.

People appreciate modesty. The greatest persons in the world are usually the most self-effacing. Their strong sense of inner worth renders unnecessary the praise of the multitudes. It is the diminutive persons, the would-be heroes, who make a show of their gifts and achievements.

PRAYER

Dear God, why is it that those of us who do least for others are most concerned to be recognized for what we have done? We desire thank-you notes, brass plaques, and public praise for all our good deeds. Help us to be more like the Master of all, who, having rendered the greatest of services, besought others to remain silent about the gift. Amen.

JESUS SPEAKS BACK

*J*esus may have been a gentle and modest person, but he was also firm with those who opposed him. In this passage are echoes of John the Baptist, whose fiery denunciation of the scribes and Pharisees once rang out along the Jordan.

The Pharisees had said that Jesus derived his power from the Evil One. How, he demanded to know, could the Evil One bring forth good works? Obviously the Pharisees themselves were related to the Evil One. They were a nest of snakes, hissing and writhing and ready to inject their poison into any victim who came near them!

It was not that Jesus minded their words against him—those would be forgiven. But their impediment to the movement of the Spirit of God, to the coming of the new realm, was unforgivable. In the day of judgment, their own words would prove their condemnation.

Here is a healthy attitude for all of us! We should not worry about what others say or think of us, but we should always be concerned about the spirit of evil, which blocks the work of God's realm in the world. *That* is the real problem we face.

PRAYER

O God, I often get steamed up over the wrong things—little slights from friends or a lack of recognition from those I work for—while I hardly think of the graft and corruption at the corporate level that are grinding down your little ones, making slums of our cities, and poisoning the atmosphere of our world. Help me to become more passionate about the important things. Through Jesus, who had the right perspective, amen.

SIMPLE FOLK REQUIRE NO PROOF

*H*ow easy it is to think, "If only I had lived in Jesus' day and seen the miracles he worked, I would have had no problem believing in him!" But Jesus said to the scribes and Pharisees that only a perverse generation needs a sign in order to believe, and he refused to accommodate their desire for a sign—except to speak of his own death and resurrection, which Matthew obviously regards as the most important sign Jesus ever gave. They would fare worse in the judgment than the people of ancient Nineveh or the Queen of the South—non-Jews who respected God more than they did.

The scribes and Pharisees had tried, in their vain efforts to be righteous, to cleanse their lives of evil. But the evil had returned to its source seven times stronger than when it began. What hope could there be for such stiff-necked people?

By contrast, there were the disciples, who had never thought of themselves as righteous or skilled in the law. They were like brothers and sisters and parents to Jesus. They had followed him without asking for signs of his power and authority. They were like the gentle, humble people of the beatitudes. Theirs would be the realm of God.

PRAYER

Forgive me, O Lord, for having ever desired signs of your favor. I am surrounded by such signs if I will only learn to see them. Life bears abundant clues of your presence, from the gentle sunlight that awakened me this morning to the water I drank from an old dipper to the lovely yellow squash on my plate at dinner and the smiles of my family around the table. Why am I so obtuse that I seldom recognize you? Thank you for being there, and for Jesus, who made such things much plainer to us. Amen.

Day 46   *Matthew 13:1-23*

SPEAKING IN PARABLES

*M*atthew 13 is given solely to parables about the realm of God and discourse about parables. It is both tantalizing in its material and enlightening about Jesus' method of teaching. Contrary to the image we received from Matthew 5:1, of Jesus addressing the multitudes with the Sermon on the Mount, we are told here that Jesus always spoke to the crowds in parables.

Why would he have spoken to the crowds only in parables? Perhaps it was so the ones God intended to hear and be saved would recognize the true meaning of the parables, while others would hear only puzzling words. Denis de Rougemont, a French scholar, once called parables "traps for meditation."

That is, they invite us inside, where they suddenly develop new meaning for us. If a person is unwilling to enter, the story remains a mere absurdity.

We can only conclude that the explanation of the parable of the seeds in verses 18-23 and the later explanation of the parable of the wheat and tares in verses 36-43 are additives or glosses on the original text for the purpose of instructing neophyte Christians in the day when the Gospel was written. Jesus clearly expected the original disciples to understand the parables without explanation; if they did not, there was no reason for him to speak in parables at all.

PRAYER

Lord, the disciples heard and understood because their lives were committed to you. But I am often like the crowds who heard but never understood. At least, like them, I am seldom swept away from my usual moorings to enter the wild seas of the Spirit. The very monotony of my existence accuses me of never having heard and responded fully to you. Please increase my power to hear these parables as I read them again, and to truly live them, from the inside out. Through Jesus, who tempts me with such mysteries, amen.

Day 47   *Matthew 13:24-30, 36-43*

THE WEEDS AND THE WHEAT

*T*his apocalyptic story has been useful ever since Jesus told it to explain why God permits good and evil to dwell together in the present age. It must have served an important purpose in the early church as an explanation of why there shouldn't be frequent purges to cleanse the church of persons who seemed not to fulfill their obligations to Christ and their fellow believers.

I have heard pastors say that the work of their churches would progress much more smoothly if So-and-So would just step in front of an oncoming truck. One woman observed that there was nothing wrong with her church that "a few Christian burials" wouldn't cure. Many of the early Christians must have felt precisely the same way about some of their colleagues in the local congregations.

But Jesus' parable suggests that it is not always possible to get rid of undesirable followers without somehow damaging the desirable ones in the process. Who is wise enough, after all, to make such decisions? In the early church, Simon Peter would certainly have been one of those ex-pelled, for denying that he even knew Jesus. But sometimes the very persons we think should be removed are the ones who turn out to be the heroes in the end.

The Pharisees were always ready to make such decisions about who belonged to God and who didn't. But Jesus taught his disciples that this is not a decision for human beings. God will separate the wheat and the weeds in the final judgment, and then the righteous "will shine like the sun in the kingdom of their Father" (v. 43).

PRAYER

I admit, O God, that I have been guilty of deciding that certain persons should not be permitted to remain in the fellowship of the redeemed. I'm afraid this condemns me as an unwise, headstrong disciple who needs to return to the Master for instruction. I can only pray, after rethinking this parable, that I shall be gathered with the wheat and not thrown into the fire with the weeds. Through Christ, my salvation, amen.

Day 48   *Matthew 13:31-35*

BRIEF STORIES ABOUT THE NEW REALM

*T*he common element in these two parables is the startling, unexpected way the kingdom or realm of God grows once it has started. First, there is the surprise involved in seeing that a mustard plant, which was once a tiny, spherical seed about the size of a large pinhead, has become so large and many-branched that it can shelter the nests of numerous birds. Then there is the image of the yeast—probably a bit of dough that has been set aside in some water to ferment, the way we make sourdough bread today—that causes the flour and water it is mixed with to expand to almost miraculous proportions.

Professor Bernard Brandon Scott, in his book *Hear Then the Parable,* observes how extremely daring—and therefore potent—this second parable actually is. Yeast was usually considered an unpleasant substance, and when the rabbis used it as an image, it was almost always to speak of the treacherous influence of something. Yet Jesus applied it to the new realm of God. By the same token, Jesus showed a *woman* mixing the bread—an allusion that would have been unpopular with the strongly male-oriented scribes and Pharisees.

And the amount of dough the woman was mixing would have produced enough bread for fifty people! She must have been preparing for a party. So there is tucked into the folds of this very brief parable even an allusion to the celebrative or banquetlike character of God's realm.

We can almost imagine Jesus' smile as he told this outrageous story.

PRAYER

What a poet Jesus was, O God! How he loved conjuring up daring new images to speak of what was almost unspeakable, to describe the mysteries of your heavenly realm. Help me to catch the playful spirit of his rich, associative mind. Let me break through to new and joyous levels of understanding. In his name, amen.

Day 49   *Matthew 13:44-52*

MORE PARABLES

or sheer joy," says the *New English Bible,* the man who found the buried treasure "went and sold everything he had, and bought that field."

We can picture the man racing about from acquaintance to acquaintance, asking what they would give him for his possessions.

"But you don't want to sell those candlesticks, Barnabas—they belonged to your uncle Joseph."

"I want to sell—give me anything!"

"But, Barnabas—your library! You have always loved it so!"

"No matter—it is nothing. What will you give?"

Joyously, confidently, vigorously selling *all* for the field with its treasures. So it is, said Jesus, with the realm of God. If a person only knew its worth, he or she would give up everything for it.

This was the difference between Jesus and the scribes and Pharisees— he was enthusiastic, filled with the Spirit of God's realm. His mind raced from image to image, describing the coming of a new creation.

Even a teacher of the law, he said, can become a learner in the realm of God. Then the teacher will not merely draw on the store of what has been written and said before, but will feel the tides of creation rise within, so that he or she speaks new things as well as old.

How beyond price this new realm is—if people would only realize it!

PRAYER

The old and the new, O God. How wonderful if all people were so open to both the past and the future, and could draw upon one while learning from the other. Grant that I may maintain a spirit that combines both reverence for what has been thought in the past and receptivity to all the emergent factors constituting a new order in my time. Through Jesus, who said we could learn from him, amen.

Day 50   *Matthew 13:53-58*

DISDAINING THE FAMILIAR

I went to school with one of the most famous theologians of modern times. We were not friends, but I used to see him frequently in the library, the halls, and the room where we ate our lunches. Like others who knew him even marginally during those days, I have great difficulty believing that he is the same man whose name is spoken with respect throughout the world. He was simply too common and unattractive to have evolved into that other person. In order to read his writings with proper reverence, I have to detach myself from any memory of the student I saw and think of him only as a renowned theologian.

Apparently it was this way for the people of Jesus' hometown. They could not believe that the profound teachings they heard from Jesus or the miraculous healings he performed came from one whom they had watched growing up as the son of Mary. And the attention they paid to the contrast between their expectancies and the man who stood before them diverted them from the things he was trying to say and do, so that his effectiveness was limited in their midst.

What they needed to remember, as we do, is that wisdom is a gift of God, whatever the vehicle, and we should not permit our incredulity toward the source to blind us to its value.

PRAYER

Sometimes, O God, others stagger me with their insights into life's mysteries. Help me never to miss the truth of what they say because I am so preoccupied with its source. Through Jesus, who both said and did the truth, amen.

THE DEATH OF THE BAPTIST

*G*od is not the only judge of human beings. History—the long look—also renders its judgment. And history reveals the vast difference between the two men at the center of this little drama.

John we know to have been a simple man of simple tastes. Herod's life was complicated by ambition, pride, and foolishness.

John was morally zealous. Herod was corrupt and entangled in his own sins. He had broken Jewish law to divorce his wife and marry Herodias, and he broke it by executing John by decapitation and without a trial.

John was totally committed to the coming realm of God. Herod was committed to keeping his own throne intact if he could.

John died with honor, and he is remembered throughout the world as the forerunner of Christ. Herod died in disgrace, banished by the emperor to the remote districts of Gaul, cut off from the very kingdom he sought so desperately to preserve.

Real security, history seems to say, does not lie in earthly thrones and fortifications, but in commitment to God and the divine righteousness. It cannot be bought by gold and jewels. It is given to those who live in the Spirit of God.

PRAYER

O God, power in the hands of a careless person is a frightening thing. It even prompts me to consider whether I do not often misuse the modest power at my disposal. Teach me to care so much for everyone affected by my power that I may not abuse it, but may turn it into a blessing shared with others. Through Jesus, who cared about the use of power, amen.

FEEDING THE CROWDS

*I*t has been estimated that in Jesus' time there were more than two hundred cities in Israel with populations of more than 15,000—all in a country no larger than many present-day counties in the United States. So it was not always easy for Jesus to get away from people to pray and rest. Here, when he crossed the lake for that purpose, the crowds merely followed him around the edge.

Feeling compassion for the people, as he always did, he told the disciples to give them something to eat. "All we have," they said, "is five loaves and two fish." "Let me have them," said Jesus.

He blessed the loaves and fish and gave them to the disciples to distribute, and when everyone had eaten, twelve baskets full of scraps remained. The miracle is reminiscent of the Israelites' receiving manna from heaven as Moses led them through the wilderness. But, as Jesus is greater than Moses, the provision is much more abundant for those he feeds.

This was an important narrative among the early Christians, not only because Jesus was the new Moses but also because the multiplication of the bread accorded so well with the eucharistic meal that was the central rite of Christian fellowship. In a time when Christians sometimes met literally in the wilderness, or at least in very private places, to avoid detection, the story spoke eloquently of the way God daily provided their food for spiritual life.

PRAYER

We are inclined, O God, to put our trust in programs organized for our future maintenance—in social security and insurance funds and savings accounts—so that we spend much of our energy providing for tomorrow's needs. Help us to rediscover the meaning of freedom and spontaneity by depending on you for our daily bread. Through Jesus, who feeds us in any wilderness place we can possibly inhabit. Amen.

Day 53   *Matthew 14:22-36*

CHRIST AND HIS CHURCH

*A*fter feeding the people and sending them away, Jesus went up the hillside that swept duskily down to the sea. The average person would have done so in order to lie down and sleep after such a strenuous day. But Jesus went up to pray. He had learned long before that prayer releases inner energies that restore the person even more than sleep. Having been restored himself, he was able to come to the rescue of the disciples in the foundering boat.

We can imagine the situation in the early church's life to which a passage like this must have spoken. Persecutions had made survival difficult for the church. Jesus' reappearance was delayed beyond their expectations, just as he was late in coming to the disciples in the boat. Peter, who was probably already known as the chief spokesman for the church, had faltered badly at the time of the crucifixion. But Jesus had steadied him and helped him back into his role, as he helped him back into the boat in this story. The story is really about the transcendent Christ—*after the resurrection*—coming to the troubled church and stilling the troubled seas around it.

It is no wonder the story reaches its climax when the disciples fall down to worship, saying, "Truly you are the Son of God" (v. 33).

The remarkable little picture in verses 34-36 is in keeping with such a passage. It too is of the transcendent Christ, this time passing among the crowds of people begging only to touch the hem of his garment. "And everyone who touched it," translates the New English Bible, "was completely cured" (v. 36).

PRAYER

Dear God, I am greatly moved by this picture of the early church and its worship. Grant that when the storms seem too much for us today we shall remember this passage and take heart. Through Jesus, who always joins us in the troubled vessel, amen.

Day 54   *Matthew 15:1-20*

THE PARABLE OF THE UNRIGHTEOUS MAN

*T*his material is closely related to Jesus' teachings in Matthew 5:17-48, where he said that he had not come to abrogate the law of Moses but to fulfill it. The scribes and Pharisees are concerned once more with the failure of the disciples, who are unobservant Jews, to keep the regulations or traditions associated with the law. The disciples do not perform the ritual ceremonies before meals.

Stung by this persistent nettling over nonessentials, Jesus replies in two ways. First, he reminds them that they have *altered* the law of Moses to make the commandment to honor one's parents avoidable, just as in Matthew 5:30-32 he reminded his audience that the law concerning divorce had been *weakened* to suit the contemporary legalists. Second, he gives his critics a brief parable: It is not what goes into the mouth that defiles a person but what comes out.

The disciples, uncomfortable with the tension building between Jesus and the legalists, ask if he realizes he has angered them. But he too is angry, and lashes back: "Let them alone; they are blind guides of the blind" (v. 14).

Peter, again the spokesman for the early church, asks for an interpretation of the parable. This is probably for the benefit of neophytes in the church of Matthew's age, who needed to understand the meaning of the saying. It isn't the food entering the body that defiles it, says Jesus, but the talk coming out of it.

As from the very beginning of the Gospel, we are reminded that religion is a matter of the heart, not of observing rules and regulations.

PRAYER

O God, I have heard that scruples over the Communion meal and how it is to be taken keep the major Christian bodies from uniting in our day. We are no better than the scribes and Pharisees, it seems, for we put our own traditions above fellowship and worshiping together. Save us from being blind guides of the blind. Through Jesus, who perennially rebukes our foolishness, amen.

Day 55   *Matthew 15:21-28*

JESUS AND A FOREIGNER

*I*f we are bothered by Jesus' tendency at this stage to define his mission in terms of Israel and not of the entire world, we must remember that Matthew's Gospel was written from a Jewish perspective to emphasize how Jesus had first fulfilled the prophecies regarding a Messiah for Israel. But this story very self-consciously represents Jesus as bringing benefits to the Gentile world as well.

The woman, a Canaanite or non-Jew, accentuates the Jewishness of Jesus by calling him Son of David, a Messianic title. The disciples' irritation with her—"Send her away," they demand of Jesus—is probably increased by the racial prejudice they instinctively feel. And even Jesus appears to refer to her with a racial epithet; the Jews referred to foreigners as "dogs."

But the woman is insistent, and she asks for so little—only the crumbs that fall from the table. It is a gentle imploring that the woman makes on behalf of her daughter.

Jesus, always compassionate, cannot resist. He grants her request, even though his first mission is to the Israelites. And the Gentile world begins in a small way to benefit from the coming of the Jewish Messiah!

PRAYER

From what small beginnings, O God, sprang the riches that have come to the Gentile world from the Jewish Savior. The mind boggles at any attempt to enumerate your blessings to our culture. Freedom, peace, love, and all they mean in specific ways are the gifts of your Spirit. We thank you through Jesus, who has broken down every wall that divided us, if we will only see that he has. Amen.

Day 56 *Matthew 15:29–16:12*

WORRYING ABOUT BREAD

*A*gain the story of the crowds and Jesus' compassion on them. Again the hesitance of the disciples—"Where are we to get enough bread in the desert to feed so great a crowd?" (15:33). Again the blessing of what there was and the feeding with abundance in the wilderness. And again the nagging question of the Pharisees, "Show us a sign," with the cryptic answer that they were to have only the sign of the prophet Jonah.

"Beware," says Jesus, "of the yeast of the Pharisees and Sadducees" (16:6). Yeast was often used by rabbis as a symbol of evil and how quickly it permeates everything. But the poor, dull disciples! They hear the word *yeast* and realize in an instant that they have failed to bring any bread with them, though so many basketfuls were left over from the feeding of the four thousand. "He has caught us unprepared," they think.

"Don't you understand?" Jesus says. "I was speaking of the evil influence of the Pharisees and Sadducees, not of real bread."

It is interesting that in the parallel passage in Mark 8:11-21, it is the *bread* and not the *yeast* that lies at the center of Jesus' meaning. Here, Matthew is concerned to point up the continuing conflict between Jesus and his legalistic enemies.

O God, I too am a dull disciple, always worrying about bread and other things when I should be concerned about issues of evil and intransigence in the world. Forgive me, and help me to be more discerning. Through Jesus, whose lot it is to have dull disciples like me, amen.

Day 57   *Matthew 16:13-20*

THE GREAT CONFESSION

Some scholars think this passage is an early attempt to bolster the papal authority of Peter, while others insist that Peter's confession is to be the real foundation of the church. Regardless of what it says about Peter, this passage provides an important picture of Jesus.

Several times in the Gospel we have noted Jesus' caution to people he has healed not to tell others about it. The fact that he remains strangely unknown, despite the crowds that gather around him, is underlined by his question, "Who do people say that the Son of Man is?" (v. 13).

When he asks, "Who do *you* say that I am?" Peter replies, "You are the Messiah, the Son of the living God" (vv. 15-16). It is a highly significant confession, registering what may have been only a slowly maturing conviction on the apostles' part. In the boat, they had recognized him as the Son of God (Matt. 14:33), but we know that time sequences were often mixed up in the writing of the Gospels, and we suspect that the boat episode may actually have been a post-Resurrection narrative. Matthew apparently construed Peter's confession as the first major recognition by the disciples of the true scope of Jesus' work and ministry. He is not merely a wonderful teacher and worker of miracles; he is the long-promised Savior of the people!

Again Jesus counsels the disciples not to tell anyone who he really is, as though the secret must not yet be disclosed. And from this time on he begins to prepare them for the events of the Passion week and beyond, which now loom palpably close.

PRAYER

O God, what a moment it must have been for the disciples when they moved to this new level of recognition. They were surely filled with exultation. I wonder if it might not be like that with me as well—that the quality of my entire life could be suddenly altered by a deepened awareness of the meaning of Christ to my existence. Let it be, I pray, through him who reveals himself to faithful disciples. Amen.

Day 58   *Matthew 16:21-28*

LETTING GO OF LIFE IN ORDER TO HAVE IT

*F*rom here on out, the shadow of the cross falls implacably across Matthew's account of Jesus' ministry. And how quickly Peter falls from the sublimity of the new order to the fear and hesitance of the old! He has barely made the great confession that Jesus is the Messiah, when Jesus speaks of his impending death and Peter counters, "God forbid it, Lord! This must never happen to you" (v. 22). He can no more fit the two things together—Messiah and death—than the crowds of unbelievers could. How can a figure of such power speak of dying a shameful death?

"Get behind me, Satan!" says Jesus, rebuking Peter as furiously as he had earlier congratulated him on his insight. "You are setting your mind not on divine things but on human things" (v. 23). Or, as the *New English Bible* translates it, "You think the thoughts of man and not of God."

If the early church described in the book of Acts had taken a motto from the sayings of Jesus, as they faced a hostile world, this might well have been the one: "The way you think is not God's way but man's." They no longer thought in the usual terms of cost, probability of success, and failure. They were like a people on fire for God, turning the world upside down, because everything seemed possible to them under God.

The secret, as Jesus explained to the disciples, is not to worry about self. It is in trying to grasp life that we lose everything; it is in living recklessly for God that we find everything!

PRAYER

I want to take risks, O God, and live unencumbered by selfish concerns. But there are many things for which I feel responsible. What am I to do about them? Help me to know the answer, because it often perplexes me. Through Jesus, whose commitment makes me feel guilty, amen.

A FORETASTE OF THE NEW ORDER

*T*his passage is especially striking in the light of Matthew's theme that Jesus is the new Moses. The event apparently occurred during the Feast of Tabernacles, as Peter wanted to erect booths or tents for the three figures. The emphasis of Jewish thinking during this time was on the new age of the Messiah. The ascent of the mountain, the appearance of Moses and Elijah, and the cloud representing the holy presence of God are all in keeping with this emphasis.

Jesus' face shines as Moses' did when he descended from Mount Sinai. The voice from the cloud, however, the same voice heard at Jesus' baptism in Matthew 3:17, announces that this is one greater than either Moses, who represents the law, or Elijah, who represents the prophets. It is the beloved Son, which in Jewish thought is the closest identity a human being could have to God.

The presence of Elijah among the transfigured ones leads naturally to the disciples' question about the popular notion that he must return to experience death before the age of the Messiah. Jesus indicates that the people of the age have already had their Elijah—John the Baptist—but failed to recognize him. And the reference to John is occasion for Jesus' reference to his own sufferings, which will be in dramatic contrast to the glory he has just shared in the Transfiguration scene.

PRAYER

Mountains, light, cloud—the symbolism of this passage is of height, loftiness, rarefication. It beckons me, dear God, from the tawdriness of my everyday concerns—from a cluttered desk, a messy laundry room, unpaid bills, a car in need of repair. Thank you for such hallowing moments, and for sending light in my darkness. Amen.

WHEN FAITH IS TOO WEAK

*T*his story must have been told for every lagging disciple in every age, including our own. The situation in the life of the early church is not hard to imagine. After all the marvelous stories of Jesus' miracles of healing, and then of the disciples', especially in the book of Acts, some followers of the Way were distressed that they could not cast out demons, cure the sick, and raise the dead as their Lord and predecessors had. Did they not share the same power? Ah, says the Gospel, coming to their rescue, even the apostles failed on occasion, because their faith was not strong enough.

We are funny creatures. Faith transforms us. When we believe something strongly, we enter a new realm of possibility. I heard a man say that in an emergency his father had picked up the side of an automobile and held it while an injured person was removed from beneath the wreck; afterward he tried to lift it again and could not budge it. The crisis had propelled him into a new dimension of strength. Is it so hard to believe that miracles occur in the lives of those whose faith accepts miracles as natural?

PRAYER

Moving mountains by faith is beyond my imagination, O God. Maybe Jesus exaggerated only to make his point. I can believe in dramatic cures, telepathic messages, and superhuman strength. Help me to move from my present level of expectancy to one where such things are the rule and not the exception. Through Jesus, for whom miracles were a way of life, amen.

Day 61   *Matthew 17:22-27*

A FISH STORY

*H*ere, set against Jesus' prediction of his death and resurrection, is a strange story. What can it mean? The intent is surely similar to that of the encounter between Jesus and the Pharisees (Matt. 22:15-22) about paying taxes to Caesar. The position of the early church was consistently pro-authority. Even though the government was corrupt and shared in the persecution of Christians, Christians were advised to pay their taxes, pray for their leaders, and live harmoniously in the temporal order. This passage involves the payment by Jewish Christians of the tax to maintain the Temple in Jerusalem. After the Jews instituted new rules that deterred the Christians from participating in synagogue and Temple worship, many Christians no doubt protested the Temple tax assessments.

Jesus and his followers, who are giving their lives to God's work, should hardly be taxed to support a place dedicated to his worship. But, says Jesus in effect, we do not want to cause difficulty for those who merely enforce the rules, so we shall pay their taxes. It is a rule of generosity for future generations, much in keeping with the teaching of Matthew 5:41: "If anyone forces you to go one mile, go also the second mile."

As for the fish story, which seems almost too fantastic to deserve a place in the Gospel, there is, of course, the possibility that it was symbolic and not realistic. We remember that the fish became a symbol for Christianity because the Greek word for "fish," *ichthus,* is an anagram of the motto *Iesus Christos Theou Huios Soter*—"Jesus Christ, God's Son, Savior." Could the story have meant that the Christian community would pay the Temple tax for its members? The early Christians, after all, did hold their goods in a common treasury.

PRAYER

It sometimes bothers me, O God, to pay taxes to corrupt authorities. I feel that I could use the money much better for humane purposes. But Jesus never seemed to worry much about money; that isn't what your realm hinges on. Give me an open and generous spirit, I pray, that I may be more like him. Amen.

Day 62   *Matthew 18:1-14*

GOD'S LITTLE ONES

This chapter constitutes another of the long discourses in Matthew that are collections of Jesus' teachings for the edification of the Christian community. This particular passage deals with the simplicity and childlikeness of his followers when compared with the learnedness and sophistication of the great scholars of the Law.

Recall that when Jesus denounced the cities that had refused his ministry he said, "I thank you, Father, Lord of heaven and earth, because you have hidden these things from the wise and the intelligent and have revealed them to infants" (Matt. 11:25). It was a point Jesus made again and again in various ways. The realm of God was a new creation; it could not be poured like new wine into old skins. It required fresh vigor and childlike imagination, untrammeled by too much devotion to mere tradition.

Perhaps Jesus anticipated criticism of the disciples and the Christian community. "Don't think too harshly of these little ones," he was cautioning in effect. "They have their guardian angels who look directly into the face of God. Of course, they resemble sheep in their simple faith. But God has sent his Good Shepherd to find the sheep that the learned shepherds of Israel have disregarded. And there is great rejoicing whenever one of them is brought home to the realm!"

PRAYER

Make me simple, dear God, as you must be simple. Let my eye be sound and my entire body full of light. Calm my thoughts, that they fly not in a thousand directions. Still my impulses, that they may wait upon you as a sheep waits upon the help of its shepherd. Make me see your world fresh-washed and magical, as a child, and I shall glorify you this day. Amen.

Day 63   *Matthew 18:15-20*

WHEN LITTLE ONES FALL OUT

*H*ow shall God's little ones deal with quarrels among themselves? Matthew here relates explicit teachings of Jesus on this subject. First, there is patient exchange with the contentious person. Go to him or her and discuss the matter in question. If the person remains alienated, take one or two other Christians along and try again; perhaps he or she will be convinced upon hearing the facts from other perspectives.

Should this not avail, then take the matter before the Christian community and let them deal with it. Perhaps the health of the entire organism is necessary to reestablish the health of the diseased tissue. But if the person remains obdurate even against the community, there is nothing left but to treat the person as an outsider.

The words spoken to Peter in the context of the great confession (Matt. 16:19) are repeated here: Decisions made in the community are decisions of God's realm as well. An ancient Jewish saying is "Two that sit together occupied in the law have the Presence among them." As the Christian community is formed by God's presence in the new creation, God is automatically involved in the decisions it makes.

PRAYER

What a beautiful picture this offers, O God, of a church where your Spirit is so strong that everyone trusts the decisions that are made by the community. Help my church to be that kind of place, and help me to be the kind of living member who will enable it to be. Through Jesus, whose wisdom was always exceptional, amen.

THE MUTUALITY OF FORGIVENESS

*I*n the preceding passage, Jesus talked about how Christians are to settle their disputes, first by talking to each other, then by involving two or three others, and finally by taking them before the entire community. Now he deals with what we are to do with those who repeatedly transgress against us or mistreat us in such monstrous fashion that we are all but beside ourselves in anger and disappointment.

Once more Peter, the spokesman for the community, voices the question: "Lord, if another member of the church sins against me, how often should I forgive? As many as seven times?" Other laws of mercy said three times; Peter was appearing to be generous. Jesus replies, "Not seven times, but, I tell you, seventy-seven times" (vv. 21-22). Other translations read "seventy times seven." Such a number is no longer literal, of course; it speaks of such depths of concern and forgiveness as cannot be measured.

There follows a parable on the realm of God to remind every member of the community that he or she is there only by divine grace. In one sense, it is a gloss on the statement in the model prayer, "Forgive us our debts as we forgive our debtors." We were all so far in debt—the poor character in this story was in by a king's ransom!—that there was no hope of ever paying. For us to be hard or unforgiving toward anyone else, then, over what in comparison can never amount to more than a beggarly amount, a few coins, is absurd. We have not truly appreciated the magnitude of God's gift to us, and cannot in fact consider ourselves part of God's realm.

PRAYER

Dear God, what a deep well of the Spirit this presumes! It reminds me with terrifying vividness of the shallow level at which I daily live. Give me a renewed consciousness of my freedom from debt, that I may respond to others always with exhilaration and joy. Through Jesus, who forgave others even from his cross, amen.

MARRIAGE MAKES ONE FLESH

*A*gain Matthew takes up the greater-than-Moses theme, this time with regard to the law about marriage and divorce. Moses had said that a man could divorce his wife if he gave her a legal notification of dismissal. But Jesus, who said that he came to perfect the law, not abolish it (Matt. 5:17-18), says that divorce is not permissible for any cause except unfaithfulness, regardless of Moses' saying.

"It was because you understand so little about of the meaning of love," says Jesus, "that Moses permitted you to divorce your wives! But that was not the original intention at all." In the creation, God ordained one wife for one husband; the two become one flesh. And in the new creation, it is clear, that is how Jesus intends it to be.

In that case, say the disciples, it is better not to marry; marriage is too final a step to take. Not everyone is capable of making that decision, says Jesus, but whoever can ought to do so. Taken together with Paul's statement in 1 Corinthians 7:9, "It is better to marry than to be aflame with passion," this passage lays the foundation for clerical celibacy as it has been practiced through the ages.

Next, as if to underline the complexity of life when it must be regulated by law, Matthew turns once more to a picture of the children or little ones in their simplicity of life-style. Mothers have brought them to Jesus for him to lay hands on them and pray for them. The disciples, who characterize the insensitivity and male chauvinism of the age, and thus reveal much about the foregoing comments on marriage and divorce, try to drive them away. But Jesus stops them. He says again, "It is to such as these that the kingdom of heaven belongs" (v. 14).

PRAYER

O God, this hard teaching on marriage would not be necessary if we had only learned the lesson about forgiveness in the preceding parable. Help me to live as if my spouse were the person in the parable who owed so little and I were the one who owed so much—for I truly think that is the way it is. Through Jesus, who commended love above everything, amen.

PROPERTY AND THE NEW REALM

*T*he French philosopher Gabriel Marcel once wrote a book called *Being and Having,* the thesis of which was that it is very difficult to *be* and to *have things* at the same time. Having inevitably succeeds in crowding out being. This is largely the point of this story in the Gospel. The nearly perfect young man has one major flaw: His possessions own him.

Perhaps the man is meant to pose a contrast between the esteemed Jew who strictly observes the law and the little ones who belong to God's realm. He has spent his entire life trying to attain salvation through the law. Yet he knows he lacks something very basic.

When Jesus tells him to sell everything and donate his money to the poor—in other words, to lead a very different kind of life—he is saying, in effect, that the righteousness of Jews before the law is not sufficient. The law is unable to measure the intent of the heart. It could not disclose the extent to which the man really worshiped his possessions, not God. The new realm, on the other hand, calls for total allegiance—the kind given by the disciples who have left their fishing boats to follow Jesus.

In the new creation, says Jesus, those who have forsaken selfish values for the realm will have their full reward. Around him in his "heavenly splendour," as the *New English Bible* translates it, the disciples will sit on twelve thrones. Those who have endured slander from the pious Jews because they are untutored in the law and tradition will rule over their learned detractors. And all the little ones will be repaid many times for their faithfulness.

PRAYER

I confess, O God, that this passage makes me uneasy. I am too much like the rich man, who wanted to keep his property and be a disciple too. Help me to renounce my dependence on material things, so that I am not possessed by my possessions. Through Jesus, who found freedom through prayer and fasting, amen.

EQUALITY IN GOD'S REALM

*T*his passage, which appears only in Matthew and not in Mark or Luke, is brilliantly placed after the story of the rich man and the disciples' discussion with Jesus. It cuts in two directions. On one hand, it is a warning to the legalistic Jews that God, because God is God, will treat the little ones of the realm, the latecomers, as well as God treats them. On the other hand, it may also be a warning to the disciples that they are not to expect special consideration because they left all to follow Jesus at an early point in the realm's coming, but will share it fully with all the little ones who enter late.

The point is—and this is always hard for work-oriented people to grasp—that the realm is God's and God decides who will enter it and what their rewards will be.

Society tries to instill in us the feeling that we are worth what we do, not what we are. We grow up estimating our own value by external standards—how hard we have worked, what we have accomplished, or how much money we have made. But God, being God, is not bound to or deceived by our ways of measuring. God gives the new realm to whomever God wills, the way a generous householder rewards the negligent servants as well as the diligent ones.

This is an important reminder in a Gospel that was written primarily to encourage the early Christians to a life of righteousness and faithfulness. As Jesus said to Peter in Matthew 19:26, the range of possibilities with God does not always coincide with ours. God is God, and above all laws—even the law of averages and the law of expectancy!

PRAYER
This is far more hopeful to me than the last passage, dear God. I am not only a latecomer to the vineyard, but I am also terribly clumsy, and often step on tender plants or prune the wrong limbs, and sometimes I cherish the illusion that I am better than other workers. I am glad you are a God of mercy as well as a God of justice. Amen.

THE WAY TO BE GREAT

A journalist who had once desired to be an artist was thrilled with the assignment to interview the great Picasso. They had shared a meal at a sidewalk cafe in Montmartre, the fabled artists' quarter of Paris, and their coffee cups were empty. The journalist kept glancing toward the waiter, attempting to get his eye. He seemed very annoyed. Noticing this, Picasso disappeared behind a curtain, emerged with a carafe, and provided a fresh cup of coffee for the astonished writer.

"Whoever wishes to be great among you," said Jesus, "must be your servant" (v. 26). It was an important word for the Christian community, which has always had as much trouble with personal pride as any institution composed of human beings.

Part of the irony of the request of the disciples and their mother, in Matthew's narrative, lay in its timing. Jesus had just spoken of his humiliating death and was on his way to Jerusalem, where it would take place. We do not know whether the other disciples were angry with James and John because of the inappropriateness of such a request at such a time or because they too wished the places of honor. Jesus' speech to them seems to indicate the latter reason.

If Matthew had known the story related in John 13:1-11, of Jesus' taking a towel and washing his disciples' feet, he surely would have told it in this Gospel, for it illustrates even more graphically than allusions to the cross the meaning of the passage. True greatness shows itself in humility, not in pride of rank or place. Whoever would be first must become a slave.

PRAYER

How easy it is, dear God, to get by in a society where rank and place are easily fixed. Then all we have to do is the proper thing. But your realm sweeps away all such defenses and leaves no rule but love. We are all servants, for your sake. Amen.

THE COMING OF THE KING

Rejoice greatly, O daughter Zion!
  Shout aloud, O daughter Jerusalem!
Lo, your king comes to you;
  triumphant and victorious is he,
humble and riding on a donkey,
  on a colt, the foal of a donkey.
(Zech. 9:9)

*T*he last line of this prophecy is a *parallelism,* merely repeating in altered form the line before it. Apparently a literal-minded translator did not understand this, and altered the text to have it in Matthew do an impossible thing—put Jesus on two animals at once! But the prophecy from Zechariah is important for comprehending the scene of Jesus' entry to Jerusalem at the beginning of Passover. No longer trying to keep his Messiahship a secret, Jesus selects this image of the king riding a beast of burden as a way of announcing his mission. He comes as the one appointed by God to save his people.

The word *Hosanna* is from Psalm 118:25-26, and is not a term of praise but a cry to "Save now!" The people do praise the Messiah. But the main shout that goes up from them is "Save now! Save now in the highest!"

Jesus and the crowds apparently go straight to the Temple, where Jesus overturns the tables of the profiteers who exchange currency and sell sacrifices. The Gospel of John locates this cleansing at the beginning of Jesus' ministry (John 2:13-22), and Mark places it in the second day of the Passover. But here in Matthew it is strategically located as Jesus' first act in this weeklong drama, perhaps underscoring his battle with the legalistic Jews. He runs off those who traffic *legally* but not *spiritually* in the Temple, and exalts it once again as a place of worship. In all the ancient prophecies, the Temple had figured as the place of convergence for the new creation, with all nations flowing to it.

Similarly, the miracles of healing in the Temple are symbolic of the new age, and the indignation of the chief priests and scribes to the cries of "Save now!" throws the conflict between old and new into sharp relief. Jesus has now seized the initiative and is forcing a showdown between the old regime and the new.

Save us now, O God, from unspiritual systems and uninspired leaders. Enter the sacred places of world finance, industry, education, and government where the poor are daily cheated, and let every house become a house of prayer. Through him who has come, still comes, and is coming, amen.

Day 70   *Matthew 21:18-22*

THE LESSON OF THE FIG TREE

*T*his magical story is hardly in keeping with the Jesus we have come to know in the Gospel. He does not go about performing miracles for his own sake or because he is angry. If he did, then he would in likelihood have yielded to the temptations described in Matthew 4. Moreover, fig trees do not normally produce fruit until early summer, and, even though the leaves were premature on this particular tree, it does not seem reasonable that Jesus would have cursed the tree for not bearing fruit out of season.

A clue to the meaning of the puzzling event may lie in verse 43, in the reference to "a people that produces the fruits of the kingdom." The fig tree probably stood for Israel. It was considered the most important tree of the land and was a symbol of fertility and prosperity. Several pictures of the wrath of God in the Old Testament referred to God's destroying the fig trees.

Jesus' cursing of the tree, then, was probably a parabolic saying or even a parabolic action having to do with the failure of Israel. It may have occurred at some other time and been drawn into the chronology of Holy Week because of its dramatic picture of God's wrath against the nation. Israel had put forth the leaves of righteousness—the scribes and Pharisees had, that is—but had not really brought forth the fruit of righteousness; Israel's heart did not truly belong to God. Therefore, God would curse the old Israel and it would never again have the chance to bear fruit.

PRAYER

Forgive me, dear God, for every time I have set forth leaves when I had no intention of bearing real fruit. Help me not only to be honest, but honestly to love you. Through Jesus, who was always what he appeared to be, amen.

THE SON WHO PLEASES THE FATHER

*J*t is Monday morning after the great entry on Sunday. When Jesus enters the Temple, he is beset by the chief religious officials of the country. "By what authority are you doing these things?" they demand (v. 23). The healings of the day before are still on their minds, but it is his act of riding into Jerusalem on the colt, announcing his Messiahship, that has really jolted them. The cries of "Hosanna—save now!" probably ring yet in their ears. "What an upstart!" they must think. "How dare he come in here as though he were God's own anointed!"

They are shrewd old men, but Jesus gives them a taste of his own shrewdness. "Did the baptism of John come from heaven, or was it of human origin?" (v. 25). They are political enough not to answer. So Jesus gives them a parable. Which is the father's delight, the son who promised a day's work and didn't give it or the son who said he wouldn't work but repented and did? They are practical fathers. There can be but one answer.

"Ah," says Jesus in effect, drawing the noose tight, "the unobservant Jews whom you condemn go into the realm of God ahead of you, for they listened to John and repented. *You* are the sons who promised to go and did not."

PRAYER

How often, O God, I have promised to enter the vineyard and did not. I meant to go, but the sun was hot or there were distractions on the way to the field. Now many less righteous than I go in ahead of me, because they acted promptly when asked to go. Forgive me, and let me go now, while there is yet time. Through Jesus, who pierces me to the heart with his stories, amen.

THE LANDOWNER'S SON

*J*his remarkable parable is probably a part of Jesus' answer to the question "By what authority are you doing these things?" His authority is that of a son—the final emissary sent from the landowner to claim the vineyard that was rightfully his.

As much as anything, the parable points to the violent death of Jesus only four days hence. The wicked squatters hurl the son outside the vineyard and there murder him. Jesus, as the writer of Hebrews is careful to point out (Heb. 13:12), was crucified outside the city walls of Jerusalem.

But the disenfranchised son becomes the foundation for a new order. He is the stone rejected by the builders but reclaimed by the architect and established as the chief cornerstone of the building.

There is no messianic secret. Jesus' meanings are all too plain to the priests and Pharisees. They want to imprison him at once but are afraid of the crowds who cried, "Save now!"

PRAYER

I like to think I would have been on Jesus' side against these selfish, evil leaders, O God. But I am not so sure. There is that in me which sides with the powers that be—with law and order and process. So I confess the possibility that I would have acted wrongly, and I ask your forgiveness. Through the Son who lost his life, amen.

Day 73   *Matthew 22:1-14*

THE WEDDING FEAST

*L*ike the story of the landowner in Matthew 20:1-16, this parable is double-edged, so that it cuts both the self-righteous Jews and the false members of the Christian community.

First, the edge toward the observant Jews. From the beginning, God, like the king in the parable, had given special invitations to the Jews. But they had not responded. So God redirected the wedding invitation. This time it was to all the people in the streets, without regard to their station or backgrounds. These people then poured into the dining hall. Clearly this was a picture of the early church; it was filled with people of many nations, some of whom had never had a relationship to the God of Israel.

But then comes the second edge of the story, the one aimed at the Christian community itself. The king enters the dining hall and finds a guest who has not even had the grace to dress for the occasion. For this breach of etiquette, the man is cast into the darkness.

The meaning for observant Jews is clear enough. But what does this portend for members of the Christian community? Taken in the context of Matthew's Gospel as a whole, it may be a warning to those who think they can be part of the banquet without conforming to the moral and ethical expectations of the host. Jesus, as the new Moses, expects his followers not only to fulfill the law but also to go beyond it. It seems likely, then, that the king in the parable is not merely capricious in his behavior toward the guest without wedding clothes, but does what he does in righteous indignation at the disrespect shown by the guest.

PRAYER

I am tested by this parable, O God. I like parties and banquets, and the idea of your realm as a wedding feast appeals to me. But I realize that I live in tattered garments—that my life is not as gentle and pure and self-denying as Jesus asks. Help me to repent and to find in Christ's righteousness a cloak for my own unseemliness. Amen.

Day 74   *Matthew 22:15-22*

A CUNNING QUESTION AND A PIERCING ANSWER

*I*t is not easy to deal with a question that is a trap and to emerge from it so victoriously that one's questioners are dumbfounded. Yet that is precisely what Jesus did in this instance.

The seriousness of the trap is underlined by the presence of the Herodians, supporters of Herod the Great, whom the Pharisees normally disliked because they curried favor with the Romans in order to maintain positions of influence. The Pharisees were staunchly opposed to the Romans, and, if Jesus said it was lawful to pay taxes to Caesar, they would lose no time in spreading the word, making Jesus unpopular with the crowds. The Herodians, on the other hand, would be unhappy if Jesus took the position that Roman taxation was unlawful, and would probably have him arrested on charges of sedition. Either way, he was bound to lose.

But the questioners did not reckon with Jesus' resourcefulness. "Show me the coin used for the tax," he said. "Whose head is this, and whose title?" (vv. 19-20). They were Caesar's, of course. Then give the emperor what is due him, said Jesus, and give God what is due to God.

It was a master stroke! Whatever bore Caesar's image must belong to Caesar. But, by the same token, anything bearing God's image belonged to God. Human beings, made in the image of God, not their own, should be doing better things than trying to trap good people with clever questions!

PRAYER

Lord, most of us prefer asking you hard questions to giving you our love and loyalty. How tawdry it is of us, and what joy we are missing. Break through our clever games and show us how life ought to be. Through Jesus, who knew what is due to whom, amen.

Day 75   *Matthew 22:23-33*

THE GOD OF THE LIVING

*H*ow strong the opposition to Jesus was growing! First came the Pharisees and Herodians with their malicious question. Then came the Sadducees, who were opposed to the Pharisees in most matters but saw Jesus as a threat to the stability of their relationship to the Romans. They were the upper-class ruling party of Israel, who numbered among themselves not only many prominent and educated families but also the chief priests as well.

The Sadducees were strong adherents of the Torah, but did not accept the rest of the Old Testament as scriptural. And because they found nothing about the resurrection of the dead in the Torah, they refused to accept it as a religious teaching. Their question to Jesus was, therefore, a mere trick, for they did not believe either the woman or the seven brothers would be alive after death.

But Jesus minced no words; he told them they knew neither the scriptures nor the power of God. In the resurrection, he said, souls become as free and marvelous as angels and have no need for legal contracts and institutions such as Moses gave.

Nor was Jesus through with that. He entered the ground where so many Pharisees had contended with the Sadducees and lost—the Torah itself. "Haven't you read what God himself said?" he asked, in effect. "I am the God of Abraham, the God of Isaac, and the God of Jacob. The verb is present tense. You admit that God is living. Then Abraham, Isaac, and Jacob must be living too!"

78

PRAYER

Somehow it seems demeaning to me, O God, that Jesus ever had to engage in such arguments. But I know life is like that. We have to contend with ignorance and absurdity and misguided people. Help me to be more patient in dealing with cranks and fools, as Jesus was. Amen.

Day 76   *Matthew 22:34-40*

THE TWIN PILLARS OF RELIGION

*M*ark's Gospel makes it clear that the lawyer who asked the next question of Jesus did so in a friendly manner because he respected the way Jesus had handled the earlier questions (Mark 12:28-34). In all sincerity the man inquires, "Which commandment in the law is the greatest?" (v. 36).

Jesus replies with the commandment most familiar to every Jew because it was part of the *Shema,* the opening sentence of every Jewish worship service: " 'You shall love the Lord your God with all your heart, and with all your soul, and with all your mind'" (v. 37; see Deut. 6:5). That is all the man asked, but Jesus is not content to stop there. The trouble with the scribes and Pharisees was that they *did* stop there. Their religion was entirely vertical, lacking human compassion.

Because the love of God is hollow and pretentious without horizontal relationships, Jesus immediately connects another commandment to the first: " 'You shall love your neighbor as yourself '" (v. 39; see Lev. 19:18). The *Shema* must be said in this light, for the two commandments are the twin pillars supporting all the law and the prophets. Take either of them away, and everything collapses.

PRAYER

I catch myself rejoicing, O God, that I am not as stiff-necked or hardhearted as the Pharisees, and I realize that is a bad sign. If I loved my neighbors as myself, I would sympathize with their human frailty. Forgive me for my pride, and grant that I may more genuinely care for all my neighbors. Through Jesus, whose love for his neighbors led him to a cross, amen.

MORE THAN THE SON OF DAVID

*T*he Pharisees are apparently stunned by Jesus' answer about the commandments, so Jesus follows with a question of his own: Whose son is the Messiah? It is a simple question. David's, they respond, for "Son of David" is the most common messianic title. The scribes and Pharisees have heard the crowds calling "Jesus, Son of David," and know he is aware that they are thinking this.

What about Psalm 110:1, asks Jesus, where David says: "The LORD says to my lord,/ 'Sit at my right hand/ until I make your enemies your footstool' "? The reference, it is agreed, is to the Messiah. If David calls him Lord, says Jesus, then isn't he more than a mere son?

If the hearers were stunned before, now they are awe-struck. Have they heard correctly? Does Jesus claim to be more than a man? Does he think he is David's *Lord?* There will be no more badgering questions. The next questioner, in fact, will be the high priest who examines Jesus for blasphemy (Matt. 26:57-68).

PRAYER

This must have been a high moment, O God—a daring moment. I appreciate the drama of it, because I know its awful consequences. Help me to follow him whom you have named Lord, and who at the end claimed the title. Amen.

THE TROUBLE WITH THE PHARISEES

*W*e recall that when Matthew wrote his Gospel, the Christian community was still struggling to establish its identity over against Judaism. This group of sayings, with its introduction, seven woes or indictments, and conclusion, was aimed at helping to show the difference between them.

The admonishment to do what the scribes and Pharisees say, but not what they do, is interesting. It is not the law that is so bad, nor even the scribal additions to it, but the attitude with which the scribes and Pharisees approach it. They have set themselves up as an elite group to make heavy burdens for others to bear.

By Jesus' time, the Pharisees had existed for two centuries. Their name meant "the separated ones." They devoted themselves to keeping all the laws extrapolated by the scribes from the Torah—so many that they filled more than fifty volumes! So being a Pharisee was a full-time job.

As Jesus saw, such zealousness was often misplaced. Separation became a source of pride to them, and they became intolerant of others who were less perfect than they. Their sin was not devotion to religion but lack of charity to others. Jesus said they were self-centered and only pretended to honor God, when what they really did was to pay homage to themselves.

PRAYER

I know it is wrong, O God, for religion ever to come between me and another human being. Yet I strongly suspect that it does—that I find it more difficult to accept and love persons whose forms of worship and ways of believing are different from mine. Forgive me for this, and help me to be like Christ, who lived so close to you that he always saw things in the right perspective. Amen.

Day 79   *Matthew 23:13-39*

THE SEVEN WOES

$\mathcal{I}$t is hard to imagine the Jesus of the beatitudes giving vent to such invective as marks this long passage. As Bible scholar William Barclay says, "It is seldom in literature that we find so unsparing and sustained an indictment as we find in this chapter." But we must remember, to understand it, that the scribes and Pharisees, more than anyone else, were poisoning the spiritual wells of Israel. And they, more than anyone, were trying to block Jesus' ministry to the people. The last verses of this chapter indicate a man on the verge of tears in his frustration to minister to the holy city. Perhaps they are the best clue of all to the outrage he felt against the ever-present religious bigots who had stoned the prophets in earlier ages and would crucify him in this one.

The description of the scribes and Pharisees is devastating: They will not enter God's realm themselves, and they keep others from entering; they scour the world to make disciples, and then make torments of the disciples' lives; they keep all the fine points of the law and miss the most important ones; they make themselves appear holy but are filled with corruption; they speak of honoring the prophets but are as hungry to murder prophets as their fathers were.

No wonder the formula for the woes begins each time, "Woe to you, scribes and Pharisees, hypocrites!" There could be no more stinging indictment of persons who held religion in high esteem. The word for "hypocrite" in Greek originally applied to an actor who carried a large mask in front of him as he played his part, one that could easily be seen by the whole audience. That was precisely the way Jesus pictured the Pharisees—they were men playing parts behind oversized masks!

PRAYER

Save us all from the burden of other people's religious expectations, O God, and save them from ours. Let us be content to meditate on our own shortcomings and spend no time searching for those of others. And grant to each of us a sense of the positive meaning of faith, that we may never lose touch with you by being negative. Through Jesus, whose religion was so healthy-minded that he could even deal with bigots, amen.

Day 80   *Matthew 24:1-14*

THE GOSPEL FOR THE WORLD

*T*he first saying, verses 1-2, may have occurred on one of the first visits Jesus made to Jerusalem with the disciples, because they come to him in amazement, like gawking tourists, to point out the Temple buildings. Although the Temple was hardly large by contemporary standards, it probably appeared gigantic to these country visitors; and it was certainly magnificent, for it was constructed of white marble overlaid with gold. When Jesus said that not a stone of it would be left standing, apparently he was not referring to the destruction of the Temple in A.D. 70, for Josephus said that the Temple was then destroyed by fire. Possibly he was making a general statement about the failure of the religion of the scribes and Pharisees (remember the "woes" of chapter 23); the Temple, as the symbol of that religion, was doomed to eventual ruin.

The next saying, placed on the Mount of Olives, which was traditionally associated with the messianic age, is in answer to a question about signs of the *parousia*, or Second Coming, and the end of the age. Jesus describes the difficult early years of the church, when Christians were persecuted for their faith and there was much confusion in the world. Perhaps the most chilling part of the description is the warning that "the love of many will grow cold" (v. 12). But the gospel will be preached to all the nations, and then—the time is not specified—the end will come.

PRAYER

Sometimes, God, I think this is the age when love has grown cold. People are so insecure and frustrated that they quarrel, cheat, and gouge one another without respect to either common morality or the love of Christ. It is a time of general distress and unhappiness. Help me to be a reservoir of strength and kindness to others this day, and to give my life in love as Jesus did. Amen.

Day 81   *Matthew 24:15-31*

A TIME OF CONFUSION

*I*t would take far more space than we have here to begin to untangle the references of these verses, some of which are to the destruction of Jerusalem and some to the end of the age. The "desolating sacrilege" of verse 15 is clearly a reference to Daniel 9:27; 11:31; and 12:11, where the prophet reflected on the desecration of the Temple by Antiochus Epiphanes, king of Syria, who erected an altar to Zeus there and sacrificed swine on it. Apparently Jesus is warning the believers to flee the city when a foreign ruler does this again, for it is a sign of the collapse of all things.

In a time of such confusion, there will naturally arise many false messiahs who will assume, because they too can see the signs of the end, that they are God's intended leaders. Even some of the chosen community will be deceived by them. "But don't listen to them," says Jesus, in effect. "Remember what I have told you. When the Son of Man appears again, it will not be in a corner, in some limited way; he will be seen from east to west, like the lightning."

As for verse 28, it is apparently a proverb, applying to the appearance of false messiahs, who, like vultures, will gather over the body of civilization.

The whole universe is seen to collapse in the terrible Day of the Lord. But in the midst of the desolation will come the one who is to rule the new creation. His angels will fly all over the heavens, gathering the chosen together.

I easily get lost, O God, in all this business of signs and predictions. I am also bothered by those who don't see its poetic character, but insist on counting the days and weeks until the end. Help me to keep what is primary in all this, though: the vision of Christ as sufficient to all his little ones, whatever comes in the world—and not lose it with all of the unsettling language. Amen.

Day 82   *Matthew 24:32-51*

MORE SAYINGS OF THE END

*T*here are obvious signs of the collapse of all things, says Jesus. The intelligent person learns to read such signs, the way he or she knows that when the fig tree puts out its leaves summer is near. But there is no way of knowing the exact time, so it is important to continue working and living as one normally does.

We know from Paul's writings that some Christians, expecting the imminent end of the world, simply quit working. Foreseeing this possibility, Jesus gave the parable of the servant who, when his master suddenly appears, is faithfully setting food before the other servants. The servant who says that because the master has been gone so long he will surely not arrive today, and therefore neglects his duties, will be punished along with the hypocrites—and we remember that the formula for the seven woes of chapter 23 was "Woe to you, scribes and Pharisees, *hypocrites!*"

PRAYER

Dear God, make us faithful servants to do the small things that are important in the daily affairs of people and save us from any tendency to resign our care for others, for whatever reasons. Through Jesus, who never asked to be waited upon, amen.

Day 83   *Matthew 25:1-13*

THE JOY OF READINESS

*I*t is possible that this parable is not about the return of Christ at all, but about the coming of God's realm to the Jews. If this is so, then

Israel was the bride of the story, and the ancient manuscripts that add "and the bride" at the end of verse 1 may be correct.

The custom was for maidens to attend the bride, not the bridegroom, and then to accompany the two as the groom took the bride from her parents' house to his. If Israel was the apparent bride, then the maidens were the religious leaders responsible for seeing her delivered to the Messiah. Some of them, because of the hard intertestamental period and the delay of the Messiah's appearance, had turned their thoughts to other things and simply were not prepared for the realm of God when Jesus came among them with his message.

Verse 13 may have been at some point a textual addition, though not an unworthy one, for the theme of watchfulness is always applicable in spiritual matters.

Most of us today are accused by a passage like this of not being properly mindful of Christ's return and the consummation of all things. After centuries of waiting, we have allowed our spirit of watchfulness to die like an unattended campfire. As much as we hate to admit it, we should probably see ourselves in the careless attendants.

PRAYER

We are all inclined to slothful spirits, O God. Our sensibilities become dulled, and we miss many opportunities each day of seeing your advent in our lives. Resensitize us, we pray, until we live on tiptoes, expecting you at any moment. Amen.

Day 84   *Matthew 25:14-30*

MISJUDGING THE MASTER

*O*nce more we have a parable subject to two interpretations. Jesus very possibly told it with the Jewish religious leaders in mind; the scribes and Pharisees were the one-talent servants who had been mere guardians of what had been given them in the law. But Matthew's placement indicates that the early church saw in the parable a challenge to faithful living in its own time, and indeed in that sense it is timeless.

The servant's error was his misreading of the master's nature. He had seen only half of that nature—the tendency of the master to be a zealous farmer, gathering in hay and grain even in places where it sprang up wild and had not been cultivated. He mistook this for miserliness, when in reality it indicated imagination, risk, and resourcefulness.

This certainly would have applied to the legalistic religious leaders of Jesus' day. They looked upon the religion God had given as something to be carefully guarded and restricted—hence their impossibly elaborated system of rules and taboos. They had completely overlooked the real dynamic of Judaism, which was able to produce John the Baptist, Jesus, and, of course, Christianity itself.

PRAYER

There is something in all of us, O God, that loves rules and prescriptions. We feel safer if we can take the measure of things and assign them to well-defined categories. But your Spirit is more than we are able to express in formulas and regulations. You transcend our definitions and dogmas. You elude our finest theologies. Help us not to be caught as the third servant was, with spirits timid and fearful. Let us ride the wild waves of your realm's coming, like surfers joyous and unafraid, because we can trust him who has come in your name. Amen.

Day 85   *Matthew 25:31-46*

THE CENTRALITY OF THE "LITTLE ONES"

*F*ew passages in Matthew's Gospel are more moving than this one. It represents the culmination of centuries of longing for justice; when justice is done, it is seen not in terms of mere legalistic righteousness, such as the scribes and Pharisees were interested in, but of care for all of God's little ones.

We tend, after centuries of habit, to read the saying as applicable to some distant future. But when the disciples first heard it, it was surely clear to them that the goats of the parable were the scribes and Pharisees, the strictly observant Jews, who had to put heavy burdens on the common people and had not really cared about their salvation (compare Matt. 23:4). The sheep, on the other hand, were the little ones of the heavenly realm. The Messiah-king identified with the little ones, and thus brought judgment on the others.

There is no sharper warning to religious people in any generation than this parable, for it reminds us of our perennial tendencies to regard the poor, the unattractive, and the powerless as outsiders in the human community. Such an attitude always carries its own judgment in God's created order.

PRAYER

God, I think of the person I most despise, and of the reasons why. Is it wrong of me to make such judgments? Am I in effect pronouncing judgment on myself, because I have not loved as I was told to? I fear it is so and ask you to forgive me—as I try to accept the person I despised. Amen.

Day 86   *Matthew 26:1-13*

A BEAUTIFUL ACT

*H*ere, set between pieces of information about the gathering storm that will break over Jesus before the week is out, is a story of tender devotion that has, as Jesus predicted, been told all over the world.

Jesus and the disciples were resting in the home of Simon the leper—probably one of the persons Jesus had healed. John's Gospel indicates that the woman with the ointment was Mary, the sister of Martha and Lazarus, which places the scene in Bethany.

With her loving intuition, Mary perceived the tragic meaning of Jesus' predictions concerning his conflict with the authorities. With characteristic generosity, she came to him in Simon's home bearing the vessel of ointment she had probably been saving for her own and her family's anointment after death. It was a costly substance, worth as much as an average man might earn in a year. Either in sympathy or in loving protest of the way Jesus was about to spend himself, Mary poured the entire amount of ointment on his head, so that it ran profusely through his hair and into his clothing. The room was immediately filled with the sweet, thick odor of death.

The disciples, sensitized to the needs of the poor, were outraged. (John's Gospel pins the blame for their outburst on Judas the traitor.) Why wasn't the ointment sold for the benefit of the poor, if she wanted to honor Jesus?

But Jesus commended the woman. She had recognized that they were in the presence of the Lord of the new creation. There were other resources for the poor—and this example was never intended to gainsay the importance of caring for them. But Mary had prepared the King for his burial. Her grasp of the situation was better than the disciples', and her deed would always be associated with the community's proclamation.

PRAYER

Dear God, increase in me the capacity for spontaneous acts of generosity, that I may do lavish, beautiful things both for the poor and for others around me. Through Jesus, who understood and approved, amen.

Day 87   *Matthew 26:14-25*

THE PERFIDY OF JUDAS

Sometimes even strong persons break under the pressure of relentless conflict. Something snaps in them, and they do unpredictable things—things absurdly out of keeping with their usual character.

It may have been that way with Judas. Surely something in him had recommended him to Jesus as a disciple. But in the constant battle with the authorities in Jerusalem he reached a point where he couldn't take it any longer. Maybe he thought Jesus was wrong to speak of dying instead of fighting; or, as some have suggested, perhaps he thought he could provoke a revolution in which Jesus would emerge victorious.

At any rate, Judas agreed to deliver Jesus into the hands of the chief priests for thirty pieces of silver, which, according to Exodus 21:32, was the price of a slave. By today's standards, the deal was cut for about four or five thousand dollars. Ironicallly, Judas enslaved himself and vilified his name forever in the transaction.

How did Jesus know? There were many telltale signs in Judas's behavior. One of them was his dipping his hand into the bowl of bitter herbs that were part of the Passover meal. The rule in the Essene community at Qumran was that people dipped their hands in the bowl in hierarchic order; that is, in the sequence of their status. Judas's dipping his hand with Jesus suggests a breach of etiquette on his part—as though he were choosing equality with his Master.

PRAYER

There is some Judas in me too, O God. I bristle with self-importance and confidence in my own opinions. Sometimes I think I know better than you what I need or should do. I crowd the bowl at such times by dipping as you do. Forgive my terrible impertinence and help me to live humbly and devotedly, that I may not betray you. Amen.

THE FIRST SUPPER

We usually call this meal the Last Supper. But why shouldn't it be called, instead, the First Supper? It was, after all, the beginning of a tradition that has been central to the Christian community ever since.

The Gospel of John accorded this meal several chapters. Why did Matthew spend so little time describing it? Perhaps he was more concerned with the actual Passion story than with its embodiment in a symbolic meal. He wanted to show the human drama being played out beyond the table, in Judas and Peter and Caiaphas and Pilate and all the others whose stories held so much interest for the Christian community. Thus he hastens on from the bare fact of the supper's institution to describe Peter's protestation of faithfulness—a protestation we know to be ill-fated.

The hymn that Jesus and the disciples sang before going out was probably Psalm 118, which contains the words:

> With the LORD on my side I do not fear.
> What can mortals do to me?
> The LORD is on my side to help me;
> I shall look in triumph on those who hate me.
> It is better to take refuge in the LORD
> than to put confidence in mortals. (Ps. 118:6-8)

But Peter and the other disciples apparently forgot what they had sung.

PRAYER

Their guilt is my guilt, O Lord. I too betray you, in a thousand small betrayals. I disappoint children who have looked to me expectantly; I fail my elders, who need my care and attention; I give less than my best to my friends, who have reason to hope for more. Forgive me and help me to do better. Through him who loved even those who let him down, amen.

PRAY TO BE SPARED THE TESTING

Professor David Daube has reminded us of a rule among the Jews that whenever one of the group celebrating the Passover fell asleep—not merely dozed but fell into a deep sleep, so that he could not answer a question—it was the end of the celebration. Perhaps this explains the puzzling way Jesus kept returning to the disciples as he prayed; he did not want the Passover celebration to come to an end.

There is great pathos in this picture of Jesus, deeply saddened by the betrayal of Judas and the impending events of the next few hours. It was entirely natural for him to seek strength through prayer, for it had been his discipline at earlier times to spend many hours in prayer.

What did he pray at this time? He prayed that the dreadful hour of testing might simply go away, if possible—that he might be wrong about the series of events he saw rapidly building to a climax.

He also instructed the three disciples to pray a similar prayer for themselves. But they were tired and did not realize the seriousness of the hour, so they failed to pray as they were bidden. And with what enormous consequences! Jesus came out of Gethsemane refreshed in spirit and ready to endure the worst the authorities could do to him. If the disciples had prayed, they too might have been refreshed, and, instead of fleeing, might have died by Jesus' side. It is a tremendous thing to ponder, isn't it? Prayer can actually get us into trouble, or it can keep us there if we are already in it!

PRAYER

Dear God, too often my prayers are mere recitations of shopping lists. I do not listen to you and learn what I should be doing with my life. Therefore, I live wastefully and in needless desperation. Help me to take my prayer life more seriously, and not to fall asleep. Through Jesus, who was crucified, amen.

Day 90   *Matthew 26:47-56*

NOT WITH SWORDS' LOUD CLASHING

*T*he irony of verse 25 is continued here as Judas calls Jesus Master and kisses him. It was considered impudent of a disciple to kiss his master before the master had first kissed him, and Judas once more demonstrated his feeling of equality with Jesus.

John 18:10 tells us that the unnamed disciple who drew his sword was Peter. The fact that a mob had followed the chief priests and elders to the site enhances the possibility that this action was very significant. It might easily have signaled the eruption of local warfare, for probably many in the crowd as well as in the entire city were prepared to follow Jesus in an armed rebellion.

Surely in the early Christian community, too, many felt that Christians should do more to defend themselves against imprisonment and persecution. Why not train secret militia to offset the power of the corrupt authorities? But the example of Jesus, and his words about not taking up the sword, have had great influence through the ages on the Christian attitude toward violence. In our own time, they were persuasive to Mahatma Gandhi and Martin Luther King, Jr., both of whom influenced millions of oppressed people.

It is the royal demeanor of Jesus here that causes us to question his use of power for selfish purposes in the stories of the fish with money in its mouth (Matt. 17:27) and the withered fig tree (Matt. 21:18-22). Such tales are simply incongruent with the behavior of one who offered himself so gracefully to his own executioners.

PRAYER

We understand so little of the nature of power, O God, and how it finally harms those who would use it selfishly against others. We are always drawing our swords against the enemies outside us. Help us to know what enemies lurk within us and to submit ourselves to you for more perfect cleansing. Through him who resisted the impulse to summon angels in a frightening moment, amen.

Day 91   *Matthew 26:57-68*

THE JUDGMENT OF THE OLD MEN

*T*he Romans, as Matthew made abundantly clear, were only incidental accessories in the death of Jesus. It was the religious leaders of the Jews, from first to last, who resented his style of ministry, his popularity with the poor, and his way of besting them in argument. There is no mention in this chapter of a Roman soldier's having been present in the capture of Jesus, despite the danger the mob scene constituted to the civil peace. It was all the work of the Jewish authorities. And now the same authorities proceed with their council meeting to try Jesus.

As the Sanhedrin, or Council of Elders, had no power to impose the death penalty except in cases of Gentile violation of the sacred area of the

Temple, it is probable that they commenced by trying to find Jesus guilty of some seditious act that they could then report to the Roman procurator. But failing this, apparently because of confusion among the false witnesses, they finally established a religious accusation against him, that of blasphemy. When Jesus admitted to being the Son of God, the high priest, following a custom prescribed for such occasions, tore his robes. The elders, shocked by the brazenness of the accused, declared that he deserved to die. Leviticus 24:16 prescribes death by stoning as the punishment for blaspheming. Perhaps because they lacked the authority to inflict the penalty they desired, the elders broke into a frenzy of petty retribution, spitting on Jesus, slapping him, and taunting him.

Jesus had said they were devoid of love, turning their professed love of God into a demonic caricature of true religion. In this wild scene, they acted out the very portrait he had painted of them.

PRAYER

What terrible things people do in the name of religion, truth, and honor, O God. Please save me from participating in such evil judgments—even when all that is involved is petty gossip or unfriendly remarks. Through Jesus, who always befriends the victims of injustice, amen.

Day 92 *Matthew 26:69-75*

THE FALL OF THE ROCK

*W*hy was the story of Peter's defection so much more important than those of the other disciples, who also ran away? Why, indeed, but that by the time the Gospels were written it was Peter who had clearly emerged as the most significant figure in the Christian community. Because he was the leader, the story of his faltering was all the more engaging to the community. It reminded them of the utter frailty of the human foundations of their movement. The man whom Jesus had called the Rock had proven unstable in a critical moment. He had slept when Jesus told him to watch and pray, and then he had lacked the courage to confess his relationship to Jesus in the very courtyard of the enemy!

Later, at Pentecost, Peter would be fired with courage and would excoriate the same elders for having crucified Jesus. He would become known for his dedication to the community, and legend would represent him as being crucified upside down because he did not deem himself worthy of dying as his Lord had.

Imagine what encouragement this biography would have been to frightened, hesitant Christians everywhere. Peter, the big fisherman, had once hesitated too. But then he had wept in repentance and become the rock Jesus called him to be. Surely every Christian can respond in the same positive manner to his or her own former acts of defection and become doubly responsible in the new realm.

PRAYER

It is good, O God, to have someone like Peter to relate to, for there are times when I am discouraged by my own faithlessness and betrayal. Forgive me for every time I have been hesitant to witness to your presence, and help me to show the fruits of my repentance, as Peter did. Through him who stands forever in the dock as we struggle in the courtyard, amen.

Day 93   *Matthew 27:1-10*

THE REPENTANCE OF JUDAS

*H*ow difficult it is to recall a word or an action once directed against another human being. Judas learned this bitterly in the case of his betrayal of Jesus. Perhaps he thought Jesus would best the elders in a showdown. But when he learned that the elders had condemned Jesus and sent him to Pilate, the raw, ugly truth of what he had done hit him with a sickening impact. Hurrying back to the chief priests, he tried to undo what he had done. Failing that, he hurled the blood money on the floor of the Temple and left despondent.

Whether he took his life that very morning, dying when Jesus did, or later, the record does not indicate. It tells us only that the money, because it was tainted with blood, was used to buy a burial site for strangers, fulfilling a prophecy from Zechariah 11:12-13. Thus the memory of Judas would always be associated with strangers and outcasts—people who had no friends to bury them.

PRAYER

O God, what a lonely position Judas was in. I pray now for all persons who think that life is so bad that they are contemplating suicide. Help them to know that somewhere, somehow, someone cares for them. Through Jesus, who was Judas's friend, amen.

A STRONG MAN BEFORE A WEAK ONE

*A*re you the King of the Jews?" asked Pilate (v. 11). It was an important question, legally at least. Apparently the chief priests and elders had translated the term *Messiah* that way for Pilate when they brought Jesus before him. Pilate was, after all, head of the Roman occupation, and would take the matter more seriously if he thought Jesus was after the throne of Herod; that would mean insurrection and trouble.

But Pilate was canny. He listened to the old men of Israel snapping off charges against Jesus, and he watched Jesus waiting silently before them. He knew that the old men did it all for envy—that they feared this strange young prophet with such deep ways.

Pilate was in a ticklish situation. He believed the man innocent. His wife had even had a dream about him and warned Pilate not to have anything to do with him. But the situation was explosive. The elders could make trouble for him among the people and with his superiors in Rome.

So Pilate did the discrete, political thing—and earned infamy as a result. Now we class him with all those persons who consider career and influence above right moral action; and Jesus, who was willing to die for a righteous cause, is revered even by non-Christians throughout the world.

PRAYER

Dear God, grant that I may never lose touch with myself to the extent that I could wash my hands of anyone whose well-being depended on me—even someone I knew as fleetingly as Pilate knew Jesus. Through Jesus, who would have acted nobly if he had been in Pilate's place, amen.

JESUS AND THE CARNIVAL

*B*rueghel the Elder once painted a crucifixion scene that captured the carnival-like qualities of that awful day. It is called *The Procession to Calvary*. It shows Jesus being led out of the city ahead of a mob of people who are excited by the smell of blood and violence. Someone is turning a somersault. A boy is pole-vaulting over a mud puddle. Two men are hanging already on distant crosses. Jesus has fallen beneath his. In the lower left quadrant of the painting, a tug of war is going on between Simon of Cyrene's grim-faced wife and the soldiers who want Simon to help Jesus with the cross. Simon is in the middle, being held by his wife and pulled by the soldiers. Most of the people are utterly indifferent to the exhausted figure of Jesus. They are simply out for a good time.

Brueghel has seen what is apparent in this passage—the cruel and ugly side of humanity that takes pleasure in the pain of others or enjoys the defeat of a famous personality. It is not a pleasant thing to behold. In fact, it makes one ashamed that fellow human beings could behave in such callous ways.

But we remember that Jesus came as the Messiah of the new creation, and creation always means pain and suffering as order is wrought out of chaos. Here was the climactic moment in his struggle with the forces of evil, and evil was making its strongest play.

PRAYER

O God, there is some strange blood lust in us that makes us take pleasure in other people's misfortunes. Forgive this dark stream and turn us to tenderness; let mercy temper justice and love replace vengeance. Teach us the ways of the one who prayed even for those who nailed him to a cross. Amen.

Day 96   *Matthew 27:45-54*

THE LAST HOURS

*W*hen the crucifixion was over, it was apparent that things had been occurring at two different levels.

At one level, the carnival level, the crowds gaped at the spectacle of a man dying. Once, when Jesus was reciting Psalm 22, which speaks of both despair and victory, they thought they heard him cry out to Elijah. Elijah was supposed to come to the aid of the righteous when they suffered. When someone brought a sponge and vinegar to lift to his mouth, others said to wait and see if Elijah really would come to help him. Then Jesus cried out with a loud voice—John's Gospel says it was a cry of overcoming—and died.

At another level, according to Matthew, there were significant occurrences in nature. The sun was darkened from noon until three o'clock. There was an earthquake, and the curtain between the Temple court and the Holy of Holies was ripped in two. The earthquake also opened many tombs, and dead persons came forth to walk through the city as predicted by Daniel 12:2 (although the phrase "after his resurrection" suggests that verses 51-54 may be out of sequence here, and belong after the resurrection). And the centurion and his men guarding Jesus were astonished and believed that he was indeed the Son of God.

PRAYER

Dear God, what a horrible death Jesus died on the cross. I cannot think about it too long without becoming ill. But what a miracle it was—that one death has done more to cure sick humanity than all the gardens ever visited, all the music ever played, and all the laws ever enacted. I can only thank you in the name of him who suffered. Amen.

Day 97   *Matthew 27:55-56*

THE WOMEN IN THE DISTANCE

*T*his is a very brief reading for today, but the revolution we have been through in the last twenty years in our thinking about men and women makes the verses especially revealing.

Jesus' well-known apostles were all men. But it is obvious from many references in the Gospels that also many women followed Jesus. And it is also obvious from numerous passages in the Gospels that Jesus was far more humane to women than was the average male of his day. He seemed to recognize that in the realm of God no distinction is made between men and women. And the early church, following his lead, was extremely open to women as leaders and sponsors of local congregations.

But in the usual politics of the day, women had little voice or power. That is what is so sad about the picture in these verses of Scripture: "Many women were also there, looking on from a distance" (v. 55). The male followers of Jesus had failed. Most of them were in hiding, or discretely hid themselves in the crowd. But the faithful women, unable to avail anything against the religious leaders and the soldiers, waited silently in the background.

Among these women were Mary Magdalene, who, legend has it, was a prostitute before she met Jesus; the mothers of some of the disciples, wondering what would happen now to their sons; and surely Mary, the mother of Jesus, whose heart was pierced by the greatest agony of all.

Some of them would be the first at the tomb when it was possible to go. Their devotion was unbounded. They would be among the most eager witnesses to the resurrection. And they were only the first among millions of women who have been devoted followers of the Messiah, and without whose faithful discipleship the heavenly realm might have remained unknown to many of us today.

PRAYER

I am grateful, O God, for the many women in my own life who have guided me to a closer relationship with you. Grant that the Christian community in all its parts may be as open and supportive of the service of women as Christ himself was, that they may no longer have to look on from a distance. Amen.

Day 98   *Matthew 27:57-66*

LAID IN A BORROWED TOMB

Joseph, according to the other Gospels, was a member of the Council of Elders (Mark 15:43) and did not give his consent to Jesus' death (Luke 23:50-51). If he was already a disciple at the time of Jesus' trial, it is possible that the meeting of the Council was called hastily and with only a select membership present. John 19:38-39 says that Joseph's relationship to Jesus was secret, and indicates that Nicodemus helped him remove the body and inter it.

Secret or not, it surely required considerable courage and devotion for Joseph to go to Pilate and request the body. Whether the disciples and the women lacked courage to do the same is beside the point; as strangers to the city, they would have had no place to bury Jesus, and a criminal's body was considered a defilement, especially on the sabbath, which was almost upon them. At least the two Marys did not hesitate to be identified with Jesus, and were present for the interment. It is highly probable that they assisted in the preparation of the body for entombment.

We can only wonder what was really in the minds of the scribes and Pharisees in requesting a guard for the tomb. Were they actually afraid of theft, or was it more that they feared?

PRAYER

O God, Jesus was laid in a borrowed crib when he was born and a borrowed tomb when he died. Truly he had no home, no place to lay his head. His life was a perfect example of the selflessness he preached—and the freedom that went with it. Now let him live in our hearts forever, for we owe him everything. Amen.

Day 99   *Matthew 28:1-10*

FALL DOWN AND WORSHIP!

*T*his is the first instance we have of followers of Jesus, other than the inner circle of disciples, actually worshiping him. Before, they no doubt admired him, listened to him, puzzled over him, perhaps even loved him. But here Matthew says explicitly that the two Marys fell at his feet and worshiped. His resurrection identified him so completely with the power of God in establishing the new creation that the women did not hesitate to share with him the kind of adoration normally reserved for God alone.

The four Gospels vary in their details of the resurrection narrative, but all agree on one thing: Mary Magdalene's devotion to Jesus caused her to be at the tomb at daybreak on the first day of the week and led to her being the first of Jesus' followers to see him in his resurrected form.

Can it be, then, that love is the only prelude to true worship? It was love that kept Mary Magdalene near the cross in the hours of agony, that brought her to the sepulcher where Joseph and Nicodemus buried Jesus, and that caused her to return at daybreak after the sabbath. And it was love's vision of the risen Christ that led her to fall down to worship him.

Here is a perfect example of Jesus' teachings about the realm of God. The scribes and Pharisees kept the law with rigorous devotion. But that was not enough. Our righteousness must exceed that of the scribes and Pharisees, said Jesus; it must be characterized by love and forgiveness and joy. Mary embodied the faith of the new order, because she loved so much.

PRAYER

O God, how this woman's life must have been transformed from the experience of the cross to the experience at the tomb. Women were no longer at a distance, beholding things from afar; now they were at the center, touching the feet of the risen Christ. Help us all to move from one experience to the other, and to fall down and worship because something extraordinary has happened to us. In his name, amen.

THE SOLDIERS TAKE A BRIBE

*W*e can only be saddened by the guards' response to the miracle they had witnessed. How typical it is of people in every age. They had been present at the most wonderful event in history; yet they resolved to treat it as a mere opportunity to make some cash and go on living as before.

Most of us, like these soldiers, regularly pass up chances to enter new dimensions of existence. We are usually so bent on earning a living or achieving status or having a good time that we don't even see the potential of great moments when they come to us. We miss the heavenly realm in our midst and fail to realize that the new creation waits at our very door to be born.

PRAYER

If I were only waiting at the tomb like the women, O God, instead of rushing around trying to make a better living like the soldiers, you would appear to me more often. Save me, I pray, from my own spiritual sloth. Through Jesus, who opens new worlds to those with eyes to see, amen.

THE NEW AGE OF THE SPIRIT

*M*atthew must have been running out of papyrus when he neared the end of his Gospel, for he condensed so much in this brief paragraph.

Jesus meets the eleven disciples at a mountain in Galilee. We recall the significance of mountains in the Gospel—especially in the Sermon on the Mount and the scene at the Mount of Transfiguration. It is fitting for the one who is greater than Moses to give his final instructions from the mountain.

The scribes and Pharisees had demanded to know Jesus' authority for what he did. Now he says, "All authority in heaven and on earth has been given to me" (v. 18). The verb is in the perfect tense—*it has already been accomplished.* The disciples are to go to all the nations, as the coming of the magi and the healing of the Canaanite woman's daughter prefigured, to make disciples of all who believe. The baptism with which they baptize, not visibly different from John's baptism, is now in the name of the Son too, and of the Holy Spirit, for all of this is in and of the Spirit.

The disciples, moreover, are to teach those they baptize. They are to instruct them in all the things Matthew has tried to set down in his Gospel. The new realm is not to be a mere charismatic movement, strong on emotion and weak in doctrine. It is to have a firm and dynamic ethical foundation, so that the law of God may truly flourish in the world.

And the most marvelous thing of all—the secret of the age of the Spirit—is that Jesus is now released from being in only one place at a time. Now he can appear freely to his disciples wherever and whenever he pleases to disclose himself. The child born in Bethlehem has become Lord of all creation!

PRAYER

O Lord, who taught and healed and broke bread with the disciples, teach, heal, and break bread with us. Renew the sense of your presence among us, that your teachings may gain new purchase on our imaginations. And let us go and make disciples of all nations, for yours is the kingdom and the power and the glory forever. Amen.

Day 102   *Mark 1:1*

A SCRIPT WITH TRUMPETS

*W*hat a world of meaning is packed into these few words: "The good news of Jesus Christ, the Son of God" (v. 1).

We can hardly appreciate the meaning of "Christ" or "Son of God" today without remembering the context. For centuries little Israel had lain at the crossroads of the ancient world, constantly battered, raped, and plundered by larger powers. The people had long dreamed of a great moment in history when God would dramatically reverse everything, bringing the old era to a close and inaugurating a new era in which the Divine Presence would rule the world from Jerusalem. Israel would become preeminent among the nations, and all roads would lead to its Holy City. But as no one could ever look directly upon God, God's Messiah—Christ—would be God's appointed one, and would be both the sign and the commander of this new age in human history.

Imagine, then, the startling, audacious character of Mark's announcement: Jesus, the Galilean who had been crucified outside the city walls of Jerusalem, was the Christ! He was the Son of God—another messianic title well known in that day. After centuries of waiting, he was the one God had promised.

This is why Mark called what he was writing "the good news." Mark was *proclaiming* this good news, lifting it up for everyone to read and hear. If this were a play, the script would call for trumpets. Jesus is the Christ, the Son of God. It is the greatest announcement in the world!

PRAYER

O God, my world is so routine and fragmented. My consciousness is preoccupied with so many things—schedules and budgets and household duties and TV programs. Help me really to hear Mark's announcement in all its true significance, so that my life is changed by it. Through Jesus, who is the Christ, amen.

Day 103   *Mark 1:2-8*

THE CALL TO A NEW BEGINNING

*T*he quotation in verse 2 is actually from Malachi 3:1, not Isaiah. But Mark would not have been troubled by such a small error. He had something much bigger in mind—the preaching of God's new realm!

John the Baptizer, the fiery prophet, was gathering a new community in the wilderness. This in itself was an important symbol, for Israelites regarded the wilderness period of their history, when Moses had led them out of Egypt, as their greatest era. Now, at a time when the land was covered by populous settlements, John took to the wilderness again, calling the people to a new beginning.

Spiritually, they were to join this new beginning through "baptism of repentance for the forgiveness of sins" (v. 4). The Greek and Hebrew words lying behind the concept of repentance suggest a "turning back" or "return," with a sense of sorrow for having gone away. Immersion, which was practiced in those days to initiate Gentiles into the Jewish religion, was offered as the ritual entrance into this new wilderness community, and even the Jews were required to come the same way.

Mark would play on this wilderness theme again in chapters 6 and 8, in the stories of Jesus' feeding of the multitudes. In both cases the crowds were in the wilderness and were fed by Christ, a picture that would have had great meaning to the church in its years of persecution.

In addition to the baptism of repentance, John preached the arrival of the Messiah, whose coming was popularly associated with the new community. "I have baptized you with water," said John, "but he will baptize you with the Holy Spirit" (v. 8).

John didn't want anyone to mistake him for the Messiah, the thongs of whose sandals he said he was not worthy to untie. Unfastening a master's footwear was the work of a slave, but John didn't even feel worthy to do that for Jesus.

PRAYER

O God, I am no more worthy than John, but I want to be part of the new community you are forming. Let me be immersed in your Spirit and know there is nothing too lowly for me to do. Through him who comes and is coming, amen.

Day 104   *Mark 1:9-11*

A TENDER MOMENT

*C*ommentators have long puzzled over Jesus' baptism. If he was the Lord, the Messiah, then why should he have submitted to baptism in the same manner as all the others who came into the new community? Matthew's Gospel, written after Mark's, explains that it was fitting for Jesus "to fulfill all righteousness" (Matt. 3:15). The Gospel of John, written still later, seems to rationalize that it was in order for John the Baptist to see the Spirit descending on Jesus and know that he was the Messiah (John 1:32-33).

There is a simple explanation, if we follow only the account in Mark. John was forming the wilderness community through baptism. Jesus wanted to identify with that community, so he was baptized by John.

It was not a time of public recognition of the Messiah, according to Mark. Jesus was the only one who saw the heavens open and the Spirit descending like a dove, and he was the only one who heard the voice. It was a private vision, in keeping with the fact that Jesus was from the obscure town of Nazareth and that Mark would make much of the so-called messianic secret, not revealing him to many persons as the Christ until shortly before the crucifixion.

The significance of the vision was a private one. It verified in Jesus' own spirit the calling of God to his ministry. The phrase "my Son, the Beloved" may have been much more personal than simple identification with the Messiah role; as Professor C. E. B. Cranfield suggests, it confirmed Jesus' "already existing filial consciousness." It was a tender, intimate moment. God confided to his Son the pleasure God felt in him—and, by extension, in the new community he represented.

PRAYER

Dear God, I am moved by this scene. I always get a lump in my throat when I behold parents watching their children being baptized. To think of your watching the baptism of Jesus is quite overwhelming. Thank you for the picture. Amen.

Day 105   *Mark 1:12-13*

AMONG THE WILD BEASTS

*W*hat a lot of drama is packed into these two verses! Jesus is driven out by the Spirit—the Greek word literally means "thrown out"— and spends forty days and nights in the wilderness.

The wilderness, in Hebrew thought, was considered the habitat of demons. Moses had spent forty years with the Israelites, wandering in the desert (Deut. 8:2, 16), and both he and Elijah had undergone forty-day fasts (Exod. 34:28; 1 Kings 19:8). As the newly baptized Messiah, Jesus was obviously undergoing a period of testing, like the trial times of all legendary heroes.

It is well known among saints and mystics that the experience of deep meditative prayer is often intimately related to temptation. The "dark night of the soul" described by St. John of the Cross, for example, was not a period of apathy derived from godless existence; on the contrary, it was a terrifying span of restiveness encountered in the very midst of a spiritual journey. Several persons who have had this experience describe it as the most deeply disturbing period of their lives, because it is a period when faith is shaken to its very core.

Mark is the only Gospel writer to allude to the "wild beasts." He may have done so to underscore the desolation of the wilderness, or because demons were believed to inhabit untamed animals. It is also possible that Mark saw this as a messianic touch, for many prophecies pictured the age of the Messiah as a time when wild beasts would become tame and docile—when "the wolf shall live with the lamb" and "the leopard shall lie down with the kid" (Isa. 11:6).

Through his faithfulness in this time of trial, Jesus proved his worthiness as the Messiah. As a result, the very messengers of God came to his service.

PRAYER

It is very difficult to be faithful to you in the wilderness, O God—maybe even harder than it is in a crowd. Let my experience of your presence be so real that I may be faithful wherever I am. Through him who always proved worthy, amen.

Day 106   *Mark 1:14-15*

TIME FOR A CHANGE

As we try to read between the lines of Mark's compressed narrative, we wonder whether Jesus had already joined John the Baptizer in preaching along the Jordan River in Judea, and now moved north into Galilee as a consequence of John's arrest. At any rate, he appears in his home country, preaching the good news from God about the nearness of the divine realm.

God had always, in theory, been the ruler of Israel. But the people were unmindful of this, and the prophets had spoken of a day when God would take this rulership in full power and authority.

"That day is at hand," Jesus announced. "The time is fulfilled." In New Testament Greek there are two words for "time"—*chronos,* meaning clock or calendar time, or time in its usual linear sense, and *kairos,* meaning time that is ripe with significance. Here the latter word is used. This is a special time. It is as though time itself were a pregnant woman and the moment had come for her to be delivered of an offspring.

The reaction to this news, Jesus announced, should be repentance, change of life, complete reorientation. It was the same message John had preached. To realize that the long-awaited realm of God was upon the world should produce a sudden revolution in people's behavior. They would show their belief in the good news by acting as though at last it were really true.

How would I have responded, O God, to Jesus' announcement that your realm was at hand? How do I respond now? For it is at hand, isn't it, growing silently in our midst even now, as Jesus taught his disciples? Grant that I may repent and lead a godly life. In the name of Jesus, who preached the new realm as good news, not bad, amen.

Day 107   *Mark 1:16-20*

NO TIME TO LOSE

*T*here are interesting parallels between this passage and 1 Kings 19:19-21, in which the prophet Elijah calls Elisha to be his follower: (1) Elijah had just spent forty days in the wilderness, where God had given him a mission to accomplish; (2) Elisha was plowing a field when Elijah came by and called him; (3) Elisha took long enough to kiss his mother and father goodbye, and to slay and cook a yoke of oxen to give to the people; (4) then Elisha followed Elijah "and ministered to him."

With the impression of his ministry fresh and strong upon him, Jesus likewise felt the importance of securing helpers. He could not possibly preach to all the people alone.

It is worth noting that he did not call unemployed folk to be his disciples. It is our tendency, when we want something done, to go to those who are unengaged or in a slack time. But Jesus picked men who were at work and offered them a higher task, "Follow me and I will make you fish for people" (v. 17). Immediately, Mark says, they went with him.

Mark liked the word *immediately*. He used it eleven times in this chapter alone (sometimes it is translated "at once"). *Immediately* this, *immediately* that. It is almost as if he wished to write the script for an old-time movie, with everything happening at double speed. Perhaps the word has theological significance in the face of what Jesus was preaching about the *kairos* and the fullness of time. With the heavenly realm breaking in, movement had to be swift. There was no time to lose.

PRAYER

I sometimes long for the days, O God, when life was simple and people made commitments just like that! Now we seem to think about everything until the time for action is past. Help us to be more spontaneous, at least when it comes to your realm. Through Jesus, who was always unwavering in his faithfulness, amen.

Day 108   *Mark 1:21-28*

TEACHING AND HEALING

*W*e were told in verses 14 and 15 that Jesus came into Galilee preaching preaching the good news. Now we are told about his teaching and healing. The three activities are inseparably linked in the Gospels, suggesting that the same ought to be true today as well.

Capernaum was a bustling town on the northwest side of the Sea of Galilee, and the Synoptic Gospels agree that it was the headquarters for most of Jesus' ministry. This may be one reason why he chose the fishermen as disciples, because their homes were apparently close by, as verse 29 indicates.

Always faithful to the worthier traditions of the Jewish religion, Jesus went to the synagogue on the sabbath. There he astonished everyone with the wisdom of his teaching. Unlike the scribes, who were laymen devoted to studying the law and developing its implications for daily life, he expounded the law with great flair and authority. Where they cited footnotes and previous interpretations, he spoke directly and emphatically.

Then, as if to underline this authority, Mark records a miracle story. There was among those in the synagogue a man with an unclean spirit—a demon. The spirit, more perceptive than ordinary persons, recognized that here was no mere itinerant rabbi but the Messiah himself. He not only spoke about the heavenly realm, but he was the very sign of the realm's presence.

"Be silent!" Jesus commanded the spirit. And the spirit left the man. Was this injunction to silence another instance of the so-called messianic secret? But the people were greatly impressed. Jesus had power as well as authority. And word about what he had done spread quickly, like a fire through dry grass.

PRAYER

Help me to understand, O God, how intimately healing is related to the presence of your realm. Grant that I may not only be healed myself, so that I am whole in your Spirit, but also that I may reach out with healing to others. Through Jesus, the worker of miracles, amen.

MORE HEALING AND MORE SECRECY

The Gospels show us very little of the private lives of Jesus and the disciples. This passage is all the more touching, then, for its allusion to Simon Peter's mother-in-law. Homes were small and unpretentious in those days, and extended families often lived together in what we would consider crowded conditions. Peter's father-in-law was probably deceased, and the mother-in-law lived in Peter's home, as indicated by the fact that when she felt better she got up and began to serve the others.

If Jesus could cure the man with the unclean spirit at the synagogue, and later the people who were brought to him at sundown, he could surely do as much for a member of his disciple's household, and especially one who had only a fever.

An interesting distinction is made between the people who are merely sick and those who are possessed of demons. Demon possession probably involved some degree of dementia or uncontrollable behavior.

Notice the expression "the whole city was gathered around the door." Contemporary accounts suggest that more than fifteen thousand people lived in Capernaum. Imagine the clamor outside Peter's house as they gathered there, all eager to see the man who worked miracles and have their illnesses cured. Yet Jesus cautioned the demons not to say who he was.

PRAYER

O God, I like the fact that Jesus attended to Peter's mother-in-law. Sometimes I forget, in my prayers for people suffering great hardship and affliction, to pray for the healing of my own family. I offer them to you now and ask that they may be whole and well and kept in your love. Through Jesus, who was never too busy or farsighted to care for those closest to him, amen.

THE CONSTANCY OF TEMPTATION

A problem we encounter in dealing with temptation is that it usually comes when we least expect it. Sometimes, as in this passage, it comes when we are in periods of great success and acceptance.

During his forty days in the wilderness, Jesus was tempted by Satan. Now, in the early days of his public ministry, he was tempted again—but this time under very different circumstances.

He had met with tremendous acceptance in Capernaum. The phrase "in the morning" does not necessarily link this day immediately to the one described in verses 21-34. Probably a number of days had elapsed, and support among the populace had been growing.

The temptation was for Jesus to stay in Capernaum and secure his reputation there as a worker of miracles. But he saw it for what it was—a temptation—and firmly resisted it. His mission was to go throughout the land, announcing the arrival of God's realm. He must not be deterred by success in one locale.

Characteristically, Jesus arrived at this decision in prayer. He had the same need that we have to be "alone with the alone." It was there that Simon and the others—Mark pointedly does not call them disciples—found him to tell him that everyone was seeking him. But his head was clear and his mind set. It was time to move on and proclaim the realm in other places.

PRAYER

I am sorry to confess, O God, that I seek you more when I fail than when I succeed. Help me to listen better in the good times, and in my thanksgiving to hear the still, small voice that directs my path. In the name of Jesus, who had heavenly integrity, amen.

THE MESSIAH AND THE LEPER

M ost of us have never known what it means to live as an outcast. But here was a man for whom most of the world was off-limits. He had leprosy, one of the most dreaded diseases of all times. The law forbade him normal contact with healthy people. He was required to remain always at a distance and call out a warning of his uncleanness.

What great faith the man must have had in Jesus' power to heal, to have transgressed this strict social rule and approached Jesus. He came and knelt, a practice usually reserved for royalty and great servants of God. What confidence he showed, in both Jesus' power and compassion!

Verse 41 is problematic in the manuscripts. Scholars agree that the ancient texts reading "moved with anger" are to be preferred to those reading "moved with pity." Some scribe, finding anger an inappropriate response by Jesus to this situation, probably changed the wording. But why would Jesus have been angry? Would it have been at the disease itself? At the man for breaching the social rules? Or because the man was intruding on his plans to continue preaching the realm of God? We can only speculate about the reason.

Whatever his feelings, though, Jesus dealt compassionately with the man. He touched him—a startling thing, for lepers brought both spiritual and physical defilement—and made him whole. Then, fearing his reputation as a healer would interfere with his preaching, Jesus enjoined the man to remain silent and go to the priest for the ritual cleansing and restoration prescribed by the law.

But the man predictably disobeyed Jesus' warning, and soon the demand on him as a wonder-worker was so great in the cities that he had to retreat to the countryside.

PRAYER

Dear God, it is easy to understand why this man could not keep silent about what had happened to him. What is hard to understand is how I can keep silent about all that has been done for me. Teach me to speak when silence would betray your generosity. Through Jesus, who touches us all in our defilement, amen.

Day 112   *Mark 2:1-12*

THE FORGIVENESS IS AMONG YOU

*H*ere we enter a strange section of Mark's Gospel. Between verses 2:1 and 3:6 he tells five stories about Jesus' conflicts with the authorities. In these stories, Jesus suspends his emphasis on being silent about the works he does; in fact, he seems intent on being known through his works. This suggests that Mark had this body of stories intact from an earlier source—perhaps from Peter—and inserted it here in a text otherwise more of his own telling.

The first story is a very dramatic one, of four friends who brought a paralyzed man to the house where Jesus was staying and found such a crowd of people that the only way they could get their friend close enough to Jesus to be healed was by digging a hole through the clay roof and letting him down from above.

Jesus saw the man's obvious condition, yet began not by healing him but by forgiving him. It isn't clear why he did this, for he did not usually equate illness with sin. But it instantly inflamed the scribes, who believed it blasphemous for any human being to arrogate to himself the power of forgiveness, which was God's alone to give. Jesus responded to their outburst by referring to himself as the Son of Man—a messianic title—and commanding the paralyzed man to take up his mat and walk home.

The fact that "they were all amazed and glorified God" (v. 12) suggests that even the scribes were won over and joined the crowd in applauding God for what had been done before their very eyes.

PRAYER

O God, I confess that I too am prone to think of forgiveness in negative terms—as though it were for failures and misdeeds. But I can see here that it has a very positive side too—that it prepares the way for life and health. Enable me to experience it daily, I pray, as the necessary precondition for my enjoyment of everything around me. Through Jesus, who has the power to amaze me even today, amen.

Day 113   *Mark 2:13-17*

JESUS AND THE OUTSIDERS

*M*any people are careful about those with whom they are seen, especially if they hold public office of any kind. We need to remember this to understand the importance of this conflict story. As the one proclaiming the long-awaited realm of God, Jesus daringly identifies himself with the wrong people, thus risking the disapproval of the scribes and Pharisees who were the solid citizens of their time.

The Gospel of Matthew speaks of the man here called Levi as Matthew. Some biblical scholars think he is the same as James, also identified as a son of Alphaeus (Mark 3:18). The important point, of course, is his occupation. He was one of Herod Antipas's customs collectors in Capernaum, the port through which northern travel around the Sea of Galilee ordinarily had to pass. Such minor tax officials were held in almost universal disdain as thieves and liars. The "sinners" of verses 15 and 16 may have been the "people of the land," who had not had the opportunity to study the law as the scribes and Pharisees had and were, therefore, shunned by them.

For Jesus to call Levi to be a follower and to eat at his home was unthinkable to the scribes and Pharisees, not only because of the character of these people but also because the meal was certain to be ritually unclean. It was virtually impossible for such officials to avoid contamination in dealing with non-Jews, and they were notorious for failing to pay tithes on their own foodstuffs and for neglecting the rules about the proper cleansing of utensils and the proper killing and preparing of food. Jesus had thus scandalized the solid citizens by his action.

Mark's point, as in the preceding conflict story and the story of the leper (1:40-45), is that the Messiah is above contamination. Instead of the sinner's rendering him sinful, he makes the sinner whole!

Jesus underscores this with an analogy. It is right for people to avoid the sick, lest they too become infected. But the same rule does not apply to the doctor, who visits the sick to make them well. Likewise, Jesus is above the ordinary rules governing righteous behavior; his mission is to restore righteousness to sinners.

PRAYER

O Lord, the source of all rightness and goodness, forgive me for expecting you always to be associated only with decent and honest people. Help me to imagine you consorting with the most unlikely persons in my community, lest I, like a scribe or a Pharisee, cut myself off from those you love. Amen.

Day 114   *Mark 2:18-22*

SONS OF THE WEDDING

*E*ach religion has its own characteristic tone. Hinduism, with its emphasis on reincarnation, reveres life. Confucianism, accenting filial piety, is conscientious. Christianity, because of its emphasis on the heavenly realm in our midst, should resound with joy and celebration!

This is the point of this conflict story involving a question about why Jesus' followers did not fast as John's disciples and the Pharisees' disciples did. Why should they fast now? Jesus asked. They were celebrating the great eschatological wedding—the ultimate wedding—that God has promised for so long.

Fasting wasn't a legal requirement among Jews except on the Day of Atonement. Those who did fast at other times had some special reason for doing so. John's followers may have been fasting because he had been taken away. This would explain Jesus' saying in verse 20 that his own disciples would fast when the bridegroom was taken away. The Greek word for "taken away" is probably a reference to Isaiah 53:8, which speaks of the Divine Servant's being "taken away" and "cut off from the land of the living." It thus implies a violent death and is a reference to the crucifixion.

The small parables of the cloth patch and the new wine, which we met in Matthew's Gospel, emphasize the newness of the experience of the first Christians.

The point of both parables, placed in this grouping, seems to be that disciples of Jesus should not be expected to be mournful and long-faced like their predecessors in Judaism, for what is happening to them is of another order. It is a time for celebration and dancing. We are, as the Greek says literally and the text translates "wedding guests," "sons of the wedding."

PRAYER

Like the scribes and Pharisees, O God, I too often am serious and gloomy in my religious faith. Help me to catch the spirit of joy and enthusiasm that ought to permeate my life because of your realm, and live daily as if at a great wedding. Through Jesus the bridegroom, amen.

Day 115   *Mark 2:23-28*

THE MOST SCANDALOUS STATEMENT

*A*s in the other conflict stories, the point here is that Jesus is the Lord of everything, including the law. He could eat with people who were not ceremonially clean (vv. 15-17) and he and his followers could pluck grain on the sabbath.

The law permitted taking as much grain from a stranger's field as one could reap with the hands (Deut. 23:25), but it also forbade reaping on the sabbath as one of the thirty-nine activities not permitted on the holy day (Exod. 34:21). The penalty for violating the sabbath was death by stoning, although violators were to be given one warning. This may have been a warning instance.

But Jesus answered with authority by citing the time David and his men entered the tabernacle and persuaded Ahimelech the priest to assuage their hunger with the holy bread consecrated for the use of priests and temple servants (1 Sam. 21:1-6). The Pharisees never spoke ill of David for this, and here was one greater than David, the Messiah himself.

"The sabbath was made for humankind," Jesus reminded them, "and not humankind for the sabbath" (v. 27). This was not an uncommon saying among rabbis at the time, but other rabbis did not behave as Jesus did. In the context, as Ernst Kässemann has said in *Jesus Means Freedom,* this is probably the most scandalous remark Jesus ever made. It cut across in an instant the artificiality of a religion that had devolved into mere law-observance. And, in the end, the attitude voiced here resulted in Jesus' crucifixion.

PRAYER

Dear God, it is the old matter of the razor's edge again: How do I know when to obey the law and when to follow the instincts I have in Christ? Help me through prayer and devotion to discern moments of obedience from moments of celebration, and to be true to you in both. In the name of Jesus, who is Lord of both. Amen.

Day 116   *Mark 3:1-6*

THE URGENCY TO DO GOOD

This is the last of the five conflict stories, and once more involves the sabbath, which lay at the heart of the Jewish legal system. The rabbis permitted healing on the sabbath only in cases where persons' lives were in danger; otherwise, healing was regarded as work and a violation of sabbath law. As no reason is given why the man with the paralyzed hand could not have waited another day, we may assume that Jesus was openly challenging the injunction against sabbath healing.

113

In one sense, Mark makes the same point in all of these stories. Jesus is encountering the scribal interpretations of the law. He is the Messiah, and therefore Lord of the law.

In Jesus' eyes, it is important to do good for people whenever possible, even on the sabbath. Doing good obviously takes precedence over doing nothing. As he puts the question in verse 4, it is no wonder the scribes and Pharisees are silent; they had either to agree with him or sound like inhuman monsters.

The healing is done very openly. The words "Come forward" in verse 3 imply that he stood the man in the middle of the crowd. The act is a purposeful demonstration of Jesus' messiahship.

If Mark counts the reprimand for reaping on the sabbath (2:24) as the single warning accorded sabbath violators before stoning them to death, his conclusion in 3:6 is a natural ending for the story as well as for the entire section of conflict stories. Now the Pharisees go out to plot Jesus' death. They counsel with the followers of Herod Antipas, who held political jurisdiction over Jesus, and whose help would be important in securing his death under the Roman occupation. The die is cast.

PRAYER

O God, give me the same kind of passion for doing good that Jesus had. Grant that selfish considerations may never deflect me from helping others, and let the exuberance of your realm determine the character of all my behavior. Through Jesus, who would have healed my hand if I had been the man in the synagogue, amen.

Day 117   *Mark 3:7-12*

THE SIMPLE FOLK RESPOND

*D*mitri, in Dostoevsky's novel *The Brothers Karamazov*, says that God will be kept alive in the prisons even if allowed to die among intellectuals and respectable people. It is an age-old truth. Again and again in history it is the little people, the outcasts, the simple folk, who understand and respond to the call of God when God is neglected in the finer circles.

After the five conflict stories that represent Jesus' failure with the religious leaders of his culture, Mark balances the account by depicting the enthusiastic response of the common people.

Jesus has withdrawn from Capernaum to more rural areas around the Sea of Galilee, and great crowds follow him. They come from every part of the Holy Land except Samaria, which most Jews disregarded, and the Decapolis, or ten Greek cities, which were less Jewish than other parts of the country.

Typically, the people want only what Jesus can do for them and show little regard for his personal well-being. There are so many of them and his ministry is so demanding that he has the disciples keep a boat handy for getting away for rest or safety.

It is the demons themselves—the agents of Satan—who recognize Jesus' real identity. They fall prostrate before him and cry out for mercy, probably in the screams of their poor victims.

And Jesus, true again to this strange theme in Mark's Gospel, orders them not to reveal his identity.

PRAYER

O God, it is the simple part of me that comes after you, that will not stop coming after you. The other part chases many phantoms, dreams, and illusions. Thank you for the simple part and its relentless return to life and health. In the name of Jesus, who casts out my demons, amen.

Day 118   *Mark 3:13-19a*

THE NEW ISRAEL

*T*hese verses assume a special force from what has preceded them. First, there are five conflict stories summarizing Israel's rejection of the Messiah. Then the Messiah turned to the common people, withdrawing to the seaside to teach and heal them. Now he goes up into the hills (going to the mountains always symbolizes an important action or event) and commissions twelve followers to be his special helpers. They too are common folk. And they are to be the pillars of the new Israel, as there had been twelve leaders of Israel in the days of tribalism.

Again, as in the calling of Peter, Andrew, James, and John (1:16-20), the initiative comes from Jesus. In the Old Testament, God called the heroes of the faith. Now the Messiah, the One coming with the heavenly realm, exercises this function.

Note the special dimensions of the call: The disciples are "to be with him, and to be sent out to proclaim the message, and to have authority to cast out demons" (vv. 14-15). Normally the disciples of rabbis followed their masters to learn their teachings, in exchange for which they provided food and a place to sleep for the rabbis. But Jesus is no ordinary rabbi; he teaches "as one having authority." Therefore, his disciples have a special assignment—to proclaim God's realm and extend the healing ministry of the Messiah.

Before anything else, though, they are to "be with him." It is a penetrating thought, isn't it? How many times we attempt to do the work of Christ without first being with him—without waiting in his presence to receive his Spirit and guidance. But being with him, or allowing him to be with us, is the only way we can really begin to do his work.

PRAYER

Lord, sometimes I am impetuous and rush out to do your work without having waited on you in prayer. Then I spin my wheels on things that don't really matter. Teach me to seek your guidance at all times, and then to follow it faithfully when it has come. Amen.

Day 119   *Mark 3:19b-30*

"THE OTHER SIDE"

*C*haim Potok, in his novel *My Name Is Asher Lev*, tells the story of a young artist who is misunderstood by his family and friends. As Hasidic Jews, they regard his enormous talent as coming from "the Other Side"—from Satan—and try to discourage him from using it.

Jesus encounters a similar response when he returns to Capernaum with his newly appointed disciples. The scribes from Jerusalem have spread the word that his power is from Beelzebub, the prince of demons. Even his family has heard this word in nearby Nazareth and has come to take him home.

But Jesus is forthright. He calls the lie-mongers to him and addresses them in parables. "Satan's work is to bind and destroy," he says in effect. "I am freeing and healing. How can you say that is of Satan? It is clearly against him."

Verse 27 may be a reference to the temptation in the wilderness (1:12-13), when Jesus won an initial victory over Satan. Having thus bound or inhibited the strong one, he is now proceeding to plunder his house, setting the captives free.

The rumor his enemies from Jerusalem have spread, says Jesus, is unforgivable. People can be forgiven almost anything. But to hinder the coming of the divine realm, which is what the scribes are guilty of, is blasphemy against the Holy Spirit and will be held against them forever.

PRAYER

This frightens me, O God. Have I ever stood in the way of your heavenly realm? Have I ever, by any word spoken, any deed done, any look of my countenance, discouraged others from believing? Have I ever stood in the way by merely being obtuse, unaware, unfeeling—by being there without joy and excitement? Please forgive me, dear God, for I know I must be guilty. Through Jesus, who was right to be angry, amen.

Day 120   *Mark 3:31-35*

THE REAL FAMILY

*T*hese verses must be read in connection with verse 21, with verses 22-30 as a long parenthesis between them. It is after the scribes have spread their slander that Jesus' mother and brothers arrive to take him home.

We should easily find sympathy for them. They have not been at the heart of the controversy all along. They are simple folk and would have a great natural respect for the opinions of the learned scribes, especially as the scribes came all the way from Jerusalem. They think their son and brother is sick, and they want to take him home and care for him.

Jesus' reply to those who tell him his family is there may seem callous if taken alone. But we must note that the Gospel writer does not tell us what may have followed in the way of a reunion with them, and that his point here is to complete the narrative about the flare-up of opposition to Jesus' ministry.

Jesus is still talking about the realm of the Spirit. "Who are my mother and my brothers?" he asks rhetorically (v. 33). His eye sweeps the room, filled with the once lame and blind and diseased he has healed, the simple folk who hang upon his teachings. "Here," he says. "Here are my mother and my brothers! Whoever does the will of God is my brother and sister and mother" (vv. 34-35).

He has appointed the twelve to be the leaders of the new Israel. In this realm of the Spirit, blood ties will not be the determining factor. The rabbis will not come in merely because they are the sons of Abraham.

Kinship will not secure a place for anyone. It is the followers—those who do the will of God—who will be Jesus' family.

PRAYER

O God, I am deeply moved by this teaching. It speaks to me of the strange intimacy I enjoy with Jesus in times of devotion and commitment. But it also reminds me of the importance of doing your will and making the way into the realm easier for others. Grant that I may not fail and that the sense of intimacy will always be there. Amen.

Day 121   *Mark 4:1-9*

THE SEED OF THE KINGDOM

*A*s there were five conflict stories (2:1–3:6), now Mark gives us five parables, which are not unrelated to the conflict stories. The conflict stories pictured Jesus' encounters with the scribes and Pharisees and ended with Mark's note about the Pharisees' counseling with the Herodians about how to destroy Jesus. Then, after Jesus' calling of the twelve, the scribes accused him of being possessed by Beelzebub. Now the overall theme of the five parables is the working of God to bring the new realm to successful fruition in the world. As Mark arranges them, in other words, they are a message of assurance in the face of the difficulties posed by Jesus' enemies.

The first parable is about the word of the heavenly realm and the kinds of people who hear it and don't hear it. It presupposes our knowing the ancient method of sowing seed *before* the ground was plowed. This is the reason the seed is sown on the path and on the rocky ground. The path will later be plowed up. The rocky ground is ground where there is a thin layer of soil over a layer of limestone—a condition characteristic of land in Israel.

Jesus' emphasis is probably not on the various kinds of ground but on the fact that some of the seed came to fruition and bore a rich harvest. Despite the opposition of the scribes and Pharisees and despite the blindness of many of those who hear him, Jesus' announcement of God's realm will find lodging in some persons and spring up abundantly.

The last verse, "Let anyone with ears to hear listen!" (v. 9), is like a gauntlet thrown down to the present hearers. It leaves us with the question "Will the heavenly realm spring up in me?"

O God, you are a prodigious sower, scattering precious seed on all kinds of ground. Prepare me, I pray, to receive more of the seed that falls on my life and to bring it to good measure for you. Through Jesus, who understood humanity well, amen.

Day 122   *Mark 4:10-12*

THE REASON FOR PARABLES

*W*e are accustomed today to thinking that everyone ought to hear the gospel and be persuaded of its truth. But there is a strong conviction in the biblical writings that God would call certain persons to his realm and not call others. It was, perhaps, a matter of preserving God's absolute sovereignty.

It is in this vein that we can understand these words of Jesus. Whereas we normally regard the parables as "earthly stories with heavenly meanings," told to illuminate some truth, they were apparently intended also to veil the truth from those God had not chosen. Thus they would fulfill Isaiah 6:9-10, which commanded:

> "Go and say to this people:
>   'Keep listening, but do not comprehend;
>   keep looking, but do not understand.' . . .
>   so that they may not . . .
>   . . . turn and be healed."

"To you has been given the secret of the kingdom of God," says Jesus to the ones gathered with him and the twelve. The word for "secret" in Greek is *mysterion,* a technical word from the so-called mystery religions to describe the very core of their belief and understanding. Paul used the word several times in his letters. Here the implication is clear: Jesus himself is the Messiah, the bringer of the heavenly realm, and his stories make sense only in the light of this understanding. Anyone who is not possessed of the mystery will hear only a clever saying or story, and is bound to misapply it.

O God, help me to dwell with the "secret" you have given until it makes all of life clear to me; there is no other way I shall understand, even though I become renowned for my knowledge and praised for my speech. Through Jesus, in whom you continue to disclose the mystery, amen.

Day 123   *Mark 4:13-20*

THE WORD IS THE SECRET

*H*ere is a rare instance in the Gospels where Jesus is shown explaining a parable. Some scholars believe the explanation is really a gloss added by a scribe or by the early church. It is not in keeping with Jesus' use of parables, they say, to provide an allegorical interpretation like this; his parables normally make a single point.

But perhaps the scholars are reading the explanation the wrong way. There really is a single point to the story, even in the explanation. The sowing of the Word finally results in the miraculous springing up of the godly realm. Some respond to the Word one way, others another way. But the sowing of the Word is central to the parable.

This is what Jesus was about, what he was doing wherever he went. It is what the disciples' ministry was to be about. It is what the church in the ages has been about. It is what *we* are to be about.

Like the generous sower in the parable, we do not sow with an eye to where the seed may spring up and produce God's realm. We do not say, "I will avoid wasting seed here, for the birds will get it," or "I will not sow here; it is too close to the path." Instead, we sow merrily wherever we go, knowing that others who come after us will plow the ground and nourish some of the seeds, confident that God will bring them to fruition in God's own time.

It is a beautiful picture of how the heavenly realm springs up in response to the broadcasting of the word about it.

PRAYER

O God, who has given the seed so abundantly, help me to sow less sparingly. I am so careful to measure what the response will be and where it will seem most affirmative. Make me profligate in sharing the news of the realm wherever I go, that it may spring up in the most unlikely places. Through Jesus, whose wisdom is beyond question, amen.

THE IMPORTANCE OF DILIGENCE

*T*his saying of Jesus in verses 21 and 22 is apparently a reference to the messianic secret and the lowliness of his appearance. "It will not always be thus," he is assuring the disciples. "No one lights a lamp in order to put it under a vessel or under a bed. Nor has God begun the work of the divine realm in me only to leave things as they are, in mystery and enigma. One day all the world will be able to see the light that shines in its midst!"

Therefore, it is very important that we pay close attention to everything Jesus says—to ponder it and turn it over and over in our minds until its secrets are ours. The more understanding we have garnered, the more we shall yet garner.

In this, the heavenly realm is like the situation in Asian societies in which the rich were always receiving gifts from others while the poor were buffeted and robbed even of what they had. If we have been careful to amass understandings from the teachings and deeds of the Master, it will act as a magnet to attract further understanding.

PRAYER

Dear God, we have seen Jesus in his resurrection and understand about the light put on the stand. Yet, he is still a secret to much of the world, and has not really come to light. Let me, therefore, be diligent in studying his words. Teach me how to meditate on them day and night, that understanding may give way to a more direct apprehension of his presence. For to know him is to know you. Amen.

THE MERRY FARMER

*T*he picture here is not greatly different from that in the earlier parable of the seeds. Mark undoubtedly coupled it with the other parable because of their similarity.

The point seems to be about the joyous abandonment with which the farmer does his work, trusting God for the mysterious power by which it all gets accomplished. He broadcasts the seed, then goes about his daily routines. As the writer quaintly puts it, he sleeps and rises night and day. Then, without his knowing how, the grain appears. The earth seems to produce of itself, "first the stalk, then the head, then the full grain in the head" (v. 28). It is a miracle.

But the farmer does not stop there. When the grain ripens, he takes his sickle, hones it, and goes into the field to cut the grain. Then he carries it to the threshing floor, where it is winnowed and separated, so that the kernels of grain may be ground into meal and used for baking.

The heavenly realm is this way, said Jesus. The seed has been sown. Miraculously, it is springing up. When we see it, it is time to be like the merry farmer and take our sickles to the field. We should not spend our time asking what happened to make the seed take root or how the growth of the ear occurred. Instead, we should be concerned for the harvest.

PRAYER

O God, we are all scholars and scientists at heart. We prefer debating the secrets of photosynthesis and maturation to taking our sickles into the field and gathering the grain. Help us to learn from this parable. You have given the divine realm. Let us go forth as simple farmers to do its work—even if we are scholars by profession. Through Jesus, who never disdained such tasks, amen.

Day 126   *Mark 4:30-34*

FROM HUMBLE BEGINNINGS

A friend once showed me a necklace someone had given her. Hanging from the chain was a small charm made of clear plastic. Inside the plastic was a small, round seed about the size of a poppy seed or a celery seed. It was, in fact, a mustard seed, said my friend, sent to her from the Holy Land.

In Palestine, the mustard seed was the subject of numerous proverbs because it was small and yet produced such a towering bush. Often the mustard plants around the Sea of Galilee rose to heights of ten feet or more and reached circumferences of as much as thirty feet.

So it will be, said Jesus, with the realm of God. Its beginnings are humble—a prophet clad in the skins of beasts and a Messiah walking from town to town with a motley band of disciples. But from this unlikely seed will spring up an incredible growth, capable of sheltering believers from all nations and ages.

Are we discouraged by the smallness of Christian efforts in our own day, especially in the large metropolitan areas? Does the world's outlay for arms and military operations far exceed the church's gifts for missions? Are there more people at ball games on Saturday than attending worship on Sunday morning? Do not despair. God guarantees that the heavenly realm will be like the mustard bush.

PRAYER

Dear God, give me courage from this simple story. Bless the small beginnings of the gospel in my life, that they may spring up like this. And grant that my efforts for your realm, however tiny and weak, may become a shelter for the souls of others. Through Jesus, who always knew how the realm would grow. Amen.

Day 127   *Mark 4:35-41*

THE MASTER OF WIND AND SEA

*W*hat a rich story this must have been for the early church! The symbolism of the boat was often used for the church itself, so that a boat floundering in high seas would have signaled, "Here's a picture of the church in trouble!" And the Lord of the church was in the boat asleep. As D. E. Nineham has pointed out, the people of Israel, during times of personal or national calamity, sometimes accused God of being asleep. Psalm 44:23-24, for example, says "Rouse yourself! Why do you sleep, O Lord?" Here in Mark's Gospel was a case of the Messiah's appearing to be thoughtlessly asleep while his followers were in imminent danger of perishing!

The disciples no doubt labored valiantly to save the boat themselves, but they were no match for the storm. Their words to Jesus were a reproach: "Teacher, do you not care that we are perishing?" (v. 38).

Jesus awoke and immediately addressed the storm. "Be still," the formula he used, is the same employed in rebuking the demon in Mark 1:25, underlining the possibility that this should be read as an encounter with satanic forces.

Immediately the scene shifts. Mark is fond of contrasts, as in the darkness suddenly made bright by the lamp put on a stand (4:21-22), the earth that was bare and then produces grain (4:26-29), and the small mustard seed that in the next glimpse has become a gigantic bush with birds nesting in it (4:30-32). Here the scene of wildness and terror suddenly gives way to one of peace and calm. And in the tranquility, Jesus asks, "Why are you afraid? Have you still no faith?" (v. 40).

There is the real clue. Faith in the God who brings the divine realm banishes fear. It enables us to sleep through storms—through misfortunes and persecutions—because then we know that God is not really asleep but is in control of our ultimate destinies.

It is small wonder that the disciples were filled with awe—they had seen one of the great secrets of life!

PRAYER

O God, I believe—*almost*. I believe—*when conditions are favorable*. I believe—*when there is no storm*. Help my unbelief. Let my faith become an abiding trust, an anchor that holds deep and steady when the winds rise and the waves threaten me. Through Jesus, whose confidence did not waver even on the cross, amen.

Day 128   *Mark 5:1-13*

AN ENCOUNTER WITH DEMONS

*P*eace! Be still!" Jesus had said to the threatening waves. "Come out of the man, you unclean spirit!" he orders the demon in this passage (v. 8). Mark is clearly concerned to show the power of the Messiah to command both natural and supernatural forces. In each case it is a storm that is quelled—only in this case it is a psychological storm.

The poor man is obviously deranged—so badly, in fact, that he shrieks night and day and does himself bodily injury on the stones. Completely desocialized, he lives in the caves along the lake, where the dead are buried.

The man runs to Jesus and falls down before him. Jesus immediately commands the demon to leave the man. "What have you to do with me, Jesus, Son of the Most High God?" asks the demon (v. 7). Like the waves of the sea, he recognizes the Messiah standing before him.

He says his name is Legion. A Roman legion numbered from four to six thousand soldiers. So a veritable host of devils had taken control of the poor man's soul.

124

Knowing they cannot win against the Son of God, the demons seek a compromise, asking to be sent into the herd of swine rooting nearby. It was not at all unusual for unclean spirits, on being cast out, to wreak mischief as they went. Jesus grants the request, and at once the herd pours grunting and squealing over the precipice and into the sea, probably very near to the spot where Jesus, the disciples, and the man are standing.

This is a clear demonstration of the Messiah's unusual power, even over the forces of evil in the world.

PRAYER

O God, there are demons in my life, some named and some unnamed, that make me hurt myself when I don't intend to. They often make me feel antisocial and unlovable. Let Jesus overpower my demons, too, and send them away from me, that I may wait before you in quietness and joy. For his very name's sake, amen.

Day 129   *Mark 5:14-20*

THE HARDEST KIND OF WITNESS

*Y*ears ago there was a man in our town who had been a notorious alcoholic. He often came home in a drunken rage and beat his young wife nearly to death. Then he was converted in a revival meeting and stopped drinking. He became an ardent worker in the church and went all over the area, witnessing to his miraculous transformation. His wife always accompanied him and sat there beaming as he told what Christ had done in his life.

I once asked him how it felt to be the object of such amazement. He said he often wished he could move away and start life over in a community where no one knew about his past, but that God wanted him to make his witness there among people who had known him.

It was the same with the man out of whom Jesus sent the demons. He wished to go with Jesus and the disciples—to leave the area where he had been so mercilessly possessed and where he was known as a madman by all the people of the region. But Jesus sent him home to witness to those who knew him.

Perhaps the man's reasons for wishing to leave are underlined by the response of the herdsmen. Fearful of anyone who talked to demons and had power over them, they begged Jesus to leave their territory. It was not because of the loss of the swine that they sent him away; it was because they did not wish to be in the vicinity of one who contended openly with the forces of evil. They knew that could be dangerous.

Notice that Jesus instructed the man to tell people how God had had mercy on him. It was not a breach of the messianic secret of which we have spoken, for this was Gentile territory, not Jewish; and Luke 8:39 makes it clear that it was God, not himself, that Jesus instructed the man to praise for his healing.

But characteristically the man spread the news about Jesus, not only about God, and soon the incident was known throughout the Gentile territory called the Decapolis. He "proclaimed" it, the Gospel says—the same word used for "preaching" throughout the New Testament.

PRAYER

O God, it is hard to live with my past mistakes among people who know me. But it glorifies you if my relationship to you has brought me beyond them to a new level of maturity and behavior. Help me thus to bear witness to your power in my daily existence. Through Jesus, who once landed on the shores of my life too, amen.

Day 130   *Mark 5:21-34*

A STORY WITHIN A STORY

*H*ere is an interesting literary occurrence, a story that takes place within the telling of another story. Jesus is approached by a Jewish leader, who asks Jesus to heal his infant daughter. As he accompanies the man to his home, an incident occurs along the way.

Imagine the distress of this poor woman. For twelve years her menstrual discharge has not ceased. And her anxiety is probably not only for her health; by Jewish law, she is also regarded as ceremonially unclean. Her strong desire to be cured is evident in the fact that she has consulted many physicians and has spent all her money and property on unsuccessful treatments.

When she hears about Jesus, her hope is stirred. She thinks that if she can only touch him as he passes she will be healed. In those days, the power to heal was believed to reside in inanimate objects as well as in people, so Jesus' robe was merely an extension of him. She touches him and is instantly healed—after many, many years of seeking help.

126

But Jesus, unwilling for the healing to remain at the level of magic, asks who touched him. With obvious fear—perhaps she is afraid he will take back the cure—she falls down before him and tells her story.

"Daughter," says Jesus, using a term of gentle affection, "your faith has made you well; go in peace, and be healed of your disease" (v. 34). The word *peace* on the lips of Jesus would have borne the meaning of the Hebrew *shalom*, which means not only an absence of strife but genuine fullness of life as well. In this case, it would not be a mere formula for parting but a phrase bursting with promise.

PRAYER

How wonderful, Lord, if I could come as this woman came and, touching your garment, be instantly transformed into wholeness of being! Help me to know it is possible. Give me faith like hers, and be there when I reach out. Amen.

Day 131   *Mark 5:35-43*

A POWER TO RAISE THE DEAD

*H*ere we resume the story of the Jewish leader's daughter, remembering that Jesus was on the way to their house when the woman touched his garment and was healed. This man's daughter's case is even more hopeless than that of the woman who had consulted many physicians, for she has died. But Mark wants us to see that there is no limit to the Messiah's power, for he can even raise the dead.

The people "weeping and wailing loudly" in verse 38 are probably professional mourners who were standing by until the moment of death. They are symbolic of our utter hopelessness in the face of death's inevitable advance.

Jesus reproaches them for their lamentations. "The child is not dead but sleeping," he says (v. 39), indicating that her death is temporary and not permanent. The mourners laugh. Don't they know death when they see it? Jesus puts them outside, and, with the child's parents and his three disciples, goes to the girl's body. Taking her hand, he speaks to her in Aramaic, the language spoken by most Jews in his day. *Talitha* is the feminine form of "lamb" or "young one." It is a tender address, probably spoken quite softly. *Cum* is the imperative "arise."

And *immediately*—how Mark likes that word!—she gets up and walks around the room. Mark probably stresses the instantaneousness to emphasize Jesus' power. Had she been only very ill or in a trance and then been revived by Jesus, she would have yet been too weak to rise. Jesus has demonstrated his authority as God's Messiah by performing the ultimate miracle: He has raised someone from the dead. It is a fitting climax to the series of stories Mark has narrated to show the Messiah's power.

The people, including the mourners, are naturally overcome by amazement. They have witnessed an epiphany, a revelation of the very power of God.

PRAYER

O God, our world, like the mourners, is inclined to laugh and scoff at any claim about raising the dead. Give us faith not to be drawn into this hopeless and joyless position. But let our constant nearness to Christ keep the memory of your power strong in our consciousness. For his name's sake, amen.

Day 132   *Mark 6:1-6*

THE POWER OF UNBELIEF

We often hear about the power of belief. The titles of countless books and articles celebrate it. But here is an instance of the opposite's being true as well. When we lack belief, we limit even the power of God in our midst.

Jesus takes the disciples home with him. He teaches in the synagogue on the sabbath—and the tongues wag. "Where does he get all this wisdom and power?" they ask in effect. "He's the son of Mary. He was a carpenter here. We know him. How can he be what he claims to be?"

The sad part of the story is the limitation the people's unbelief puts on their ability to participate in the benefits of the heavenly commonwealth. It is not that Jesus' power is restrained, but there is no great believing hunger there, no enthusiasm of faith, to call it forth. It lies essentially dormant, and Jesus himself marvels at the obtuseness of the populace.

Think of the blind woman there, destined to remain in darkness the rest of her life, the leper who would never be clean, the invalid who would never walk. It was a terrible tragedy.

Day 133   *Mark 6:7-13*

THE SENDING OF THE TWELVE

*E*ven as the people in Jesus' home region failed to respond to his messiahship, he intensified efforts to prepare for the heavenly realm by sending out his disciples.

They went in twos, an old biblical custom. They went simply, with no food, no bag, and no money—not even a coin in their belts or girdles. They were allowed sandals and a staff—the latter to ward off brigands along the way—but were not allowed so much as an extra undergarment.

They were instructed to claim hospitality in only one house in a village, and, when their work in that village was done, to move on. If people refused the message they preached and taught, they were not to argue or waste time trying to persuade them but were to observe the ancient Middle Eastern custom of shaking the dust from their feet and moving on, thus declaring the place heathen and leaving the people responsible for their own fate.

The whole emphasis was on the urgency of the mission. Time was short. The word must be spread quickly. People must be warned to repent and prepare their hearts for the new era.

As agents of the Messiah, the disciples were also empowered to cast out demons and heal the sick. Wherever they went, it was as if static electricity were being discharged in advance of a great weather front. The heavenly realm was arriving in Christ, and they were his emissaries.

PRAYER

What an ideal, O God, that these early missionaries of the faith left for successive generations. To go as they went, with nothing but a staff and the clothes and sandals they were wearing, challenges my desire for security and comfort in the service of Christ. Help me so to live in Christ's presence that I too shall be ready to live sacrificially. For in him we have beheld your new realm. Amen.

Day 134 *Mark 6:14-29*

VIOLENCE AND THE COMMONWEALTH

*T*his is the only story in Mark's Gospel in which the spotlight seems to be turned away from Jesus to someone else. But Mark's purpose may be to underscore the violence that occurs in the collision between the earthly realm and the realm of God. John the Baptizer was an early victim of that collision.

This Herod was not the same one who tried to kill Jesus when he was born; he was only sixteen years old at that time. Nor was he technically a king. He was the ranking Jewish ruler over Galilee and Perea, though the Romans actually controlled the area.

John had fearlessly denounced Herod for marrying his brother's wife despite the fact that, by Jewish law at least, Herodias had not been divorced from her first husband. Herod had imprisoned John, but had apparently become fond of visiting him in prison and talking with him. He had also refused Herodias's demands that John be killed.

Like a tale from the *Arabian Nights,* this story relates how Herodias's daughter, Salome, dances for Herod and his guests at a birthday dinner and charms them so completely that Herod offers her anything she wants, up to half his kingdom. The bloodthirsty Herodias tells her to ask for John's head on a platter.

When Jesus' fame grows, Herod thinks it is John come back to life.

For Mark, the whole episode is surely like the establishing of a theme in a musical work. The sense of violence and conflict can only increase as God's realm looms nearer. In the end it will reach its crescendo in the death of the Messiah himself, for earthly powers will not take lightly this invasion of the realm they have held so selfishly and tenaciously through the centuries.

PRAYER

O God, I cringe from such bloody violence as this; it is not in my nature, and I do not like it. I forget how many have died for the faith I claim, and for my very freedom to claim it. Heighten my awareness of the areas where belief still brings people into open conflict with the powers of this world, and give me the courage to be part of the battle. Through Jesus, who was crucified, amen.

Day 135   *Mark 6:30-44*

BREAD IN THE WILDERNESS

*W*hat happens in this passage would be readily recognized by early Christians as the pattern for the Eucharist, the feeding of the people by God. The leader asks the people to be seated. He says the blessing for bread, breaks it, and has his assistants distribute it among the people. They all eat and are filled, and a dozen basketfuls of fragments are gathered afterward.

There were precedents for this miracle. Exodus 16 and Numbers 11 record God's feeling of the Israelites in the wilderness, with an emphasis on the abundance of the food provided. Second Kings 4:42-44 tells of Elisha's feeding a hundred men with the twenty loaves of barley and fresh grain brought by the man from Baalshalishah, stating that they all "ate and had some left." The story in Mark is thus set against the providence of God throughout Jewish history, and it relates the Messiah to Moses and the prophets.

But it obviously goes beyond the precedents, for Jesus is much more special than Moses or Elisha. His presence as Host raises the feeding to the character of a messianic banquet and relates the messianic banquet to the Eucharist, or Lord's Supper, observed in all the churches of Christendom as a remembrance of his presence with the people.

How many times local congregations of Christians have found them-selves in wilderness situations—poor, resourceless, destitute, separated from influential society—and have experienced a similar feast in the bread and wine of Communion. Merely curious readers or scholars may argue over whether the miracle of the feeding could actually have taken place and how it might have done so. But anyone who has ever received Communion at a particularly desolate moment in his or her life will recognize in an instant the inward truth of the passage. Jesus cares for his flock in the wilderness!

PRAYER
Dear God, there is no greater miracle in the world than the lifting of a heart, and my heart soars at rereading this glorious passage. My cup runs

over, and I cannot eat all that you place before me. I can only thank you and bow my head in the name of Jesus, whose new community is forever. Amen.

Day 136   *Mark 6:45-56*

JESUS IN THE DARK HOURS

*W*e can easily imagine the situation in the early church for which Mark intended this narrative. Progress was not easy for the young church. Persecutions were frequent, causing defections from the membership. It must have seemed at times as if the church were a helpless little boat on a large and stormy sea, unable to go forward and constantly threatened with imminent destruction.

In the very darkest hour when the storm is worst, between three and six in the morning, Jesus comes to those in danger. He has a resurrection-like appearance. They think he is a ghost and are as frightened of him as they are of the storm.

"Take heart," says Jesus, "it is I; do not be afraid" (v. 50). The Greek words for "It is I" mean, more literally, "I am." They are thus reminiscent of what God told Moses when Moses asked who he should say had sent him to the Egyptians. God said to tell them, "I AM has sent me to you" (Exod. 3:14). This connection with Moses is enforced by the information that Jesus intended to pass by the disciples; in the Greek version of the Old Testament, the same word for "pass by" is used in Exodus 33:18-23 and 1 Kings 19:11-12 to speak of God's glory passing by Moses and Elijah.

The ghostly appearance of Jesus, coupled with this probable reference to God's glory passing by, assures us that this is a picture of the exalted Christ—the Christ who was raised from the dead by the power of God. And the final verses of the passage show the messianic I AM moving among the common people, healing all who touched even "the fringe of his garment." The message is plain: Jesus the risen Lord comes to his people when they are in trouble and brings them hope and comfort!

PRAYER

God, help me to remember this vivid story whenever things seem to be going badly; then I shall behold your glory passing by and become aware of Christ's presence in the ship with me, so that I shall neither despair nor be afraid. Amen.

THE TRUE SPIRIT OF THE LAW

*H*ere is sharply drawn the major issue between Jesus and the scribes and Pharisees from Jerusalem. Jesus is not a nontraditionalist, as indicated by the verse preceding this passage (6:56), which refers to the fringe of blue tassels he wore on his robe to indicate that he was a son of the law (see Num. 15:37-41; Deut. 22:12). But neither is he a strict traditionalist, as they are. He does not insist that his disciples, who are simply men from the country, follow the ceremonies so rigidly observed by the legalists.

When the scribes and Pharisees attack the looseness of Jesus and his apostles, Jesus neither defends nor condones their practice. Instead, he counterattacks at his enemies' weakest point: their hypocrisy. They make a fine show of being holy and pious, he says, but they distort the very idea of the commandments.

The illustration he gives is penetrating. A *Corban* was an offering made to God. It was something set apart from ordinary use. The owner could continue to use it, but it was then technically God's and could not be given to anyone else. Jesus cites a suppositional case (though perhaps a very common one) in which a young man declares his property Corban in order to avoid helping his parents. Later, he repents of this injustice to his parents and tries to have the Corban returned to ordinary use. But the scribes and Pharisees refuse to permit it, even though they profess to uphold the commandment about honoring one's father and mother.

Thus, says Jesus, they make void the Word of God—the written Law— for the sake of their flimsy tradition. And they "do many things like this," confirming Jesus' accusation that they do not have the true spirit of God's law in their hearts.

PRAYER

Deliver me, dear God, from the small loyalties of habit or tradition that would keep me from larger loyalties of the spirit. Let your presence in my life determine both what I think and what I do. Through Jesus, who understood the deeper meaning of piety, amen.

ATTACKING THE SOURCE OF EVIL

*M*ark has arranged this saying or parable of Jesus to follow the conflict with the scribes and Pharisees (7:1-13) because it is a natural extension of that story. "It isn't what goes into your mouths," says Jesus in effect, "—food that hasn't been ceremonially cleansed—that renders you ungodly, but what comes out of your mouths from the heart."

This establishes the real order of righteousness, which the scribes and Pharisees seem to have forgotten. As all the Old Testament prophets insisted, it isn't careful attention to ceremonial regulations, burnt offerings, and the like that God desires, but basic human goodness, moral decency, and compassion for others.

It seems to be a simple matter. But it was an issue of continued debate in the early church, and remains so even today. Paul was to battle legalism as a form of self-justification throughout his ministry to the churches in Asia Minor. Martin Luther fought against it in the age of the Reformation. And even in our own day there are those who insist that being a Christian requires a particular stance on such matters as the role of women in church and society, drinking alcoholic beverages, and attending church and Sunday school.

Any schematizations for salvation invented by human beings lead to our self-deception, as they did with the scribes and Pharisees. Only full submission to the realm of God, so that our hearts are filled with light, will suffice to induce true holiness in us.

PRAYER

O God, keep my mind and heart from petty rationalizations about my worth or goodness. My only hope for salvation is in you. Therefore, let me be charitable to all persons, forgiving and anxious to love them, for in this only do I experience your realm as a present and eternal reality. Amen.

A WOMAN OUTWITS THE RABBI

*H*ere is another healing story, only one made doubly interesting by the close reporting of the exchange between Jesus and the Syrophoenician woman. Jesus has gone to the seacoast area for a rest, and is therefore among many people who, like this woman, are non-Jews. This becomes very significant as Mark's Gospel unfolds, for the woman is the pivot on which Jesus' ministry turns from its Jewish base to a wider concern for people of other backgrounds.

Our sympathies are immediately drawn to the woman, for her daughter is ill and she seeks Jesus' help. Race and traditions don't stand in the way of a mother who cares about her child's welfare.

Jesus is coy, and at first refuses to help her. The children's bread shouldn't be thrown to the dogs, he says. "Dogs" was an epithet used by the Jews of their Gentile neighbors. But the woman is clever. Yes, she replies, but the little dogs under the table (the Greek word indicates small lapdogs, as opposed to larger canines) get the crumbs that fall from the children's plates. Jesus is surely delighted by her wit. "For this saying," he says, "you may go your way; the demon has left your daughter."

On the face of the passage, it is a simple encounter between Jesus and an unnamed woman. But when we get to Mark 8:1-10, the story of another feeding miracle, this time on non-Jewish soil, we shall see how important this encounter really was. The history of the entire world often turns on apparently small and insignificant events.

PRAYER

O God, I who am also an outsider, a non-Jew, am grateful for this little story of a woman who recognized Jesus' messianic powers and implored his help. You have given me far more than "crumbs" in my lifetime, and I owe you everything. Amen.

Day 140   *Mark 7:31-37*

THE MIRACLE OF HEARING AND SPEAKING

*J*t is probable that this story and the one of the blind man in Mark 8:22-26 were included with Isaiah 35:5 in mind:

> Then the eyes of the blind shall be opened,
> and the ears of the deaf unstopped.

The story is also related to Mark 6:52, which says the disciples did not understand about the miraculous feeding in the wilderness, and 8:17-21, which discusses this lack of understanding. The whole section of Mark is about not being able to see, hear, or understand what is happening in Jesus the Messiah.

Jesus' method in this healing became part of the baptismal rite practiced in many local churches during the early years of Christianity. The bishop or presiding officer conducting the baptism would spit on his fingers, then touch them to the candidate's ears, eyes, and mouth, symbolizing the person's new ability to hear the gospel and witness to his or her faith.

We are told that Jesus sighed before performing this wonder. The word translated *sighed* is used by Paul in Romans 8:22-26 and 2 Corinthians 5:2-4 to express an intense struggle of the soul. Apparently Jesus was contending with the whole host of demonic powers in effecting this cure. This would have been very much in keeping with Mark's consciousness of Isaiah's prophecy and how it had come to a head in Jesus' ministry.

PRAYER

This would be the miracle of miracles in my case, O God, to make me truly hear what my ears hear and to liberate my tongue to give thanks and to speak generously of others. I ask you to do it again for me—and again and again, if necessary. For yours is the realm that makes all of life meaningful. Amen.

Day 141   *Mark 8:1-10*

THE SECOND GREAT FEEDING

*M*ark 6:30-44 tells about the feeding of five thousand people in the wilderness. Now here is a story about the feeding of four thousand people in another wilderness area. It might seem anticlimactic after the first feeding. But if we see what Mark was up to, we find that it is quite the opposite.

The first feeding was on Jewish soil; this one is in the Decapolis, which was regarded as Gentile. There were five thousand people in the first crowd, a multiple of the sacred number five, the number of books in the Torah; there were four thousand people in the second crowd, a multiple of the number four, symbolizing the four corners of the earth. Twelve baskets full of fragments were collected in the first instance—the number of the tribes of Israel; and seven in the second experience, for the seventy nations of the world. Moreover, the Greek word used for "basket" in the first story is *kophinos,* a distinctly Jewish type of basket, while in the second story it is *spyris,* an ordinary kind of basket known throughout the Greco-Roman world.

Add to all this evidence the story of the Gentile woman in Mark 7:24-30, midway between the two feeding stories, whom Jesus first refused and whose persistence led him to do a miracle for a non-Jew. She thus became the pivot on which Jesus' ministry turned from the Jews to the Gentiles. And here, in the second feeding miracle, he confirmed that the new realm of God was for the whole world, not just for the Jews.

PRAYER

O God, this is thrilling material! What a gifted interpreter Mark was to weave these insights into such a provocative narrative. Thank you for his vision of Christ feeding the nations. Lift my eyes to this vision whenever I come to the table of blessing, that my own dedication may be more commensurate with the breadth and depth of its meaning. Through him who feeds us all, amen.

Day 142   *Mark 8:11-21*

THE SIGNS WE ALREADY HAVE

I once knew a woman who could not quite believe that her husband loved her. He was very tender toward her and showed her every consideration. He provided her with a lovely home and continually showered her with manifestations of affection. Yet nothing—none of his gifts and expressions of love—was ever enough. She constantly demanded new and more convincing proof.

It was the same with the Pharisees in their attitude toward Jesus. He had recently performed two stupendous miracles in feeding the multitudes, and, if the hints in Mark are reliable, lived in a constant situation of wonder-working. Yet, the Pharisees came seeking a special sign, perhaps some apocalyptic token in the skies, such as halting the sun in its course or turning the moon to blood.

Jesus' deep sigh is a key to his disappointment and his resolution not to pander to such a desire for the merely sensational. But the disciples were another matter. They too were slow to perceive what it meant that the Messiah was in their midst. In the boat, when he spoke to them about "the yeast of the Pharisees and the yeast of Herod"—remember that yeast often symbolized pernicious influence—they suddenly remembered that they had forgotten to bring any bread and fell to discussing the matter. Jesus interrupted them and chided them for their anxiety.

How many baskets of fragments had they collected after the first feeding? Twelve. And after the second feeding? Seven. There in the boat with them was the breadmaker himself, the one whom the Fourth Gospel would eventually identify as the very Bread of Life. Why were they worried? Had their eyes not seen what passed before them, or their ears heard the exclamations of the crowds?

Jesus himself was the sign of the heavenly realm. How could anyone ask for more?

PRAYER

It is the same in every generation, O God. Doubt rises in us like the yeast in the dough, and we continually ask for signs and wonders. Teach us instead to give thanks for the signs and wonders already surrounding us—for daily bread and changing seasons and tender care. Then we shall know the presence of Christ, and who it is that said, "I am the Bread of Life." Amen.

Day 143   *Mark 8:22-26*

THE MIRACLE THAT JESUS DID TWICE

*T*his story is in some details similar to the one in Mark 7:31-37, which also followed a feeding narrative. Interestingly, the first story was about the healing of a deaf man, and this one is about the restoring of a blind man's sight—with Mark 8:18 between them asking, "Do you have eyes, and fail to see? Do you have ears, and fail to hear?"

Above and beyond recording the two incidents as bona fide healings by Jesus, the Evangelist obviously uses them in a symbolic sense as well. They clearly bespeak Jesus' power to make us hear and see with a spiritual insight we have been missing.

One of the most captivating details of this particular story is Jesus' asking whether the man sees anything. "I can see people," he says, "but they look like trees, walking" (v. 24). His sight is not perfect. So Jesus again anoints his eyes with spittle, and this time the cure is complete.

This is the only instance in the Gospels of a healing miracle that is incomplete the first time. It is so out of keeping with the usual peremptory character of Jesus' miracles, in fact, that it prompts us to consider its special meaning here.

Surely it is Mark's way of saying to those who have once been anointed with the vision of Christ but who still do not see all things clearly, "He will anoint you again, this time with perfect vision."

PRAYER

Lord, I have seen part of the wonder and beauty of your heavenly realm, but my cure has not been complete. I still struggle with imperfect ideas and an uncommitted will. Touch me again, and again if necessary, that I may behold everything as I should. For your name's sake, amen.

Day 144   *Mark 8:27-33*

THE NECESSITY OF SUFFERING

*A*t this point in the Gospel, Mark begins to build toward the crucifixion and resurrection of Jesus by having the disciples define their understanding of who he is. Their response to his question is identical to the information given in Mark 6:14-16, introducing the story of John's death: Some say he is John the Baptist, others Elijah, and still others that he is one of the prophets. When Jesus presses them for *their* response, Peter answers, "You are the Messiah" (v. 29).

Now a strange thing occurs. Jesus does not congratulate Peter, as Matthew's Gospel represents him as doing (Matt. 16:17-19). Instead, he "sternly" orders the disciples not to tell anyone about him. Why? Apparently we are still dealing with the so-called messianic secret.

It may be, too, that Jesus thinks the disciples know too little about what they have seen and heard, for he begins to instruct them about his death and resurrection. Peter demonstrates how little they understand by protesting that this must not happen.

Then, in a flash, Jesus rebukes Peter, seeing in Peter's words such temptation as he felt in the wilderness at the beginning of his ministry: "Get behind me, Satan! For you are setting your mind not on divine things but on human things" (v. 33). It seems an unkind thing to say to a friend who cares about your welfare. But just as Jesus has seen Satan's power at work in the ill persons he has healed, so also now he sees Satan behind the kindness of Peter.

It is not merely Peter's understanding that is at stake; it is the whole battle with demonic forces. The cross will be not only an unfortunate episode in which justice miscarries, but it will also be the last cruel effort Satan can make to avert the coming of God's new realm!

PRAYER

I sympathize with Peter, O God. I, too, would have protested such pessimism from the Master. But I often fail to recognize the cosmic drama going on behind the surface of things. Help me to look more sharply and to be ready to die in the fight against the demonic. Through Jesus, who saw clearly and did die, amen.

Day 145   *Mark 8:34–9:1*

THE PRICE OF DISCIPLESHIP

*N*ow Jesus widens the circle of those who must understand about his death and resurrection, calling in a crowd of followers. He wants them to know the hardships facing them after he has left them.

Admittedly, it is questionable whether he would have used precisely this language, particularly about the cross, for such concepts would have had little meaning before he actually lost his own life on a cross. Perhaps the statement is an amalgam of an actual warning spoken by Jesus and the later awareness on the part of the Christian community of the way Jesus had died.

At any rate, Jesus is depicted as a leader fully aware of the awful toll his people are about to pay in God's battle with the demonic forces. It is too late to back down, he says; the climax is inexorable. Any who try to forsake him will effectually lose all they have. But all those who pay with their lives will actually be saving their lives.

The last verse (9:1) testifies to the intensity to which Jesus sees matters as having come. Some of those standing near him, he says, will still be alive when God's realm will have come in power. This word has led some scholars to think that Jesus was flatly mistaken in his apocalyptic vision; clearly, they argue, the new order did not come in the sense that he expected.

But we must remember that Mark was writing this years afterward. What did *he* think? Surely, if he thought Jesus' expectations had been misplaced, he would not have added this verse. He would simply have omitted it. But he did not. As far as he was concerned, Jesus had been right. The new order *had* come in power. If we do not think it has, that is because the quality of our experience of Christ is not what Mark's was. It is a test of what we see and understand!

PRAYER

It is easy to think, O God, that the great wars of faith were waged years ago, and that this is an age of drabness and dullness. Help me to see what cosmic battles are being waged in my own day and in the very environment where I live. Then let me make my commitment to follow Christ and fulfill it every hour, that I may not lose my soul in the mindless routines of daily existence. Amen.

Day 146   *Mark 9:2-13*

A FORETASTE OF GLORY

*T*his is a dramatic passage with which Mark follows Jesus' announcement to the disciples that he and they must suffer. It is essentially a picture of Jesus transformed as he would be in the resurrection. What could be more encouraging after the warning he has sounded?

Everything in the narrative conspires to depict the arrival of the heavenly realm. First, Jesus' clothing is transformed. Popular belief about the end of time was filled with the idea that people's final glorification would extend even to their clothing. Then there is the appearance of Elijah and Moses, who were popularly expected to reappear at the end of time to preside over the changes in the world. And finally there is the matter of the cloud, reminiscent of God's presence, which appeared as a cloud to the Hebrews in the exodus.

When the voice from the cloud testifies, "This is my Son, the Beloved; listen to him!" (v. 7), there can be no doubt. The climax of Jesus' ministry and the arrival of the new realm are at hand.

In the light of all this, Peter's desire to build booths or tabernacles and stay on the mountain is more than the mere human desire to prolong an exciting experience. It was widely believed that in the last days God would pitch a tent and dwell with Israel as the holy presence had in the time of the wilderness wanderings. The disciples thought the end had come, and it was, therefore, fitting to dwell on the mountain in tents.

But suddenly it was over. It had been momentary—a vision out of time. Jesus was alone. His garments no longer shone. Thoughtfully the men descended the mountain. They were full of questions. Jesus warned them not to speak of this until after his resurrection. He must still "go through many sufferings" (v. 12). Yet, through it all they would have this to remember. It was an unforgettable experience.

PRAYER

O God, there are experiences like this for all of us who spend time with you. If I have had none, it accuses me of being a lazy, undisciplined follower. Make me faithful in my devotions, that I may ascend more often to the mountaintop. Through Jesus, who was transfigured, amen.

Day 147   *Mark 9:14-29*

THE POWER OF BELIEF

This is the final exorcism story in the Gospel of Mark, and an absorbing story it is. Jesus and the three apostles come back from the Mount of Transfiguration and find the other disciples being taunted by the scribes because the disciples were unable to heal a boy of an apparent case of epilepsy. Jesus flares up, possibly at the demons possessing the boy, but certainly also at the disciples, who could not help him. We must remember that these are the same disciples described in Mark 8:14-21, who could not see or comprehend. "You faithless generation," says Jesus, "how much longer must I be among you?" (v. 19).

But then his sympathies for the boy overtake his wrath. "How long has this been happening to him?" he asks. From childhood, the father replies, but adds that he hopes Jesus is able to help. "All things can be done for the one who believes," says Jesus (vv. 21-23).

Many sermons have been preached on this text suggesting that a positive attitude goes a long way toward helping any desperate situation. But Jesus has more than this in mind. He is surely thinking of the new order of God, and suggesting that anyone who truly believes it is at hand will see miracles in his or her life.

Why does the boy remain in a trance after the demon has left him? It may be that Mark intended Jesus' raising him by the hand to prefigure the way Christ shall raise all believers in the day of resurrection.

And what does Jesus mean, at the end of the story, when he tells the disciples that this kind of demon "can come out only through prayer"? Weren't they men of prayer? What he undoubtedly means is that utter belief in God's new order is necessary for this power, and that kind of belief results only from hours of practicing the presence of God.

PRAYER

O God, this passage, like so many others, is frightening in what it demands. It asks nothing less than my total commitment and unreserved belief. Help me to give myself to you in prayer and love and excitement— and so to believe radically in your new order. Through Jesus, who led the way in such belief, amen.

Day 148   *Mark 9:30-37*

WHAT IT MEANS TO SERVE GOD

*J*esus was passing secretly through Galilee so that the crowds would leave him alone and let him continue teaching the disciples, preparing them for his death. Typically, the disciples were having a hard time understanding what he was talking about, but—and this is a warmly human note—they "were afraid to ask him" (v. 32).

Mark seems to have seen a connection between the suffering of the Messiah and the passage that follows. The disciples had been arguing about who was the greatest. When Jesus asked what they were talking about, they were embarrassed and kept their silence. So he gave them an object lesson. Taking a small child—perhaps the child was playing nearby or was borne in its mother's arms—he held it up before them. "Whoever welcomes one such child in my name," he said, "welcomes me, and whoever welcomes me welcomes not me but the one who sent me" (v. 37).

It was a wonderful lesson. "If you want to be the greatest," he was saying, "then be the humblest—put yourself down on the level of a child, where your reputation doesn't mean a thing. That way, you welcome the Savior of the world. Not only that, you welcome God."

Henri Nouwen tells in his book *In the Name of Jesus* how he left the world of the university to become the chaplain of a school for special children, called Daybreak. The biggest adjustment he had to make was to the loss of the status he had enjoyed as a professor. The children at Daybreak didn't recognize any of his attainments—his degrees, the books he had written, his renown as a lecturer all over the world. All they cared about was whether he loved them and could be comfortable with them.

This is what Jesus was trying to get the disciples to see. The only status that matters in God's new realm is love and vulnerability.

PRAYER

There is so much I do not know about service, O God. I talk about the poor, but do not give them my possessions. I talk about the hungry, but do not share my food. I talk about the little children, but do not spend time with them. Forgive me, dear God, and help me to really love all of these. Through Jesus, who does, amen.

Day 149   *Mark 9:38-41*

USING JESUS' NAME

Some scholars do not believe that these verses are a genuine part of the early Christian tradition because they seem to conflict with the behavior of the Christians. If the incident really happened, then why were the Christians so exclusivist? Acts 19:13-17, which is about some Jewish exorcists who tried to use the name of Jesus, is clearly not sympathetic with such usage.

But such contradiction is all the more reason to accept the validity of this passage. Surely no scribe would have undertaken to add to the tradition something that contravened the actual practice of the church.

It is probably another case of Jesus' insight and understanding going so far beyond our own. In his perception of the way the new order was breaking forth all around him, he was not worried about the presence of unauthorized wonder-workers who used his name. It is when we lack faith in the overpowering nature of the heavenly realm that we begin to worry about the purity of our organization and its methods of operating.

Think of the guilt we bear for our prejudices regarding denominations and forms of church governance, modes of piety and patterns of worship. We have often behaved as if our own forms and methods were the only ones, and all the others were less than Christian. Yet, Jesus was tolerant of those who used his name though they had never been with him, and said, "Whoever is not against us is for us" (v. 40).

We tend to be overly frightened, O God, by those who are not of our camp and manners. Teach us to be open and tolerant, and to recognize as your children also the many people who have come to you by routes unknown to us. Through Jesus, who acknowledges the least favor done for his little ones, amen.

Day 150   *Mark 9:42-50*

SOME HARD SAYINGS

*J*esus said early in the Gospel of Matthew that he had not come to destroy the law but to fulfill it. Here Mark reminds us that despite our tendency to think of Jesus as a gentle, kind figure, he could be very hard and demanding. The sayings are quite aphoristic, and may have been grouped together from a variety of utterances during his ministry.

First is a warning about doing anything to disturb the faith or hope of any of the "little ones" who believe in the Messiah. This would appear to be a word of caution to any Jew who attempted to turn a weak Christian away from belief in Christ. But it would also apply to a Christian who carelessly wounded or implanted doubt in another Christian. It would be better, says Jesus, for that person to have a great millstone—the kind turned by a donkey, not one of the small ones turned by hand—tied around his or her neck and be dropped in the sea. It would be a kinder judgment than the one awaiting the person.

The theme of judgment, then, becomes a pivot for the next series of verses—only this time it is undoubtedly the Christian who is threatened by judgment. The "hell" that is mentioned is hardly an apt basis for a doctrine of eternal punishment. The word used is literally *Gehenna,* the name of the valley southwest of Jerusalem that had been desecrated by Josiah (2 Kings 23:10) and was afterward used as a place to burn refuse. It was thus a dump infested with maggots and characterized by smoldering fires, and had become identified in Enoch 27:2 and 4 Ezra 7:36 as a place of divine retribution.

It is better, said Jesus, to lose a part of your life quite dear to you than to be led astray by that part and so lose everything.

The phrase "salted with fire" is probably a reference to Leviticus 2:13 and other Old Testament passages indicating that Jewish sacrifices were to be accompanied by salt. Christians in this time of persecution would be seen as human sacrifices purified by fire. The word *fire* probably led Mark to place this saying after the one before it. Unrelated sayings were often connected this way to make them easy to remember by certain catchwords.

The last saying, verse 50, is added for the same reason. This time the catchword is *salt*. It is a plea for Christians not to lose their saltiness—the heavenly quality in their lives—and so become useless to the world.

PRAYER

The world is a hard place, O God, and the demands upon me as a Christian are great. I cannot meet them alone. Be with me and give me a sense of your presence at all times. Then I shall be able to withstand the pressures and care for your little ones. Amen.

Day 151   *Mark 10:1-12*

MARRIAGE AND THE HEART

The Pharisees come at Jesus again, this time with a question about divorce. "What did Moses command you?" asks Jesus. "Moses allowed a man to write a certificate of dismissal and to divorce her," they said (vv. 3-4).

The reference is to Deuteronomy 24:1-4, which speaks of a man's divorcing his wife if he finds "some indecency" in her. He is to give her a bill of divorce, which she can then present as proof of her divorce should another man wish to marry her. One school of Jewish thought held that "some indecency" meant adultery; another said it meant any cause of displeasure the husband felt toward the wife, such as unattractiveness or inability to cook.

Although this was the text to which the Pharisees' legalistic minds immediately flew, Jesus apparently was thinking about a more basic text in the law—the commandment "You shall not commit adultery." The more lenient ruling, he says, was given because of people's "hardness of heart." But God never intended for male and female relationships to end that way. God created a man and a woman, and in marriage they become one flesh. What God has joined, then, let no one put asunder.

Jesus' theology of the new order is obviously at work here. In the heavenly realm, God will be so exalted that we will not sit around worrying about whether we are finding fulfillment with the man or woman we married. Our hearts will simply be occupied by other things.

PRAYER

When you are close to my consciousness, dear God, my whole world is beautiful. Then it is easy to fulfill the highest expectations for my life. Help me, therefore, not to dwell on my problems but on the fact of your presence, and I shall glorify you with my joy. Through Jesus, who understood this perfectly, amen.

Day 152 *Mark 10:13-16*

A KINGDOM OF CHILDREN

*H*ow much poorer we should be if this story had not been preserved! And what an accusation it is of our pretentious, complicated lives as adult Christians!

The wise have always spoken well of the open, receptive nature of children, and of the importance of our maintaining their best qualities in our mature years. It has been said that we are most truly ourselves when we are playful and spontaneous in the manner of children.

Many authorities believe, however, that Mark's story is more than a benediction on childhood. It is a beautiful picture of God's new order as a realm of joyous, childlike persons, to be sure; but it may also be an early apologetic for accepting children in baptism. The command "do not stop them" (v. 14), sometimes translated "do not hinder them," echoes a part of the liturgy of baptism, which asked the question "What hinders?" In Acts 8:36, the same question occurs with reference to the Ethiopian eunuch who wishes to be baptized. The fact that Jesus is described in verse 16 as laying his hands on them also suggests liturgical meaning, for the laying-on of hands was a part of the baptismal ceremony.

Whether or not we see this additional meaning in the story, it is a rich and lovely little narrative. Jesus was rejected by most of the responsible Jews of his day, and he was often misunderstood by his own disciples. He could well hold up the happy, responsive children as examples of those who truly belong to God's new order!

PRAYER

O God, teach me the joy of the simple and uncomplicated life in which I accept the blessing of your presence the way a child accepts the presence

147

of a dear friend. Then I shall gladden your heart by the renewed innocence of my spirit. Through Jesus, who lays his hands on me, amen.

Day 153   Mark 10:17-31

SURRENDERING ALL IMPEDIMENTS

*I*n contrast to the preceding passage about little children, here we have
a striking example of someone who could not enter God's realm
like a little child. It is a man whose wealth and possessions have become
the basis of his security. He *wants* to become a follower of Jesus, but he
cannot meet the test of commitment when Jesus tells him he must sell
everything and give his riches to the poor.

Throughout the Gospel, we have seen the conflict between those who
keep the law and Jesus, who demands that people go beyond the law and
have God's Spirit in their hearts. This man has kept the law in exceptional
fashion, but he is not prepared to demonstrate absolute commitment to
the Messiah.

Jesus and the disciples talk about it after the man has gone away. The
disciples are amazed, for like most people they have always regarded
wealth as a sign of God's favor. But Jesus tries to make them understand.
Entering the divine realm is not easy. It requires complete confidence in
God. If we depend on anything else, we must forsake that. As Jesus said
in Mark 9:43-48, if any part of our being—even a hand or an eye or a
foot—interferes with our complete devotion to God, we are better off to
cut that part away and hurl it into the flames.

Peter reminds Jesus that he and the disciples have left all. Yes, says Jesus,
and the reward will be commensurate with the sacrifice. What is given up
will be restored a hundredfold. The persecution endured now will be
replaced by eternal life in the age to come, and the tables will be turned
for many people.

PRAYER

Dear God, help me to look hard into my own life and recognize the
dependencies I have not surrendered. Are they my home, my family, my
work, my travel? They are all dear to me. But grant that I may love you so
much that none of them stands between us, now or in the future. Through
Jesus, who gave up all from the very beginning, amen.

JESUS GOES AHEAD OF US

*T*his is the third and most specific of Mark's predictions of the suffering of Jesus. It is the first time Jerusalem has been mentioned as the place where Jesus will be crucified. In Mark, the holy city is ironically the center of the evil power in the world. It is from there that have come the scribes and Pharisees who oppose Jesus and refuse to understand him. Now, as he approaches the city, we feel a natural heightening of suspense and conflict. It is little wonder that the disciples are afraid.

What a powerful image Mark gives the early Christians, though, with Jesus going ahead of his followers. This would surely have been comforting to those facing persecution and death for their faith. Jesus always precedes his disciples. Ministers, missionaries, and lay workers have often commented that this is their experience. Wherever they have gone, into jungles, foreign countries, palaces, or ghettos, they have been anticipated by the presence of Christ. Christ is always there first.

Perhaps the most interesting feature of this prediction of the passion is the reference to Jesus' being delivered to the Gentiles—the Romans— who will mock him, spit on him, scourge him, and kill him. This is a literal preview of events Mark will describe in 14:65 and 15:15. Whether Jesus predicted the very details of his trial and death or Mark added them after the fact is beside the point. The important thing in the narrative is Jesus'—and the disciples'—apprehension of his coming execution.

As for the resurrection, this must have been a dark mystery indeed to the disciples at this point. As Mark says very tersely in 14:50, when Jesus had been captured by the priests and their guards, "All of them deserted him and fled."

PRAYER

Lord, you go ahead of me into the strangest places. Often they are places where there is pain or conflict or misunderstanding, and I am afraid to follow you. Teach me faithfulness, that I may not desert you, but follow with courage and love. For you are with me, even to the end of the world. Amen.

FOLLOWING A SERVANT LORD

*H*ow often we make the same mistake James and John made, of thinking that our religion exists for us. "We want you to do for us whatever we ask of you," they said to Jesus (v. 35). Doesn't that sound like us? Some of us even judge the efficacy of our religion by how dependable God is to do that. If God gives us what we ask for, we think our belief is good and true; if not, we begin to doubt.

But Jesus turns the thinking of his disciples around. That is not the way it is in God's realm, he says; there, the greatest are those who exist to serve others. Jesus himself is the prime example. Even though he is the Messiah, the Son of God, he came "not to be served but to serve" (v. 45).

Can James and John drink the cup Jesus will drink or be baptized with the baptism facing him? The references are two-pronged. On the surface, they allude to Jesus' impending death. At another level, they surely spoke to the early church about the Lord's Supper and the ritual of baptism. To engage in either was a dangerous act, and might involve the participant in following Jesus to a premature death, especially during times of heavy persecution.

Even if the disciples can follow Jesus in this, he says, it is not his to say who will sit at the places of honor with him. The realm is God's, and God will decide such matters.

We are back to the matter of entering the new order like little children. In the world, people race and strain to enter ahead of others, to be number one, to hold the place of honor. In God's realm, it is enough to be a mere servant, to be the "slave of all." Joy comes not from place or position but from the presence of God in our midst.

PRAYER

O Lord, who walked humbly among us, teaching with patience yet suffering indignities and pain beyond telling, help me—proud, ambitious, and selfish—to learn to be gentle, restrained, and self-emptying, even as you are. Amen.

THE GIFT OF SIGHT

*I*n a Gospel that has had so much to say about seeing and not seeing, this is an important narrative, especially as it occurs while Jesus is on his way to Jerusalem for his final encounter with the scribes and Pharisees. "Jesus, Son of David," the blind man calls out, "have mercy on me!" (v. 47). Even though his eyes do not see, he recognizes what many do not: that the one on his way to the holy city is the Messiah.

Others try to shush him. He is creating a disturbance. But as he has all the way through the Gospel, Jesus has compassion on the poor and suffering, and calls for the man to be brought to him.

"What do you want me to do for you?" Jesus asks. It is the same question he asked James and John in the preceding passage. There he said that their request was not his to grant. Now, when the man says, "My teacher, let me see again," Jesus bestows the favor (v. 51).

This request is different. It comes not from the disciples, who have been with Jesus for many months and still don't understand his ways, but from a poor, untutored blind man whose faith has leaped up to embrace the new order. "Go," says Jesus, "your faith has made you well" (v. 52). The Greek word meaning "to make well" refers to salvation as well as to healing.

Immediately—how Mark loves that word!—the man receives his sight and follows Jesus "on the way." He joins him in the final part of the great pilgrimage to Jerusalem, and will be among those spreading palm branches in the road. Jesus no longer cautions the one who is healed not to speak. There will be no more messianic secret. It is time to recognize the Messiah approaching the holy city. The realm of God is at hand!

PRAYER

Dear God, remove my blindness too, and let my faith leap up as this man's did. I, too, am a beggar beside life's road, waiting for your salvation. But let me see you with the inner eye, and I shall confess you to all the world and follow you in the way. For you are the redeemer of everything! Amen.

JESUS ENTERS THE CITY

*J*esus' entry into the holy city, which in Mark's Gospel occurs now for the very first time, is intricately related to scriptural prophecies. Zechariah 9:9, for example, praises the king who comes riding on the foal of an ass. And Psalm 118, which apparently derives from an occasion when a king came to the Temple to offer thanks for a great victory in battle, speaks of opening the gates of righteousness and of the stone rejected by the builders that has become a great cornerstone. This psalm, moreover, had come to be used always with the Jewish Feast of Dedication, commemorating the cleansing of the Temple in 165 B.C. by Judas Maccabeus, and was associated with the waving of bundles of green branches, actually called "hosannas," by the people.

Perhaps the most striking thing about Mark's account of the entry is the comparative quietness of it. It is not accompanied by the great crowds of Matthew's account and does not appear to upset the city officials. Nor does Jesus create an immediate disturbance in the Temple. He merely enters it, looks around, and retires to Bethany, two or three miles away, to spend the night. The greeting in verses 9 and 10 derives from Psalm 119:26; and, though it seems messianic in nature, it was probably spoken by a band of disciples, not by great crowds of people, as in Matthew's account.

Mark apparently was not concerned to depict this as a tumultuous occasion, but as one of deep symbolic significance. Jesus chose the colt and entered the city as a king; whether crowds were present does not matter. It was a victorious moment in the spiritual sense. Jesus' ministry had reached a climax, and he had been utterly faithful to God. Now the scene was being set for the greatest drama of all.

PRAYER

O God, I would like to have been there to behold Jesus' entry into the holy city; it is always exciting to watch history being made. But it is far more important that I shall see the coming of the Son of God when all history is consummated. Then the shouts will be deafening indeed. Prepare my heart for that moment, I pray, through him who rode on the foal of an ass. Amen.

A JUDGMENT ON THE JEWISH RELIGION

*A*s we have observed before, Mark was fond of inserting a story within another story he was telling. Here, the story of the cleansing of the Temple is sandwiched between two parts of the fig-tree narrative. But the two are actually related in theme and effect.

The fig tree was often regarded as a symbol of the nation Israel. Luke 13:6-9 is a parable in which this connection is obvious. It is highly probable, therefore, that this story is set at the beginning of the Passion narrative as a symbol of Israel's failure. This is the only instance we have of Jesus' performing a *destructive* miracle. It is thus really out of character for him, signaling that its meaning is to be sought beyond any superficial reason for the act. Like the fig tree, Israel had put out leaves indicating the presence of fruit—among these were Israel's many religious rituals and observances. But in the encounter with God's Messiah, Israel was found lacking fruit.

The Temple story fits closely with this theme, for the scene of desecration, with moneychangers and sellers of birds and animals at exorbitant prices, reveals how far even this symbolic center of Israel's worship had departed from the true spirit of faith and worship. So Jesus' anger is kindled again at the sight of this prostitution.

Returning to the fig tree as Jesus and the disciples retire for the night to Bethany, Mark shows us in the barren tree what will happen to Jerusalem and Israel as a result of their falling away from true holiness.

Jesus' final comments about faith and prayer in the last segment of the passage may have been appended here because of the demonstration of his miraculous power we have just witnessed. If so, we need to be cautious in quoting these verses in support of just any prayer requests we make, regardless of the sincerity of our belief; for Mark attaches the remarks to a miracle that is intimately associated with the coming of the new order and the condemnation of the old. This would suggest that our prayers for miraculous results are effective when attached to eagerness for the new order to arrive, not when they are offered for merely selfish reasons.

PRAYER

O God, it is easy enough for me to side with Jesus in his indignation about the profanation of the Temple. What is harder is to hear a similar judgment against my own lack of spirituality. Like the Temple in this story, my own existence is often profaned by economic considerations. Forgive me and make my heart a place of true prayer. Through him who saw to the depths of everything, amen.

Day 159   *Mark 11:27-33*

A QUESTION OF AUTHORITY

*M*ark sets here the first of several "conflict stories" between Jesus and the authorities, which will end with Jesus' crucifixion. In this instance, the encounter appears to arise from the cleansing of the Temple. The chief priests, scribes, and elders would doubtless represent the Sanhedrin, the high religious court of Israel, and, as it was in charge of the Temple police, would be responding to a complaint about Jesus' behavior.

The question of authority is vital. Israel was in theory a theocracy, with God at its head. The Jewish ruler (if we ignore the Roman occupation) derived his authority from God. So did the Sanhedrin. The question asked of Jesus may have been designed to see whether he considered himself a prophet sent from God. It probably was not intended to test his messiahship.

Jesus' answer is typically rabbinical. He poses another question, about the authority of John the Baptist, who was generally accepted by the people as a true prophet. "Did the baptism of John come from heaven, or was it of human origin?" (v. 30).

The crafty old men see that they are bested. They cannot answer the question either way without committing themselves to an outcome with which they would be uncomfortable. So they do not answer, and Jesus refuses to continue the matter.

It is interesting to note that this first conflict story turns on a reference to John the Baptist. As we have seen in earlier passages, John's violent end seems to have brought Jesus to the first realization of his own probable death by violence. This story, set at the beginning of the Passion week, thus provides a theme that will culminate in the crucifixion itself.

PRAYER

God, I am too often like these old men from the Sanhedrin, and like to argue fine points of religious philosophy when I should simply open my heart to you. I listen to sermons and pick at their grammar while evading

154

the deeper issues they raise. Make me stop this play-acting and be ready to meet you everywhere. Through Jesus, in whom I see you most clearly, amen.

Day 160   *Mark 12:1-12*

THE REJECTION OF THE OWNER'S SON

*T*his allegorical parable has its source in Isaiah 5:1-30, which describes an owner lovingly establishing a vineyard and clearing it of stones. While he hopes for wonderful grapes from the vineyard, it yields only wild grapes. In both Isaiah and Mark, the reference is, of course, to Israel, which despite God's tender care has produced only bitter fruit.

The part of the parable original to Jesus is the story of the owner's repeated attempts to collect some of the vineyard's profits from the churlish tenants. Jesus' hearers would have readily identified with such a story, for Israel had many foreign landowners in that day, and it was surely not uncommon for their emissaries to be poorly treated by those managing their properties. There was even a law that if the only heir to a piece of property was killed, the occupants would have first claim on it.

The religious leaders of Jerusalem doubtless saw the point of the parable, as we are told in verse 12. The attempt to arrest Jesus could have been made only on the charge of identifying himself as the owner's son. Here he was, right in the center of the vineyard, and the tenants were plotting how to get rid of him. It was an ingeniously self-fulfilling prophecy.

Verse 9, about the owner's vengeance, is a reinforcement of the prophecy in Isaiah, that the owner will make waste of the vineyard, so that only briars and thorns will grow in it.

Verses 10 and 11 are a direct quotation from Psalm 118:22-23, which we have seen plays a substantial part in Mark's understanding of the Passion. The religious authorities have rejected the son, but—from a post-resurrection viewpoint—he has now become the cornerstone of the building or the keystone of the archway (the Greek allows either interpretation).

PRAYER

I too, O God, am prone to think I own the things I use form day to day—my home, my clothes, my money, my body, my mind. Forgive my presumptuousness and lack of sensitivity. Help me to remember that all I have is a trust from you, and that every person I meet is potentially your messenger. In your Son's own name, amen.

Day 161   *Mark 12:13-17*

AN HONEST ANSWER TO A DISHONEST QUESTION

*T*he anonymous "they" of this passage we assume again to be the religious leaders actively seeking to destroy Jesus. By asking whether they should pay taxes to Caesar, they hoped to elicit from Jesus a self-incriminating answer.

Most Jews passionately resented having to pay the universal poll tax imposed by Caesar. The most galling part of this was that the tax had to be paid in silver coins bearing Caesar's image, not in the normal Jewish coinage, which bore no image at all. The laurel wreath above Caesar's head and the inscription on the coin proclaimed Caesar divine. This was an unbearable affront to Yahweh-worshiping Hebrews.

If Jesus answered that it was right to pay taxes to Caesar, he would incur the immediate wrath of the nationalistic populace. If, on the other hand, he said it was wrong to pay the taxes, he would be reported to the Romans on the charge of sedition.

But Jesus once more proved too clever for them. Asking for a Roman coin, he demanded to know whose image was on it. The answer was obvious: it was Caesar's. Very well, then, said Jesus, give it to Caesar; but, at the same time, give whatever is God's to God.

It was understood that anything bearing Caesar's image was literally and legally his. Others might use it temporarily, yet in fact it belonged to him. But by the same token, God's sacred image is implanted in every one of us, meaning that we all belong to God.

PRAYER
How many times, O God, have I been indignant about some injustice in the world—something done to the poor or the powerless—when I myself was less than sensitive to your presence or your requirements of me? Help me to pay what is due in the world, but also to render to you what is due to you. Through Jesus, who lived in complete awareness of your ownership, amen.

THE GOD OF THE LIVING

*T*his time Mark pits the Sadducees against Jesus, possibly to show how completely rejected he was by all the leading factions in Jerusalem. The Sadducees were a wealthy social class with strong traditionalist leanings, and the high priest was always chosen from among them. Doctrinally they rejected the relatively "liberal" theology of the Pharisees, who were much closer to Jesus on teachings about eternal life, the Spirit of God, and even the new realm. They accepted only the Pentateuch, or first five books of the Old Testament, as binding on their beliefs, and discounted all further developments.

Hence they begin by citing Moses in Deuteronomy 25:5 and pose a question that seems to demolish the possibility of Moses' having believed in the resurrection. If a woman had seven husbands, as Moses' law would have ordered, whose wife would she be in eternity? It appears to be a clever question.

Jesus is cutting in his reply, and twice tells the Sadducees they are wrong. They fail to see that those who rise from the dead are like angels, who have no need of wives or progeny to be immortal. Then Jesus turns their own pride in Moses upon them: Moses says in Exodus 3:6 (the story about the burning bush) that God said, "I am the God of . . . Abraham, the God of Isaac, and the God of Jacob." Not I *was*, but I *am*. God is not the God of those who have died, but of those who live.

PRAYER

O God, help me to escape the snares of my own wit and cleverness, which would entangle me in questions like those of the Pharisees and Sadducees. Let my meditation be upon you and your power, so that my mind sails like a silver ship through the dark waters, calm and steady in the sense of your presence. For you have the words of life. Amen.

THE HEART OF THE MATTER

*I*n Eugene Ionesco's play *The Chairs*, an old man prepares to give a summary of his philosophy to a group of important people. He has hired a professional orator to make the speech for him, lest it be lost through poor delivery. When the orator arrives, the suspense is terrific. He stands with his back to the audience, composing himself. Then he turns and begins to deliver the old man's message. "Mmm, mmm, mmm, gueue, gou, gu," he says. He is speech impaired, and cannot produce a single syllable. This is the playwright's way of saying that there is no meaning at the heart of human existence—only emptiness and silence.

How different is the positive note at the center of Jesus' life and belief. Asked to point to the central commandment, he replies with this remarkable combination of answers, one from Deuteronomy 6:4-5 and the other from Leviticus 19:18. First we are to love God with everything in us, and then we are to love others as solicitously as we care for ourselves.

Rabbis in that time often tried to summarize the law. The famous Hillel, for example, had said, "What you yourself hate, do not do to your fellow; this is the whole law; the rest is commentary; go and learn it." That Jesus' summary was so much more positive than this is very revealing of the healthiness at the core of his being. In an instant, he had brought to focus the essential message of both the law and the prophets: God prefers loving-kindness to all religious rites and sacrifices.

PRAYER

What a simple thing love is, O God. It is so much less complicated than great ethical philosophies. It cuts through all the knotty, difficult problems as if they weren't there at all. Help me to feel your love at all times, so that in turn I may love everyone else around me. Through Jesus, who lived by the law he cited, amen.

Day 164   *Mark 12:35-44*

SMALL CAN BE BEAUTIFUL

*T*he first three verses of this passage are somewhat enigmatic. Scholars think they may be the concluding part of another conflict story that has been lost. Jesus appears to be insisting that the Messiah is more God's son than David's, and, therefore, of greater importance than the Jewish leaders realized.

But the next section is much clearer. It is a warning against mere legalistic religion. The scribes were the very caricature of legalism. They liked parading around in their long robes, which were supposed to represent great learning. They enjoyed receiving the deferential salutations of others in the streets, for the rule was that the less learned people greeted the more learned first. They always took the front seats in synagogues, where everyone could see them. They took advantage of the piety and generosity of widows, who probably listened to them more readily than others. They used their prayers, which should have been addressed to God, to gain attention and admiration in public.

Such behavior, said Jesus, only heaps up condemnation before God. How much more admirable is the illustration provided by the simple woman, a widow, who quietly approached the Temple coffers and dropped in her two small coins. The Greek word for "coin" used here, *lepton,* meant a coin so tiny and worthless that it bore no image or inscription; it was merely a round bit of metal and alloy. But the woman's spirit was so magnanimous—that was all the money she had in the world—that Jesus praised her and said she had given more than all the wealthy people who put in much larger sums of money.

Her religion, unlike that of the scribes and Pharisees, was heartfelt and real.

PRAYER

I am afraid I am a calculator, O God, and I live in a calculating kind of world. I am always figuring out what I can afford to give you or others. Help me to be instead like this wonderful woman who asked what she could afford to keep and then gave everything she had. Through Jesus, who did the same, amen.

Day 165   *Mark 13:1-13*

AN INJUNCTION TO FAITHFULNESS

*T*his chapter is often called "the little Apocalypse," because it deals with the end of all history and how Christians are to behave until that moment. It is set at a turning point in the Gospel. Chapters 1–12 are the story of Jesus' ministry. Chapters 14–16 are the account of the crucifixion and resurrection. This chapter forms a transition between the two parts and serves as a farewell discourse.

The discourse begins with a disciple's exclamation about the size of the Temple and its surroundings. Jesus says that they are marked for destruction. The discourse then continues on the Mount of Olives, from which the Temple and the city can both be clearly seen. "When?" the disciples want to know. When will this great destruction come?

It was common in those days to ask prophets what the sign of the last days would be. Jesus does not give them a single sign, but many. Others will come claiming to be Messiah. There will be wars and rumors of wars, earthquakes and famines. But these are only the beginning.

The important thing, says Jesus, is not their knowledge of when the end is, but their behavior in the interim. They have much to bear for the gospel. There will be persecutions and imprisonments. The disciples will stand before rulers to give an account of their faith. Families will be torn apart as some stand up for the new order, and Christians will be hated by others.

"But the one who endures to the end will be saved" (v. 13). It is not knowing when that saves; it is being faithful.

PRAYER

It is even harder to be faithful now than it was then, dear God. Wars and disease and natural disasters have been our lot for centuries. Temples have come, and temples have gone. Cultures have risen and fallen. Give us courage to wait despite all these things. Through him who knew that cleaving to you is everything, amen.

Day 166   *Mark 13:14-27*

GREAT POWER AND GLORY

*L*ike most people who have lived in California, I have experienced several earthquakes. One night my wife and I were literally thrown out of bed by a quake, she on one side and I on the other. It is a terrifying experience.

Jesus warns his disciples that the great Day of the Lord will be a time of such terror. It will be a time to flee to the mountains. The person on the housetop who comes down the side stairs should not take time to enter the house. The person working in the fields should not stop to retrieve a cloak laid aside in the warm hours. Only God's mercy will prevent the utter destruction of everyone.

An unmistakable sign of the end, says Jesus, is "the desolating sacrilege set up where it ought not to be" (v. 14). This is thought to be a reference to Daniel 9:27, 11:37, and 12:11, which describe the profanation of the

Temple by Antiochus Epiphanes in 168 B.C. Antiochus set up a statue of Zeus in the Temple, outraging Jewish sensibilities. Mark may be thinking here of the establishment of the Antichrist in the Temple—some power utterly devoted to the destruction of the old Judaic worship.

The heavens themselves will reflect the darkness on earth. It will be a time of horrible chaos.

Then—the imagery is from Daniel 7:13-14—the Son of Man will come in clouds "with great power and glory." When it is all over, the Son of Man will send forth his messengers to gather the saints from all directions, "from the ends of the earth to the ends of heaven" (v. 27).

This is the eternal hope of every Christian: after the wars and rumors of wars, after the quakes and famines, after all sufferings, the coming of the Son in power and glory. Then justice will reign forever.

PRAYER

Apocalypse is strange to our time, O God, and it is hard for me to think about. Speak to my heart of its true meaning, lest I miss its promise and its hope. Through Jesus, who never shrank from using its language, amen.

Day 167   *Mark 13:28-37*

THE IMPORTANCE OF WATCHING

*T*his passage doesn't actually contradict the previous one, where Jesus seemed to be announcing "signs" of the end. Actually the signs he gave were of a very poetic, imaginative sort and did not remove the necessity of watching for the end. And the signs were to occur before the end, leaving the end time itself unknown.

A characteristic prophetic note is the imminence of the end. The true Christian posture, therefore, is always one of expectancy, of standing on tiptoe for the arrival of the Day of the Lord. This does not mean letting all one's duties go; on the contrary, it means heightened attention to all responsibilities. This is the point of the short parable in verse 34: When the master is away, the servants are to be at work, though one servant waits at the door and all are excited at the prospects of the master's imminent return. We are all to be about our jobs, but with a keen sense of watchfulness.

Verse 30 has been the subject of much speculation. Did Jesus really expect the end of all things to come in his own time? It is possible that he did. But he may also have meant that the *signs* of the end, which he had been discussing, would appear before the present generation had died. Certainly this was true. The Temple was destroyed by the Romans in A.D. 70, and many people suffered calamities described in verses 5-23.

If this interpretation is correct, the end itself could come at any time, and faithful servants will always be ready, regardless of how long we have already waited.

PRAYER

We forget, O God, that all time—past, present, and future—is forever *now* to you. Help us to live in your presence so faithfully that it becomes *now* to us as well, and we live on tiptoe, watching for your new order. Through Jesus, who told us to watch, amen.

Day 168   *Mark 14:1-11*

CONFLICTING PASSIONS

*I*n these brief verses we see how two different persons responded to Jesus under the gathering pressures of the Passover week.

The woman, whom John's Gospel identifies as Mary the sister of Martha and Lazarus, anoints Jesus with her own burial ointment. It is a costly gift—three hundred denarii was nearly a year's wages for a worker. By today's standards, it was worth between twenty and thirty thousand dollars. As flasks were often broken and left behind in burial sites, her anointing is clearly associated with Jesus' approaching death.

The word *messiah* literally means "anointed one." Therefore, the woman confirms God's anointment of Jesus in what amounts to a confessional act. This is emphasized by the fact that she anoints his head, while Luke 7:38 and John 12:3 picture her anointing his feet. Anointing the head is a gesture akin to crowning.

Some persons present do not perceive the ritual significance of the act—Mark shrouds these persons in anonymity. They protest that it is a waste, that many poor persons could have used the money from the spilled perfume. But Jesus identifies the act with his going away from them: "You will not always have me," he says (v. 7).

Judas's behavior is exactly opposite that of the woman. Instead of treating Jesus as the Messiah and mourning his approaching death, Judas goes out and betrays him in an act of infamy. Wherever the gospel is preached, as Jesus said, the woman's beautiful story is told. And wherever Judas's name is mentioned, his deed of treachery is remembered. In fact, his very name has become synonymous with betrayal.

PRAYER

Lord, there is both Judas and Mary in me: I betray you, and I love you. I wish it weren't so; I want only to love you. Forgive the dark side of me and help me, by exposing it constantly to your light, to reduce its power over me. For your name's sake, amen.

Day 169   *Mark 14:12-16*

PREPARING FOR THE PASSOVER

*A*s we have seen, the Gospel of Mark places strong emphasis on the eating of bread in Jesus' presence. In chapter 6 the five thousand are fed. In chapter 7 the Syrophoenician woman asks for the crumbs from the children's table. In chapter 8 the four thousand are fed. And afterward the disciples are in the boat without bread and must be reminded that Jesus is able to provide bread whenever he is present with them.

Now all of these allusions to the Eucharist come to a head in the passage about the Last Supper, reminiscent of the feeding stories in chapters 6 and 8. Once more the disciples come to Jesus to inquire about how to prepare for the meal.

Jesus has prearranged a place for the meal. The two disciples are to find a man carrying a water pitcher; he will lead them to an upper room furnished for the occasion. In a country where only women carried water jars, the man would have been easy to find.

The meal itself is highly charged with symbolism, for it is a Passover meal, celebrating the escape of the Jews from bondage in Egypt. Jesus is to be the lamb for the new Passover. As the blood of the first Passover lambs was smeared on the door frames to keep Jewish children safe, Jesus' blood will keep his followers from eternal harm. He later calls the cup of wine "my blood of the covenant" (v. 24).

The emphasis in this passage on *preparing* is a reminder of how much preparation had truly gone into getting ready for this hour. The whole Gospel has led up to it. Not only the "bread" passages we have alluded to, but also Jesus' entire ministry of preaching, teaching, and healing has been a prelude to this important occasion.

In my rushing about, O God, I often fail to reflect on what deep meanings lie behind simple occurrences. Teach me to pause and see your hand behind history, working out your loving will for our world. Through Jesus, who saw the importance of preparation, amen.

Day 170   *Mark 14:17-21*

EXAMINING OURSELVES

*W*hat inward pain it must have been to Jesus to think that one of his twelve intimate associates was conspiring with his enemies to bring about his doom. Mark must have sensed this, for the phrase "one of the twelve" is twice used to describe the betrayer (vv. 20 and 43). Twelve men whom he had called and taught. Twelve with whom he had walked and worked and eaten and slept. Twelve with whom he had prayed. And one of them would deliver him for death.

But the passage suggests two levels of betrayal. One is the level of ultimate betrayal, leading to death. The other is less final. It is the level represented by the other disciples. We could call it the level of failing a friend. Before the night is over, each of the disciples will have betrayed Jesus this way.

"Surely, not I?" each asks.

This may have been a liturgical question in the early church. Paul had written to the Corinthians about the importance of self-examination before taking Communion. "Examine yourselves," he said, "and only then eat of the bread and drink of the cup" (1 Cor. 11:28).

Imagine a section of liturgy that might have gone like this:

LEADER: And Jesus sat at the table, eating with his disciples.
PEOPLE: Disciples like us.
LEADER: And he said to them, "One of you will betray me."
PEOPLE: Who, Lord? Surely, not I.
LEADER: One who is eating with me.
PEOPLE: Oh surely, Lord, not I.

Which of us can believe that he or she has never betrayed the Lord, that he or she does not betray him now, that he or she will not betray him before the day is out?

164

Lord, it is I. There is no question about it. I have failed to understand; I have missed the vision; I have not loved my neighbor; I have not glorified your name. It is I, O Lord, and I am heartily ashamed. How can you forgive me, who has betrayed innocent blood? Amen.

Day 171   *Mark 14:22-25*

THE JEWEL OF THE LITURGY

*I*t is remarkable how quickly our author tells the story of the table once he has gotten to it. It seems almost anticlimactic. First we had all those great stories about bread—bread in the wilderness, bread for a Syrophoenician woman, bread for the disciples in the boat—and now this. Four scant verses.

The reason, it has been suggested, is that these words are part of a solemn tradition Mark had inherited—like the words Paul wrote to the Corinthians about the Communion (1 Cor. 11:23-26). They, too, comprised four scant verses.

These few words are like a precious jewel for which the goldsmith prepares an elaborate setting. The setting is much larger than the jewel. It carries images and stories designed to enhance the luster of the jewel. But it is the jewel that counts. Without it, the setting would be worthless. Here is a priceless treasure—the words of institution for the central rite of the Christian church—and their simple beauty dignifies everything around them.

What words of ours could enhance it further? It is one of the world's masterpieces. We can only read or say it with awe.

PRAYER
Thank you, dear Lord, for the bread and cup of your presence. There is no worth in me, that I should eat or drink at your table. But you have loved me, and in accepting that I reflect your worthiness. Amen.

A SAD PREDICTION

We can never overlook the importance of the psalms as a background for the final events in the life of Jesus. It is almost as if the bittersweet music of the nation were distilled into life through the upper room, the crucifixion, and the resurrection. The hymn Jesus and the disciples sang before leaving the upper room was almost certainly from the last of the great Hillel psalms, possibly Psalm 118, which contains the words "It is better to take refuge in the LORD/ than to put confidence in mortals" (Ps. 118:8).

It may have been these very words that led Jesus to say to the disciples, "You will all become deserters" (v. 27). The Greek word used here is derived from *skandalizein,* "to scandalize" or "to cause offense," and means "you will be offended." The corresponding noun, *skandalon,* means a trap or something that causes one to trip or fall. The idea of tripping or falling because of something in the nature of the Messiah was common in Christian usage. Mark is saying here that even the disciples were about to stumble in their understanding of the Messiah's suffering.

The word about the shepherd and the sheep is from Zechariah 13:7-9, which says that after God allows the shepherd to be stricken, the sheep will go in many directions. But eventually some of them will call on God, and God will answer them. The disciples are entering a time of severe testing. Even Jesus' promise to be raised up and reunited with them in Galilee will not allay their deep fears and confusion.

Typically, Peter does not understand. He thinks he knows himself well, and will not give way before Jesus' enemies. But Jesus knows better. Before the cock crows twice, announcing the new day, Peter will have denied his Messiah three times.

PRAYER

It is a sad fact, dear God, that we cannot put our ultimate confidence in other human beings or even in ourselves. I want to believe in others and trust their love, but I am often disappointed. Help me to forgive them, as Jesus forgave Peter, and to put my confidence in you, for your heavenly order and your promises are forever and ever. Amen.

THE TESTING OF THE DISCIPLES

*T*his well-known story is about Jesus' wrestling with God over the death he is to die. He has come to the crossroads—to the last possible moment of escape—and elects the hard way, laying down his life for the good of the world. It is a beautiful and enduring picture of the greatest sacrifice in all of human history.

But in one sense it is the disciples who are really tempted in the garden—not Jesus. He prays that the cup of his suffering may be removed; yet in the end he submits to what God has willed for him. But the disciples face the cup, too. Jesus earlier asked James and John, when they asked to sit at his side in the new realm, "Are you able to drink the cup that I drink?" (Mark 10:38). In Gethsemane, it is apparent that they are not ready. Later they will drink it, as martyrs for the faith. But not now, when Jesus drinks his. They do not yet understand all things.

Three times Jesus leaves them to watch and pray. It is an eschatological picture like the parable in chapter 13, with a man going on a journey, putting his servants to watch, and charging his doorkeeper to stay awake and watch for him at any hour. Watching and praying and understanding are keys to salvation.

Do you see what a pointed message this was for Christians in the early centuries? They, too, were being tested for faithfulness. Like the disciples, they were often asleep when they should have been watching. And what about us? Isn't it a message for us as well?

PRAYER

I am accused, O God. I do not maintain the sharp edge of watchfulness required of a Christian. Your new order breaks in around me, and I do not even see it. The Son comes and stands beside me, and I snore in his presence. Help me to be more faithful, both for his sake and for my own. Amen.

THE PERFIDY OF A FRIEND

*E*ven my bosom friend in whom I trusted," says Psalm 41:9, "who ate of my bread, has lifted the heel against me." Jesus had said that one of those close enough to dip bread with him in the dish would betray him.

Now it happens. Judas comes forward and plants a kiss on Jesus' face. There is impudence in this act, an arrogance, for disciples usually waited for their master to kiss them. It is as if he couldn't wait to finish his treachery.

The other disciples make a brief stand. One, at least—identified in John 18:10 as Simon Peter—strikes out with a sword and cuts off the ear of the high priest's slave. But as Jesus reprimands his enemies for the manner in which they have seized him, coming in with swords and staves in the garden instead of taking him among the crowds in the daytime, all the disciples take flight.

Verses 51-52 have long puzzled commentators. It has traditionally been assumed that the "certain young man" was Mark himself, but there is no evidence to support the view. If it had indeed been the author, he would surely have given a reason for his being clad only in a linen cloth on a cold night. Some think the verses are a reference to Amos 2:16, in which God says of the day of judgment against Israel that "those who are stout of heart among the mighty/ shall flee away naked in that day."

At any rate, the picture is of Jesus' complete forsakenness. Everyone, even the hapless young man, flees into the darkness, leaving Jesus alone with his captors.

PRAYER

O Lord, I am no better than they, for I have often forsaken you in times of real testing. You have gone to your cross alone more than once. Forgive me, I pray, and grant that I shall be more stalwart when I am tested again, for I cannot live without you. Amen.

NO LONGER A SECRET

*T*his passage is a climax in Mark's narrative. From very early in the Gospel, Jesus' ministry has been depicted in terms of his conflict with Jerusalem. It has also been characterized as a secret ministry, probably to avoid a final contest until Jesus is ready for it. Now he is ready—his hour has come—and the conflict reaches its fulfillment in the encounter with the high priest, who is the embodiment of the Jewish religious system.

The report that Jesus said he would destroy the Temple, whether true or not, is important, for the Temple is the very symbol of Jerusalem. It was from there that the scribes and Pharisees had come who showed up in the crowds when Jesus healed and taught in Galilee. When he came to Jerusalem, he went straight to the Temple; and the next day he drove the moneychangers and pigeon sellers from the Temple. It was while sitting on the Mount of Olives, where the view was dominated by the Temple, that he delivered his "little Apocalypse," which had as a fundamental feature the destruction of the Temple. The Temple stood as a tangible reminder of Israel's failure. At the moment of Jesus' death, Mark will observe that the veil in the Temple has been split completely in two, symbolizing the demise of Temple worship.

It is fitting, then, that the encounter with the high priest brings an end to the note of messianic secrecy. "Are you the Messiah, the Son of the Blessed One?" asks the high priest (v. 61). "I am," says Jesus, "and 'you will see the Son of Man seated at the right hand of the Power,' and 'coming with the clouds of heaven' " (v. 62). It is a total announcement of his messianic identity.

The high priest reacts predictably. The council of elders cannot pronounce the death penalty—they fear usurping the Roman prerogative—but they find him "deserving of death" and begin plotting how to accomplish it.

Jesus approaches his final humiliation. The disciples could not understand that he is the *suffering* servant of God.

PRAYER

O God, a blind man in Jericho recognized Jesus as the Messiah, but the religious leaders didn't. Help me to listen to the blind ones I know, and see Christ always through their eyes. For the sake of your new order, amen.

THE FALL OF A LEADER

I ronically, at the very moment when Jesus is inside the house of the high priest confessing his identity as the Messiah, Peter is on the outside denying that he even knows Jesus.

What was Mark's interest in this full account of Peter's denial of Jesus? Peter became a leader in the early church. In Acts 2, he is portrayed as standing courageously before the Jewish populace and preaching Jesus as the Messiah of God. In Acts 3:13, he even accuses others of denying Jesus in the presence of Pilate. But Mark consistently shows Peter's failure to understand and follow Jesus. In 8:31-33, when Jesus spoke of his suffering and death, Mark pictured Peter as protesting, and Jesus even identifying him as Satan! What point was Mark trying to make with his constant downgrading of the chief apostle?

Some scholars have suggested that Mark was probably encountering a tendency in the early church to deemphasize the suffering of Jesus in favor of his triumphal resurrection. If so, Mark made Peter and the other disciples into models of misunderstanding in order to dramatize the unswerving way Jesus himself faced the humiliation of his trial and crucifixion.

Whether this theory is correct or not, Peter's failure and brokenness have always been a great inspiration to ordinary Christians. Here was the number-one apostle, the chief spokesman for the early church, floundering about like an unsure adolescent, denying his Master to preserve his own safety. If Peter could be forgiven and make the recovery he made, there is hope for every faltering Christian in the world!

PRAYER

Thank you for the gift of tears in times of failure and frustration, O God, for they bring relief and cleansing. Help me to come to that point now. Let my denials of Christ move me to the abyss of deep reflection and produce such a purging of my conflicting emotions that I may weep and begin anew in your service. For Jesus' sake, amen.

THE PROCURATOR AND THE KING

*I*n this passage we come upon another messianic title, "King of the Jews." The Jewish leaders realized that this title would be more inflammatory to the Roman governor than Messiah or Son of Man, because it sounded more political. For Mark, the term would also have been apt in the light of his references to David (2:25-26; 10:46-48), the greatest of the Jewish kings, who was linked to Jesus by the messianic title "Son of David."

Pilate, whose residence was normally in Caesarea, was probably in Jerusalem to keep an eye on the crowds during the Passover feast; therefore, Jesus was sent to him. Contemporary history was less kind to him than are the Gospels, and he was described by Agrippa I as "inflexible, merciless, and obstinate." But Mark was doubtless concerned to put as benign a face on the Roman government as possible, for Christians needed the favor of Rome merely to exist. Thus Mark pictured Pilate as unusually respectful of Jesus in this interview. Pilate is even said to be amazed or to wonder at him—a word that in Greek had very religious undertones.

The cause of Pilate's wonder was apparently Jesus' silence before his accusers. The early Christians would have understood and appreciated this in the light of Isaiah 53:7:

> He was oppressed, and he was afflicted,
>   yet he did not open his mouth;
> like a lamb that is led to the slaughter,
>   and like a sheep that before its shearers is silent,
>   so he did not open his mouth.

PRAYER

The truth of Jesus' messiahship was never more evident in his miracles, O God, than it was in his behavior before his accusers. Grant that I, as your child, may develop the same inner bearing in the world. For your name's sake, amen.

TWO SONS OF THE FATHER

*B*arabbas is an Aramaic name meaning "son of the father." In usual usage, it was a surname. In some early manuscripts of Matthew's Gospel, Barabbas's full name is shown as "Jesus Barabbas" (Matt. 27:16). *Jesus* was not an uncommon name, and it is entirely possible that it was Barabbas's given name. If that was the case, subsequent Christian scribes may have piously deleted the name of their Lord when they found it attached to the insurrectionist who was released in the Messiah's place.

How ironic it would have been. Two Jesuses, two sons of the father. Did Pilate see the irony? Was it a clever act on his part to put the two before the Jewish crowd and offer to release whichever one they asked for? Jesus the murderer, or Jesus the Messiah. Which would they free?

The chief priests did their work among the crowd. Mark could imagine them moving in and out like weasels, like creatures of evil, persuading the people to ask for Barabbas.

"And the King of the Jews?" asks Pilate. "What shall I do with him?"

"Crucify him!" they shout.

So one Jesus is turned loose in the world as a murderer, while the other, innocent of all crimes, is tied to a post and scourged. Then he is delivered up to be crucified.

PRAYER

There is so much cruelty in the world, O God; some people's instincts are unbelievably barbaric. For the most part, I tend not to see this because I don't like to see it. Forgive me for that, and help me in the name of Jesus, who suffered unjustly, not to avoid instances of similar suffering today, but to pit myself against them with all my mind and heart and strength. For it is one way of giving meaning to his terrible suffering. Amen.

THE MOCKERY

*S*ir James Frazer's *The Golden Bough* describes ancient rites in which a fool or a prisoner was dressed as a king, given a scepter, and made the center of a mock court. Perhaps such pagan practices lay behind the soldiers' behavior in this passage.

The entire battalion—two to six hundred men—witnessed the spectacle. Some may have felt sympathetic toward the poor figure being abused. Most probably took up the game with delight. A purple soldier's cloak was thrown over Jesus' bleeding back, a crown of thorns pressed on his head. In mock gravity, the soldiers saluted as if greeting Caesar. "Hail, King of the Jews," they shouted.

They struck him, spat upon him, and fell at his feet, pretending to pay homage. Then, their brutal hunger either sated or transmuted into a blood thirstiness that could be quenched by nothing less than the victim's death, they reclaimed the purple cloak, draped Jesus' own robe about him, and led him away to crucify him.

Through it all, apparently, he uttered no sound, but suffered in the same silence that had brought even the callous heart of Pilate to wonder at him.

PRAYER

Lord, do I mock you, too? When I claim you as my King and then serve my own interests instead, is that a mockery? Forgive me, Lord, and restore me to a full measure of devotion, lest I end by mocking only myself. For your name's sake, amen.

Day 180   *Mark 15:21-25*

THE SHAMEFUL DEATH

*M*ark is incredibly terse about the crucifixion, despite the fact that his Gospel has been building relentlessly toward it from the beginning. It is likely that Simon of Cyrene, who helped to carry the cross, either was a follower at the time or later became one. It may even be he who provided the information about the crucifixion, as most of the disciples had fled or were at a distance. Offering wine and myrrh as an analgesic mixture to persons about to be crucified was customary. Jesus' refusal of it was probably part of his resolution to drink to the full the cup of suffering set before him.

The part of the cross that was carried by the victim was the heavy crossbeam. The upright beam would have been in place already in the ground. The victim's hands were then nailed or strapped to the cross-beam, and it was raised to the top of the upright beam.

After Jesus' body had been affixed to the upright cross, the soldiers cast lots for his clothes, as it was their legal prerogative to do. Part of the shame of public execution was the victim's nakedness, especially in a condition of such extremity that he could not control his own bodily functions. This also fulfilled the prophecy in Psalm 22:18, which pictures the evildoers casting lots for the victim's garments.

It was only nine o'clock in the morning when they crucified him, says Mark. The long hours of dying were ahead. Crucifixion was noted for the slowness with which death claimed its victim.

PRAYER

Golgotha. The name is heavy, evil, forbidding, dear God. A place of death, blood, suffering, loneliness. The depth of human experience. Keep it before me and let me never forget it. Christ paid too much in suffering for me to lose sight of it for a single day. Amen.

Day 181   *Mark 15:26-32*

THE KING UPON HIS THRONE

*W*hen criminals were led out to be executed, they always bore or were preceded by placards stating their names, places of origin, and offenses. Whether Jesus' inscription carried the full information or was limited to the ironic title "King of the Jews" we have no way of knowing. It is possible that it charged him with threatening to destroy the Temple, for all the people seemed to know the charge and taunted him with it.

Some of the scribes mocking him were possibly the ones mentioned as early as Mark 2:6, who had dogged him all the way through his ministry and were now feeling triumphant at seeing him suspended on a cross. "He saved others," they said (they had seen the miracles!), but "he cannot save himself. Let the Messiah, the King of Israel, come down from the cross now, so that we may see and believe" (vv. 31-32). It was not a taunt to be taken seriously. They did not want to believe, or they would have believed already.

Even the robbers on the other crosses joined in the chorus of jests and insults. First the passersby, then the chief priests and scribes, and now the robbers. It makes Jesus' humiliation complete, that even his fellow victims should turn on him.

The supreme irony, of course, is that Jesus is indeed the King of the Jews, the long-awaited Messiah. Yet, as Mark understood, he is the Suffering Servant, who must remain silent and drink the awful cup to the dregs. Only then can he truly fulfill the prophecies about him, that he is the King of an entirely new order of Kingdom.

PRAYER

Lord, words are poor, inadequate things to speak of your great suffering, with all its shame and loneliness and agony. Help me to feel it now like a terrible weight on my soul. Then I shall weep and praise your name, for you are a King like no other the world has ever known. May your kingdom come, now and forever. Amen.

Day 182   *Mark 15:33-39*

TRIUMPH OUT OF DARKNESS

*T*he three-hour period of darkness from noon until midafternoon had been predicted in Amos 8:9:

> On that day, says the Lord GOD,
> I will make the sun go down at noon,
> and darken the earth in broad daylight.

It was at the end of this eerie period that Jesus cried out, "My God, my God, why have you forsaken me?" (v. 34). Fitting as they were, these words were probably not a testament of despair. On the contrary, when seen in the context of Psalm 22, from which they are taken, they become part of a great affirmation of faith, a wonderful doxology about God's dominion over all the earth.

Jesus' use of the Aramaic word *Eloi* caused the bystanders to think he was calling Elijah, who was traditionally thought to come to the aid of sufferers. The sour wine-filled sponge was probably the cheap *posca* normally drunk by Roman legionnaires. It fulfilled the prophecy in Psalm 69:21*b:* "For my thirst they gave me vinegar to drink."

Mark saw the splitting of the veil, which kept common people from the Holy of Holies, as the climax of Jesus' conflict with Temple religion. In a certain sense, at least, God had destroyed the Temple, and Jesus would build a more spiritual one in the community of believers.

If the rending of the veil had significance for Jewish readers, the conversion of the centurion had similar meaning for Gentile followers. Unlike the Jews, he needed no special sign to believe. Facing Jesus as he died, this man discerned from his appearance and manner of dying that he was indeed the Son of God. He saw an epiphany in a corpse!

PRAYER

O God, this passage is crammed with deep emotion and great significance. What a thrill it is to imagine Jesus crying out in triumph as he died. Help me so to practice your presence that I too may cry out when I am dying, not in pain, but in victory; not in regret, but in unspeakable joy. For yours is the new order forever and ever. Amen.

Day 183   *Mark 15:40-41*

THE WOMEN WHO SERVED HIM

*C*uriously, this is Mark's first mention of the women who followed Jesus. But the women were obviously part of the entourage of disciples throughout much of the Galilean ministry, and they had traveled with Jesus and the other disciples to Jerusalem for the confrontation with the religious leaders.

Magdala, the home of one Mary, was an area on the west side of the Sea of Galilee. The other Mary was apparently known to Mark's readers by her sons, James "the younger" and Joses, just as Simon of Cyrene was known to them by his sons, Alexander and Rufus (15:21). Matthew 27:56 identifies Salome likewise as the mother of the sons of Zebedee.

The picture, in other words, is of mothers who raised their children in the faith and saw them become well-known figures in the early church. We cannot help wondering what the history of Christianity might have been had it not been for them and countless women like them, who, often nameless and unhonored, provided the stability of belief and the progeny that enabled the church to perdure.

The fact that "there were many other women who had come up with him to Jerusalem" (v. 41) suggests that there may even have been more women than men among Jesus' followers and that the staying power of the church in those trying years owed more to them than we are usually aware of.

Certainly, the women's movement in our day has derived great impetus from Jesus' attitude toward women. Unlike many males of his time, he seems to have looked beyond gender in valuing persons. His realm has always transcended the world's way of distinguishing between Jew and Gentile, slave and free, male and female, for it regards all as being "one in Christ Jesus" (Gal. 3:28).

PRAYER

Dear God, help me always to be sensitive to persons who have not been accorded full status in the world. I want to appreciate their feelings and communicate with their needs, through him who reaches out to me in my own. Amen.

Day 184   *Mark 15:42-47*

THE BURIAL OF THE KING

*W*e have little information about Joseph. Even the location of Arimathea is uncertain. The fact that Joseph was "waiting expectantly for the kingdom of God" (v. 43) may mean only that he was a pious Jew, not necessarily that he was a follower of Jesus. But there was an element of risk in what he did, both by exposing himself to the curse of handling a body and by identifying himself as a Jesus-sympathizer to the other members of the Sanhedrin.

Two things appear to be clear. First, Mark was dealing with a fragment of tradition that did not fit precisely into the timetable of events as he was describing them, for preparing and entombing a body on the Passover would have been as problematic as doing so on the sabbath.

Second, what Mark was really interested in was to underscore the fact that Jesus had *died*. The word for "body" in verse 45 should really be translated "corpse," as the Jerusalem Bible has it. Mark wanted his readers to understand that Jesus did not merely *appear* to die—his death was a cold, hard fact!

Sometimes those on crosses died slowly. Pilate was apparently surprised that Jesus had already expired. When he had sent a man to verify the fact, he consented to Joseph's burying the remains. Joseph bought a shroud, took down the corpse, rolled it in the shroud, and laid it in a tomb carved out of rock. Then he rolled the large disk-like stone in front of the tomb.

Finis—a real death, a real corpse, a real shroud, a real tomb, a real stone before it.

And one final touch: The two Marys watched the entombment from a distance. This note was necessary to inform us of how they would know which tomb Jesus was in when they went to anoint his body the day after the sabbath.

PRAYER

O God, death is an overpowering fact when it claims someone close to us. Until then, it may seem remote and unreal. But in that moment its reality is uncontestable. Help me to remember this passage when death comes to a person near me. Then I shall know that Jesus has entered the heart of the same reality and reigns triumphant over it. In his glorious name, amen.

Day 185   *Mark 16:1-8*

A QUERULOUS ENDING

*I*n the most reliable ancient manuscripts, Mark's Gospel actually ends with verse 8; it is supposed that some scribe later added the more traditional ending of verses 9-20. If this is so, we must ask what Mark had in mind with such an unconventional conclusion. Perhaps the problem is not really as difficult as it first appears.

The three women—two Marys and Salome—who watched the crucifixion from a distance (15:40-41) and then followed Joseph of Arimathea to see where he had laid the corpse (15:47), come at first light when the sabbath ends to anoint the body with spices. They are startled to see the huge stone rolled away, which they had expected to be a problem, and to be met by a "young man" who is apparently an angelic messenger. (Is the "young man" the same one we met in 14:51-52, who fled in nakedness? Did he give up earthly clothing then for the heavenly raiment he now wears?) His words to them should be familiar, for they are essentially what Jesus had been trying to teach his followers for weeks, that he must be crucified and buried, but would then be raised from the dead.

Jesus would meet the followers in Galilee, said the young man. This was consistent with the fact that Mark set most of the important ministry of Jesus there, bringing him to Jerusalem only for the final confrontation and the crucifixion. Mark saw Jerusalem as a citadel of evil. Galilee, on the other hand, was the home of Jesus' "little ones," those who welcomed the new realm of God.

But the women do not understand, and they run away in fear without telling anyone anything. This is why this ending seems inappropriate. There is no real triumph in it, no picture of the great missionary stance of the early church. But wait. Isn't this precisely the picture Mark has endeavored to show of the disciples all along, that they could not understand what Jesus was doing or talking about? Maybe Mark handled the ending of his Gospel this way in order to emphasize that the success of the Messiah's work depended entirely on God, not on any human instrumentation.

Isn't it easy for us to identify with this kind of ending today? Most of the time we, too, don't understand and we, too, fail to witness. Yet God continues to introduce the new order into the world.

PRAYER

Ever since the resurrection, O God, Jesus has been meeting us in Galilee—in the ghetto kitchens, hospital wards, schoolrooms, and other places of service to your new order in the world. Help me not to be blind, the way the disciples often were; open my eyes and let me see Jesus as I work for him. In his name, amen.

Day 186   *Mark 6:45-52*

A DISPLACED RESURRECTION APPEARANCE

*Y*es, you have read this passage before. No, it is not a mistake that it is set here, and you are asked to read it again. Actually, it is a displaced resurrection appearance of Jesus. It may be part of the reason why Mark didn't end his Gospel in the traditional way; he had hidden an ending elsewhere in the narrative.

The sea, in ancient literature, was often a symbol of evil and chaos. Early Christians, by the same token, saw in ships the symbol of the church itself. This passage, then, may very well have been about the hard times experienced by the early church as it made its way in a chaotic, unfriendly world.

When Jesus came walking toward the ship in the night, the disciples at first thought he was a ghost—an apparition.

"Tharseite," said Jesus. "Take heart" or "Have courage"—the same word spoken to Paul by the risen Christ the night after Paul was imprisoned by the soldiers (Acts 23:11)! Or, as we commented earlier, "Take heart, *I am*"—the same word given to Moses when he asked who God was—"I AM WHO I AM" (Exod. 3:14). Jesus got into the boat with them, and the winds ceased.

The reason the disciples had been afraid in the storm, says Mark, was that they didn't understand about the loaves—about the feeding miracle. In fact, they didn't understand much of anything. Remember, too, that the women who came to the empty tomb were afraid and didn't tell anyone anything about it—again because they didn't understand.

Mark wasn't against using resurrection appearances to tell the story of Jesus; this selection from 6:45-52 indicates that. But he wanted us—his readers—to understand something he pictured the disciples as never understanding: The real proof of the resurrection is not in the appearances to certain women and apostles, but in the bread we eat in the wilderness and the way Christ comes to ease our hearts when the nights are dark and the seas are stormy.

PRAYER

Lord, this is a great mystery. I have eaten your bread in the wilderness and sensed your presence at the height of the storm. Help me to remember always that you are with me, not by outward appearances, but in the spirit within. For you have proven yourself on countless occasions. Amen.

Day 187   *Mark 16:9-20*

THE TRADITION OF APPEARANCES

*H*ere, as we have said, is some scribe's addition to the original ending of the Gospel. We are not sure when it was made, but it was done by the time of Irenaeus, who referred to it in the middle of the second century.

We are first told, in contradiction to 16:1-8, which said that Jesus had gone ahead of his followers to Galilee, that he appeared to Mary Magdalene (not to the other Mary and Salome), and that she, instead of keeping silent as in verse 8, came and told the other disciples. Then we are told about the appearance to two followers as they walked in the country. These were possibly the disciples from Emmaus, identified in

Luke 24:13-35. Finally, Jesus appeared to the eleven themselves, as they would not believe either Mary Magdalene or the two men from the country, and chided them for their "lack of faith and stubbornness" (v. 14).

Jesus gave the eleven a commissioning similar to that in Matthew 28:18-20, telling them to "Go into all the world and proclaim the good news to the whole creation" (v. 15). Some commentators believe that this kind of saying would not actually have come from Jesus to the first disciples; otherwise, Peter would not have needed his vision about the Gentiles in Acts 10:9-16, and the early church would not have required the Council of Jerusalem in Acts 15 to determine that the gospel should be extended to the nations.

Most scholars are also convinced that the so-called signs of believers in verses 17-18—especially speaking in tongues, picking up serpents, and drinking poison—are later descriptions of the Christian experience based on instances of these occurrences in various congregations.

How much more powerful was Mark's original ending, which simply sent the disciples and other followers off to Galilee with the promise that he would meet them there. Mark's real message is not that Jesus is in heaven at God's right hand, but that he meets us in the highways and byways of life as we go about ministering to people in his name.

PRAYER

Lord, your power is beyond description, turning the world upside down and standing all expectancies on their heads. But save me, I pray, from needing special signs of this power to know that you are alive and with me. Give me, instead, the gift of quiet reflection, of meditation on your presence, that I may truly see and understand where you are at work in the world where I live. Yours be the power and the glory forever. Amen.

Day 188   *Luke 1:1-4*

A DEFINITIVE ACCOUNT

*E*very biographer and historian," says the essayist Northrup James, "attempts to write the best account yet. Drawing on all that has gone before, yet adding that unique quality which he alone can give, he seeks to say the definitive word, the one that will marshal all the others into gleaming perspective. Even though additional writers may come after him, assaying the same task, his story, he hopes, will provide the unavoidable focus for theirs."

This must have been the feeling of Luke as he began his account of the life of Jesus and the early church. Many others, he said, had already written their accounts. But he wanted to write his, putting it together with his own unique touch.

Theophilus, to whom both the Gospel of Luke and the book of Acts are addressed, may have been a well-to-do patron or benefactor of Luke, as suggested by the courteous form of address. His name, which means "beloved of God," could indicate that he was born of Christian parents and was younger than Luke. If this is the case, then the Gospel and Acts were written by Luke as an effort to lay before his young friend the salient facts of the early Christian movement as he had received them from both eyewitness reports and the writings of others who were ministers or servants of the Word. Theophilus had already heard reports of the origins and progress of the movement, but Luke wished him to have a very careful account and to "know the truth."

PRAYER

Thank you, O God, for the men and women who have had enough care for the truth to write reports about matters for those of us who would come after them. Help me to cherish their efforts and ponder their accounts for the meaning they may have in my own life. Then help me to love my children and their children and their children's children enough to pass on to them my own testimony on these things. For the sake of your heavenly realm, amen.

Day 189   *Luke 1:5-25*

STARTING WITH THE TEMPLE

Significantly, Luke begins his Gospel in the Temple. He uses a similar technique in the book of Acts, which begins in Jerusalem and moves out to the world beyond. In other words, Luke has a *spatial* vision. A Gentile himself, he is interested in how a religious movement that begins with a Jewish system centered in Temple worship moves out from there to the nations.

How Zechariah happened to be in the Temple at this time is fascinating. As a male member of the tribe of Aaron, he was entitled to offer sacrifice in the Temple. But there were so many descendants of Aaron that they were divided into groups and allowed to serve only two weeks each year. Within each group, lots were cast to see which priest would be allowed to officiate. No priest was permitted to do this more than once in a lifetime, and some never had the opportunity. We can imagine Zechariah's excitement, then, when the lot fell to him "to enter the sanctuary of the Lord and offer incense" (v. 9). It was a supreme honor—even enough to offset the sense of shame Zechariah had felt at having had no child.

Then it happened! As the prayers of the people were being offered, an angel appeared to Zechariah in the midst of the smoke from the incense. God would answer both the prayers of the people for deliverance and Zechariah's prayers for a son. The son's name would be John. He would take the ascetic vows of a Nazirite and would go out "with the spirit and power of Elijah" (v. 17), who was regarded as the greatest of the prophets.

Zechariah couldn't believe it. Like so many Jews depicted later in the Gospel, he asked for a sign of proof and received a very personal one—he was struck speechless until the baby's birth! How the people must have talked that day about the priest who had seen a vision at the altar and was left voiceless by the experience. But aren't all great mystical experiences finally unspeakable?

PRAYER

I have been speechless a few times in my life, O God, but never like this. Lead me through prayer and contemplation to greater depths of spiritual experience, so that I may talk less and hear more. Through him whose story is at the heart of this mystery, amen.

Day 190   *Luke 1:26-38*

THE GREATER MIRACLE

*F*rom the miracle of birth to the elderly, God now turns to the miracle of birth to an unmarried young woman. If John's birth was special, the Savior's birth must be even more special. He would be born as the offspring not of an aged priest of the Temple but of the Holy Spirit of God.

"Hail, Mary, full of grace," Jerome translated the Greek in the Latin Vulgate edition, and a tradition arose that venerated Mary as the receptacle of grace that could be dispensed to others. But the New Revised Standard Version more properly translates, "Greetings, favored one! The Lord is with you" (v. 28). It was indeed an incredible honor; she had been chosen to bear the Savior of the world.

Luke, with characteristic human understanding, shows us the puzzled, frightened side of Mary's reaction. She was greatly perplexed by it all. But the angel assured her, reminding her of her nation's great hope through the centuries for a Messiah, a Savior in the line of David whose kingdom, unlike David's, would be forever.

Mary was still puzzled. How could this be, for she was a virgin? God's Spirit would accomplish it, said the angel; therefore, her son would be the Son of God, and would be holy. Moreover, her relative Elizabeth, who had been barren for years, was already with child. It was a time of great miracles. "For nothing will be impossible with God" (v. 37).

Mary's response, in the end, was touchingly modest and humble: "Here am I, the servant of the Lord; let it be with me according to your word" (v. 38).

PRAYER

This story seems fanciful and untrue, O God, to the kind of world we live in today. Yet, you still send your word to those you favor, and your Holy Spirit upon those who are devout in their own spirits. Teach me to say with Mary, "Let it be with me according to your word," that I may know your will in my affairs and submit to it in simple humility. In the name of him whose new order is forever, amen.

Day 191   *Luke 1:39-56*

THE BLESSEDNESS OF BELIEVING

*T*his is a remarkable passage, especially in view of the low general estate of women in New Testament times. With continuing sensitivity, Luke describes the gentle, feminine side of this mighty event that was taking place in the history of Israel and the world.

Luke attempts to relate the later ministry of Jesus to the entire context of prophecy and expectancy in Israel's long history. God is working behind the scenes, so to speak, to coordinate the events that will finally culminate in the birth, death, and resurrection of the Savior.

Mary, in all of this, personifies the faithful remnant in Israel who persist in believing in the promises of God. As Elizabeth says, "Blessed is she who believed that there would be a fulfillment of what was spoken to her by the Lord" (v. 45).

The song attributed to Mary is called the Magnificat, which is the first word in the song's Latin version. It is a psalm of thanksgiving very much like many of the poems in the book of Psalms. It speaks of God's covenant-faithfulness; as God has chosen Mary over all the highborn ladies of the age to be the mother of the Savior, so God is now ready to exalt the low, the poor, and the hungry over the high, the rich, and the well fed. As the psalm concludes, this is no new promise, but the fulfillment of the one made to Abraham long ago.

Luke does not say it directly, but he implies that Mary remained with Elizabeth until Elizabeth delivered her child. It would have been the kinlike thing to do, and three months should have brought them just about to that time. What wonders we can imagine the two women sharing during this period!

PRAYER

O God, fulfillment must have been hard for these people to wait on, and then hard to believe when it was almost upon them. Strengthen my faith in the promises you have given, that I too may live in the blessedness of expectancy. Through Jesus, who is and will be the fulfillment of everything, amen.

Day 192   *Luke 1:57-80*

THE GRACIOUS GIFT OF GOD

*H*ere, especially in verse 65, we are given a clue about where Luke got these stories that are not told in the other Gospels. They circulated among the people in the little hill communities near Judea, where John was born. Luke apparently heard them from Christians in this region.

Like the other stories, this one provides interesting personal details whose ultimate meanings reflect universal truths. Zechariah and Elizabeth's neighbors came to rejoice with them at the birth of their son and to be present for his ritual circumcision. At the moment in the rite when the child is to receive his name, the neighbors and kinsfolk, assuming the boy will be named for his father, proceed in the father's silence to name him. But Elizabeth speaks up to say that his name will be John, meaning "gracious gift of God." It is an understandable gesture, given the parents' elderly status. But their friends and kin brush Elizabeth's answer aside, deferring to Zechariah. They fully expect a sign from him confirming that the child should bear his name.

Zechariah startles them—twice. Writing on a tablet, he indicates that the child will indeed be called John, not Zechariah. Then he surprises them again by suddenly regaining his voice. He begins to speak, and his first words are expressions of praise to God. The neighbors and kinsfolk are filled with fear. They know that something far beyond the ordinary is going on here. They are dealing not with human beings but with God.

Given the gift of prophesying, Zechariah delivers a poetic utterance, praising God and predicting that John will be the forerunner of the Messiah himself, preparing his way by calling people to repentance and forgiveness of their sins.

PRAYER

A birth is a sacred occasion, O God, and so is receiving a name. Make me more aware of the sacredness of my own life, and let me know that it is a gift from you. Through him who calls us to new life in your will, amen.

Day 193   *Luke 2:1-7*

NO ROOM IN THE INN

*W*e often think of this passage in terms of a quiet scene in a stable. But look at it again. It is a picture of crowdedness, busyness, noise, commotion.

First, there is the decree of the emperor, which sets the whole world in an uproar. The Roman Empire extended all the way from the British Isles in the west to Persia and parts of India in the east. Thousands of tribes were scattered across it, many of them living in out-of-the-way valleys and having little to do with the Roman government. The emperor knew that only a fraction of the people were paying the taxes due to Rome for the upkeep of the roads, garrisons, theaters, and other public services. Someone suggested that if there were a roll of all the citizens it would be easier to collect the taxes. So the emperor ordered a roll to be made and required everyone to return to his or her home area for registration. The roads all over the empire were filled with pilgrims—pilgrims going home to be duly registered.

Then there is the other picture here, that of a small town in the hill country below Jerusalem. It is as if the camera that has been taking a wide-angle picture suddenly zooms in for a close-up to show what the census means in the life of a single village. It focuses on Bethlehem. We see the crowds of people filling the streets, along with the sheep and goats and donkeys they have brought with them; we hear the cacophony of human voices and animal sounds alike rising over the scene.

And it is within this melée, this hubbub, that the Savior of the world is born. Finding no room in the inn because of the unusual crowdedness, the parents seek refuge in a cattle stall behind the inn. There, in the cold of the night, with the smell of animals strong in the air, Mary gives birth to the Messiah and wraps him in strips of cloth and lays him gently in a manger.

It is a beautiful picture, and the entire world is indebted to Luke for sharing it with us.

PRAYER

My life is as busy as those of Caesar's world, O God, and I am as likely as most of the people then to miss the coming of Christ in my life. Teach me to be quiet, to see and to hear, that I may be aware of his approach and make a throne for him in my heart. For he is the King of kings. Amen.

Day 194   *Luke 2:8-20*

NEWS OF A GREAT JOY

*I*n this passage, Luke reveals a major theme of his Gospel: the joy that is associated with Jesus and the new order. Gabriel had promised "joy and gladness" to Zechariah (1:14). The babe in Elizabeth's womb leapt for joy at the visit of Mary (1:44), and Mary's psalm rejoices in God (1:47). When the seventy disciples return from their preaching mission, they announce with joy that even the demons are subject to them (10:17). Jesus tells them to rejoice that their names are written in heaven (10:20). He himself rejoices in the Holy Spirit (10:21), and then declares to them, "Blessed are the eyes that see what you see!" (10:23). After Jesus heals the woman bent with an infirmity, all the people rejoice at the glorious things he does (13:17). And, of course, there are the three stories of great joy in chapter 15, about the finding of the lost coin, the lost sheep, and the lost boy. More than any other New Testament writer, Luke is captivated by the notion of joy, and his Gospel resounds with it from one end to the other.

Here in our present passage is the central occasion for joy: the coming of the Savior in human flesh to inaugurate the long-awaited new age of God. Appropriately, he is identified by birth with the poor, who have no place to lay their heads, and with the religious pariahs—the shepherds—who are socially despised by the religious rulers of Israel.

And the religious outcasts see the shining glory of God's presence and hear the voice of an angel. "I am bringing you good news of great joy," says the angel, "for all the people" (v. 10). When the announcement is made, the whole sky is suddenly filled with the music of heavenly choirs, praising God and promising peace among "those whom he favors" (v. 14).

The peace they speak of is more than the absence of war; it is the Hebrew *shalom,* meaning fullness and blessedness. And characteristically for Luke, the shepherds, having learned the joyful news, in turn become its bearers. They return to the hills, glorifying and praising God for all they have heard and seen. The joy of the new age is that contagious!

PRAYER

I am heartily sorry, O God, for the lack of joy in my life. I am too frequently tired, depressed, or annoyed. My life should be a continual psalm of praise, for I have both heard and seen the coming of your new order. Forgive my obtuseness and return me to the passion of your salvation. Through Jesus, who took his place among the poor and rejected of the world, amen.

Day 195   *Luke 2:21-39*

THE REWARD FOR WAITING

*L*uke seems to know nothing of the massacre of the innocents and the flight into Egypt reported by Matthew's Gospel (Matt. 2:13-23). He is concerned instead to show us the relationship between the newborn Savior and the holy city, so he represents Mary and Joseph taking Jesus there many times—for his circumcision, for Mary's purification (required by Jewish law forty days after childbirth), and every year for Passover (v. 41).

On the second visit, for Mary's purification, Luke shows us the Messiah's recognition and acceptance by two faithful persons who have been waiting, the way all good Jews have been waiting, to see God's salvation.

First we are introduced to Simeon, a "righteous and devout" man in the city who is guided by the Holy Spirit to come to the Temple. When he sees the holy child, who is now several weeks old, he takes him in his arms—imagine cradling the Savior of the world in your arms!—and praises God with a song of ecstasy. Then he blesses the astonished parents and speaks prophetically to them, warning them that their son is a "sign" who will be "opposed so that the inner thoughts of many will be revealed" (v. 35) and that a sword of pain will pierce Mary's heart through it all.

Next we meet an eighty-four-year-old-woman, a prophet, who in her widowhood spends all her days and even nights in the Temple, fasting and praying. She comes into the Temple while the holy family is there and immediately begins to praise God and speak about the child "to all who were looking for the redemption of Jerusalem" (v. 38). Presumably these latter persons were scattered about the city, or at least her neighborhood, and were not confined to persons in the Temple.

PRAYER

I wonder, O God, if I truly understand what it means that Jesus is the Savior of the world. It is such a huge concept, and the world seems so resistant to being saved. Help me to fast and pray—to lead a life of ordered devotion—in order that I may comprehend more fully in all my being what my mind already knows about Jesus. For the sake of your great realm, amen.

Day 196   *Luke 2:40-52*

A SIGN OF THE FUTURE

*H*ow eagerly some parents observe their children to determine what their life's work will be. "Doctor, lawyer, merchant, chief" is an old game based on this eagerness to know the future. Today it has been replaced by aptitude tests and counseling services designed to point young people in the most appropriate directions.

In this passage, Luke reveals the early direction taken by Jesus. At the age of twelve, like every Jewish boy, he became *bar mitzvah,* a son of the law. Probably it was in celebration of this important occasion that Jesus' parents took him to Jerusalem for the annual Passover festival.

The fact that the family had traveled homeward for an entire day before missing Jesus does not mean that they were careless parents. Theirs was probably a large, extended family, and Jesus would have moved freely among aunts, uncles, and cousins. His parents would have assumed he was with them as they started homeward.

He was, in fact, in the Temple, revealing his leaning toward a future rabbinical life. He gravitated toward the learned teachers the way youngsters today incline toward business offices, laboratories, or movie sets. When his mother reprimanded him for being thoughtless, he replied with a significant answer: They should have known they would find him in his Father's house. Already he understood his place as the Son of God.

Mary, says Luke, pondered all these things in her heart. Apparently she was the source of this story, and it became part of the oral legend of Jesus, kept alive among the Christian communities in the Judean hills.

PRAYER

Grant to the children I know, O God, the sense of direction and inner identity that Jesus had by the time he was *bar mitzvah*; and let Jesus himself stand at the center of where they are going with their lives. For his name's sake, amen.

Day 197   *Luke 3:1-14*

NO HIDING PLACE

*W*hatever image we may have of John the Baptist, it certainly isn't that of a soft-soaper! "You brood of vipers!" he called the people who came out to see and hear him (v. 7). The wonder is that so many came to receive such abuse.

But John had a clear vision of the judgment that was coming on Israel as part of the appearance of God's Messiah. He knew there would be no hiding for the guilty. And many people obviously recognized the authenticity of his warning and asked what they could do.

It is interesting that John's answer was couched in terms of simple justice. People who had more property than they needed were to divide with those who had none. Those who had food were to share with those who were hungry. Tax collectors were to do their duty but forgo the often exorbitant fees they were accustomed to extracting for personal use. Soldiers were to live simply and honestly, and not use their positions to rob or falsely accuse people of crimes and confiscate their property.

The injunctions were not different from those Jesus would give later for citizens of the heavenly realm. They implied a new orientation in life, a new spirit, so that God, not personal profit, became the center of a person's life.

And, interestingly, Luke sets his account of the great wilderness prophet into a universal context. He begins by locating John's ministry in the reign of Tiberius, the Roman emperor, and then names the local governor and religious leaders. John's message of repentance and justice was not meant for the little land of Judah alone, but for the world!

PRAYER

Do I have more than others, O God? Then I, too, need to hear John's message and prepare the way of the Savior in my life by sharing what I have. Grant me the grace, imagination, and resoluteness to do this acceptably. In the name of him who has come and is always coming, amen.

Day 198   *Luke 3:15-20*

A GREAT HUMILITY

*O*nly persons with a special quality of inner assurance and self-identity are capable of true humility. I once knew such a person. He was a powerful man who controlled the affairs of many employees. Yet he was always modest and invariably acknowledged the abilities of other persons. I once heard him, when accepting an honor, enthusiastically credit his superior in another city with the leadership and insight responsible for the honor.

John was obviously in touch with himself in this way. When people came asking if he were the Messiah, it must occasionally have been tempting to suggest that he was, or at least to wonder in his heart if indeed God was not preparing him for this great station. But he was apparently quite resolute on the matter, pointing people instead to the one whose ministry would follow his.

"I baptize you with water," he said, "but one who is more powerful than I is coming," and "he will baptize you with the Holy Spirit and fire" (v. 16).

As Luke was also the author of Acts, we cannot help associating this verse with the description of what occurred at Pentecost, when a sound "like the rush of a violent wind" filled the house where the followers were; "divided tongues, as of fire," rested on each of them; and the Holy Spirit welled up in them and they began to speak in other languages (Acts 2:1-4). John's followers had experienced baptism by water. So had Jesus' disciples. But the *real* baptism, the one that would be the sure sign of the new order's presence, would be the baptism of the Spirit and fire, and that was the baptism Christ would bring.

John the Baptist, as theologian Karl Barth has said, was content to be a signpost pointing the way to Jesus.

PRAYER

Make me a signpost too, O God. Let the joy of my spirit and the helpfulness of my actions point others unmistakably to Jesus, who stands at the center of everything. Amen.

Day 199   *Luke 3:21-38*

A GREAT MOMENT

*T*here is no more tender moment in a parent's life than when his or her child undergoes a rite of initiation or passage. Baptism, confirmation, first communion, *bar mitzvah*, graduation, marriage—each is a time of deep and satisfying emotion, combining reflection on the past and anticipation of the future.

It is surely no wonder that the Gospel tradition represented God as speaking with delight at the moment when Jesus, the "only begotten Son," was baptized by the prophet John. It is beside the point whether Jesus needed to be baptized "for the forgiveness of sins" (Luke 3:3); the important thing is that by accepting baptism from John he identified himself with penitent Israel, the Israel whose hope was still in God.

Luke apparently has the Holy Spirit descending on Jesus while he is praying, probably after the baptism when he entered the wilderness (see 4:1-13). The words spoken by the heavenly voice, "You are my Son, the Beloved" (v. 22), echo Psalm 2:7. Psalm 2 is a hymn exalting the king whom God has set over the nations to rule with a rod of iron and dash his enemies to pieces. The second phrase, "with you I am well pleased," is probably from Isaiah 42:1, in which God is speaking of his servant who will redeem Israel through the ministry of suffering. So the two motifs are combined—exaltation and suffering—and are set at the very beginning of Jesus' ministry.

Then Luke gives a long genealogy, relating Jesus to David, Abraham, Adam, and thence to God, the father of Adam. The justification for placing the list of names here is the phrase "son of God," which may be linked to the voice saying, "You are my Son, the Beloved." And by relating Jesus to Adam, as well as to David and Abraham, Luke underlines again his proclamation of Jesus as a universal Savior, not merely the Savior of the Jews.

PRAYER

O God, the early Christians must have been thrilled by this picture of their Lord being baptized as they were baptized. Generate a similar excitement in me now as I contemplate the scene. Arouse in me a new enthusiasm for your heavenly order and for the leadership of your Holy Spirit in my own life. Through Jesus, whose lineage relates him to everyone, amen.

Day 200   *Luke 4:1-13*

TRIAL IN THE WILDERNESS

*Y*ou are my Son, the Beloved," God said when Jesus was baptized. *"If you are the Son of God,"* the devil challenges him in two of the temptations recorded here. It is an attack on Jesus' understanding of his identity and of the confidence God has in him to fulfill his ministry.

Accordingly, each temptation is extremely basic to human nature.

The first is for *bread.* Jesus has been fasting for days and is very hungry. But he resolutely answers the devil with the words of Moses in Deuteronomy 8:2-3, about how God humbled the Israelites in the wilderness and let them hunger in order that they might understand that people don't live merely by bread, but by the words of God.

The second temptation is to *power and glory.* The devil promises to make Jesus a great king if he will fall down and worship the prince of darkness. Again Jesus cites Moses, reminding him that we are to worship only God because God is a jealous deity (Deut. 6:13-15).

The third and final temptation is to *put God to the test.* Whisked to the top of the Temple, 450 feet above the Valley of Gehinnom, Jesus is urged to throw himself down. Psalm 91, after all, promises complete protection to God's anointed. But again Jesus refuses to yield to temptation, and the devil departs to wait for another opportunity.

In all three temptations—bread, glory, religious certainty—Jesus responds with the need for absolute obedience to God. What an important passage this must have been to early Christians who, for one reason or another, were tempted to defect from the faith! It places temptations squarely in eternal perspective; enduring them now in the wilderness of life leads eventually to the realm that God alone can give.

PRAYER

I, too, have often forgotten, O God, the meaning of real obedience. My age knows far more about freedom than it does about obedience; yet, it often misses the very first principle of freedom: that freedom is lost the minute we fail to obey you. Help me to discover again how to be faithful to the heavenly vision, and thus to be truly free. Through Jesus, who fulfilled this paradox magnificently, amen.

Day 201   *Luke 4:14-21*

THE DESIGN OF JESUS' MINISTRY

*H*aving flatly denied the devil's attempts to make him into a self-gratifying, power-hungry, earthly king (Luke 4:1-13), Jesus now clearly defines the kind of ministry he intends to pursue. It is to be a ministry to the poor and outcast, the blind and unaffirmed. God's new realm will exist for precisely those people the old realm has consistently neglected!

Luke places the announcement of the servant ministry in a synagogue service in Nazareth. The synagogue was the heart of Jewish educational and religious life. A sabbath service there usually consisted of a call to worship, known as the *Shema* (Deut. 6:4-9); an assigned passage from the law; a free passage from the Prophets; a sermon or interpretation of one of the passages; and assorted prayers. Any man in the synagogue might be given a scroll and asked to read or preach, even if he were a visitor. The sermon was always preached from a seated position, and might be followed by questions from the others present.

On this occasion, Jesus was obviously invited to read the free selection from the prophets and then to provide the sermon. He selected Isaiah 61:1-2, which begins a long poem about the mission of God's mighty

194

servant who is to restore Israel. It is a beautiful passage, and quite revolutionary in its emphasis on the poor and outcast; but the hearers, long familiar with it, would have nodded happily at hearing it read again.

The stunning thing happened after the reading, when Jesus began to speak his own words. "Today," he said, "this scripture has been fulfilled in your hearing" (v. 21). That is, the anointed one predicted by Isaiah was there in their very midst!

PRAYER

Release to captives, oppressed people going free, blind people seeing, good news preached to the poor and not to the rich—O God, this is indeed new and revolutionary in every age. How we long for it even today. Let Christ come quickly, that what began to be fulfilled in him may be consummated in our own time. For yours is the power to bring it to pass. Amen.

Day 202   *Luke 4:22-30*

THE TYPICAL REACTION

*Y*esterday we read about Jesus' design for his ministry, based on Isaiah's vision of good news being preached to the poor, release for the captives, recovery of sight for the blind, freedom for the oppressed, and the coming of the Lord's year of favor. Today we have seen how the people in his hometown reacted to this.

First they were pleased at the graciousness of his speech and at the prospect that he would perform in Nazareth the kinds of miracles he had performed in nearby Capernaum. Perhaps the year of the Lord's favor was indeed at hand.

Then doubt began to creep in. Wasn't this Jesus, the son of Joseph the carpenter? The Messiah was supposed to be a regal figure. How could Joseph's son be the Messiah?

The text appears to be garbled and unclear, so that we must surmise what happened next. Probably Jesus found too much skepticism among the people to do any great works for them. They were not really prepared for the coming of God's new order. Mark tells us as much in his Gospel (Mark 6:5-6).

Jesus even suggests, in keeping with Luke's general emphasis on the worldwide mission of the Savior, that the Jews might entirely miss the great blessings of God. Israel had been full of widows in Elijah's day; yet Elijah went to the house of a widow in Sidon, a Gentile area. Similarly, Israel had many lepers in Elisha's time; yet Elisha had given the blessing of God to a man from Syria.

Enraged, the proud Jews rose up and carried the brash young prophet out to throw him to his death, possibly on the charge that he had uttered blasphemy. Somehow, though—Luke doesn't trouble to be more specific—Jesus managed to walk through their midst and escape.

The tone of the entire passage is consistent with that of the temptation narrative. Jesus is faithful to what God wants and will not swerve aside for anything—not to feed himself, not to gain personal glory, not to test God, and not to please the citizens of the town where he grew up!

PRAYER

O God, how would I receive Jesus if he were to come into my life as he came into these people's lives, speaking of things that would upset my patterns and practices? Wouldn't I be as unkind and unreceptive as they? Forgive my selfishness and help me to prepare to change everything in my life and environment for you. Through him who knew what you wanted and sought it despite all consequences, amen.

Day 203   *Luke 4:31-44*

TEACHING AND PREACHING THE KINGDOM

We tend to think of the teaching and preaching of the new order as primarily an oral matter—communicating through speech. But for Jesus the new order was coming in power, not mere talk. Therefore, his teaching and preaching were interfused with miraculous acts of healing. When he announced in the synagogue at Nazareth that he was anointed to proclaim release to the captives and recovery of sight to the blind, he obviously had in mind more than mere announcement of the coming of the new order. For him, preaching and teaching meant participating in the power of the new order itself! This passage, then, is the logical one to follow his declaration in the synagogue. It shows the preacher of the new order in action.

Luke seems to have taken over this particular collection of material almost verbatim from the Gospel of Mark (1:21-39), or from some source of stories available to both Mark and himself. The purpose of the selection in both Mark and Luke is to relate Jesus' healing ministry to the "authority" with which he taught and preached. When he spoke, it was not the carefully guarded speech of the scribes and Pharisees; it was the penetrating, free-ranging discourse of one obviously in touch with his subject—and the miracles were simply further proof of this.

The demons recognized Jesus as the true Son of God, and they knew his coming shook their power and authority to the very depths. Their cries as they left their victims were filled with awe and respect: "You are the Son of God!" (v. 41). They realized that it was the beginning of the end for them. The scribes and Pharisees had never had any power over them. But they knew it was different with Jesus. He was the Holy One of God, and the arrival of his heavenly reign meant the collapse of theirs.

PRAYER

Sometimes, O God, I think the demons showed more respect to Jesus than we show him today. We sing "Oh, How I Love Jesus" and buy car plates bearing his name, then live as if he hadn't died for our sins and been raised to live as an eternal presence in our midst. At least the demons went away in hushed respect, forsaking even their dwelling places. Let him matter more to me, I pray, for his name's sake. Amen.

Day 204   *Luke 5:1-11*

AN ASTONISHING CATCH

*T*he two boats in this story apparently belonged to Simon and Andrew and, we suspect, James and John. The incident occurred before Jesus called them to be his disciples. He had been teaching near the lake when the boats came in from the night's fishing, and he saw that they were empty. As the fishermen tended their nets, pulling seaweed from them and mending the broken places, Jesus stepped into Simon Peter's boat and asked him to take it a little way off shore so Jesus would have room to breathe as he continued to teach the people.

Then, after his teaching was done, he told Simon to take the boat out again and let down the nets, promising a great catch. Simon was reluctant; he was doubtless tired from the fruitless night's work. Yet he obeyed—Jesus was the sort of man one listened to. And this time, when the nets were drawn up, they were so full that Simon had to call for the other boat to help bring them to shore.

The enormity of the miracle stunned Simon Peter. Falling down at Jesus' feet, he cried, "Go away from me, Lord, for I am a sinful man!" (v. 8). His words are reminiscent of Isaiah's when he saw God high and lifted up in a vision (Isa. 6:5); he was terrified of his own unworthiness.

"Do not be afraid," said Jesus, "from now on you will be catching people" (v. 10). The abundance of the catch was surely a sign of the number of people who would come into the church under the ministry of Peter and the other disciples. From that time on, the men left their boats and followed Jesus. Luke has given us a beautiful explanation of their call.

PRAYER

Like these fishermen, O God, I am often tired when nothing is happening in my life. Teach me to hear your voice at such times and to steer for the deep water again. In the name of him who can keep my nets full, amen.

Day 205   *Luke 5:12-16*

RELEASE FOR A CAPTIVE

*I*n the dialogue following his sermon at the synagogue in Nazareth, Jesus had alluded to Elisha's healing of the leper Naaman. Now Jesus heals a man "covered with leprosy" (v. 12).

Leprosy was one of the most dreaded diseases of that time, not only because of the way it wasted the body but because it isolated the victim socially and religiously. This man clearly became one of the "captives" referred to in Jesus' reading from Isaiah (Luke 4:18). According to Leviticus 13–14, which gives specific rules governing leprous persons, the leper was declared unclean by the priest and cast out from normal society.

Jesus is shown doing what most Jews would never do: touching the leper, risking social and religious contamination for himself. But then the miracle occurred. Instead of his being contaminated by the leper, Jesus cleansed the man. He reversed the usual direction of effect and opened a new future for the man.

Jesus' instruction that the man go to the priest and conform to the Levitical law and be pronounced well was probably for the man's sake socially; he would then be reintegrated into the normal fabric of Jewish society.

The verbs in the final sentences of the passage are interesting. They are all in the imperfect tense, denoting continuing activity. The word about Jesus *kept* going out; great crowds *kept* gathering around him; and he *kept* withdrawing and praying. This is the picture of Jesus we have seen in Matthew and Mark as well—he constantly alternated between a busy life of healing and time alone for prayer and inner renewal.

PRAYER

I often forget this dialectic, O God, and try to meet the demands of life without times of prayer and reflection. Please help me to see once and for all that I simply can't do it—that only the continued refreshment of your presence will enable me to deal adequately with the burden of busy days. Through Jesus, who fully understood this, amen.

Day 206   *Luke 5:17-26*

A CHARACTERISTIC DETAIL

*T*his is a highly charged setting, with a number of scribes and Pharisees from all over Israel observing as Jesus heals people in a great crowd. Then comes the dramatic moment when "some men" (Mark specifies four) lower a paralyzed friend through the roof to reach Jesus. In Mark's Gospel, the roof is of the clay-and-wattle variety typical of Palestinian homes, but Luke speaks of tiles, suggesting a Roman style of house. The friends of the paralyzed man are so confident that Jesus can heal him that they tear up a roof to bring him to the Master!

Jesus, seeing their great faith, immediately forgives the man's sins, and thus provokes controversy with the scribes and Pharisees, who say it is blasphemous to usurp the power of God to forgive sin. Why did Jesus do this? Perhaps he reacted spontaneously to the men's faith that the new order of God had indeed entered their midst; and the most immediate barrier to entering that new order is always sin, not a physical condition.

When the scribes and Pharisees object, Jesus gives them a demonstration of power and authority they can understand and measure visibly: He commands the paralyzed one to stand up, take his bed, and walk home. The man does as he is told. And Luke adds a characteristic detail that is missing in Mark's Gospel—the man is "glorifying God" as he goes home. This is the note of joyous discovery that runs through the Gospel of Luke, from the announcement of the Savior's birth to the story of his resurrection. We are told, moreover, that they were *all* amazed and glorified God—presumably even the querulous scribes and Pharisees!

PRAYER

I think I understand, O God, why Jesus forgave the man before healing him. I am inwardly paralyzed by my sins and failures, and it is only as I experience your forgiveness that I begin to sense wholeness and joy. Then even my body feels better. Thank you, dear God, and hallelujah! Amen.

Day 207 *Luke 5:27-39*

A NEW MOOD OF REJOICING

*T*hese verses have to do with the new order that has come in Jesus. He is not a mere continuation of the old religious tradition, represented by the scribes and Pharisees and their restrictive view of the law. Instead, he brings an air of liberation, a fresh spirit of joy and celebration in life.

The people who have been cast away from the religious center because they could not keep the law perfectly are brought back with joy (note the "great banquet" in Levi's house), just as the prodigal son is received in the parable (Luke 15:20-24). And the disciples who follow the Master, themselves common, unreligious persons, likewise live joyfully instead of ascetically, celebrating their Lord's presence in their midst.

The brief parables of the garment and the wineskin, then, are metaphorical ways of saying that this exhilarating movement of Jesus cannot be merely appended to or enclosed in the traditional forms of religion; it is too dynamic, too volatile, and can only end by destroying the old way, as an unshrunken patch of cloth will do when sewn to a shrunken garment, or as active new wine will do when poured into old, dry skins.

Verse 39 appears only in Luke, and not in the parallel versions of Matthew and Mark. It seems to be a comment on those who find the old religion adequate—especially the scribes and Pharisees. They find the old wine to be good, so simply do not try the new wine. Jesus understood the difficulty of giving up old habits and traditions.

PRAYER

O God, my problem is that I have allowed the "new" religion of Jesus and the disciples to become old in my life. My responses to you have become dull and routine, and I no longer have a continual sense of delight in my faith. Come as new wine in my life, tearing up old wineskins; break me open to current joys in your realm. For Jesus' sake—and mine—amen.

Day 208   *Luke 6:1-11*

THE PRIORITY OF PEOPLE OVER TRADITIONS

*T*his passage should be read as a continuation of Luke 5:27-39, for it is further commentary on what Jesus said there about the new mood of joy and excitement in the realm of God. Fussiness about sabbath law was part of the strict religious tradition developed by the scribes and Pharisees. Jesus did not violate the law of Moses, for he was a humble observer of divine law; but he was certainly not about to conform to the miserly elaborations of that law that had become such a burden to observant Jews.

The first incident, plucking and eating grain on the sabbath, revolves about a regulation against milling corn on the holy day. It seems silly to us that rolling a few grains of wheat in one's hand to separate the kernels from the husks should be construed as milling or grinding. Jesus' answer to the scribes and Pharisees did not try to argue with the absurdity of this interpretation. Instead, it cited another "offense," recorded in 1 Samuel 21:1-6, in which David and his men had eaten the sacred bread of the Presence in the temple. What this illustrated as Jesus used it was the priority of human need over any commandment. Thus the summation, "The Son of Man is Lord of the sabbath" (v. 5).

The second incident, healing on the sabbath, defies the rule that a person could be doctored on the sabbath only if his or her life were in danger. Again Jesus challenged the priority of the law over human need by effecting the cure on the sabbath. It was a direct reflection of his declaration of ministry in Luke 4:16-30: Healing the sick and releasing the captive were to have top priority in the new order of God!

Verse 11 is a dark hint of what is to come. Those who cherished the old traditions could not bear to see them broken in this manner. They would eventually have their pound of flesh.

O God, forbid that I should ever follow in the footsteps of the legalists by making any *Christian* regulation more important than the people I meet in life. Fill my heart with such love and exultation that I shall never become defensive about mere traditions or habits of thinking. Through Jesus, who drew fresh dedication from everything, amen.

Day 209   *Luke 6:12-19*

THE PEOPLE OF THE NEW SPIRIT

*F*ollowing his controversies with the religious leaders of Israel and their rancorous discussion of what to do to him, Jesus formally appoints the twelve disciples who are to be the pillars of the new movement. The importance of this act is underlined by his spending the night praying in the hills. These are to be men whom God wants and who will be entrusted with the power to heal and to preach the new order. And the number twelve, the same as the tribes of Israel, indicates that they are to constitute a new Israel, one rejoicing in the presence of God instead of moribund regulations and traditions.

With his newly appointed cabinet around him, Jesus then descends and meets the people "on a level place" to teach and heal them. This contrasts sharply with the emphasis in Matthew 5, where Jesus goes up into the mountain to give the sermon partially recorded here. Possibly the source from which both writers drew did not specify a place and each provided a different location from pure conjecture. Luke's basis for setting the sermon on the plain would seem to be the pattern from Exodus 24, where Moses received the law on the mountain but then descended to give it to the people.

Luke is obviously concerned to emphasize two things. First, the wide territory represented by the crowd—it embraces all of Palestine and even the outlying districts of Tyre and Sidon. And, second, the continued connection of Jesus' activities with the program he announced in the synagogue at Nazareth; he uses his power from God to effect healing for the sick and release for the captives.

PRAYER

O God, Jesus obviously saw a link between choosing disciples and his ongoing work of healing and liberating people. Have I served that link in my own time? Enable me to ponder this to my edification, that I may be used in any way that pleases you, for the sake of your new order. Amen.

A SERMON FOR THE NEW ISRAEL

*L*ike Matthew's Sermon on the Mount (Matthew 5–7), Luke's Sermon on the Plain begins with the beatitudes, describing the blessedness of those who are gathered up in the new realm of God. This section forms a natural extension of Luke 4:16-30, in which Jesus defines his ministry as being to the poor, the sick, the outcast, and the oppressed.

Thus the "woes" that follow in Luke's version (Matthew does not report any woes in the sermon) are most appropriate, for they are spoken rhetorically of all those who will miss the heavenly realm because their riches, fine foods, present joys, and respectability deafen them to the word of the gospel. Some commentators have conjectured that this section of woes was added to the text by the early church and was not really spoken by Jesus. But if we recall the extensive list of woes Jesus directed against the Pharisees in Matthew 23, we should not so readily question the authenticity of these woes.

Matthew lists nine beatitudes, while Luke provides only four. And there is another notable difference in the two lists: Matthew has *spiritualized* his. That is, he has Jesus speak of "the poor in spirit" and those who "hunger and thirst after righteousness." Luke's Jesus, however, speaks of real poverty, real hunger, and real sorrow. The point he thus preserves is that God is going to look after the little ones of the earth and produce a great revolution in which the poor will receive what the rich have possessed. This is consistent with what John the Baptist predicted in Luke 3, that the high places would be brought low and the low places raised up, as well as with Jesus' sermon in the synagogue at Nazareth (Luke 4).

PRAYER

I am frightened again, dear God, by Luke's insistence that your realm is for those at the other end of the human spectrum from myself. Grant that my fear may be instructive and that I may learn to share what I have and who I am with all of your little ones. For my redemption's sake, amen.

THE LAW OF LOVE

This passage of the Sermon on the Plain is Luke's equivalent of Paul's famous "love chapter," 1 Corinthians 13. It is set here in Jesus' sermon to indicate the absolute centrality of the loving spirit in God's new realm.

To appreciate it fully, we must recall the ethic of the old Israel with which it contrasts, which taught "an eye for an eye and a tooth for a tooth." The heart of the Mosaic law was the love of God and a careful adherence to the commandments. In practice, respect for the commandments had deteriorated into mere legalism—doing precisely what was required of one and not a smidgen more!

Jesus takes away nothing from loving God—in fact, on another occasion he says that loving God is the first commandment (Luke 10:25-28). But he seeks to avoid the spiritual and ethical impasse of the old legal system by describing those who are under God's new rule as people who love and who, therefore, go beyond the requirements in their generous concern for others. They bless those who curse them, pray for those who abuse them, lend goods where there is little hope of return, and forgive those whom the law would never forgive. In short, they are inwardly motivated to behave in a manner that completely transcends the rule of law.

The genius of this way of life, of course, is that it rewards the person who has a loving spirit with joy and peace that cannot be had on other terms. The person who keeps the law faithfully may feel self-satisfied and righteous. But the one with a loving spirit feels something even better: an exuberance and sense of life akin to that of "the Most High"!

PRAYER

My mind has known the truth of these words for a long time, O God, but I have forgotten it in my spirit. Rescue me, I pray, from the inadequacy of merely doing what is required, and give me the great joy of living selflessly, as you live. Through Jesus, who is a perfect example, amen.

LIVING GENEROUSLY

The "law of love" summarized in the preceding verses is now par-ticularized in two very concrete ways.

First, love is applied to the critical spirit. For most of us, this is one of the most difficult matters in living the Christian life. Even if we manage to appear outwardly generous to people, it is hard to keep critical thoughts and opinions from cropping up in our mind. We quickly think, "Oh, that is the wrong thing to say or do," when we see others behaving as they do. We keep mental notebooks on the actions and speeches of others, and later hold these against the persons. But Jesus says that if we are truly caught up in the sense of love engendered by the new reign of God, we will experience an over-whelming feeling of generosity toward others and their faults or mistakes.

Second, love is applied to the matter of forgiveness. The Jewish law required equitable treatment of others, and compensation when equity was breached. But it did not extend to the matter of true forgiveness. Forgiveness was thought to belong to God alone, and was sought by individuals who had sinned against God's holiness. When we really expe-rience the presence of God in the heavenly realm, Jesus was teaching, we not only have our own forgiveness but readily extend it to others as well.

The overall result of this loving spirit will be a fullness of life we can only begin to imagine now. As we learn to give full measure—a wonderful term from the marketplace, common to every Jew's daily experience—we shall find heaping measures coming back to us. There is a delightful reciprocity in things. When we share the good life of God's Spirit, we begin to find it everywhere.

PRAYER

A careful holding of grudges is too often the bane of my existence, O God. Teach me to be more profligate, more spontaneous, as I reflect on how generous you have been to me. Then I shall find all existence spiced with your presence. Amen.

WORDS FOR DISCIPLES

*J*esus had said that part of his ministry had to do with "recovering of sight to the blind" (Luke 4:18). While he meant this literally, it also had a great deal of figurative truth, as we see from this passage. Being able to see matters clearly was regarded as essential in a disciple. Otherwise, Jesus' followers would produce the wrong kind of followers of their own.

If they had truly learned all they could from him, then they would produce good fruit, the way healthy trees do. Filled with the Spirit of God, they would exude that Spirit of sweetness and goodness wherever they went. If that Spirit was not in them, they would misrepresent the new realm by saying they were Jesus' disciples when in fact they were merely providing inferior fruit.

The person who is truly a follower of the Messiah, and has learned the deep truths of the Spirit, will be like one who lays a solid foundation for a house, not like one who is in haste to get the house up and so builds it on a flat sandbar by the river without troubling to dig down and lay the foundation on the bedrock.

As Luke has arranged this material, it is an extended exhortation to thorough learning and discipleship, so that the follower of Jesus really becomes like the Master. Then God's realm will truly flourish in the world.

PRAYER

I realize, O God, that I am too prone to give you second-rate obedience instead of wholehearted discipleship. I am lazy about studying and learning what a follower of Jesus should know and practice. I do not spend enough time each day in prayer and meditation. Help me to begin again and lay a better foundation before the floods of life come and sweep away the little I have done. I want to see clearly and behave lovingly, for Jesus' sake. Amen.

THE FAITH OF A FOREIGNER

*L*uke has already ended his report of Jesus' Sermon on the Plain, but he may well have placed this story of the Roman centurion here as an illustration of the kind of life advocated in the sermon. The centurion is clearly a remarkable human being. Although technically an officer of the enemy occupation forces, he has behaved respectfully and lovingly toward the captive citizenry under his command. He has constructed a synagogue for their worship and educational needs, even though their religion differs vastly from his own, and has apparently shown his love for the people in other ways. When the elders from the synagogue come to bring Jesus to heal his slave who is very ill—possibly a Jew who is a member of the synagogue—the centurion treats Jesus with the kind of respect normally reserved for kings and potentates. "I am not worthy to have you come under my roof," he says. "Only speak the word, and let my servant be healed" (vv. 6-7). Beneath these humble words lay a great thoughtfulness. If Jesus were an Orthodox Jew, entering the home of a foreigner would have been considered defilement for him. The centurion probably expected that this was the case and wished to spare Jesus this transgression of his native custom.

"I tell you," exclaimed Jesus, "not even in Israel have I found such faith" (v. 9). The faith was obviously in Jesus' power to cure the man's slave. But it was also in a way of life that lay at the heart of Jesus' teaching. This centurion was a great example of the loving spirit of the heavenly realm.

PRAYER
Dear God, give me a loving spirit like this. Help me to see that the essence of true religion is in how I respond to the poor, weak, and oppressed of the world—not in how faultless I am about matters of religious dogma. Through Jesus, who lived this way himself, amen.

AN ACT OF COMPASSION

*T*his story of a dramatic resuscitation has rather clear theological import. Like Elijah in 1 Kings 17:17-24 and Elisha in 2 Kings 3:32-37, Jesus is seen as a prophet acting in the power of God to raise the dead. In this regard, the story serves as a preparation for the passage to follow, in which John the Baptist questions whether Jesus is the one "who is to come."

But Luke is obviously carried away in the telling by more than theological consideration. The picture is enough to bring tears to the eyes of the sternest of viewers. Jesus comes upon a funeral procession in a small town. In the slow, mournful custom of the region, the procession winds through the narrow streets, led by the family, the professional weepers, and the coffin or bier of the deceased. Apparently the poor widow is in this case the only family member and so will be left alone in the world—a terrible lot for an older woman in her culture.

It is a stark drama that greets Jesus as he arrives upon the scene—the mourning clothes, the loud wails of lamentation, the sight of the single woman accompanying the body of her son. It is precisely the kind of setting he has said the new order of God addresses.

"Do not weep," he comforts the mother (v. 13). He puts his hand on the coffin—considered a defilement in traditional religion—and halts the procession.

"Young man," he says, "rise!" (v. 14). And the young man does.

It would be impossible to describe accurately the scene that follows. The people are jubilant—not merely because their friend's son has been raised, but because God has sent "a great prophet" into their midst! Small wonder that word about him spread like a windswept fire in dry grass to all the surrounding areas.

PRAYER

Your new order, O God, has power even over death. Let this beautiful story dwell in my heart and mind until I am no longer afraid of my own mortality. In the name of him who bids the dead to rise, amen.

WHAT YOU HAVE SEEN AND HEARD

*T*his is a wonderful summary passage in the Gospel. Luke began his narrative by telling about the birth of John the Baptist and the relationship between Mary and Elizabeth, John's mother. Now he weaves John into the story again, this time to send his disciples to Jesus to ask if he is really the one to come or if they should be looking for another.

Jesus had been busy, as usual, curing the sick, giving sight to the blind, and driving out evil spirits. The timing of the arrival of the men from John couldn't have been better.

"Look around you," Jesus said in effect. "See what has been happening here. There are two men who were blind a few minutes ago. That man over there, the one hopping about, had been lame all his life. Here is a little band of people who came from a leper colony. There is no trace of their disease. This woman was dead. This child was not even breathing when her father brought her to me, and now she is playing with her friends. And these people are not wealthy land owners. They are all the poor, the little people, the forgotten ones.

"Go back and tell your master John what your eyes have seen. Then let him judge whether I am the one or he should wait for another."

Of course, the entire scenario conforms perfectly to what Jesus had promised in the synagogue at Nazareth when he read from the scroll of Isaiah. It was all now being fulfilled in their midst.

PRAYER

Like John the Baptist, O God, I long for confirmation. I want to know for sure that Jesus is the one all history was waiting for, and that now all history looks back to. Give me eyes to see what he has done and is doing in the world around me. And then let me praise your goodness and wisdom for the new order that is among us. For his name's sake, amen.

MORE THAN A PROPHET

*W*hen John's men have gone back to tell the Baptist what wonderful things they have seen Jesus doing, and how he must undoubtedly be the Messiah sent from God, Jesus ruminates about John and what a great figure he is. Perhaps some of his own followers have expressed disdain for John because he was such an unattractive figure living in the wilderness. "What did you expect?" Jesus asks them. He isn't a soft, well-groomed city man. He lives in the desert where he listens to the voice of God. He is a prophet—and more than a prophet. He is the forerunner of the new realm, which means that he is even greater than the prophetic figures of old. God has highly honored him.

And yet, Jesus adds, even the least of his own followers who has seen the heavenly realm is greater than John. This is Luke's way of emphasizing that John was the last of the old order and Jesus the beginning of the new.

Jesus' commendation of John apparently pleases many in the crowd who were once disciples of John, but it raises murmurs of dissent among the scribes and Pharisees, who have been unwilling to accept the baptism of repentance. Noting this, Jesus muses about the ones who hold back and are unwilling to be caught up in a renewal movement. They are like children who hang around the marketplace—perhaps Jesus is watching some as he speaks—and complain that others will not do things their way. They have not liked John because he is too strict and ascetic, and they do not like Jesus because he is too free and uninhibited in both his actions and his relationships.

The last word, "Nevertheless, wisdom is vindicated by all her children" (v. 35), is probably a proverb expressing a spirit of tolerance. We would say, "It takes all kinds to make a world."

PRAYER

O God, I am often as fickle as the scribes and Pharisees, liking in one person what I dislike in another. Give me a heart of compassion, that I may accept even my enemies in prayer and thanksgiving. Through Jesus, who forgave from his cross, amen.

A LESSON IN JOY

*P*erhaps this passage should be entitled "Guess Who's Coming to Dinner." Simon the Pharisee was probably a wealthy man who liked to give lavish dinners and have interesting guests. He no doubt invited Jesus because Jesus was the most talked-about person in the city. The men were apparently reclining in the Roman manner, with their shoulders toward the table and their feet behind them, and the woman with the jar of ointment simply approached Jesus in the courtyard or through an open door without his seeing her. Before she could get the flask open to anoint him, she began weeping, so that her tears fell on his feet. Overcome by emotion, she loosened her long hair (as no ordinary woman would have done) and began wiping the tears with her hair.

Simon, who knew the woman, was inwardly outraged, and Jesus could read it in his face. Perhaps with genuine compassion for Simon, and not as a rebuke, Jesus told him the parable of the two debtors and then applied it to the present situation. The nameless woman was like the debtor who had been forgiven a king's ransom—she had much to celebrate and be grateful for. Simon, on the other hand, had had no such difficulties in his life. He was a man of careful behavior and suspicious nature who did not know how to love and rejoice as she did.

There is a similar story in Mark 14:3-9 about a woman who came into the house of Simon the leper and anointed Jesus' head in anticipation of his death and burial; John 12:1-8 identifies her as Mary, the sister of Lazarus, and again indicates it is for his burial, but changes the story to an anointing of the feet. Luke is possibly drawing on the same story, but uses it to proclaim Jesus' compassion, not his death and burial. In this version, he defends the woman against the unfriendly attitude of Simon the Pharisee and tells her that her sin—the behavior that has cut her off from "decent" society—is forgiven.

Luke's picture is clear: Jesus is forming the new Israel out of people summarily rejected by the legalists of the old Israel.

PRAYER

Thank you, dear God, for the grace of this story. I am more like Simon than the woman, I fear. Help me to see that my sin is as great as hers, and, therefore, my forgiveness even more to be prized. Through him who said we should celebrate whenever we have the bridegroom with us, amen.

THOSE WHO PROVIDE

When I was a very young minister, I sometimes resented the way the churches I served depended on the donations of certain wealthy or powerful people in the community. It seemed to me that these people often took too much pride in the fact that they were able out of their plenty to give what was needed while others could not.

As I have grown older, however, I have come to think differently about this matter. It is simply part of the stewardship of the wealthy that they help to support the church in noticeable ways. Often their gifts are their honest efforts to give back to God something that bespeaks their appreciation for the blessings of God in their lives.

This passage of Scripture has helped me to understand that this practice has roots in the very ministry of Jesus himself. Here we learn that, in addition to the twelve men who followed Jesus, there were certain women in his entourage as well—women, like Mary Magdalene, whose lives had been greatly changed by his ministry—who actually "provided for them out of their resources" (v. 3). In other words, they were supporting the work of Jesus and the disciples with their monetary gifts.

Now, when I enter a great church building like Westminster Abbey or the cathedral at Chartres or Riverside Church, I usually breathe a prayer of thanksgiving for the provenance of the great benefactors whose devotion to Christ was such that they helped to erect those beautiful monuments to his name. The wealthy as well as the poor have a stake in the new realm of God.

PRAYER

Sometimes I forget, O God, how important my own gifts are to the maintenance and support of the work of Christ in the world. Make me more sensitive to the places and institutions and activities that could make wonderful use of my resources, and give me a generous spirit. In the name of Jesus, who elicits the best from all of us, amen.

THE SOWER GOES OUT

*A*t this point in the Gospel, Luke represents Jesus as leaving the synagogue setting and moving more actively through the country-side, stopping in villages and cities along the way. He is like the sower in his parable, widely scattering seeds as he goes. Not everyone is able to hear the good news he preaches. And he knows that not everyone who seems to hear will be faithful to his message to the end. But that does not deter him from doing his work, for he knows that some will hear and believe and hold fast whatever the circumstances.

Many ministers, missionaries, and teachers I have known have been discouraged along their journeys by how few people seem to have under-stood and have been significantly affected by what they were trying to teach. It is easy to become discouraged when working with human beings, for we are so fickle and unpredictable.

But Jesus looked beyond the human situation to a rule of nature itself: It is only by sowing seed that one can expect any results at all. So he pictured a farmer striding through his fields, scattering seed from side to side. Some of the seed, the farmer knows, will fall on the rocks and not take root at all. Other seed will land on shallow soil where it may root superficially, germinate, and grow for a brief time; then when the season grows hot and there is no rain, it will wither and die. But a residue of the seed—perhaps only a small portion of it—will find its way into good soil deep enough to support its growth and maturity. The whole process is worth it for this last batch of seed and what it will bring forth from the good soil.

The work of God's realm can always be read in terms of this parable.

PRAYER

It frightens me, O God, to think that I might be the kind of soil in which the gospel springs up and then dies. Help me to ply my life with prayer and study and good relationships, that it may be enriched enough to support forever the good news that has had a beginning in it. Through him who understood about seeds and soils, amen.

LIGHTING OTHERS' WAYS

*T*he material in this brief passage is greatly compressed. Either Luke received it in this form and did not care to expand it, or he was simply in a hurry to get on to more narrative material—he was very fond of stories—and so alluded to some of Jesus' teachings in very telegraphic form.

The bit about the lamp and the lampstand we have met before, in the Sermon on the Mount in Matthew's Gospel (5:14-16), where it was introduced by the saying, "You are the light of the world." Seen in this perspective, what Luke says would follow very nicely the parable of the sower and the seeds, for it would relate the disciple's letting his or her light shine to being good soil for the seed of the gospel. That is, those who are good soil will also let their witnesses be seen by others.

Verse 17 is more problematic. As a saying, it is probably not related to the saying before it, but its location next to the saying in verse 16 was possibly suggested by the word *light* in each. It seems to be an apocalyptic saying, a reminder that in the judgment all things will come to light. This becomes sufficient warrant for another apocalyptic saying, verse 18, which warns that at the end there will be a terrible shakeup in which the possessions of some folks will be taken from them and given to others who already seem to have more.

The theme uniting all three sayings is the extreme seriousness and urgency with which receiving the new order of God should be treated. The new realm, after all, takes precedence over everything in our lives. We should, therefore, take care to live as faithfully as we can, letting our lights light the ways of others seeking to find the realm for themselves.

PRAYER

No matter how long I study the Bible and my faith, O God, there are always puzzles and mysteries remaining in both. Let them suffice to remind me that life is often deeper than I suspect, and you alone hold the key to life eternal. Through Jesus, who understood everything, amen.

CHRIST'S MOTHER AND BROTHERS

*O*nce more Luke gives us a very abbreviated piece of the tradition that had grown up around Jesus, this time about the occasion when Jesus' mother and brothers came to see him and take him home. There is a much fuller account in Mark 3:20-35, which sets the incident in a larger context where Jesus is healing and casting out demons and his enemies are circulating the rumor that he himself has a demon and is out of his mind. Mary and the other family members appear out of concern for him, probably wishing to take him home and care for him until he is better.

In Mark, the crowds are so great that the family cannot get inside where Jesus is teaching, so they send him word that they are there. Jesus' comment that those gathered around him are his family is not intended as a rebuke to his blood family, but only as a comment about the nature of the Messiah, who belongs to all the believers and followers.

The same, more generous meaning surely applies here in the Lukan passage as well, and would be clearer if Luke had given the space to the incident to amplify it. It is strange that he didn't, as we know from the beautiful stories about Mary at the beginning of the Gospel that he was extremely sympathetic with her role in the coming of the Messiah.

Still, there is a possibility that, having shown us Mary's involvement in the birth of the Messiah, Luke thought it important to stress that she was a mere vessel and that the important thing was that Jesus was God's Son. Jesus' mild rebuke to her in Luke 2:49, when she chided him for not being with the family as it returned to Galilee from Jerusalem and he said she should have expected that he would be in his Father's house, would have been a clue to the psychological distancing of the Messiah from his earthly mother. Our present passage, then, could have been deliberately shortened from the Markan version in order to reinforce this distancing.

PRAYER

There is often pain and misunderstanding in human relationships, O God. But it is wonderful to know that we are all the brothers and sisters of Jesus—a holy family in him—and that we shall enjoy being united in your heavenly realm. Amen.

AUTHORITY OVER THE ELEMENTS

*M*uch of the conflict in Jesus' ministry was over his authority to do the things he did, especially forgiving sins and teaching things contrary to the emphases of the scribes and Pharisees. When he healed the paralyzed man who was let down through the roof (Luke 5:17-26), he first told the man his sins were forgiven. The scribes and Pharisees present were outraged at this and demanded to know how he could presume to forgive anyone's sins; that was God's domain alone. Jesus then told the man to take up his bed and walk home, demonstrating Jesus' power and authority in a visible way.

This story of quelling the storm at sea is a similar witness to his singular authority. As it follows a section of the Gospel concerned with his teachings, the quelling of the storm actually functions like the restoration of the paralyzed man's ambulatory functions: It validates what has preceded it, in this case the teachings.

On the whole, Luke is less concerned about the theological ramifications of the story than are Matthew and Mark (Matt. 8:23-27; Mark 4:35-41), and more interested in the simple human emotions displayed in it. He shows us Jesus as the obvious master of the situation, undismayed by the storm, in fact sleeping through it until awakened by the frightened disciples. And the disciples' fear, which is obvious, is actually less interesting than their astonishment after Jesus has calmed the sea and the winds. "Who then is this," they stammer, "that he commands even the winds and the water, and they obey him?" (v. 25).

The very men who have not appeared astonished at his ability to heal the sick, to cast out demons, and to preach the approaching realm of God have been signally amazed at two events involving their own natural element, the sea: first, when he commanded them to let down their nets into the deep and they caught a great draught of fish (Luke 5:1-11); and now here, when he rebukes the wind and the waves, and they obey him.

PRAYER

Who, indeed, is this, O God, that he has such power in the natural world? His gift was obviously more than psychological or polemical; it extended even to the inanimate things of nature. Draw me again to his mystery, and let me bow down in fear and wonder. For I am unworthy to form my own conclusions, but must rely on your Spirit. Amen.

THE LORD OF ALL

*L*uke probably saw real significance in telling this story after the one about Jesus' calming of the sea. In a sense, the two events are linked by the fact that they are parts of the same excursion. Jesus crosses the Sea of Galilee to the country around Gerasa, on the eastern coast of the sea, and then, after healing the Gerasene man, returns to the Galilean side of the sea, probably near Capernaum. The point of it all is that Jesus shows his mastery of both the sea and the demons in the land beyond the sea. In keeping with Luke's continuous emphasis, he is master everywhere in the world, not only in Galilee and Judea.

As a doctor, Luke probably found great personal interest in the stories of Jesus' healings, and he surely was fascinated by this report featuring a man so devastated by his demons that he could no longer live at home, but had to dwell away from other people in the tombs along the coast. It also suited Luke's purpose that there was a kind of universal symbolism in the name of the unclean spirits inhabiting the man, which was Legion. A legion was a Roman division of soldiers numbering four to six thousand men. If the man had this many demons in him, he was far more afflicted than any other person in the Gospels, and thus a real challenge to Jesus' authority. For Jesus to conquer thousands of demons at once, and on a foreign shore, clearly spelled his universal power.

When we remember Luke's feeling for the foreign mission of the church in the book of Acts, we know what special interest he must have had in the witnessing of the cured man to the people of his own region. It would have been important preparation for the later establishment of a Christian colony there.

PRAYER

It is a wonder, O God, that the power of Jesus not only crossed the Sea of Galilee to cure the demon-ridden man of Geresa but also crossed an ocean to touch my life. Teach me to live more constantly in awe of this power and mystery, that I, like the Gerasene, may share my awareness of it with others. For your realm's sake, amen.

A DAUGHTER OF THE OPPOSITION

*T*here was probably some human drama behind this story that did not get told in the Gospel, for Jairus was president of his local synagogue, probably in Capernaum, at a time when the religious leaders were crystallizing their opposition to Jesus. He may well have been torn between his political position and his personal need for Jesus' power to cure his daughter—his *only* daughter. When he at last decided to throw political caution to the winds and approach Jesus, he desperately threw himself at the Master's feet.

The story is interrupted midway by the story of the woman who touched Jesus in a crowd and was healed. Her condition has been identified as menorrhagia, an unceasing menstrual flow. Under the law, this made her as unclean as if she had leprosy or some other dreaded disease. It was, therefore, daring of her to touch Jesus, for the law forbade her to touch anyone. But again, as in the case of the leper Jesus touched in Luke 5:12-13, instead of his being infected by the unclean person, power went out from him to heal the unclean one.

It is amusing to note that Luke, in telling this story, omits a note from Mark 5:26, that the woman had suffered much at the hands of many physicians who had taken all her money. As a physician himself, Luke is perhaps protecting the reputation of his fraternity!

When Jesus had healed the woman and sent her away in peace, word came that Jairus's daughter had died. Jairus informed Jesus, releasing him from going further. But Jesus challenged the synagogue leader to have as much faith as the woman who had worked her way through the crowd to touch him. "Only believe in the arrival of God's new order," he said in effect, "and she will be well." Taking the inner circle of disciples and the girl's parents with him, and brushing aside the scoffers, he entered where the girl was, took her by the hand, and lifted her up as though he had awakened her from a mere nap.

PRAYER

Thank you, dear God, for these marvelous vignettes from the life of Jesus. What knowledge of people he had, and what compassion and power! Let me have faith like this woman's, that, if I will but reach out to touch him, life-giving power will flow into me. Amen.

THE ROLE OF THE DISCIPLES

*T*his passage serves as a pivot between the first part of Luke's Gospel and the preparation of the disciples to go to Jerusalem and experience the Passion there. It is essentially a picture of how the disciples helped in the ministry of Jesus and how he sustained them as a community.

The missionary thrust of verses 1-6 is obviously different from that of Luke 8:1-3, in which Jesus and a large company of followers moved together in an itinerant ministry financed by some wealthy women. Now the disciples are sent out in twos, in order to cover a wider territory, and are given orders to take nothing along for the journey but to move swiftly from place to place, depending on the hospitality of friends where they can. When people are unreceptive to their preaching of God's new order and performing acts of healing, they are to use the ancient Jewish ritual of shaking Gentile dust from their feet when reentering the holy land by shaking the dust of unbelievers from their sandals. The disciples represent, after all, the new Israel of God.

The hubbub raised around the country by this intensive, all-out mission attracted the attention of Herod, who had put John the Baptist to death. Now his uneasy conscience made him wonder if the flurry of new religious fervor caused by Jesus and the disciples was the work of John come back to life. The terse statement that Herod "tried to see him" is a foreshadowing of his meeting with Jesus during the Passover in Jerusalem (Luke 23:8).

The return of the disciples from their barnstorming ministry became an occasion for Jesus to draw aside with them in order to hear reports of their activities and offer them spiritual renewal. The crowds learned about Jesus' presence, as usual, and surrounded him and the disciples, bringing their sick who needed to be cured.

PRAYER

O God, the church itself is one of your greatest miracles—the long line of preachers, teachers, healers, pastors, and others who do your work of ministry among the people; and the many laypersons who witness and pray and support the work in every way. Let me never lose sight of this, in spite of the failure of particular persons and congregations I have known. Through Jesus, who commissions all of us, amen.

A MEAL AT THE END OF THE DAY

*I*n our last passage, the disciples had just returned from their first missionary journey, bringing reports of all that had happened and drawing aside with Jesus, when the crowds of people appeared. Now, at the end of the day when everyone is tired and hungry, Jesus orders the disciples to feed the crowds. They protest that they have only five loaves of bread and two fish. Jesus tells them to have the people sit down "in groups of about fifty each" (v. 14). He blesses the food, breaks it, and gives it to the disciples to set before the crowd.

Following hard upon the story of the disciples' return, this narrative not only shows the power of the Savior to feed his people in the wilderness, but also displays a key role to be played by the disciples in the liturgical life of the future church. As the feeding is a clear foreshadowing of the Lord's Supper, which is always a miraculous meal in the midst of human wilderness, so they are to conceive of themselves as the agents of Christ at the table as well as in the pulpit or by the sickbed.

The twelve baskets of fragments left over at the end of the meal—one for each of the disciples—bespeak the abundance of life we find in the Messiah. And, if the disciples were to eat the leftovers in the days to come, they also indicate that he will provide with great sufficiency for the needs of his servants.

PRAYER

Much of my life, O God, seems to be spent in wilderness places of the spirit. And yet you are always there, creating abundance out of little and feeding my soul until it can eat no more. Help me to respond by being a faithful follower. Through him who always looked up to heaven before breaking his bread, amen.

A NEW STAGE OF UNDERSTANDING

*J*esus had been teaching the disciples for months now, and had even sent them out on their own to preach and heal. It was time to raise their understanding of his mission to a new level. He himself had doubtless begun to see the future more clearly since John's violent death at the hands of Herod. The conversation began on the reports of the disciples' missionary journeys. Who were the people saying Jesus was? Accustomed to thinking of the future in terms of the past, they had said he must surely be John or Elijah or another prophet already dead.

Next, Jesus pressed them on their own thinking. Peter spoke for the group. They had come to the conclusion that he must be "the Messiah of God." Jesus surely approved this response, as Matthew has him doing (Matt. 16:17-19), but warned them not to tell anyone, lest it provoke an official reaction before he was ready. He must suffer and die, he said, and the disciples themselves would also suffer; but God would give them victory, symbolized in Jesus' resurrection.

There can be little doubt that Luke used the next story about the transfiguration as an illustration to the disciples of what Jesus' resurrection would be like. They beheld him in strangely altered form, with face and clothing dazzlingly radiant, conversing with Moses and Elijah, the two most popular figures in Hebrew history. They were speaking of Jesus' "departure"—actually, in the Greek, his *exodus*. As Moses had led the Israelites out of Egypt to form a new nation, Jesus was about to lead his followers into a new realm. Clearly, God was giving the disciples a picture of the transcendent Christ to verify Jesus' prediction that he would be raised up shortly after being slain.

A cloud, like the one that came over the Israelites in the wilderness, came over them and terrified them. And out of it they heard a voice saying, "This is my Son, my Chosen; listen to him!" (v. 35). It was a rare mystical experience, and it would later help them to perceive what was happening after the crucifixion.

PRAYER

O God, I wonder how many experiences like this I miss because I do not spend my nights and days in prayer as the disciples did. Teach me to apply myself to acts of devotion, that the mysteries of the faith may become more palpable in my own life. Through him who has shown us the way, amen.

A TINGE OF DISAPPOINTMENT

*T*he new level of understanding among some disciples appears to have been unmatched among others. When Jesus, James, John, and Peter came down from their mountaintop experience, a man came to Jesus who had been feeling great frustration with the other disciples. They had been unable to heal his only son of the epileptic convulsions that often seized him.

Jesus cured the boy, but not before erupting angrily at the failure of the disciples to trust completely enough in the presence of the new order to do the work themselves. His anxiety is clearly the product of the urgency he now felt. The time was short, and they must be able to carry on when he was gone.

How little they understood is emphasized by the argument they had about which was the greatest. Jesus had only recently spoken of his own suffering role; now they were contending about their honor and glory. Jesus gave them an object lesson they would never forget. Setting a little child beside him—perhaps the one he had just cured of epilepsy—he told them that there was no such traditional status in God's realm. Anyone who was kind to a child in his name was great in the eyes of God.

The phrase "in my name" evidently spurred John to comment that they had seen a stranger using Jesus' name to perform exorcisms and had forbidden this unauthorized association. But Jesus wasn't concerned. It was the religious leaders who would not use his name that really troubled him.

PRAYER

O God, I, too, am prone to worry about my greatness. Forgive me for this smallness in my character, and lead me into deeper faith and commitment, in order that my dearest joy may lie in serving your little ones. Through Jesus, who died humbly at the hands of those who lived proudly, amen.

ON TO JERUSALEM

*A*t this point, Luke pictures Jesus as turning toward Jerusalem for the final encounter with the religious leaders there. But the trip is anything but direct, and really appears to be a kind of suspense vehicle within which Luke can continue to impart many of Jesus' teachings.

The trip from Galilee to Jerusalem normally took travelers through Samaria. The Samaritans and Jews had long been at odds, one side claiming that the holy center of life was at Mt. Gerizim and the other that it was in Jerusalem. Jesus' intention of climaxing his ministry in Jerusalem, therefore, provoked the hostilities of the Samaritans in one village, and this in turn stirred the wrath of James and John. As Elijah had called down fire from heaven (2 Kings 1:9-16), they wanted to do so now, proving the authenticity of their mission for God. But Jesus had rejected such temptations of power early in his ministry (Luke 4:1-13), and now rebuked the disciples for entertaining such a notion.

The commitment to God's realm required of followers is revealed in Luke 9:57-62. What was happening was of such intense consequence that there was no room for self-consideration or even for the traditional properties of life. Jesus saw the conflict with evil coming to a head in a very short time. The nearest analogy would be that of a military call-up; in a moment of national crisis, there is no time for personal errands.

PRAYER

I am accused, O God, by these verses. I, too, am likely to wish fire on those who resist the gospel. Yet, at the same time, I am prone to put personal errands and requirements ahead of serving you. Forgive me on both counts, I pray, and create a new spirit within me, that I may both respect the rights of others and act with a proper urgency for your new order. Amen.

THE FALL OF SATAN

*T*he urgency of this particular phase of Jesus' mission is now shown by the appointment of seventy others to help with his work. The number is symbolic, for there were thought to be seventy nations in the world at that time. These new appointees are to go simply, without encumbrance, not worrying about personal properties. Their message is simple: The kingdom of God has come near to you. This will alert the devout but infuriate others. Against the latter, they are to shake the dust from their feet.

The seventy return from their mission in great joy—one of Luke's dominant themes—reporting that even the demons were powerless before them. Jesus' response is to tell them of a vision he has had, of Satan plunging from heaven. Hebrew thought had always pictured Satan as being located in heaven, where he acted as a kind of prosecuting lawyer against the godly (cf. Job 1 and Zech. 3:1-5). Jesus in this vision foresaw Satan's complete defeat and expulsion from heaven, so that he could no longer trouble the sons and daughters of men. A great victory was in the offing. This was, and still is, the good news of God's realm.

Jesus is exultant, sensing the nearness of God's victory. He gives thanks to God that God has entrusted the realm to good, simple folk like these messengers and not to the religious masters of the land. They are so fresh, so jubilant, so willing to accept at face value what God is doing. In the same mood, he reflects that only God could choose the one who would be his Son. The old men of Israel, with all their wisdom, could not do it. Only God.

Turning again to the disciples, his companions in the mission, he exclaims, "Blessed are the eyes that see what you see!" (v. 23). How many prophets and kings of Israel had wanted to see it and could not! Simeon in the Temple had seen it—and Anna—and now they are seeing it. There will never be anything in the history of the world more wonderful to see!

PRAYER

When I shut my eyes, O God, I can see it, too: the lion lying down with the lamb, the armaments of the world beaten into plowshares, the hungry fed, and the poor walking through the city like rulers. Satan has fallen, and is falling, and will one day fall for good. Your realm come, amen.

THE REAL WAY TO LIFE

*T*his wonderful story has been told and retold around the world, and has no doubt in its artless simplicity converted the attitudes of millions of people about what obeying the law of God really means.

The lawyer—a scribe—probably asked his question about eternal life more to test Jesus than to get a true answer. He got far more than he bargained for. First, Jesus turned the question on him. Then, when he pressed further, Jesus gave him the story of the generous Samaritan.

The characters of the parable are interesting: a priest and a Levite, both central members of the religious elite of Israel, and a Samaritan, one of the people whom Jews regarded with hostility and prejudice. Luke may have located the story here because of the unfavorable mention of Samaritans a few verses earlier (Luke 9:51-56). He may also have had in mind the movement of the gospel outward from Judea to Samaria and "the end of the earth" (Acts 1:8).

The man who was beaten was heading away from Jerusalem, toward Jericho. The fact that the priest and the Levite each passed on the other side indicates that they were going in the opposite direction, toward Jerusalem, possibly to serve their turns in the Temple. As the poor victim was half-dead, there was no way that they could be certain without touching him that he had not already died, and to do that would have defiled them, according to ceremonial law. They obeyed the law, but missed the whole point of it.

The unorthodox Samaritan, on the other hand, really fulfilled the law while not even being concerned to obey it. The lawyer could only admit that the Samaritan was the real neighbor to the man, not the priest or the Levite.

When we think about it, we realize that Jesus' entire ministry is summarized in the action of the Samaritan. From the very outset, he chose to have compassion on the poor and oppressed rather than conform to the hundreds of rules and regulations governing the lives of the scribes and Pharisees.

PRAYER

O God, I have always admired Samaritans—people who live on the edge of respectable society, yet respond magnanimously to the needs of others. Help me to live more generously and spontaneously myself, that I may better understand the heart of Jesus. In his name, amen.

Day 233   *Luke 10:38-42*

THE MOST IMPORTANT THING

*T*he village Jesus is here reported to have entered is doubtless Bethany, which we know from John 11:1 to have been the home of Mary, Martha, and Lazarus. In terms of Luke's travel narrative it is highly unlikely that Jesus would have been in Bethany at this point, as it lay barely outside Jerusalem. What Luke has obviously done, then, is to place the story here, omitting the name of Bethany, because he sees a direct relationship between this little narrative and the parable of the Samaritan, which immediately precedes it. This helps us to identify more precisely Luke's own interpretation of the story.

In a way, the story is a gloss or comment on the parable of the Samaritan. Martha, who is anxious to serve Jesus properly, is really a Christian version of the priest and Levite in the parable. That is, she is deeply concerned to fulfill the law of proprieties. Mary, on the other hand, has the soul of the Samaritan. She is more concerned to respond in love than to conform to the rules or duties of the household.

It is surely unfair to brand the Marthas of the world unfavorably because of this passage—in her way, Martha was trying as hard as Mary to be a compassionate host. Our homes, churches, and other institutions would soon be in pitiable shape if it were not for the selfless service of caretaking persons.

Jesus' point—and Luke's—was more specific than that; namely, that the *first* obligation of a person is to give responsive love or compassion. When following the rules is put first, the most needful part—love—is often missed or omitted.

We should be actively involved in society for God—but not before we have taken time to pray and worship. We should work zealously for the church—but not put it before the people who lie outside the membership of the church. We should strive to improve human conditions for the poor, the weak, and the sick—but not without first truly caring for them as persons.

226

PRAYER

O God, it is much easier to feel self-righteous when I am Martha than when I am Mary. But I see through this story that love and adoration are more to be desired than busyness. Help me to be more like Mary, without forgetting the value of Martha. Amen.

Day 234   *Luke 11:1-13*

THE SPIRIT OF PRAYER

*I*t is helpful, if we wish to know how Luke felt about this material on prayer, to remember how prayer is treated in the book of Acts. Never in Acts does any Christian pray for anything for himself or herself. Always prayer is for God's realm and other persons. It is for the sick, the imprisoned, the unconverted.

Viewed in this light, the present passage is quickly understood to center on God's new order. "Your kingdom come" is the central petition of the model prayer Jesus gives the disciples. All the other phrases derive from this one. As kingdom people, we ask little for ourselves—only daily bread, not expensive feasts and clothes and property. The emphasis on *daily* bread reminds us of God's provision of manna to the Israelites during their wilderness years; like them, we are a pilgrim people. Our other concerns are to be compassionate and forgiving, as befits those who in the kingdom are forgiven and accepted, and not to be tested so severely that we abandon the faith.

Luke's version of the model prayer is considerably briefer than the one in Matthew 6:9-13, and scholars are confident that it is the more original of the two. Matthew's version has merely added liturgical phrases that do not significantly alter the meaning.

After giving the disciples a form of prayer based on the intimacy between children and their father—*Abba,* "father" or "daddy," was the everyday form of address for children to their beloved fathers—Jesus proceeded to speak of God's willingness to hear their prayers and respond to them. God will surely be as attentive as a friend who hears us knocking for help in the night, or as earthly fathers who try to give their children the foods they ask for.

While it is clear that we may ask for whatever we need, verse 13 makes it equally clear that the gift all Christians are to seek in their praying is the Holy Spirit. The overall emphasis of the passage, then, is a spiritual one, in keeping with the coming of the new order and the submission of the one praying to God's will. This is borne out again and again in the book of Acts.

PRAYER

Too much of my praying, dear God, has always been of an unspiritual nature, seeking what I wanted and not what I needed. What I have ever needed is a greater sense of your Spirit in my life. Help me to pray for that now, and to find the true joy to be known through prayer. For Jesus' sake, amen.

Day 235   *Luke 11:14-36*

THE SIGN OF JONAH

*I*f we are inclined to despair today over the shallowness of popular Christianity, we need only read this passage to know that things have not changed greatly since Jesus' time.

First, there were people who doubted the miracles Jesus was performing, and others who attributed them to Beelzebub, the prince of demons. Would Satan work against himself, Jesus asked, by casting out his own agents? What the people should see was that "the finger of God" (Exod. 8:19) was at work in their midst; then they would realize how near the realm of God was. Jesus had really entered Satan's citadel and was plundering it of souls.

Verses 24-26 appear to be a warning to those who had been cleansed of demons, lest they find themselves, like empty houses, suddenly invaded and filled with new demons.

As Jesus was talking, a woman in the crowd called out a word of praise roughly equivalent to "Your mother must really be proud of you." But Jesus turned off this word as a bit of mere sentimentality. What is important, he said, is to hear and keep God's Word.

Reflecting on those who kept asking for some kind of sign from heaven, Jesus then said that no sign would be given such an evil generation except the sign of Jonah the preacher. Jonah had gone to wicked Nineveh and preached the need for repentance, and the people of Nineveh had repented in sackcloth and ashes. Here was Jesus in a similar role, preaching the realm of God. That should be enough, if the people of his day were truly spiritual. But, as they were not, the people of Nineveh would accuse them in the day of judgment, for they had repented without special signs.

The sayings about light in verses 33-36 seem to fit the foregoing themes, although the last two verses have proven difficult for all commentators. They appear to recommend being truly able to see—which is the problem of most of the people in the crowd before Jesus, that they cannot see.

PRAYER

It is never easy, O God, to live a faithful spiritual life. Deliver me from error, I pray, and help me to cleave to what is good and true. Through him whose life is my most important guide, amen.

Day 236   *Luke 11:37–12:12*

WARNINGS AGAINST HYPOCRISY

*H*ere are several sayings of Jesus grouped around the general theme of hypocrisy and truth.

First are a number of scathing remarks about Pharisees and scribes, roughly paralleling those found in Matthew 23. The primary thrust of all the rebukes, or "woes," is that the highly orthodox Jews paid much attention to inconsequential matters of the law while neglecting the important matters—a charge in keeping with other teachings of Jesus. They fastidiously scoured the outside of the cup while completely neglecting the inside, which was more important. They went beyond the expectations of the law, tithing even their tiny herb gardens that were not worth bothering about; yet they completely ignored the question of justice for the poor and the matter of loving God. They were like unmarked graves, onto which unwary persons might stumble, defiling themselves by the contact. They constructed enormous burdens for the common folk to bear, and then refused to help them at all. Having held the key to salvation, they themselves refused to enter the door and, moreover, blocked the way so that others could not go in.

Clearly, they were obstructing the work of the Holy Spirit and would not be forgiven for this (Luke 12:10).

The disciples were warned to beware of the same kind of hypocrisy in their own lives. They would be tempted, when brought before the courts and tribunals, to lie and put on falsehoods to save themselves. But Jesus warned them not to join the hypocrites in this manner; they should not fear those who had only the power to hurt their bodies, but the One who had power to punish them by abandoning them forever. The God who cared even for the cheap, insignificant little sparrows could certainly be trusted to care about them when they suffered for the faith!

PRAYER

Being in love with your realm, O God, converts our natures, so that we no longer niggle over things of small consequence but address ourselves to larger issues, such as feeding the hungry, sheltering the homeless, healing the sick, and befriending the lonely. Help me to become an ambassador of your joy, disdaining all cost to myself. Through Jesus, in whom your light shines purely, amen.

Day 237   *Luke 12:13-24*

A WARNING IN A PARABLE

*D*iogenes is said to have given away all his possessions except a shard of pottery, which he used for drinking. Then he saw a small boy cupping his hands to drink, and threw away the shard.

Wise people have always realized that possessions can encumber life until it is barely fit for living. Jesus constantly warned the disciples of the tendency in all of us to enslave ourselves to what we have.

The man who came to him asking for a judgment did so because Mosaic law was always being interpreted by rabbis. But Jesus refused to accept the problem as a mere civil problem that could be solved by a judge's decision. Instead, he threw the burden back on the man himself, pointing out the importance of caring less about money and property.

The parable of the rich man is still a striking vehicle of truth for people who are careful about providing fiscally for their futures, yet absurdly heedless of their spiritual conditions. One wonders what would become of the capitalist way of life and an economy that depends on Detroit and Madison Avenue if many persons took the story as seriously as it deserves.

Considering Jesus' teachings to the disciples about trusting God to provide their daily needs—the model is still that of the Israelites' being fed each day in the wilderness—it is no wonder that Luke later pictures the early church as a fellowship of voluntary poverty, sharing from a common treasury. It raises an unavoidable question about our stewardship in the church today. Some churches hold more property than many business corporations, and have their most serious congregational squabbles over the maintenance of buildings. It is hard to believe that they have really considered the ravens or the lilies.

PRAYER

O God, I have never thought of myself as greedy; yet I am seriously concerned about financial security. Teach me so to apply myself to your new order that I may rise above my concern and be always free to live simply and generously. Through Jesus, who left a great spiritual legacy but no property, amen.

Day 238   *Luke 12:25-48*

LIVING FOR THE MASTER

*T*he picture here is of genuine enthusiasm in the Master's service. Being dressed for action meant wearing suitable clothes and not the usual long robes that would impede hard work or swift movement. Having the lamps burning also implied readiness, for the wicks must be trimmed and the lamps filled with oil. The disciples were to be like eager servants waiting up in the night for the master's return from a wedding feast. On returning and finding them so devoted, he would be so happy that he would reverse the normal roles, tucking his own robes into his belt and serving them at the table.

Possibly Luke knew the tradition on which John 13:2-10 is based, about Jesus' taking a towel and serving his disciples. But the symbolism of the feast and serving is not completely clear. Was Jesus going away for the feast and then returning to the disciples? Is this a picture of the *parousia*, or Second Coming? Peter's question in verse 41 is well put, but the answer seems enigmatic. In a way, the lessons apply to both the disciples and the crowds, including the scribes and Pharisees. Doubtless, too, the church saw meaning in them for itself.

It seems probable that Jesus saw the signs of a dark time coming for Israel, and, therefore, expected an imminent arrival of the great day of the Lord. In the face of this, he warned his followers to faithfully obey God's will at all times, so that no sudden cataclysm could take them unaware and result in spiritual disaster. As the special recipients of Christ's teachings, they would be held more accountable than others.

231

O God, I tremble to think how accountable I am; you have given me so many insights into the nature of your realm and your desire for my life. Yet, I am daily out of harmony with those insights. Help me to be motivated in new ways to fulfill your expectations for me, that I may rejoice in the coming of my Master. In his name I pray. Amen.

Day 239   *Luke 12:49–13:9*

A FIRE IN THE EARTH

*I*t is sometimes argued that Jesus and John the Baptist saw the coming of God's new order differently, but here is proof that Jesus, like John before him, viewed it as an occasion of extreme stress and suffering for many.

The "baptism" he said he must be baptized with was his death. Apparently he saw that as only the beginning of the apocalyptic horror. His very dying would divide households and nations. And we know how true a word that has been.

The signs of the coming of this difficult time, Jesus told the crowds, were all around them. They considered themselves good prophets of the weather; a cloud drifting in from the Mediterranean was enough to cause them to forecast rain. They should be more sensitive to the changing times, and should actively try to appease God, as one would try to appease a person suing him, even on the way to the magistrate's house!

Some people in the crowd raised a question about some Galileans Pilate had ordered killed in Jerusalem. Were they terrible sinners that this had happened to them? No, said Jesus, and he cited a tragedy involving Judeans themselves, when a tower collapsed, killing eighteen of them. They were no worse than other Jerusalemites, said Jesus, and it was useless to point to cases like this. What he meant, he said, was that they were *all* in for terrible times unless they repented. God would destroy an entire nation.

The parable of the fig tree was exactly to the point. The fig tree was a symbol of Israel. This tree was unproductive, taking nourishment from the soil and returning nothing, as Israel had from God. The owner said to destroy it. The foreman asked for a year in which to fertilize it and see if he could not make it productive. This is what the ministries of John and

Jesus were attempting to do for Israel. But if they could not turn the people toward the new order, the old nation was finished.

PRAYER

It is easy for me to be judgmental about Israel, O God, and to say that the people got precisely what they deserved. It is much harder for me to see that Jesus' words apply to my own moral and spiritual life as well. Help me to return to true worship in my life, and to feed others with the fruits of my devotion, lest I, too, be destroyed. Through him who was baptized in the flames, amen.

Day 240   *Luke 13:10-21*

THE SABBATH AND THE KINGDOM

*H*ow often we have seen people like this poor deformed woman and wished we could do something for them. We can imagine their wretchedness, and our compassion flows out to them. So it was with Jesus and this woman. When he saw her in her terrible condition, he instinctively called out to her and healed her. It was an impulsive act of love.

The behavior of the synagogue leader may also have been instinctive. He was accustomed to rules and regulations, and these dictated that no work was to be done on the sabbath—not even healing. "There are six days on which work ought to be done," he said over and over to the crowd. "Come on those days and be cured, and not on the sabbath day" (v. 14).

Some of the others were probably beginning to shake their heads in agreement. Jesus called them all hypocrites. "You take care of your animals on the sabbath," he said, in effect. "Isn't this poor woman worth more than they?"

At this the people rejoiced—one of Luke's favorite verbs—and Luke's recalling that rejoicing led him to report Jesus' sayings about the kingdom. Both sayings are about the enormous growth of God's realm. It is like the great tree that springs from the tiny mustard seed, making room for the birds of many nations to rest on its branches; and it is like the small lump of yeast in a bowl of batter, that makes the bread swell and regenerate until it is several times its original size. This was truly a cause for joy!

PRAYER

I confess, O God, that I have some sympathy for the poor synagogue leader, who was only trying to do his job. But what a wonderful sense of joy and marvel he was missing because of his job. Help me never to miss the wonder of your realm because of the work I have to do. Through Jesus, who was constantly reshaping people's attitudes toward everything, amen.

Day 241   *Luke 13:22-35*

THE MASTER AND HIS HOUSE

The person who asked Jesus the question in verse 23 was merely being curious. Speculating about when the end would be and how many would be saved had long been the pastime of the idle and pseudo-religious. But Jesus characteristically formed his answer in such a way as to involve the questioner in a life-or-death situation. Brushing aside the question of how many, he pointed to the importance of entering God's realm when one has the opportunity. Otherwise, the person may find himself or herself on the outside, unable to get in through a superficial acquaintance with the Master.

The picture Jesus gave was one of eternal disappointment—of looking in and seeing the great patriarchs of Israel sitting at the heavenly banquet not with them but with outsiders, people from all the other nations. Jesus had already demonstrated this in his ministry by dining with prostitutes and tax collectors—sinners before the law. But in God's realm even the hated Gentiles would go in before the unbelieving Israelites.

Some friendly Pharisees—perhaps the only friendly ones in the Gospels!—came and warned Jesus to leave town, for Herod wanted to kill him. But Jesus said they could tell Herod that he would not be hurried. No earthly monarch was going to set the agenda for God's anointed!

The lament for Jerusalem in verse 34 is placed by Matthew at the entrance into Jerusalem itself, not in another village, as Luke has it. Luke uses it here as a preface to Jesus' remark that he will not show up in Jerusalem until the Passover, when the people would shout "Hosanna!" at his entry (Luke 19:37-38).

PRAYER
The apocalyptic pictures and sayings in this passage are disturbing to me, O God. They speak of the shadowy side of your goodness and mercy. Let them keep alive in me a genuine sense of urgency to preach the gospel to everyone who has not yet heard and responded. Through Jesus, who never blanched at the full truth, amen.

SOME TABLE TALK

*T*hey were watching him closely" (v. 1). Weren't they, though? They wanted to catch Jesus at something. And he didn't disappoint them. He did another healing on the sabbath. Then he silenced them with basically the same argument he had used in Luke 13:15-16, when he healed the bent woman on the sabbath.

But we learn that Jesus was also watching them closely. What he saw was their jealousy about the seating arrangements—each was anxious to have a place above the others. Always take the low place, Jesus advised; it is better to be called up than put down.

Jesus also noticed that the host had carefully invited his best friends, kinsfolk, and most prominent acquaintances to the meal. That is a mistake, he cautioned; one ought, rather, to invite the poor, the maimed, the blind, the outcast, who cannot possibly repay the favor. Then God will repay at the time of the resurrection. The host had been socially careful but had completely missed the way of God's realm.

It is possible that the early church read in these last verses a lesson to itself, not to strive to have only the finest citizens at the Lord's table, for the Lord had announced that the joy of the gospel is for the poor, the blind, and the oppressed (Luke 4:14-30).

And this is precisely the point of the parable in verses 16-24. The parable is given in response to the pious remark of one of the dinner guests. Doubtless, the man supposed himself to be included in the heavenly banquet. But Jesus used the occasion to point out again, as he did consistently in all his ministry, that everyone would be surprised when he or she saw the guests at that banquet. They would be the very persons the good Jews were ignoring, while the religious leaders themselves would not taste a morsel!

PRAYER

O God, the politics of your realm and the politics of this world are often at odds with each other. Help me always to seek the way of your realm in my affairs, that I may rejoice with those who will enjoy the heavenly feast with you. Through Jesus, who watches me as I watch him, amen.

FACING THE HARD REALITIES

*D*espite his continuous conflict with religious leaders wherever he went, Jesus was still extremely popular and had an immense following among the common folk. Yet he was bothered by their lack of comprehension. They did not seem to appreciate the danger of his mission, either to him or to themselves. Therefore, he turned on them and attempted to make them face the truth. Discipleship would not be easy, he warned; in fact, it would demand every ounce of loyalty they could summon.

Hating one's father and mother did not mean to the Jewish mind precisely what it means to us. As G. B. Caird has put it, "The Semitic mind is comfortable only with extremes—light and darkness, truth and falsehood, love and hate—primary colours with no half-shades of compromise in between. The Semitic way of saying 'I prefer this to that' is 'I like this and hate that.' " What Jesus said, thus, was that their families must take second place to the realm of God.

Being a disciple, he told them in a daring metaphor, is like bearing your own cross—committing yourself to the gallows, to execution, to death among strangers.

Count the cost, he warned. Even a builder does that before erecting a tower. A king does it before engaging in war. Any reasonable person does it. Therefore, disciples should do it too—they ought not to begin a discipleship they cannot complete. To be a disciple but not follow Jesus through times of stress and danger would be like being salt without the real power of salt—and that is to be worthless and thrown away.

PRAYER

These bracing words, O God, sting my conscience like nettles. Could I follow Jesus to the death, or am I only a disciple of convenience? Increase my devotion, I pray, lest I betray you in a moment of stress or an hour of indecision. Amen.

THE KINGDOM OF JOY

*H*ere is what is for many the heart of Luke's Gospel. No other Gospel writer recorded all three of the beautiful parables in this chapter. (Matthew 18:12-14 gives the parable of the lost sheep.) More than any other stories, they seem to represent what God was working out through Jesus' ministry.

The setting is not unlike the one in which Jesus was frequently pictured: teaching and healing the poor, the blind, the outcast, with the scribes and Pharisees looking on to criticize. This time, as on other occasions, they were complaining about the unsanctified company Jesus kept. It was to answer the criticisms of the religious Jews that Jesus told these rare stories—the parables of the lost sheep, the lost coin, and the lost boy. Each would have been readily understood by those who heard it.

The essential note in each story is joy. The shepherd tracks his errant sheep out in the wilderness where it has wandered and "lays it on his shoulders and rejoices." When he comes back, he calls to his friends, saying, "Rejoice with me." Even so, says Jesus, "there will be more joy in heaven" over the sinner who repents (vv. 5-7).

The woman loses a single coin, a silver drachma, worth slightly more than a day's wages in ancient Palestine. Probably it has fallen among the straws or rushes on her earthen floor and is difficult to find in her dark, almost windowless house. She lights a lamp, sifts through the straws, and even sweeps the house in search of the coin. At last her eye falls on it. She calls her friends together, saying "Rejoice with me." In the same manner, says Jesus, "there is joy in the presence of the angels of God" when a lost sinner is recovered (vv. 9-10).

The angel who announced the birth of Jesus to the shepherds on the hillside brought them "good news of great joy" that would come to all the people (Luke 2:10). When Jesus announced the design of his ministry at the synagogue in Nazareth, he identified it with the poor and broken and neglected of the world. Here in these parables Luke has drawn these themes together in a climactic fashion. God's realm is a realm of joy!

PRAYER

Thank you, O God, for the unrestrained joy of your realm. How wonderful it is to be part of an order in which everyone has been brought in with rejoicing. Help me to ponder this today and to realize what it means for my relations with others in your realm. Through Jesus, who led the search for all of us, amen.

Day 245 *Luke 15:11-24*

THE BOY WHO CAME HOME

*T*here is only one way to the Father—through the far country! Each of us, to appreciate the love and generosity of God, must at some point experience disillusionment with self and the world, come to the point of despair, and then return to the Father in penitence, only to discover that he has been waiting all along with open arms to welcome us.

That is the genius of this story, for it is truly one of the most remarkable stories ever told, and certainly one of the best loved. It is rich in human insights. And the picture of God as a father—warm, tolerant, compassionate, forgiving, rejoicing—is surely one of the most compelling we have ever known. It is a perfect story—literary, economical in detail, universal in application, and full of human warmth and understanding.

We do not know why the younger son wanted to go away; perhaps his scrupulous elder brother was getting on his nerves. But he requested and received, according to an ancient tradition of property settlement, his share of the family estate. Off he went to the far country, where he lived like a prince until his money ran out and the country entered a period of famine. At last, in sheer desperation, he found himself in the utterly degrading position of caring for a Gentile master's pigs. Staring at the pods of the carob tree, a kind of nutrient bean fed to cattle and swine, he thought how hungry he was and what good food there was at his father's house, even for the hired servants.

Composing a contrite speech, he arose and returned home. His father, apparently watching the road with a parent's wistful eye, saw him at a distance and ran out and embraced and kissed him, despite his obviously broken condition. The boy tried to recite his speech but was interrupted by the father, who gave bristling commands to the servants to come and care for his son. The fatted calf that was ordered slain was a specially grown calf reserved for the most honored guests in the home. It was time to rejoice and celebrate!

PRAYER

My heart still leaps up at reading this story, dear God, the way it did when I first heard it. To think that you love me like the father in this parable, and that you celebrate each day's return to you, is more moving than I can say. I have sinned, O God, and am unworthy of such love. Make me one of your servants. Through Jesus, who would have been your Messiah if he had done no more than tell this beautiful tale, amen.

Day 246   *Luke 15:25-32*

THE SECOND LOST BOY

*T*he parable of the prodigal son was a story in itself. But Jesus' point in telling it was not served by that episode alone. He wanted the scribes and Pharisees to see themselves in this second episode, when the self-righteous elder brother discovered the party his father was giving for the son who had returned. There was no compassion or joy at all in the elder brother—only a feeling of resentment that his upstart sibling, who had earned no place in the home, had come back and was being treated so royally.

Perhaps the elder brother would not have minded if the father had taken the boy at his own bargain and hired him as a menial. But to restore him to full sonship and give a feast in his honor was an outrageous affront to the elder brother's sense of worth and justice. He would have no part of it, and he complained that he had never had such special treatment, even though he had lived carefully and responsibly all his life.

Can't we imagine the scribes and Pharisees bristling at this? They had spent their lives trying to live by all the rules and regulations of the Father's house—or what they thought was the Father's house. And they deeply resented the Messiah's saying that the common people, who had not had instruction in the law and had not even attempted to live as purely as they, would be welcomed into God's realm ahead of the scribes and Pharisees.

The point is that the father in the story had the right to decide as he wished. Near Eastern fathers were supreme in their households. And he had welcomed his son back. It was too bad that the elder son was such a selfish, calculating type and could not enter the merriment; he was cutting off his own nose, as the saying goes, to spite his face. It would have been more fitting, from a human, compassionate standpoint, if he could have joined in the rejoicing with his father and the servants. After all, it was as if a dead man had come back to life again. In the end, the son who stayed home proved to be more lost to the father's heart than the one who had wandered away.

PRAYER

There is a streak of the elder brother in me, O God. I, too, watch what others are receiving and measure their good fortune by my own. I am grudging when they come off better than I, though I should rejoice for them and enjoy their parties. Help me to feel your presence so strongly in my daily life that I realize there is nothing richer in the world, and I can find joy in others' success. Through Jesus, whose stories are filled with remarkable insights, amen.

Day 247 *Luke 16:1-13*

THE CLEVER STEWARD

*T*his parable seems out of place following the stories in chapter 15. Contextually, it may seem to follow more appropriately after chapter 14, with its warnings about the radical demands on those who would enter God's realm. This passage, too, is directed toward the disciples, though we learn in verse 14 that the Pharisees were listening in.

The point of the parable is the shrewdness with which ordinary businesspersons act when confronted with a crisis situation, and an exhortation to the disciples to act similarly in the face of their nation's spiritual crisis.

The steward, probably a middle manager who oversees his employer's tenant farms, learns that he is about to be sacked. Hustling about, he makes quick (and, in our minds, unethical) bargains with the master's tenants that drastically reduce their rents and thus ingratiate him with the tenants. The idea is that they will then take care of him when his employment has been terminated.

Even the man's master is impressed by this bit of clever maneuvering, and praises the servant for his ingenuity. Jesus' comment is that the children of the world are often more enterprising in dealing with their crises than the children of light are in dealing with theirs.

What did Jesus mean by making friends by means of "dishonest wealth" (v. 11)? The phrase "dishonest wealth" or "unrighteous mammon" was often used by rabbis to denote money that was legally obtained but not spiritually blessed. Interest money or usury often fell under this category. Verse 9 draws the conclusion from the parable that, like the steward, we should take every opportunity to create friendships with our money or profits, thus earning eternal merit. Verses 10-12, then, suggest that if we do not behave in this manner with the world's goods, God can surely not entrust to us the greater spiritual riches of the new realm.

The final verse, 13, links the whole business again to the call to radical commitment in chapter 14, because it restates the importance of whole-hearted allegiance. If we love God, we will use our money for spiritual purposes. But if we love money, we cannot use God to further our business situations. God will not be a party to our selfish designs.

PRAYER

This ingenious and daring story, O God, invades the world of profit and loss to illustrate the great importance of living creatively for your new order. Teach me to think prudently, as the steward did, and to use all my resources and energy in behalf of those who matter to you. Through Jesus, who served you completely, amen.

Day 248   *Luke 16:14-31*

THE EVIDENCE OF THE HEART

*T*he Pharisees, listening in to Jesus' story of the clever steward, scoffed at him. Luke points out that they loved money, and the records show that they often used their knowledge of the law to establish financial advantage for themselves. Jesus' response to them was pointed: They might know how to justify themselves legally before others, but God would not be fooled. The law was still the law, and they would be judged by it. Even though they had devised ways to obtain legal divorces, God would find them guilty of adultery.

To show how God judges by the heart, Jesus then told the parable of the rich man and Lazarus. The Pharisees would have respected the rich man and had no use for Lazarus. But God had no respect at all for the rich man, for God saw how he treated the poor man at his gate.

The rich man's pleas from Hades reinforce the point of how it will be in the afterlife for people like the Pharisees: They will cry out for help, but receive none. They have chosen the wrong way in life and will not be able to alter it.

241

The message should have been a powerful one to the Pharisees, who were always asking for "signs." They would not behave differently, Jesus said, even if someone returned from the dead to warn them. Their hearts were not right with God. They simply twisted the Scriptures and the law to suit their purposes, and they must answer for it.

PRAYER

How could it be any clearer, dear God? Your will for me is to use all I have for your little ones. No law or rationalization can protect my selfish interest from your condemnation. Have mercy on me, O God, and teach me to give myself completely. Amen.

Day 249   *Luke 17:1-10*

A MISCELLANY OF SAYINGS

*H*ere Luke recorded an assortment of Jesus' sayings that bear on discipleship—perhaps because the previous chapter dealt partly with that subject.

The first saying (vv. 1-2) is about causing "little ones" to sin. This is a tender appellation, much in keeping with the pictures of the lost sheep, lost coin, and lost boy of chapter 15. Causing little ones to stumble probably means doing anything to discourage them from walking in the way of God's new order.

The second saying (vv. 3-4) is about forgiving a brother or sister in Christ. Seven times a day is a figure of speech implying endless patience and forbearance, qualities expected of disciples who have themselves been forgiven enormous debts (cf. Luke 7:40-47).

The third saying (vv. 5-6) regards the power of faith. The reason for Jesus' reference to the sycamore tree may be its reputation for an extremely large and intricate root system, making it especially difficult to dislodge.

The fourth saying (vv. 7-10) is not commonly known or preached about today, but it is an extremely rich one for contemplation. It may originally have been spoken for the Pharisees, though it applies equally well to disciples of that or any age. Its point is that as servants of God we should never expect special attention for duties we have performed. Instead, we should maintain attitudes of humility, knowing that no works can ever make us worthy of the grace and presence of God.

O God, the irony of this Scripture is that—unworthy as I am—you have prepared a table for me and invited me to eat and drink. I am overwhelmed by your grace and what the banquet has cost you. May the dedication of my life reveal in a small way how enormously grateful I am. Through your Son Jesus, who provides the bread and the wine, amen.

Day 250   *Luke 17:11-19*

THE GRATEFUL FOREIGNER

G ratitude has always been closely allied to realizing the presence of God. People who are negative and ungrateful can be counted on to be insensitive to the mystery on which their lives really border. If they only knew—only realized—how near God is to them, it would make all the difference in the world for them.

This little story puts the rate of thoughtful, grateful persons at one in ten. There were ten lepers—all men—thrown together by their affliction. Because leprosy cut people off from all other social contact—even from their families—contact with each other was all they had.

We note that these lepers were "standing at a distance" when they called to Jesus for help. They must have been a pathetic sight, and it is no wonder he had compassion on them and healed them. "Go and show yourselves to the priests," he said (v. 14). This was in keeping with Leviticus 13:9-17, which gave explicit instructions for those having leprosy and desiring a clean bill of health. In Luke 5:12-14 Jesus healed a leper and then sent him to the priest. Here the lepers were ordered to go to the priest in the faith that they would be whole. As they were on their way the leprosy left them.

One of the ten, a Samaritan, returned to thank Jesus. He was "praising God with a loud voice," says Luke (v. 15). Jesus spoke words tinged with irony when he saw the man return. "Where are the others?" he asked in effect. "Weren't there ten? Where are all the Jews? Is this Samaritan the only one who is grateful for what happened?"

The implication is probably wider than the healing incident and the story of gratitude. To Luke, the narrative was undoubtedly a harbinger of the times recorded in Acts when the recognition of God's realm would often fare better among the Samaritans and Gentiles than in Israel itself.

PRAYER

Teach me to seek your face each morning and evening, O God, that I may daily live in sensitivity to the countless gifts surrounding me—gifts I perceive only when I am aware of your presence in my life. Through Jesus, who always lived this way, amen.

Day 251   *Luke 17:20–18:8*

THE GREAT DAY AT THE END

*T*hese sayings are all related to the end of all things, a subject of much speculation among the ancient Jews. They remind us that while the coming of God's new order meant joy and fullness to the poor, blind, sick, and oppressed, it means sudden terror and destruction to others.

First, the Pharisees asked Jesus when God's rule was coming. They probably wanted to know the signs of the end. Jesus replied that it was already in their very midst. Then Jesus addressed the disciples about the end. What he said to them was not really different from what he told the Pharisees; it was merely said from a different perspective. They knew that God's rule was already among them, but he spoke to them about how it would be in the final hours of the present world order. They shouldn't be anxious, he said; they would know when the end had come. When it did, it would happen swiftly. There would be no time to do anything.

As in times of natural calamity, some persons would appear to be absurdly singled out for destruction, while others would be untouched. Of two people asleep in the same bed, one would be taken and the other not. Such a picture intensifies the sense of divine power involved—human intervention will be futile when the end occurs.

The disciples wanted to know when the end would come. The answer is somber: The vultures will gather where the corpse lies. Israel is a charnel house, full of death and putrefaction. Vultures have an uncanny way of finding their prey.

Finally, Jesus told a parable encouraging the disciples to pray constantly for the end to come. As the judge eventually gave in to the persistent woman, so God would one day accede to their prayers.

PRAYER

It will surely help to shape my daily existence, O God, if I pray sincerely for the day of the Lamb to come. My very being will strain toward that great event. Grant, therefore, that these images may remain vivid in my mind, both consciously and unconsciously, and that I may truly pray for your realm to come. In the name of the Lamb himself, amen.

Day 252   *Luke 18:9-14*

THE BRAGGART AND THE BEGGAR

*T*he essence of this poignant little story derives from the Pharisee's failure to realize that he stood in the presence of God. Had he known that—had he felt even an inkling of it—it would surely have caused him to fall prostrate on the ground, tearing his garments and bewailing his unworthiness, as the humble tax collector did. But his religion itself blinded him to the possibility of God's unspeakable presence. He was so busy congratulating himself for fulfilling all the rules of piety—he fasted even when it was not required and paid tithes even on the smaller things in his possession, though the law did not require it—that he had no real thought for the awesome activity in which he was engaged, speaking to God, the Creator of the universe. Ironically, he saw the tax collector prostrating himself and suffering the remorse of sin, and instead of being reminded of his own need for forgiveness, he idly added to his prayers that he was grateful not to be like that poor fellow over there.

How aptly this story fitted many of the Pharisees Jesus encountered in his ministry. They, too, counted their days of fasting and were scrupulous in their tithing, but missed the real secret of spirituality, which is to dwell sensitively in the presence of the living God. It was no wonder that Jesus said God's new order would be taken from them and given to prostitutes and tax collectors. At least the latter would have some feeling for the majesty of God when they came into the divine presence!

PRAYER

Dear God, save me from pretentiousness and self-deception when I pray. Let the sublime mystery of your presence radically humble my spirit, bringing me into a new alignment with the world around me. For you are the living God, and greatly to be feared. Amen.

THE SADNESS OF A RULER

*T*here is an obvious contrast in this passage between the carefree innocence of the children and the sad, responsible nature of the ruler. Luke, like Mark, has set them side by side in order to point up this difference. The poor and oppressed are able to hear the good news of God's rule because they have nothing to lose and everything to gain. They are like children. But there are others, like this ruler, who find it difficult to enter the realm of God because it will mean surrendering their trust in earthly possessions.

The ruler was probably a leader of a synagogue, not a ruler in the sense of being a king or potentate. He was apparently an impressive man, possibly a Pharisee who had kept the law fastidiously, yet had a lot of money.

The tip-off to his attitude, in Luke's version, is the way he addresses Jesus as "good." He sees Jesus as a man who knows the law well, too. But Jesus immediately tries to relocate his sense of values, reminding him that beside God there is nothing that is truly good.

Jesus' demand that the man sell all his possessions and give the money to the poor is designed to jar his dependency from his earthly power and respectability so that he may begin to place it on God instead. It is the fact that this dependency on worldly values has sunk such deep roots in him over the years that leads to his sadness. Perhaps he realizes the great good he is missing, but cannot shake his need for power and property.

We don't know Peter's motivation for reminding Jesus that the disciples had left all to follow Jesus. Perhaps it was a bit of self-congratulation; or perhaps he saw Jesus looking wistfully after the man and wanted to speak a consoling word, such as, "Don't feel too bad, Master. Not everyone responds that way. Look at us—we left everything to come with you." And out of his reverie, Jesus replies, in effect, "You're right—and everyone who has left anything will have more than he left, both now and in the age to come."

PRAYER

I have more than I need to live, O God. Grant that I may feel your presence so intimately that I shall not be dependent on what I have, but may become more generous with it, sharing with those who have less. In Jesus' name, amen.

WHAT A BLIND MAN SEES

*L*uke now concludes the long section of teachings, begun in 9:51, during which Jesus and the disciples were supposed to be moving constantly toward Jerusalem. Before the section began, Peter had confessed that Jesus was "the Messiah of God" (Luke 9:20), and Jesus had taken Peter, James, and John onto the mountain with him, where they had witnessed a prefiguring of his resurrection (Luke 9:28-36). Jesus now reminds the twelve that he must suffer and die, but they are not able to understand any of what he is talking about.

It is ironic, then, that the person who greets Jesus as Son of David while he passes through Jericho is a blind man. The disciples, who have been with Jesus for months, and whose eyes are perfectly good, cannot "see" what Jesus tries to tell them. But the blind man "sees" perfectly well who Jesus is, and will not be silenced by those who try to stifle his outcry.

This is the only time in the Gospel when this messianic title is used. It is as if God had revealed the secret of the messiahship to a man who could not behold a sunset or look into the faces of people passing him in the road. And how appropriate it was that he should be the one to announce the Savior's approach to the holy city, for Jesus had said at the beginning of his ministry that the coming of God's new order meant restoration of sight to the blind (Luke 4:18).

Jesus restored the man's vision. But he would never again see with more genuine perception than he had shown in recognizing the One who was drawing near to Jerusalem.

PRAYER

Dear God, many things pass within the angles of my vision; yet I fear that I do not always see with true perception. Sight does not often enough become insight. Help me to listen better and watch more intently in your presence, that I may learn to see as this blind man did. Through Jesus, who is able to restore sight to the sightless, amen.

AN OUTSTANDING SINNER

*T*his is the only time in the Gospels that we encounter the title "chief tax collector." Apparently Zacchaeus was in charge of all collections for the Roman government in the city of Jericho. This means that he was free to keep part of all the revenues collected by the other tax officials in the city and perhaps in the entire region, and it accounts for the fact that he was extremely rich.

Tax collectors were considered unclean and sinful by the Jews because it was necessary for them to enter the homes of Gentiles and common people of the land, where strict food ceremonies were not practiced, and also because they dealt in Roman coinage bearing the image of Caesar. A chief tax collector was probably regarded, therefore, as the chief of sinners!

This story's appearing where it does, as Jesus is on the verge of entering Jerusalem for his Passion, is highly significant. It emphasizes once more the point reiterated throughout Luke's Gospel, that God's new order was coming for people the religious leaders didn't think would have any part in it.

Zacchaeus was so moved by Jesus' visit that his entire economic behavior was drastically changed. He went far beyond the law in Leviticus 6:5, which required that anything falsely taken from another be restored in full plus one-fifth as penalty—he would make restitution at the rate of 400 percent! Besides that, he would give half of all his wealth to the poor.

This was surely a great object lesson for any wealthy persons who became Christians in the early centuries; they could see that sharing with the poor and living in honest simplicity were part of the ethics of God's new realm. And the story contrasts markedly with the narrative about the wealthy synagogue ruler in Luke 18:18-25, who could not readjust his priorities enough to give to the poor and enter God's realm.

PRAYER

Dear God, I understand Zacchaeus's great joy at receiving Jesus in his home. Help me to receive him daily, that my spirit, too, may be utterly converted to generosity and good works. For his name's sake, amen.

A DOUBLE PARABLE

*I*n Matthew's Gospel (25:14-30) this parable was obviously directed against the Pharisees, who had received gifts in trust from God but had unimaginatively buried them under a protective, legalistic system, so that now God's realm was being taken from them and given to others. But Luke has a different application in mind, as he indicates in verse 11; he wishes to use the parable as a comment both on Jesus' absence and on the expectation of many disciples that the new order would come immediately. And the story cuts two ways—to those who are appointed servants of the Lord and to those who have strongly opposed his rule all along.

As for the servants, it is probable that Luke sees them as representing the servants of Jesus—possibly even the disciples—and not of the Pharisees. While Jesus is away (clearly he is the nobleman) receiving his kingship, they are to act wisely and resourcefully with the small sums of money he gives them. When he does return as a king, the Lord will call them to account and reward the faithful ones with the rulership of cities, while depriving the unfaithful ones of everything.

The unruly citizens in this parable are probably the scribes and Pharisees and any other persons who for any reason have refused the new order. There was a historical precedent that may have formed the basis for this part of the parable. When Herod the Great died in 4 B.C., his son Archelaus went to Rome to ask Augustus Caesar to appoint him King of Judea, and a deputation of Jewish citizens followed to oppose his appointment. Augustus did not appoint Archelaus, and, although history is silent about whether he exercised reprisals against his opponents, it is almost unthinkable that he did not. The harshness of verse 27 would suggest that he did, if the parable owes anything to the story of Archelaus, because it does not seem characteristic of the Jesus of Luke's Gospel. At any rate, the story promises an unhappy end for those who stand in the way of Jesus' coming rulership.

PRAYER

O God, do I ever stand in the way of your new order? I fear that I do, not out of any intentional opposition, but because I am not as thoroughly committed to your will as I ought to be. Forgive me, and help me to be converted to your way, so that the new order may come more swiftly. In Jesus' name, amen.

A TIME OF JOY AND SADNESS

*T*o appreciate fully Jesus' use of the colt here, we must remember the stress ancient societies placed on dramatic action. Prophets often used symbolic, nonverbal actions to signify important moments or messages. For months now, Jesus had been on his way to Jerusalem, warning his disciples that the final conflict with the authorities would occur there. His concern to dramatize his entrance, therefore, was most appropriate. He was entering the city as a king on a peaceful mission, even though certain parties would bitterly oppose him, just as the citizens refused the reign of the newly appointed king in the parable of Luke 19:11-28.

The words of praise and acclamation used by the multitude of Jesus' followers were from Psalm 118:26—words probably spoken originally as a priestly blessing on a king coming to the Temple after a great victory in the field. Jesus had won a victory in the field and had arrived in Jerusalem for the final contest.

Although Jesus' followers apparently thought the heavenly realm was about to come in all its glory, the Pharisees did not. Either they considered the disciples' words blasphemous, or they feared that the Romans would regard them as seditious and take reprisals against the Jews, so they demanded that Jesus silence the elated crowd. But Jesus knew how natural the disciples' excitement was. If they were muzzled, he said, nature itself would have to cry out. The time was at that point of fullness.

Still, Jesus could not share the people's elation. He knew that they would soon prove fickle. Looking ahead at the city's imposing profile, he began to weep. Because the city would refuse him, there was only one course open to them: They would be overrun by the Romans during a time of rebellion. The Roman soldiers would push dirt ramparts up to the great walls, rush in over them, slay the inhabitants, and then systematically lay the city in ruins—all because the people did not fully recognize the time of their "visitation from God."

PRAYER

O God, how many times have I missed a visitation in my own life because I did not stop to watch for you and recognize your approach? How often have I failed to see you in a beggar, a mourner, or a little child? I am sad for myself, the way Jesus was sad for the city. Grant that I may be far more sensitive to your comings and goings. Through him who always knew, amen.

Day 258   *Luke 19:45–20:8*

INTENSIFYING THE CONFLICT

*M*ark locates the cleansing of the Temple on the day *following* Jesus' entry into Jerusalem (Mark 11:12-17). Matthew (21:12-13) and Luke both place it together with the entry, indicating that they regarded it as a significant overture to the week of conflict leading to the crucifixion. It was an act of authority that clearly provoked the wrath of the religious leaders of the nation.

Throughout his ministry, Jesus was dogged by pietistic scribes and Pharisees, complaining that he and his disciples were not strict enough in their religious observances. Now, in this passage, he turns the tables on them, reminding them that Isaiah 56:7 said God's house was to be a place of prayer and chiding them for having turned it into a thieves' warren where religious pilgrims were overcharged.

Luke doesn't have a cleansing scene, as Mark does, but he does show us the priests' and scribes' displeasure at Jesus' presence. They were seeking ways to crush their strong, resourceful opponent. But they had to be careful because of his popularity, so they would proceed for several days to try to entrap him with clever questions.

One of these questions concerned his authority to do the works he did. They probably expected Jesus to assert his messiahship. If he did, they would run to the Romans and charge him with sedition, for the Romans were always wary during the volatile Passover season.

But Jesus was cagey. He returned a question for a question. Whence was *John's* authority—his baptism—from heaven or from human sources? The questioners were stupefied. If their answer was heaven, it would validate Jesus' own ministry. If they answered from men, then the people would react angrily, because they held John in high esteem. Lacking the moral courage to grasp either horn of this well-posed dilemma, they simply refrained from answering.

"If you won't give me an answer," Jesus said, in effect, "then you won't have one from me."

251

O God, why is it that we resent anybody who doesn't fit into our systems? What compels us to oppose, harass, and even destroy that person? Help me to live so completely in your presence that I shall be more compassionate and tolerant of those who differ from me. Through Jesus, who bids me enter your realm, amen.

Day 259   *Luke 20:9-18*

THE COMING OF THE SON AND HEIR

*A*s citizens of occupied territory, Palestinians were doubtless very familiar with absentee landlords. Many farms and vineyards in their country were owned by people who lived in Asia Minor, or even in Rome, and were worked by local tenants who did pretty much as they liked. Sometimes representatives of the owners were assaulted and killed by the tenants, just as the parable describes.

The "hook" in the parable, of course, was the line about the owner's sending his son to the tenants, who summarily rejected him, as they had the earlier emissaries, and killed him. It was true in real life that if the owners of property died or were killed, the tenants living on the property had first legal claim on it. Jesus was accusing the religious establishment of Israel of wanting to be rid of him in order that their complete proprietary rights to the nation's life and spirit would not be contested. But God was not some powerless owner residing at an impossible distance from Israel; God would come and destroy the tenants, and give the vineyard to others.

The quotation about the rejected stone in verse 17 is from Psalm 118:22-23, and was apparently a favorite text among early Christians, who associated it with the Resurrection. Luke quotes it again in Acts 4:11, in the sermon of Peter before the high priests, scribes, and elders. The last verse of our passage is clear enough: Anyone (such as the wicked tenants) who falls afoul of the One who is the cornerstone will be broken by the encounter!

Interestingly, Mark's account of the parable (12:1-12) has the son's death occurring inside the vineyard. But both Matthew (21:33-46) and Luke have altered the wording to make the parable conform to the fact that Jesus was crucified outside the walls of the city (Heb. 13:12).

O God, for me the terrible thing about this story is the realization that my life is your vineyard, too, and that I have often turned away your servants and your beloved Son from taking control of it. Forgive me for my rudeness and possessiveness, and help me in the future to surrender gladly whatever you wish from your vineyard, for it is rightfully yours and your Son's. Amen.

Day 260   *Luke 20:19-26*

THE THINGS THAT BELONG TO GOD

*J*esus' enemies had to proceed with caution against him, lest the people rise up to defend him. So they watched him carefully and sent "spies who pretended to be honest" to entrap him. The question the spies asked him turned on the annual poll tax paid to the Roman government. It was paid in silver denarii bearing Caesar's image.

If Jesus gave a popular answer, that it was wrong for God's people to handle money extolling the divinity of Caesar and to pay for the support of a heathen government, his enemies would instantly bring him before Pilate on the charge of sedition. If, on the other hand, he approved payment of the tax, it would surely cost him popular support. It is obvious from the way the questioners approached the subject—you "teach the way of God in accordance with truth" (v. 21)—that they wanted him to take the popular stand against the government, giving them the political ammunition they needed.

Cooly and shrewdly, Jesus returned an answer that acceded to neither of their desires. Hearing that Caesar's image was on the coin, he said it should be given to Caesar. Technically, it *was* Caesar's—all coinage issued by an emperor remained legally his, although used by his subjects. But there was another part of the answer: They should also give to God whatever bore God's image.

At a stroke, Jesus had not only ingeniously eluded the trap set for him, but had reaffirmed the nature of the new realm he was preaching as well. It was not to be a commonwealth in rivalry with earthly realms, commandeering their thrones and taking possession of their coinage. Jesus had settled that when he rejected the temptation to have power and glory from all the nations of the world (Luke 4:5-8). His was a realm of another dimension, to be won through suffering and death. It is no wonder that his enemies marveled at his answer and became silent.

PRAYER

Caesar's realm bothers me a lot, O God. I spend much of my energy worrying about taxes and reports and making ends meet. Perhaps, if I spent more time contemplating your realm, I would have more energy for dealing with Caesar, as Jesus obviously did. I am going to try to do that, with your help. Amen.

Day 261   *Luke 20:27-44*

THE LORD OF THE LIVING

*I*t is hard to imagine a group of people more conservative than the Pharisees, who were always complaining about Jesus' liberal ways, but the Sadducees were. Completely unprogressive, they held rigidly to the Torah and refused to admit any doctrine not expressly contained in the so-called books of Moses. Therefore, they ridiculed Jesus' teachings about resurrection by citing a law in Deuteronomy 25:5-6, decreeing that a man should marry his brother's widow in order to guarantee progeny to the family. By imagining an almost absurd instance in which the law would apply, they produced a ridiculous picture of a woman with seven husbands in the resurrection.

Jesus first observed that in the resurrection people are like the angels and thus are free from mundane necessities. They have no worry about progeny to carry on their names. Then he turned on them their own trick of reading the Torah literally. Citing Exodus 3:6, when God told Moses that God was the deity of Abraham, Isaac, and Jacob, Jesus observed that there must be a resurrection, else these men could not be living and God could not truly be their God; for God had indeed put it in the present tense, "I am the God of your father. . . . "

Some of the scribes, whose business it was to deal in the minutiae of the law, were obviously impressed by such an answer. They may have been Pharisees rather than Sadducees. Jesus had proven himself more than a match for any of them.

When they fell silent, he asked them a question: How could they, in the face of Psalm 110:1, where David called the Messiah "Lord," think of the Messiah as David's "son"? The point was that they expected the

254

Messiah, as David's offspring, to have an earthly kingdom like David's. But Jesus was not only David's son; he was his Lord as well, and his new order would transcend the kingdom of David.

PRAYER

O God, I am often impatient with people like these who want to ask fussy questions about religion. Give me more tolerance, like Jesus, and help me to respond with wisdom. For his name's sake, amen.

Day 262   *Luke 20:45–21:4*

A MODEL FOR LIVING

*E*verywhere in Jerusalem, and especially around the Temple, Jesus and the disciples would have seen the figures of the scribes moving through the streets in their long robes with tassels that touched the ground. After the encounter with them recorded in Luke 20:39-44, Jesus commented on these familiar figures to the disciples. They liked to be noticed, he said. They loved the special greetings of "Rabbi" or "Master" that others gave them in the marketplaces, and they liked the seats of honor at banquets. Rabbinical writings, in fact, gave very precise regulations for the seating of scribes, so that the oldest and most authoritative had the greatest places. But, in matter of fact, said Jesus, for all their respectability, they used their positions of influence and knowledge of the law to bilk poor, trusting widows out of their inheritances. And their long prayers, often delivered in public places, were mostly hollow pretense aimed solely at increasing their level of honor among the populace.

How much more appropriate in God's eyes was the behavior of the poor widow Jesus happened to see placing her two small coins in the offering chest at the Temple. The coins were not worth much by most people's standards—they were the small Jewish "coppers" that bore no image of Caesar—but they were obviously worth a great deal to the woman, whose appearance marked her as one in very meager circumstances.

In God's eyes, indicated Jesus, she had given more than all the self-important religious people, even though they probably made a great display of dropping their silver denarii into the offering chests. God looks on the heart of a person, not on the elaborate piety developed for outward show.

Thank you, dear God, for simple people who are able to love you in simple but profound ways. They help to correct the vision of those of us who are more complicated and less natural. Enable me to be more like them. In the name of Jesus, who also gave all he had, amen.

Day 263   *Luke 21:5-19*

PATTERNS OF SUFFERING AND HOPE

*E*ach of the so-called Synoptic Gospels contains a lengthy section of apocalyptic sayings—predictions of Jesus concerning a time of great destruction before the end of the old order and the beginning of the new. In Matthew it is chapter 24. In Mark it is chapter 13. In Luke it is this chapter, 21. One of the most interesting facts about Luke's record of these sayings is the way he has made them parallel descriptions of Jesus' trial, crucifixion, and resurrection in chapters 22–24.

The reference to false messiahs in 21:8, for example, is balanced by a reference to Jesus as the true Messiah in 24:26. Jesus warns in 21:12 that the disciples will be imprisoned; and in 22:54 he himself is taken prisoner. Jesus says in 21:16 that the disciples will be betrayed by friends and relatives; and in 22:47-48 he is betrayed by Judas. In 21:7 he says the disciples will be hated; in 22:63 and 23:18, 35-39, he is hated. In 21:19 he says the disciples must have endurance; in 22:7–23:46 he demonstrates endurance. And there are numerous other instances of such paralleling.

Luke appears to have been emphasizing that the suffering of the disciples would essentially parallel that of Jesus himself, and that they must, therefore, brace themselves to endure the calamities and hardships as Jesus endured the trial and crucifixion. If they were faithful as he was faithful, they would then share in the glory and triumph of the One who had been raised from the dead. And, through it all, the God who raised up Jesus would prove more than adequate to their needs, giving them words to say at their trials and preserving them from harm.

PRAYER
O God, the pattern of Jesus' suffering, death, and resurrection has been extremely meaningful to me whenever my own spirit has suffered in the human condition. I know there is hope in your power to bring good

out of evil and light out of darkness. Grant that I may be more dedicated to spreading the good news of this hope. In Jesus' name, amen.

Day 264   *Luke 21:20-38*

WHEN THE SUMMER IS NEAR

*W*e must remember that in the age when the New Testament was written, as existence for both individuals and nations was somewhat tenuous, apocalyptic predictions like these were very popular. Jesus often spoke of the destruction of Jerusalem. And indeed the city was destroyed by the Romans in A.D. 70, although Jesus' description of the destruction fits the destruction of 586 B.C. better than that one.

Verses 25-26 tell of an age of great natural calamities. The "roaring of the sea and the waves" suggests a temporary eruption of primeval chaos, when the waters God tamed in the Genesis story of creation rise out of their boundaries and threaten to swallow the land again.

But in all the disruption and horror, the Son of man will return, coming in a cloud with power and glory. Therefore, Jesus' followers should not be afraid, but should have confidence that their redemption is drawing near. How near seems to be indicated in verse 32, which is admittedly a problematic saying for us, suggesting as it does that Jesus expected a precipitous arrival of the end. Some interpreters believe these words apply to the destruction of Jerusalem and not to the end of all things.

The important practical consideration, as verses 34-36 observe, is to live in joyous expectation of God's new order, so that when the time of the end does come it does not catch us unaware. Having hearts "weighed down with dissipation and drunkenness and the worries of this life" (v. 34) is the opposite of living in the mood of ecstasy Luke has so frequently depicted as being appropriate to God's heavenly realm.

PRAYER

I am often weighed down, O God, by the cares of this life. My spirit is depressed by news of violence and greed and upheaval in the world. Sometimes it seems as if the ancient chaos has broken out again. Grant me the faith to watch through it all, living expectantly for the Son of man, who has already been revealed in history. Amen.

A WICKED AGREEMENT

*A*s Passover approached and "Messiah-fever" in Jerusalem ran higher and higher, the chief priests and scribes were feeling desperate. They could not arrest Jesus in the daytime without provoking an uprising. And they probably could not find him at night. Until—Judas became their answer.

Why did Judas do it? Some think, as John 12:6 indicates, he had embezzled money from the disciples' treasury and needed a cover. Others believe he was a Zealot, a member of a party of fierce nationalists, and hoped to produce a bloody revolution when Jesus was captured. Still others defend him by suggesting that he was impatient and wished to provoke the immediate arrival of God's realm. Jesus had, after all, repeatedly spoken of the necessity of his being delivered up and crucified; perhaps Judas understood this better than the others.

Luke did not trouble with such human alternatives. In his view, the betrayal had theological significance. Judas turned Jesus over to his enemies because Satan had entered into him. Unable to deflect Jesus from his goal of God's new order (Luke 4:1-13), Satan found one of the disciples of softer metal, and was working through him to prevent the preaching of the new order.

It was done for money. After all Jesus' talk about riches—the story of the rich man and Lazarus (Luke 16:19-31); the encounter with the rich ruler (Luke 18:18-30); the joyous meeting with Zacchaeus, who gave so much of his property to the poor (Luke 19:1-10); the commendation of the poor widow who gave all she had to the Temple treasury (Luke 21:1-4)—Judas defected for money. As a doctor, Luke probably knew people well. He knew how often economic considerations become the fulcrum on which people's whole lives turn. Again and again, in the book of Acts, he would note how the greed for money and property was an acid destroying people's lives. It is no wonder that Satan got to one of the disciples through this age-old door.

PRAYER

O God, I am suddenly fearful of this door in my own life. How ready am I to put economic considerations above everything else—above personal friendships, family values, even my dedication to your new order? I blush and pray for forgiveness. Envelop me in your presence until I am safe from temptation. Through Jesus, who withstood all trials, amen.

EATING THE PASSOVER

$\mathcal{N}$o meal in the entire year was more important to Hebrews than the Passover meal. It was a sacred meal, for it symbolized the birth of the Jewish nation. But it was also a social meal, the highlight of family life and joy.

It is much in keeping with Luke's picture of the human, compassionate Jesus that he shows him wanting to eat the Passover one last time with the disciples. Other Gospels possibly make more of the theological significance of the Last Supper. Luke obviously sees the human depths of it.

Normally one ate this meal with members of the family. But we remember that Jesus had said that those committed to the new order of God *were* his family (Luke 8:19-21). Similarly, he had told the disciples that he must come first with them, even before their families (Luke 14:25-26). Thus they established a precedent to be remembered in the Christian fellowship, especially at the time of Communion—that the followers of Jesus are a special family together, transcending all other relationships.

It may seem strange that Luke has reversed the order of the bread and the cup, putting the sharing of the cup before the breaking of bread. But 1 Corinthians 10:16-21 suggests a similar order, as does the *Didache*, a second-century book of teachings for the church. It is possible that these orders existed side by side in the early church.

Verses 21-23 refer, of course, to the betrayal by Judas. But the key words are in verse 22: "as it has been determined." Luke was invariably concerned to point out that everything that happened in Jesus' life and suffering had been prophesied and preordained by God. Even the betrayal itself was assimilated into the divine plan and purpose.

PRAYER

Dear God, how much this Passover meal must have meant to Jesus. How the joy and the sadness must have mingled in his heart that night! Help me to remember this strong personal emotion when I receive the cup and the bread and join with him in a prayer for the great banquet in your heavenly realm. Amen.

Day 267   *Luke 22:24-38*

THE WAY OF THE KINGDOM

*T*here is a sadness in these verses. Jesus has been with the disciples for months, instructing them, sharing himself with them, modeling ministry for them. Yet they are still like children who cannot understand. They are like the scribes and Pharisees, who love to have the best places at the table, and they fall to arguing about it. Jesus reminds them that the ideal of the new order is to serve, not to be served.

If the disciples will maintain this posture of obedient service, they will become the pillars of the new Israel. But they will not do so without interruption. First they will all fall away—even Simon Peter, who thinks he is ready to go to prison and the grave for his Master. As Satan entered Judas, he has also demanded to try Peter. But Jesus has prayed for Peter, and Satan will not be able to hold him.

Verses 35-38 are a warning to the disciples. When Jesus sent them out before, they were able to live off the hospitality of others wherever they went. But when Jesus has been crucified and his name maligned throughout the land, doors will be shut to them that were open before. They will have to carry provisions with them, and even go about armed for self-protection. Taking him quite literally, the disciples produce two swords. "It is enough," he says—probably meaning to let the matter go; enough has been said about it.

PRAYER

I want to serve you, O God, until those I am serving become hostile or arrogant or undeserving. Then I want to stop being a servant and become a ruler. Help me to remember Jesus in his passion, and humbly take my place beside him, for it is the way of the new order. Amen.

THE CUSTOM OF PRAYING

*L*uke alone, among the Gospel writers, records that it was Jesus' custom to go to the Mount of Olives to pray. Were it not for this, we might suppose that this experience on the night of the Passover was an isolated incident. But apparently it was not. Each evening through the week, as Jesus and the disciples returned from the Temple to the place of their lodging, they stopped here to commune with God, to feel the presence that recomposed their minds and restored their energies.

Mark in his Gospel (14:26-42) was more interested in the disciples' failure to understand the cruciality of the hour and to pray than he was in the agony of Jesus. But not so Luke! Unlike both Mark and Matthew, he does not record how Jesus three times returned and found the disciples asleep when they should have been praying. Instead, he describes, as they do not, the manner of Jesus' personal anguish—how a heavenly messenger appeared to strengthen him in his praying, as one would be joined in a mighty task by an ethereal stranger, and how the very pores of his body exuded drops of blood because of the enormous stress and intensity of the prayer.

Luke wished us to see, without question, the terrible human struggle going on in Jesus as the devil made a last mighty effort to deter him from purchasing a new realm with his own suffering and death.

PRAYER
O God, I am grateful for this warm, poignant picture of Jesus struggling through prayer with the destiny he knew was coming. It enables me to enter my own times of crisis-praying with more courage and confidence, for I see that the important outcome is not release from suffering but obedience to your will. Amen.

THE POWER OF DARKNESS

*P*rofessor Harry Levin once wrote a book called *The Power of Blackness*. A study of the fiction of Hawthorne, Melville, and Poe, it was designed to reveal how much of the power in their writing derived from their ability to tap the dark side of events and the world. The phrase with which Luke concludes this passage is similar to Professor Levin's title, for Luke, as much as Professor Levin, appreciated the way evil forces are at work in the world we live in.

Here, the evil triumph comes as the culmination of many battles with Jesus throughout his ministry. The devil never managed to touch Jesus himself in a vulnerable spot, but he had reached to the heart of Judas, one of his disciples. And he was using the religious establishment of Jerusalem—the chief priests, scribes, and Pharisees—as a veritable phalanx to move against Jesus. Here they were, massed together with torches, knives, and clubs, closing in on the Master at his place of prayer. Judas had been with him there before, so he knew precisely where to lead the others.

The disciples moved instinctively to protect their Master. But Jesus had already decreed that the new order was not to come by force. Healing the wounded ear of an enemy, he bade the disciples not to offer further resistance. He was, after all, no common criminal, that they should come for him with staves and swords.

Perhaps the saddest note of all is in verses 47-48. It was the custom for rabbis and their followers to greet each other with a kiss. But Jesus, knowing what Judas had conspired to do, was unwilling for him to add to his perfidy the hypocrisy of a kiss.

It was indeed the enemies' hour—and Satan's. But Jesus' hour would come.

PRAYER

It has been said, O God, that the brave person murders with a sword, the coward with a kiss. How many times have I betrayed you with a kiss, saying a pious word, acting as if I were on your side, when in fact I was weakly committed to you, if at all. Grant me the courage to be honest in my expression of feelings, and, above all, give me the grace to love you devotedly. Through Jesus, who refused a kiss that wasn't meant, amen.

A BITTER REMINDER

*I*n Mark's account of this part of the Gospel, Jesus was taken immediately before the Sanhedrin for trial, and Peter's denial occurred in the courtyard outside while the trial was going on. Luke's account, which is more probable, has Jesus being held in the courtyard of the high priest's house until morning, when he was brought to the Sanhedrin. This means that Peter was very close to where Jesus was being mocked and beaten by the soldiers—perhaps only a few yards away, in full view of it all—and that Jesus could hear each of his denials.

The courtyard would not have been large—perhaps sixty by seventy feet. The fire would have been lit for warmth as well as light, for the early spring nights are frosty in Israel. Peter showed a certain courage in entering the courtyard and then in staying after the scrutiny of a maid first identified him as one of Jesus' followers. But his courage did not run deep enough. Three times he denied that he had been with Jesus. And then, the third time, before the words had died on his lips, the cock crowed. Jesus, who all through the night had been the object of ridicule and mistreatment by men who were holding him for the dawn, heard it too, and looked at Peter. Their eyes met, and Peter remembered.

What could he do? He remembered all the good days together—how proud he had been to be first among the disciples during the months of triumph and popularity—"and he went out and wept bitterly" (v. 62).

PRAYER
This is the saddest passage, O God. I know how Peter felt in the courtyard—and how he felt when he realized he had betrayed a friend who loved him. But thank you for the story. It reminds us that we can return to faithfulness even after we have disappointed you. Help me to be faithful. Through Jesus, who prays for his own, amen.

JESUS AND THE OLD MEN

*T*he assembly of elders was composed of priests, scribes, Pharisees, and Sadducees—the main power blocs in Jewish life. As in other occupied countries, the Roman government permitted the local assembly to transact most of the business affecting its nation's internal affairs.

The members were not all evil men. Many were probably persons of deep conscience and moral conviction. They were like the members of any court or tribunal, who must live with their own personal, business, and family problems at the same time that they take the bench and make decisions affecting others.

They wanted to hear only one thing from Jesus: Did he claim to be the Messiah? "Why should I tell you?" Jesus replied, in effect. "If I did, you would not believe me." But he did tell them one thing—that from then on the Son of man would be seated at God's right hand, enthroned in power. His hour of glory had come; Satan's dominion would be shaken.

"Are you, then, the Son of God?" they wanted to know (v. 70). Mark says that he replied, "I am" (14:62). But both Matthew and Luke have altered the account to read "You have said so" (Matt. 26:64) and "You say that I am" (Luke 22:70), as though Jesus were simply resigning the matter, and implying "Think what you will."

The elders accepted this as an admission of his claim to be the Messiah and bound him over to Pilate's jurisdiction. Their own charge against him was theological, that he was guilty of blasphemy; but the charge on which they would present him to Pilate was political, that he was guilty of sedition.

PRAYER

To be human, O God, is to be involved in a network of complicity and guilt from which there is never complete extrication. We all make decisions—sometimes wrongly—affecting the lives and destinies of others. Help me to be sensitive to this and always have the courage to act honestly and compassionately in matters involving others. Through Jesus, who suffered the greatest injustice at the hands of "good" men, amen.

A BASIS FOR FRIENDSHIP

*L*acking the authority to pronounce a death penalty on Jesus, the council members came clattering into Pilate's hall to put the case before him. They made three accusations, all related to the charge of sedition: Jesus was stirring up the people, had advised the crowds not to pay the annual poll tax, and had proclaimed himself a Messiah-King. The first two charges were absolutely false. Jesus had consistently refused to excite the populace about his messiahship, and had attempted to keep it secret. The agents for the chief priests and scribes had tried to get him to say that the people should not pay taxes to Caesar, but he had not been caught in their trap (Luke 20:20-26). And we have seen in Luke 22:66-71 how the assembly drew from him the admission—if indeed it was an admission—that he was the Messiah. But the Sanhedrin was not after truth in this matter, only action. It translated everything into a language it believed would move Pilate to do as they wished.

Pilate attempted to understand the matter as well as he could. When he questioned Jesus, Jesus remained silent, knowing his words would not avail against those of the entire council of old men. Pilate said he seemed innocent enough. But the Sanhedrin declared that he was going through the whole country, from Galilee to Judea, stirring up the populace.

The mention of Galilee gave Pilate the out he needed. Learning that Jesus was a Galilean, he declared that Herod should have jurisdiction over him, for Herod was tetrarch of Galilee. And Herod, we recall, had long been interested in Jesus, wondering if he were John the Baptist come back to life (Luke 9:7-9). But Jesus was no more talkative before Herod than he had been before Pilate. So, after some mockery and buffoonery at Jesus' expense, the soldiers sent him back again to Pilate.

PRAYER

O God, I pray for every innocent person who must bear this kind of treatment today from authorities in the law or government. Give such persons the grace to behave with inner composure as Jesus did, that the indignities may not wound deeply. And hasten the day of your new order, that all people may dwell together as brothers and sisters with mutual respect. Amen.

THE MASTER AND A MURDERER

*T*he goddess Justice is usually depicted wearing a blindfold to emphasize her impartiality in rendering judgments. But our experiences in life sometimes make us think it is a sign of her blindness to the facts that would really make for justice.

The story of Barabbas's release fits the latter interpretation. He was in prison for precisely the same charges as those on which Jesus had been arraigned—sedition and insurrection. Yet he went free, and Jesus, who was innocent, was crucified.

Verse 17, which has been omitted from the RSV and the NRSV translations because it is missing from the oldest, most reliable texts of the Gospel, is necessary to explain Pilate's action. The Romans, to curry favor with the Jews, had a practice of releasing a prisoner of the people's choice during the Passover festival. When Jesus was found innocent by both Pilate and Herod, therefore, the Jews set up a clamor to release Barabbas and crucify Jesus.

Mark 15:11 informs us that the chief priests stirred up the crowd to have Pilate release Barabbas instead of Jesus. We can imagine, when Luke says "they kept urgently demanding with loud shouts that he should be crucified" (v. 23), that the priests and elders were among those crying the loudest. Clever men that they were, they incited the crowd to do their evil work for them.

PRAYER
O God, it is a fearful responsibility to be a leader of any kind. I pray for those who have roles of leadership today, especially in the world community. Grant to them a fierce respect for human rights and justice, so that they always put the good of others ahead of their own self-interest. In Jesus' name, amen.

THE CRYING OF THE WOMEN

*S*imon of Cyrene is one of those special people who, by happening to be at a particular place in a given moment, are cast by unexpected circumstances into the spotlight of history. We know almost nothing about him—he may have been a Jewish pilgrim arriving in Jerusalem after taking the Passover with relatives or friends in the country, or he may have been a one-time inhabitant of Cyrene now living near Jerusalem—but he has since become the subject of hundreds of paintings, poems, and sermons. The cross the soldiers ordered him to carry behind Jesus was the crossbar, which would be hoisted and affixed to an upright pole or scaffolding at the scene of execution.

The women who followed with the crowd had commenced the funeral custom of loud public mourning even in advance of Jesus' death. Apparently they were not the same women who had accompanied him as disciples, but local residents, as he called them "daughters of Jerusalem" (v. 28). Jesus was not angry with them; he merely used their wailing as the basis for a prophetic warning about the future destruction of the city by the Romans. It was considered a curse for a woman to remain barren and have no children. But Jesus reversed that popular standard, saying that in the day of catastrophe the barren ones would be thought blessed, for they would not have to witness the cruel slaughter of their children. If a miscarriage of justice such as one resulting in Jesus' death could occur under presently calm conditions, what would happen in that time of national disaster?

Of course, Jesus was right. Descriptions of the sacking of a city under siege are among the most horrifying accounts in all history, and the Roman demolition of Jerusalem would have offered no exception. The people of Jerusalem bought no favor with anyone with their failure to rise up in support of Jesus. Evil simply increased its hold on them until, a few years later, their beloved city was mercilessly destroyed.

PRAYER

O God, I understand the feelings of the women of Jerusalem. They were helpless against the will of those in power. Teach me to listen to the voices of those who are powerless, that I may more often know what justice is. Through Jesus, who is on the side of the little ones, amen.

PARADISE IN THE WILDERNESS

*N*o other scene in all of history has drawn the attention of artists as this one has. And no wonder—considering all the faces to be viewed here.

There are the faces of the two criminals, one bitter and derisive, the other wondering and hopeful. "Remember me," said the second (v. 42). And Jesus promised him a place in paradise, in the garden of delights.

There are the faces of the crowd. They stood "watching," says Luke. Some probably showed entertainment and enjoyment. Others probably showed horror and revulsion. Perhaps some revealed attitudes of wonder and expectancy. Was this really the Messiah? Would the new order of God appear as he hung on the cross?

There are the faces of the rulers—the priests and scribes and Pharisees. Most of them were scoffing. "He saved others," they called derisively, "let him save himself if he is the Messiah of God, his chosen one!" (v. 35). They thought they had taken care of the blasphemous upstart from the northern provinces.

There are the faces of the soldiers—tough, battle-hardened, unflinching before death and suffering. They joined in the mocking, saying that if he were the King of the Jews, as his inscription read, he should rescue himself.

And there is the face of Jesus himself, the focus of every artist's inspiration. It was regal, quietly confident, and forgiving of those who did not understand how Satan was using them as pawns and dupes in his last great bid for supremacy. Even from his cross, Jesus spoke with authority, as when he told the criminal, "Today you will be with me in Paradise" (v. 43). He knew the irony of the situation, that what appeared to most of those around him as utter defeat was really a prelude to God's mighty victory.

Paradise, he had promised the criminal. The Aramaic word for "paradise" was a form of an old Persian word, *pardes,* meaning "garden." To the Jewish mind, it spoke of both the Garden of Eden and the heavenly abode of God, where no evil existed but all was made innocent again in the divine presence. The criminal who believed would go from the cross to the realm, from the wilderness to the garden, that very day.

O God, it is easy for me to take the right side as I read this story, but it is quite another matter when I stand in the crowd at the various times when Christ is crucified today. Often I take the wrong side and realize only afterward that he was being put to death in this or that legislative bill or referendum, this or that argument among my friends. Make me more sensitive to the way he is treated in the world around me, that I may not end up mocking when I should have worshiped. Amen.

Day 276   *Luke 23:44-49*

SIGNS, PORTENTS, AND SADNESS

Signs in nature, the ancient peoples believed, often corroborated events in human life. Therefore, the darkness that came over the earth at midday was a fitting natural symbol for the death of God's Messiah. And the curtain alluded to in verse 45 was the great veil separating the outer part of the Temple from the inner part, the holy of holies, where only the high priest entered to perform sacrifices once each year on the Day of Atonement. The rending of this veil was a dramatic sign of the end of the old system and the free access to the divine presence now available to all, even persons ritually unclean.

Jesus' final words are from Psalm 31:5, whose context expresses strong assurance in God's care and delivery for the faithful one beset by suffering. God is spoken of as a "rock" and a "fortress" and a "refuge." "Into your hand I commit my spirit," the psalm reads. "You have redeemed me, O LORD, faithful God" (Ps. 31:5).

Mark 15:39 says that when Jesus had died, the centurion declared that Jesus was truly the Son of God. Apparently it suited Luke's purpose better to interpret his remark as a testimony to Jesus' innocence. This would have been important to a Roman audience, as it confirmed what Pilate, the Roman governor, had already decided (Luke 23:4, 13-16).

Luke alone records the information in verse 48 about the crowd's returning home in a mood of lamentation and penitence. Taken with verse 35, which says they were "watching" the crucifixion in an attitude unlike that of the rulers, who scoffed and mocked, it indicates that the people were generally convinced that injustice had prevailed and that Jesus was a good man. Even if they were not sure he was the Messiah, they knew a prophet and wonder-worker had been put to death that day.

And there is a mellow sadness in verse 49, which says that all those who had followed him from Galilee "stood at a distance" and saw everything that happened. If Jesus could have spoken to them from the cross, perhaps he would have quoted to them the last verse of Psalm 31—the ending of the psalm he had cited in dying: "Be strong, and let your heart take courage,/ all you who wait for the LORD" (Ps. 31:24).

PRAYER

Dear God, sometimes I wish the curtain in the Temple were still there. It is such a responsibility to have your holy presence meeting me everywhere I turn. You are there in my morning shower, in the meals I eat, in the persons I meet, in the games I play, in the way I do my work. Give me courage not only to wait for you but to meet you where you already are! In Jesus' name, amen.

Day 277   *Luke 23:50-56*

AN ACT OF RESTITUTION

*M*any times in life the only thing we can do is try in some small way to make amends for the wrong done to another—to put an arm around the student who has been unfairly treated, to invite to dinner an employee who has been unjustly fired, to treat generously the victim of racial prejudice or social inequity. It does not undo the wrong or compensate in any way for the sacrilege committed. But it is all we can do, in our feeble manner, to reach out and say, "I am sorry; I wish it hadn't happened."

This is essentially what Joseph of Arimathea did in caring for the body of Jesus. Matthew 27:57 and John 19:38 say that Joseph was a disciple of Jesus. Luke is more concerned to stress his humanitarian quality, his honest resistance to the Sanhedrin's "plan and action," and his basic Jewish hope in God's new realm. His act took some courage in the face of Pharisaic piety and the laws about touching the dead, who were considered unclean—and in Jesus' case, accursed as well. The tomb may have been Joseph's own, in which case the devotion shown would be similar to that of the woman in Mark 14:3-9 who anointed Jesus' head with her own expensive burial perfume. It was his way of saying he was sorry, that Jesus had not deserved the treatment he had received.

270

While Joseph was taking the body to the tomb, the Galilean women followed—perhaps performing traditional mourning rites along the way—and saw where it was buried. Then, returning to the marketplace, they purchased spices and ointments for anointing the body and retired to their lodging places as the sun was setting, to wait through the sabbath to come again to the tomb.

PRAYER

Dear God, what a long day it must have been through which the women waited! I pray for all who wait now for their return to the grave where a loved one has just been buried. The hours drag for them, too. Let them discover in this heavy time the hope that we hold through him who was laid in a borrowed tomb, yet could not be held by death. Amen.

Day 278   *Luke 24:1-12*

A THROWAWAY SCENE

*T*he account of the empty tomb in the Gospel of Mark contains some significant differences from Luke's version: Mark has a single messenger at the tomb (Mark 16:5), not two (Luke 24:4); the messenger tells the women that Jesus has gone ahead of them to Galilee (Mark 16:7), instead of reminding them of what Jesus said to them in Galilee (Luke 24:6-7); the women are afraid and tell no one what they have found (Mark 16:8), instead of telling the others what they have seen and not being believed (Luke 24:10-11).

It accorded with Mark's themes and theology to end his Gospel with the women's fear and silence. But how does Luke's interpretation of this final event fit into his overall message? As Mark's narrative of the life and ministry of Jesus focused on its strange power and the disciples' inability to grasp its meaning, so Luke's has centered on the theme of the great joy that has come to those who received the new order of God. Thus this passage serves as a mere prelude to the joy experienced by the disciples from Emmaus when Jesus eats with them (Luke 24:28-32) and by the followers when they realize what has taken place (Luke 24:52). In dramatic terms, it is a "throwaway" scene—one that sacrifices any particular significance of its own to the building of plot and intrigue further on in the play.

The women find the tomb empty and are reminded that Jesus told them he must die and would not be held by the grave. Then they go to report this to all the other followers—but are not believed. It is the negative moment from which the joyous, positive ones will soon follow.

PRAYER

O God, help me to recognize the throwaway scenes in my own life— those whose significance lies in what is about to happen—and thus to give thanks for those otherwise negative or less exciting times and wait in humble expectancy for what will be revealed. Through Jesus, who sanctifies all times, even the time when little seems to occur, amen.

Day 279   *Luke 24:13-35*

A REMARKABLE VISITOR

*L*uke alone, of the Gospel writers, has preserved this lovely story of the two disciples from Emmaus. They had probably been among those who "stood at a distance" and observed the crucifixion (Luke 23:49). As Jewish law forbade traveling on the sabbath, they would have had to wait until its end to begin their sad trek home.

We have normally thought of the two disciples as male, for the Greek word used to describe them in verse 25 is masculine. But there is nothing in the Greek usage to forbid the possibility that one was a woman. In fact, as they lived together, it is likely that they were either two brothers or a man and his wife.

At any rate, Jesus gave his two followers an extended lesson in Old Testament prophecy. He showed them that the entire pattern of Hebrew thought should have pointed the Jews to understand Israel's mission in terms of suffering and servanthood; if they had only seen this, they would not have been put off by his death, for only by suffering could he enter the kind of glory God intended for him.

It would have been meaningful to early Christians that the two followers recognized Jesus in the breaking of bread after the long lesson in Old Testament prophecies. This pattern was not unlike that of their own worship—first having the Scriptures explained and then meeting the risen Lord in the eucharistic meal.

Verse 32 speaks of the unusual sense of joy the two disciples felt even before they recognized their strange visitor, and it was in this mood of ecstasy that they retraced their steps to Jerusalem that very hour—in the dark!—and found the eleven to tell them what had happened. The eleven were not entirely surprised, for Peter had already reported a similar visitation.

The Resurrection clearly meant one thing: Jesus was no longer confined by normal restrictions of time and space in which mortal lives are framed, but was free to appear wherever and whenever he pleased, to this disciple and that, in this place and another.

PRAYER

How often, Lord, you probably walk with me in my way and I do not recognize you. Forgive my lack of perception, and help me, through careful study of the Scriptures and a life of prayerful reflection, to discern your presence more regularly. Your only limits are the ones I impose upon you. Amen.

Day 280   *Luke 24:36-43*

THE SPIRIT WHO ATE FISH

*W*e are like the disciples in this passage. Our views about reality are largely set by the society around us and what it has taught us to expect. Therefore, even if Jesus were to appear to us as he did to the disciples, we would believe him to be a hallucination of some kind, not a real flesh-and-blood person.

It was especially important, in the early church, to emphasize that the resurrected Jesus was truly corporeal and not a mere phantom. A heretical branch of the faith, called Docetism, maintained that Christ's Spirit came into his flesh at birth and forsook it at death. This was counter to the teaching of his incarnation, which maintained that Jesus was resurrected in body, not merely in spirit. Luke was here trying to enforce correct belief. The Gospel of John, which is believed to have been written as a defense against the Docetists, contains similar stories emphasizing the true bodily nature of the resurrected Jesus (see John 20:24-29; 21:1-14).

Jesus invited the disciples to touch and handle him—to know him nonverbally. It was a marvelous invitation, for it is quite possible that our deepest "knowings" are tactile rather than aural or intellectual. Jesus wanted the disciples to be satisfied in the most basic way possible that it was really he who stood before them. He even took fish and ate it to show them he was no ghost. He was a vital, living person.

The phrase Luke used in verse 41, "in their joy they were disbelieving, and still wondering," is characteristic of the thrust of his Gospel. What had come to pass was simply too great to believe! Nothing in the disciples' experience of life had fully prepared them for it. They could only shake their heads in wonder at the outcome.

PRAYER

O God, I become excited merely reading about the disciples' great joy. How could the church become so lethargic and apathetic in the wake of such a report? Help me to be open to the same "joy in disbelieving" in my own life. Through him who is the cause for such joy, Jesus our Lord, amen.

Day 281   *Luke 24:44-49*

THE CHARGING OF WITNESSES

*T*he disciples took seriously Jesus' charge to be witnesses to all they had seen and heard of his ministry, death, and resurrection. Later, as recorded in Acts 10:39-41, Peter declared to Cornelius, the man who sought his help for the Gentiles: "We are witnesses to all that he did both in Judea and in Jerusalem. They put him to death by hanging him on a tree; but God raised him on the third day and allowed him to appear, not to all the people but to us who were chosen by God as witnesses, and who ate and drank with him after he rose from the dead."

The Old Testament is full of references to witnesses. Usually the word had a legal sense, as of those who testified to the truth of a matter. But perhaps the most important ancient prototype for the Christian witness is to be found in Isaiah 43, where God charges the prophet with being a witness to everything disclosed in the councils of heaven. The prophet describes God's intention of saving Israel and gathering all the people to testify that God is indeed God.

Jesus' disciples were commissioned to be witnesses of the new Israel, the spiritual community God would gather from the four corners of the earth. They would begin in Jerusalem, but eventually their message would go out to all the nations. The "promise" of God was of a great people, and the fulfilling of the promise would bring the "great joy" of which the angels had spoken to the shepherds when Jesus was born (Luke 2:10-11).

Ironically, the Greek word translated "witness" is the same word from which we derive our word *martyr*. In making their faithful witness, many of the disciples would suffer or lose their lives, for the evil one would not give up his world without a struggle. But the joy was never diminished by this. It was like a lamp whose wick was always trimmed and made to burn even brighter by slander and persecution.

PRAYER

I am a witness in my way too, O God, for I have heard and seen things of your new order. Make me daily more conscious of this, that I may give my testimony to others. Clothe me with power as you did the disciples, and use me in the fulfillment of your promise. Through Jesus, who will be Lord of lords and King of kings, amen.

Day 282   *Luke 24:50-53*

THE BLESSING AND THE JOY

*B*efore Moses died at the edge of the promised land, he raised his hands and pronounced a blessing over the tribes of Israel (Deuteronomy 33). Jesus may well have been following this practice in blessing his disciples before leaving them. He had walked with them to Bethany. Some ancient manuscripts omit the phrase "and was carried up into heaven" from verse 51. Luke may indeed have omitted the phrase himself, preferring to picture Jesus as being on the road to somewhere; for that is where the disciples would often find him as they traveled with the gospel—he would appear to them in this place and that, as he had to the ones going to Emmaus, and strengthen them for the task he had given them.

However it was, he blessed and left them, and they returned to Jerusalem to worship in the Temple and wait for the outpouring of God's power. Mark, it will be recalled, saw Jerusalem as an evil place and represented Jesus as ordering the disciples immediately to Galilee (Mark 16:7). But Luke viewed the city differently; he remembered the prophecies picturing it as the center of God's renewing activity in the world (see Isa. 35:8-10). Therefore, he had the disciples return to the city and the Temple, where the stage was set for the descent of the Spirit in Acts 2 and the beginning of a vast missionary enterprise that would eventually carry the gospel into all the world.

The Gospel of Luke ends on the note that has been so characteristic of it all along: the "great joy" of those who have seen what God is doing and have become a part of it. It has been a Gospel of angels' songs, great feasts, stories of glad returns, excitement about healings and resurrections, and the ecstasy of those who have recognized the arrival of God's new realm. No wonder the last words are that "they were continually in the temple blessing God."

PRAYER

O God, this whole Gospel has accused me of being far less joyous and excited about your new order than I have every right to be. Teach me to set my days in the light of your presence, that they may become storehouses of delight, and to see the world as the arena of your great victory, that I may hope even in the face of despair. Through Jesus, who blesses me and helps me to worship, amen.

Day 283   *John 1:1-18*

JESUS IS THE LIGHT

ord, light, power, grace, truth, glory, fullness. Like the overture to a musical play, the prologue of John's Gospel gives hints of all the themes to be developed later. It is a tremendous introduction—one of the greatest poems ever written. Frederick Buechner once called it "a hymn to perform surgery with, a heart-transplanting voice."

John knew he was writing nothing less than the story of a new creation. His words "in the beginning" instantly recall the opening of the book of Genesis. The other Gospels emphasized the continuity between the ancient prophets and Jesus. John went further; for him, Jesus was the Word that existed before the creation of the world itself!

The brightest note in the prologue, after the coming of the eternal Word, is that some have accepted the light and become children of God. These are born, as John says, "not of blood or of the will of the flesh or of the will of man, but of God" (v. 13). Yet many of these, in John's day, were having great difficulties. Jewish Christians were being excluded from the synagogues, and thus had to choose between Judaism and following Jesus.

The Gospel of John was written primarily to encourage these Jewish Christians not to renounce their faith in order to be accepted in the synagogues. The Jewish people were born of flesh and blood—"of the will

276

of man." But the children of light are born of God. Moses, who saw only the "back" of God, conveyed the law. But Jesus, who not only saw God but came from the very bosom of God, brought grace and truth.

What more ultimate word could be spoken? Jesus, the incarnate Word of God, was the very essence of the covenant God had made with the Jewish people in the beginning of their relationship. He was *word, light, power, grace, truth, glory,* and *fullness.* He fulfilled every promise God had ever made to the children of Israel.

PRAYER

O God, this is indeed a hymn for performing life-saving surgery! It carries my mind beyond its limits, and I am shown mysteries too great for me to comprehend. I can only bow my head and worship you, content in the knowledge that your light will lead me to salvation through Jesus Christ, the same yesterday, today, and forever. Amen.

Day 284   *John 1:19-28*

THE TESTIMONY OF JOHN

*W*hen the delegates from Jerusalem, men versed in the law and traditions, asked John the Baptist who he was, he gave a curious response. Instead of naming himself, he said, "I am not the Messiah" (v. 20). The words, besides being emphatic, foreshadow a series of statements Jesus will make in the Gospel in which he says, "I am the bread of life," "I am the light of the world," "I am the door of the sheep," and so forth.

Then the delegation wished to know if he was Elijah. Baptism was an eschatological symbol—a sign of the end of all things. Popular belief said Elijah would return at the end of history (Mal. 4:5) or that some other prophet would be present to lead the people (Deut. 18:15). Again John uttered denials. "Then who are you?" pressed the questioners. The answer was appropriately modest: He was a voice crying in the wilderness for the people to make a straight road for the Lord. John was citing a prophecy in Isaiah 40:3. The image was not uncommon; kings and emperors often sent slaves in advance of their coming to secure the roads on which they would travel.

There was only one question left: Why was John baptizing if he was not the Messiah or Elijah or another prophet? John didn't hesitate. "I baptize with water," he said. "Among you stands one whom you do not know, the one who is coming after me; I am not worthy to untie the thong of his sandal" (vv. 26-27).

What drama this suggests! Perhaps Jesus was even then standing on the bank among the crowds. And John, according to the practice of rabbis and their students in those days, classified himself among the rabbi's followers, who were deigned unworthy to remove the rabbi's shoes.

PRAYER

O Lord, I who am not even as worthy as John beg to be your disciple. Grant that I may never get in your way, so that people see me when they should be seeing you. Baptize me with your Holy Spirit, that all my thoughts and deeds may glorify you, this day and forever. Amen.

Day 285   *John 1:29-34*

THE WITNESS OF THE SPIRIT

*M*atthew, Mark, and Luke all represent Jesus as receiving John the Baptist's baptism. John's Gospel, however, tactfully avoids any scene in which Jesus is baptized. Its Messiah is too exalted to receive baptism at John's hands. He is the preexistent Word (1:1-3, 30). He and the Father are one (17:11, 20-23). He does not suffer in Gethsemane as does the Christ of the other Gospels. He is the transcendent Messiah, the ruler of the cosmos. It would not be appropriate for John the Baptist to baptize him.

In the Synoptic tradition, John recognized Jesus as the Messiah after the baptism, when the Spirit descended on him like a dove. Here, John purports to have witnessed the Spirit, but does not link it to Jesus' having been baptized. Apparently the descent occurred at some past time, so that John knew Jesus' real identity when the priests and Levites from Jerusalem came to see him.

John makes three statements about Jesus: (1) Jesus is the Lamb of God who takes away the sin of the world; (2) even though Jesus comes later than John, he existed before John and ranks above him; (3) the Spirit has descended on Jesus, and he is the one who baptizes with the Holy Spirit.

What is meant by the phrase "Lamb of God"? Some scholars believe it refers to the apocalyptic lamb mentioned in Revelation 7:17 and 17:14, which is an object of terror and will destroy evil in the world. Others see it as the Suffering Servant of Isaiah 52–53, who gives his life for the people

278

of God, or as the paschal lamb, whose blood was smeared on the door posts of the Israelites to save their children from the death angel (Exod. 12:22). The latter interpretation fits especially well with the sacramentalism of the Fourth Gospel, which has Jesus condemned to death at noon on the day before Passover (19:4), the very hour when the priests began to sacrifice the lambs in the Temple. But all of the interpretations are fitting, and it is possible that the author, with his great literary imagination, used the phrase for precisely this reason.

PRAYER

O Lamb of God, I worship you. I praise your name for this rich image of your saving power, and for the Holy Spirit with which you baptize your true followers. Help me to witness faithfully to your coming in my life, as John the Baptist witnessed to your coming in his; for you are indeed the Son of God. Amen.

Day 286   *John 1:35-42*

A TRANSFERENCE OF DISCIPLES

*T*his is the only Gospel that represents any of Jesus' disciples as having originally been disciples of John the Baptist. The other Gospels depict the calling of Andrew, Simon Peter, James, and John at the seashore in Galilee. Many scholars are inclined to believe John's version is more accurate, or that the calling in Galilee occurred after the one in Judea, and the disciples had gone home to fish for a while. This would explain the apparent abruptness of the calling in the Synoptics.

The scene is quiet but powerful. The two disciples walk away from John the Baptist and follow Jesus. Jesus looks back, sees them, and asks what they are seeking. They call him rabbi, or great teacher, and ask where he is staying. He invites them to come and see. They do, and end by staying the entire day with him.

It is beautiful the way Andrew then goes to find his brother Simon Peter and says, "We have found the Messiah" (v. 41). Peter is to figure much more prominently in the early Christian movement than Andrew, but Peter might not have met Jesus at all if it had not been for Andrew. "We have found the Messiah" could be the most important message ever spoken by a disciple of Jesus, whether in their age or ours.

Jesus changes Simon's name to Cephas, which is translated "Peter" and means "rock," possibly expressing something Jesus saw in his character. In Matthew 16:18 Jesus infers that he calls Simon "rock" because Jesus intends to build his church on him. The Fourth Gospel does not explain the meaning, but we recall that an act of renaming in the Old Testament (e.g., Abram to Abraham or Jacob to Israel) presaged some mighty use of the person renamed.

PRAYER

O God of Abraham and Israel, of Andrew and Simon Peter, what would you like to call me? What name might evoke the gift I am able to give you? Teach it to me as I pray, and let us have it between us as our secret, that I may hear when you call me in the night, and respond, "Here am I, Lord." Through Jesus, whose name is greatest of all, amen.

Day 287   *John 1:43-51*

A PUZZLING DISCIPLE

None of the other Gospels mentions Nathanael as a disciple of Jesus. It is possible that he was included in their lists under another name—some think he may have been Matthew, as Matthew means "gift of Yahweh" and Nathanael means "God has given." But it is also possible that John is trying to represent something special with this story, for he calls Nathanael "truly an Israelite in whom there is no deceit" (v. 47). Nathanael may well stand for the new Israel, those born "not of blood or of the will of the flesh or of the will of man, but of God" (1:13). This interpretation is reinforced by Jesus' saying he saw Nathanael under the fig tree, for the fig tree in the Old Testament was often a symbol of a prosperous Israel.

Nathanael's response to Jesus' call is beautiful. First he addresses Jesus as rabbi, or teacher. Then he calls him Son of God. And finally he names him King of Israel, which involves a play on the fact that Jesus earlier called Nathanael "truly an Israelite."

Jesus' response to Nathanael is to tell him that the best is yet to come. If Nathanael believes on the basis of the simple encounter they have had, his heart will swell at all he will behold in months to come. What he will see will be utterly convincing—as if angels danced from heaven to earth and back again above the head of this man he has taken as his King!

280

O God, this is an inspiring passage. Help me to take Jesus as my teacher and king, that I, too, may be "truly an Israelite" in your new realm. And as I pray and meditate in the weeks ahead, let me see with spiritual eyes this confirming vision of the Messiah with angels dancing above his head. For yours is the new order and the power and the glory forever. Amen.

Day 288   *John 2:1-12*

THE BEST WINE OF ALL

*H*ere again we are into material not mentioned in the other Gospels. This is extraordinary, when we consider that John says it is the very first miracle Jesus performed. Moreover, John leaps into the story by saying "On the third day there was a wedding" (v. 1). The third day from what? From Jesus' baptism? From the calling of Philip and Nathanael? It has even been suggested that it is a reference to the third day after Jesus' death, when the resurrection occurred. Thus the wedding feast would be intended as a symbol of the new realm of God.

Whether we accept this interpretation or not, it is no doubt significant that the miracle involved six stone jars that held water for the Jewish rite of purification. The number six meant incompleteness to the Jews, as the number seven signaled completeness. If we assume that the wine had sacramental significance—as a symbol of the Christian Eucharist, or Communion—we see the contrast between the inadequacy of the old religion and the fullness of the new. The steward of the feast—probably a friend of the bridegroom—pronounced the new wine even better than the wine they had already had, though it was customary to serve the best wine first at a feast.

Each of us must decide individually whether the author of the Gospel intended the story literally or symbolically. But either way it is impossible to miss a certain symbolic level in the passage. Early Christians could hardly have heard the account without finding eucharistic meaning in it. Jesus is the one who gives the new wine of the heavenly realm. Wedding feasts were often used as a sign of God's ultimate banquet—the great ingathering of God at the end of time. And Nathanael, the true Israelite, must surely have seen this.

O Lord, the old wine of my life has failed me. I thirst for the new wine of your presence and power. Come into my daily affairs and give me a banqueting spirit. Transform the inadequate forms of religion in my life into well springs of faith and joy, for your wine is above all wines, and your realm beyond compare. Amen.

Day 289   *John 2:13-22*

TALKING ABOUT TEMPLES

*T*here may be significance in the placement of this story near the account of the wedding in Cana (in the Synoptic Gospels, it comes near the end of Jesus' ministry, not at the beginning). The miracle at Cana demonstrates the superiority of the new order over the old. Here Jesus moves from talking about the old Temple to speaking of the new one—his body—which would be raised up in three days.

We remember that the Gospel was written to encourage Christian Jews not to return to Judaism in order to continue worshiping in the synagogues. This passage had obvious meaning for such persons, for it effectually relocates holy space from the Temple to Jesus himself.

The cleansing of the Temple becomes a mere launching point for the conversation with "the Jews," which is the weightier part of the passage. The Jews, who lack spiritual understanding, ask for a sign of Jesus' authority—a miracle to attest to his messiahship. He answers with a dare: "Destroy this temple, and in three days I will raise it up" (v. 19). The Jews assume he is referring to the great building that is still under construction, the one from which he has driven the money changers and sacrifice-vendors. In fact, he was referring to his own body.

Again there is a possible connection to the passage about the wedding feast at Cana. It, too, took place "on the third day" and was suggestive of the fullness of life to come through Jesus' resurrection.

It is little wonder, when Jesus had been raised from the dead, that his disciples remembered all these things and reconsidered them in the context of resurrection faith. Then such incidents made sense to them in new and dynamic ways.

Lord, the old temple of my life is cluttered with things that dishonor you. Come in your cleansing presence, I pray, and drive them out. Resacralize my heart as a dwelling place for your Holy Spirit, and I shall praise you in word and deed, for yours is the glory forever. Amen.

Day 290   *John 2:23-25*

A WARY JESUS

*T*he Gospel of John emphasizes a few signs or miracles of Jesus to the exclusion of many others described in the Synoptic Gospels. Here the others are at least mentioned. But we also receive an insight into the importance of signs in John. They are significant for their spiritual teachings, not as proofs of Jesus' authority. Jesus himself disdains those who believe in him merely because they have seen some unusual act of power. This fits well with the saying in 20:29: "Blessed are those who have not seen and yet have come to believe." The premium is on understanding, not on excitation by signs and miracles.

Verses 24-25 are a sad note on human nature. Jesus knew better than to trust the applause of the crowd, because he knew "what was in everyone." He understood the fickleness and selfishness of which we are all capable, and he knew it could rise in an instant at the least provocation. The very people who would shout "Hosanna!" as he rode into Jerusalem would be crying for his crucifixion only a few days later.

Against the ephemeral nature of popular approval, we can better evaluate the devotion of the few disciples who remained faithful to Jesus through his ministry, trial, and death. They clung to him not because of what they had seen but because of what they understood about the coming of a new order. This is why John so preferred the title of rabbi for Jesus—because he taught the disciples understanding.

PRAYER
If I understand why Jesus was wary of popular acclaim, O God, it is because I know the fickleness of my own heart. Like the people of Jerusalem, I am inclined to be more excited about outward signs than inner meanings. Teach me to be quiet and to study hidden connections, that I may be faithful in all things. Through Jesus the Christ, amen.

A TEACHER OF SPIRITUAL THINGS

*T*his is a dramatic meeting, for Nicodemus was a member of the Sanhedrin, one of the seventy ruling elders of Israel. He comes as a teacher to the master teacher. And he comes at night. The Gospel makes a lot of light-and-dark symbolism throughout. Here one of the teachers of Israel comes in the darkness, and Jesus tries to enlighten him.

It is difficult in an English translation to get the verbal play that lay at the center of the conversation. The Greek word *anōthen* may be translated either "again" or "above." When Jesus said it is necessary to be born *anō* then to enter God's new order, Nicodemus took the word to mean "again" and questioned how that was possible. But Jesus was talking about being born from above, by God's Spirit. This was the difference between him and the rulers of Israel: He represented the Spirit of God, and they were locked in earthly traditions.

It is like the wind, says Jesus, that blows wherever it pleases. Again there was word play. The Greek word he used means both "wind" and "spirit." Here is the master of the winds and the waves toying with a learned teacher of Israel. If Nicodemus could not understand either the wind or the spirit, how could he possibly understand what God was up to in the new realm?

We should consider the effect of this story on John's audience of Christian Jews. Why would any Christian forsake Jesus to return to Judaism, which did not understand the mysteries of God? No wonder Jesus called Nathanael a true Israelite; it was through him and others like him, not the elderly rulers of Israel, that God's realm would be realized.

Nicodemus makes two later appearances in the Gospel. In 7:50-51 he tries to restrain the Pharisees in their attempts to silence Jesus. And in 19:38-41 he helps Joseph of Arimathea prepare the body of Jesus for burial. The effect is to suggest that he became a cryptodisciple, a secret follower of Jesus. But there is something sad about the stealthiness of his discipleship. Those who have most to lose are least likely to identify themselves wholeheartedly with Jesus. Being born from above is not as easy for them as for the simple folk, like Simon and Nathanael.

PRAYER

O God, it frightens me that I may know many things, as Nicodemus did, and still miss the truths of the Spirit. Teach me to be open to your presence, that I may discern what you are doing in my world and worship you. Through Jesus your Son, amen.

Day 292   *John 3:13-21*

A WORD FROM THE AUTHOR

*A*lthough traditionally treated as part of Jesus' words to Nicodemus, these verses are probably a gloss by the author himself—a short sermon prompted by Jesus' encounter with the Jewish ruler. Verse 13, "No one has ascended into heaven except the one who descended from heaven, the Son of Man," makes little sense if spoken by Jesus.

John picks up the ancient image of Moses' brazen serpent and applies it to Jesus. God instructed Moses to make the serpent and raise it up on a pole to save the Israelites who were dying of a plague in the wilderness (Num. 21:4-9). The word for "pole" in Numbers 21:9 is also the word for "sign," and this was surely in John's mind. The real sign that Jesus gives, finally, is his being lifted up like the serpent, and anyone who regards this sign faithfully will have not merely life, but eternal life.

The phrase "eternal life" dominates the Gospel of John. It means more than life without end; it means a certain quality of life, something in the Spirit of God that transcends ordinary experience. God wants all the world to have this kind of life, says John, to become what God intended from the very beginning of time.

Verse 19, with its reference to "the light" that has "come into the world," takes us back to the theme of the prologue, of the light entering the darkness. The people who have seen the great sign—Jesus' being lifted up and received back into the bosom of the Father—have escaped the condemnation of the darkness. Those who have not accepted the sign— notably the Jewish leaders—are condemned for loving the darkness more than the light.

PRAYER
O God of brightness and glory, I tremble to think how I am inclined to darkness and shadow in my life. My spirit is lazy, and my deeds are often selfish. Forgive me and teach me to love the light who has come into the world, for he has been lifted up and set above all darkness forever and ever. Amen.

THE FRIEND OF THE BRIDEGROOM

*T*here is a hint here of what we have seen before, the attempt to draw John the Baptist into jealousy over Jesus' popularity. Here it comes when some of John's disciples, who have been engaged in conversations with "a Jew" (they were, of course, Jews too; this is John's word for the enemies of Jesus), come with the report that many of John's followers are leaving him to follow Jesus.

But John, great spiritual leader that he is, responds calmly and confidently. Jesus is receiving the people because God is giving them to him. This is a consistent theme in the Fourth Gospel (6:39; 10:29; 17:2, 9, 11, 24). God is sovereign, and any whom God gives to Jesus must come to him; conversely, any who are not given may not come.

Jesus, after all, is the bridegroom of God's new realm, and John is only the friend of the bridegroom. It was the friend's job, in Jewish culture, to prepare the wedding feast and have everything in readiness for the nuptials. It would have been a great impropriety for the friend of the groom to try in any way to take the groom's place with the bride. Instead, the friend waited with the bride until other friends of the groom came and brought her to the groom. Then the friend rejoiced to hear the sound of the groom's voice, and turned his charge over to the groom. At that moment, the groom became everything to the bride, and it was time for the friend to fade away. Therefore, John said, "He must increase, but I must decrease" (v. 30).

The author may have included this remarkable passage to remind disciples of John the Baptist that he deferred to Jesus and surrendered his ministry to him. But it is also an effective reminder to us about our own places in the new order of God. We worry more than we should about being recognized for our contributions to Christ's ministry in the world. But Christ is the bridegroom, and we are only his friends; it is appropriate for us to do our duty and then retire from the limelight. The real focus of spiritual joy is on Christ and his church.

PRAYER

Thank you, dear God, for this beautiful picture of the relationship between Jesus and John. Help me also to be a friend of the groom and do everything I can for his bride. In his glorious name, amen.

THE WITNESS FROM ABOVE

*T*his is another of John's editorial comments. Just as he followed the account of Nicodemus's visit with the short sermon about Jesus (3:13-21), he follows the story of John's waning popularity with a brief homily. "The one who comes from above is above all," says the author (v. 31). The emphasis is similar to that in Jesus' words to Nicodemus, that one must be born from above to see God's new realm (3:3). Jesus is above all earthly teachers—John the Baptist as well as Nicodemus—and whoever accepts his teachings has eternal life.

The phrase in verse 32, "no one accepts his testimony," is obviously an exaggeration, for the next verse refers to those who have already accepted it. But the remark may indicate a feeling of depression experienced by many Christians both then and now because so few persons have actually responded to the light.

Verse 36 is a statement parallel to verse 18: Whoever believes in the Son has eternal life, but whoever does not is already experiencing the wrath of God. In the Synoptic Gospels, the wrath of God is spoken of as occurring in the future. In John, it is already operative, just as eternal life is a quality of being in believers' lives now, not only in the life beyond death. We fashion our own judgments, both now and in the world to come, by the way we respond to our present opportunities.

PRAYER

Dear God, I am concerned about all the people who even now are experiencing your wrath. How terrible it must be to live from day to day with darkness and hopelessness. I pray for your grace and mercy in their lives, that somehow they may turn to the light and find a new quality of being. Through Jesus Christ, amen.

ONE GREATER THAN JACOB

*T*he average Jew would have considered a Samaritan's drinking vessels unclean—ritually impure—and yet Jesus asked to drink from this woman's water jar. But the biggest scandal of all, as evidenced by the disciples' amazement in verse 27, was that Jesus should speak publicly to a woman, whatever her race. Men of that day did not even address their own wives in public—much less a strange woman.

Like the authors of the other Gospels, John apparently viewed Jesus' behavior as evidence of his messiahship. The Lord of creation transcended the parochial rules by which other men lived.

The "gift of God" to which Jesus refers in verse 10 probably means the Spirit of God or the spirit of truth, which in the Johannine literature is always treated as a divine gift. Had the woman only known that the final age had come and she was standing in the presence of the Lord of that age, she would have been seeking the water of life from him.

But she typically misunderstands—just as Nicodemus misunderstood in 3:1-12. Her reply in verse 11 indicates that she has taken his words "living water" to mean more running water or flowing water, not the water of eternal life. Is he greater than their common ancestor Jacob, she asks, who discovered the well where they stand? Even for Jacob it was not a place of running water, but a mere cistern, from which water had always been drawn by hand.

Jesus' reply underscores the difference between the old order and the new: "Everyone who drinks of this water will be thirsty again, but those who drink of the water that I will give them will never be thirsty. The water that I will give will become in them a spring of water gushing up to eternal life" (vv. 13-14). What a declaration this must have been to Christian Jews tempted to forsake their Christianity to return to the synagogues. The faith that had reached them through Jacob and the patriarchs would leave them always thirsting for more; what had come to them in Jesus was fully satisfying, and would be so forever.

PRAYER

God, I am as guilty as "the Jews" of forgetting how far above tradition Jesus is—how much nearer the center of your being, how much wiser, and how much more compassionate. Let me now, in the quietness of my meditation, experience his transcendent glory, that my life may be transformed by his presence. For his name's sake, amen.

THE MEANING OF TRUE WORSHIP

*A*s in the story of Nicodemus, there is probably word play here. When the woman says she has no husband, Jesus says she has had five. The Hebrew word for husband is *ba'al*, which is also the popular word for "deity." The implication is that the woman has not only lived loosely (Jewish law permitted women to marry only three times) but has had many gods.

Jesus exhibits the kind of insight into her affairs that he showed with Nathanael (1:45-51) and Nicodemus (3:1-12). As John said in 2:25, he "knew what was in people." His extraordinary perception leads the woman to think him a prophet, and she initiates a conversation about worship. She alludes to the fact of religious pluralism—people have varying ideas about where to worship and how to do it.

But Jesus uses her words as a springboard for the most important truth of these few verses: that the hour is now at hand when worship at all holy places is superseded by a new kind of worship. "God is spirit," says Jesus, "and those who worship him must worship in spirit and truth" (v. 24).

This was precisely the message needed by Christians who were being forced out of synagogue worship; the time had come when God's rule was everywhere and there was no more requirement for sacred locations. The coming of the new order had rendered the old dependence on holy places null and void.

The woman's understanding is growing. Does she dare to hope that Jesus is the Messiah? "I know that Messiah is coming," she says. "When he comes, he will proclaim all things to us" (v. 25).

"I am he," says Jesus, "the one who is speaking to you" (v. 26). "I am" is an expression we shall meet again and again in John. "I am the bread of life" (6:35). "I am the light of the world" (8:12). "I am the gate for the sheep" (10:7, 9). "I am the good shepherd" (10:11, 14). "I am the resurrection and the life" (11:25). "I am the way, the truth, and the life" (14:6). "I am the vine" (15:1, 5). Used alone in this passage, without any modifier, the words *I am* carry a definitive, regal impact—as when God said to Moses, when Moses asked God's name, "I AM WHO I AM" (Exod. 3:14). The one speaking to the woman at the well is the eternal Word, present at the creation of the world!

PRAYER

O God, it often seems easy to worship you in church, where everything reminds me to look for your presence. Teach me instead to watch for you everywhere, for every place is holy if you are there, and there is no place where you may not be found. Amen.

Day 297   *John 4:27-42*

THE BEGINNING OF THE HARVEST

*W*hen the woman saw the disciples returning, she left her water jar and ran into the city to tell the people about the extraordinary stranger she had met. Why did she go so abruptly? Perhaps because the appearance of the disciples convinced her that Jesus was a special person; or because she knew they would not approve of her talking with their Master. Some interpreters have seen in the forsaken water jar a symbol of her inadequate religion, similar to the symbolic meaning of the six stone jars at the wedding feast in Cana (2:6). For the moment, at least, she had lost all interest in water from the well of Jacob; she had discovered the one who could give her "living water."

"Come," the woman exclaimed to the townspeople, "and see a man who told me everything I have ever done! He cannot be the Messiah, can he?" (v. 29; the RSV translation is "Can this be the Christ?").

Had Jesus indeed told her everything? If so, we have received only fragments of the conversation. Considering the time required for the disciples to purchase food, we can imagine a much more extensive interchange. Jesus apparently touched the woman's deepest feelings, causing her to become excited and voluble about the experience.

Meanwhile, the disciples set food in front of Jesus and were worried that he didn't eat. But Jesus was feeding on something else. He was beholding the arrival of the new order, and the vision nourished him. He saw coming to fruition the work of the prophets in sowing the seeds of the new order. It was harvest time, and the disciples were his field hands.

The Samaritan village was among the first fruits of the harvest season. The people entreated Jesus to remain with them, and he stayed for two days. When he left they said to the woman, in effect, "At first we believed because of what you said; now we believe because we have experienced the man himself, and are convinced that he is the Savior of the world!"

PRAYER

Lord, it was this way in my life too. At first I believed because others spoke of you; then I experienced your presence for myself. It was like nothing else that has ever happened to me. Grant that the memory of the event may remain strong and fresh in my mind, and that your presence may continue with me always. For your name's sake, amen.

Day 298   *John 4:43-54*

MORE FRUITS OF THE NEW ORDER

*P*erhaps the Roman official in this story had heard the news of the water Jesus changed to wine, as John mentions it again in verse 46, and thought that the great wonder-worker could save his ailing son. Jesus' response to him is tinged with rebuke: "Unless you see signs and wonders you will not believe" (v. 48). But the official is not a Jew and is clearly not interested in signs for the sake of signs. "Sir," or Lord, he says, "come down before my little boy dies" (v. 49).

"Go," says Jesus, "your son will live" (v. 50).

When the official matches the time of his son's recovery with the time he heard the word from Jesus, he realizes that Jesus was responsible for the cure. "So he himself believed," says John, "along with his whole household" (v. 53).

There are two significant things about this passage. First, assuming that the official was a centurion (cf. Matt. 8:5-13; Luke 7:2-10) or a Gentile, the passage completes an idea begun with the visit of Nicodemus in chapter 3. Jesus presented himself first to the Jews (Nicodemus), then to the Samaritans (the woman at the well and the people of her village), and finally to the Gentiles. This is the model of the Gospel's progress as noted in Acts 1:8: "You will be my witnesses in Jerusalem, in all Judea and Samaria, and to the ends of the earth." And the conversion of a man's household foreshadows a pattern found in Acts 10:2; 11:14; 16:15, 31, 34; and 18:8. So the passage is an example of the way Christianity moved out from Jerusalem and Jesus became identified as "the Savior of the world" (John 4:42).

Second, the emphasis of the passage is on life, a central theme in John. "What has come into being in him was life," said the prologue, "and the life was the light of all people" (1:4). "Very truly, I tell you," Jesus will say in John 5:25, "the hour is coming, and is now here, when the dead will hear the voice of the Son of God, and those who hear will live." This story of the official's son forms a transition to a section of the Gospel even more strongly concerned with the subject of life than the one we have been reading.

PRAYER

O God, it is so easy for me to confuse mere living with life itself. Like the father in this story, I become concerned about survival only. Help me to transcend this understanding, I pray, and learn to focus on your presence in such a way that I can happily say, "Whether I live or die, I am the Lord's." You are the God of the living, not of the dead. Amen.

Day 299 *John 5:1-9a*

A HEALING ON THE SABBATH

We can imagine the scene around this pool on a typical day. There would have been dozens of poor, unfortunate people lying or sitting about on their mats, waiting for the stirring of the waters. Most would have shown signs of poverty or squalor. Some would have had twisted limbs. Others would have suffered varying degrees of paralysis. For hours at a time, they would have lain there, some waiting impassively, others moaning or talking.

Whenever the waters began to move—either from an angel or an underground current—those who lay closest would scream and claw to get in. Relatives or friends waiting nearby would hasten to assist their loved ones into the water.

The poor man singled out by Jesus was utterly pathetic. He was "blind, lame, and paralyzed." Totally helpless. He had never been able to get into the water in time. Jesus knew his circumstances—that he had been lame for thirty-eight years—in the same uncanny way that he knew all about Nathanael (2:47) and the woman at the well (4:39). Stopping before the man, Jesus looked at him intently, then told him to take up his mat and walk.

How surprised the man must have been to feel the surge of life again in his long-unused limbs! What trembling steps he must have taken, as if he were a baby first learning to walk. And what a shockwave must have swept over all those who lay about the pool and witnessed what happened.

The early church evidently saw a symbolic relationship between this story and Christian baptism, because the scripture, along with the story of Nicodemus in 3:1-21 and that of the blind man in 9:1-40, was one of three Johannine passages used to prepare new Christians for their baptismal rites. Perhaps the story was viewed in the same manner as the water-into-wine story of 2:1-11, as showing the superiority of Jesus over the old order of Judaism. The man had lain by the pool with five doorways (symbolizing the five books of the law) for thirty-eight years, and Jesus, the Son of the new order, had healed him in a moment!

PRAYER

Lord, my heart swells for what happened to this man by the pool. What power you have to transform the lives of those who depend on insufficient forms of religion! Touch the areas of my life that have not responded to you, and cause them to respond to your glory. You are the hope of all who have waited a long time. Amen.

Day 300   *John 5:9b-18*

THE FURY OF THE JEWS

*I*nstead of rejoicing in the healed man's good fortune, "the Jews" in this story were angry at seeing their sabbath laws flouted. The law expressly forbade carrying an empty bed on the sabbath. The Jews, therefore, immediately verbally attacked the man as he carried his mat home. The man in turn replied that he was only doing what his benefactor had instructed him to do. He didn't even know Jesus' name.

Jesus later saw the man in the Temple, possibly making a sacrifice of thanksgiving for having been healed. "See, you have been made well!" Jesus said. "Do not sin any more, so that nothing worse happens to you" (v. 14). This is a curious saying, and difficult to interpret, for it is directly opposed to Luke 13:1-5 and John 9:3, in which Jesus refuses to draw a connection between sin and human affliction. It may have been added by a well-meaning scribe who thought the moral lesson should not go amiss.

Having seen Jesus again, the man went to "the Jews" and told them it was Jesus who had healed him. He had no apparent motive for doing this, and seems to have been ignorant of any consequences of the act. Characteristically, in John's Gospel, people do what they have to do to fulfill the drama of salvation.

"The Jews" then went to Jesus and raised objections to the sabbath healing. His reply was pointed: God did not stop working on the sabbath; why should he, as the Son of God? This naturally irritated the Jews even more. Jesus not only healed on the sabbath, but also claimed to be equal with God. John had said in the prologue of the Gospel that Jesus was in the beginning with God and participated in the creation of everything. But this was something "the Jews" could never believe. Therefore, a conflict between them and Jesus was inevitable, and would lead eventually to Jesus' death.

PRAYER

O God, grant that I may never care more about religious rules and practices than about any human being. As Jesus transcended all earthly forms and places of worship, so let my spirit rise above all petty and parochial concerns, that you may be glorified in a loving care for all the world. Amen.

Day 301   *John 5:19-30*

THE AUTHORITY OF THE SON

These verses continue a discourse obviously begun in verse 17, when Jesus answered "the Jews" after healing a crippled man on the sabbath. They explain in more detail the authority of the Son to heal and give life, as well as to condemn those who refuse to believe in him.

The argument is essentially from analogy. In primitive Israel a son learned his father's trade; he could literally do only what his father had done before him. Jesus said he had done only what he had seen his Father doing—healing on the sabbath. Not only that, said Jesus. Now the Father has turned his work over to the Son, just as earthly fathers turn their businesses over to their sons. And this means that the Son has the power to judge as well as to heal.

Now that Jesus is in charge of the judging, those who hear him and believe his word receive eternal life; those who do not are condemned accordingly. Moreover, this power of Jesus extends not only to the living but to the dead as well. Even people in their tombs will hear the voice of the Son and come forth to be judged by him. Those who have led good lives will receive "resurrection of life," and those who have done evil will receive "resurrection of condemnation." That is, the good will go on living, and the bad will have their evil deeds raised against them, and, presumably, return to their torpid states.

The guarantee of the Son's justice lies in the fact that he does none of the judging for himself, according to his own will, but does it all for the Father who sent him. Again, it is the good name of the Father that ensures the validity of the Son's work.

PRAYER

Teach me, O God, to do your work as Jesus did. Not that I may be set in judgment over others, but that I may be used to bring life to those who do not have it. Let me show love to those who have not experienced it freely and joy to those whose hearts are sullen. Through Jesus the Son, amen.

Day 302   *John 5:31-40*

WITNESSES TO JESUS' AUTHORITY

*I*n the continued discourse on his authority, Jesus refers to a principle in the law calling for more than one witness in a civil case (Num. 35:30; Deut. 17:6; 19:15). If he were the only one testifying to his authority, he says, his word would be untrue. But there is another who bears witness. Some interpreters take this to mean John the Baptist, of whom Jesus speaks in the next verse. But the sense of the passage requires it to be God, for the reference to John is parenthetical to a longer reference to God.

"You sent messengers to John," Jesus says, "and he testified to the truth" (v. 33). John had said that he was not the Christ, but was sent before him (John 3:25-30). Not that the word of a mere human being is adequate, says Jesus; he cites John's witness only because "the Jews" seemed to delight in him and because, if they could believe through him, they would be saved.

It is really the Father's testimony that counts most, and the Father has witnessed to Jesus' authority in three ways: (1) by letting Jesus do the works he has done in their midst; (2) by bearing personal witness to Jesus' sonship—the reference is possibly to John 1:32-33, in which the Spirit of God descended like a dove on the Son; and (3) by the witness of Scripture, which foretold the coming of the Son and the things he would do.

"The Jews," however, are insensitive. They have seen the signs and wonders in their midst but have not believed. They cannot hear the voice of God and so do not accept God's confirmation of the Son. And, though they search the scriptures constantly, hoping to find eternal life, they miss the clues and do not come to the Son, who can give them life.

PRAYER

Lord, teach me to listen faithfully for your voice, that I may learn to trust it above my own opinions or the opinions of those around me. Let your witness be the measure by which I evaluate all other voices, for you have the words of eternal life. Amen.

Day 303   *John 5:41-47*

THE GLORY OF GOD

*T*he Jews in Jesus' day accorded exceptional honor to famous rabbis, many of whom lived like princes among their countrymen. They were given large banquets and attended by the wealthiest citizens. Their words were repeated in the best society, and they were respected as the wisest men in the world.

The rabbis themselves contributed to this aura by the way they continually quoted one another's words and praised one another's sagacity.

Jesus, as John indicates, did not take part in this self-serving exchange of praise. His glory was not the cheap demi-glow of human commendation, but the glory and honor of God the Creator. And because he did not play the little game the rabbis played, they did not speak well of him, and "the Jews" did not accept him.

"I know," said Jesus, in effect, "that you do not have God's love in you, for I have come in God's name and you have refused to receive me. But if some rabbi comes among you in his own name, puffed up with human conceit, you fall over yourselves to receive him. You are full of pride and love to exchange praise for one another instead of seeking the glory of God."

What shame verse 44 strikes into our hearts if we but ponder it. Which of us is not guilty of having had more regard for what other persons think of us than what God thinks? Even in Christian congregations, we are often influenced more by what the minister or other well-placed persons think than by what God desires.

O God, I am certainly guilty of caring what other persons think of me. I know I have done things to receive their honor and good opinion when I should have done them for you and your realm alone. Forgive me and restore a right spirit within me. Through Jesus, who knows what is in the hearts of people, amen.

Day 304   *John 6:1-14*

COMMUNION BY THE SEA

*T*his is the only miracle of Jesus recorded by all four Gospels (Matt. 14:13-21; Mark 6:32-44; Luke 9:10-17), and John's account is probably the best loved, for it alone provides the detail about the small boy who surrendered his lunch to feed the multitude.

Actually there are numerous significant details in the story, including the information in verse 4 that Passover was at hand. This note was doubtless for the Christian Jews reading the Gospel, who were unable to attend Passover services in the synagogues any longer. John wanted them to know that the Messiah had given them a meal that transcended even Passover itself in significance.

Eucharistic reminders abound in the story. First, Jesus gave thanks over the bread. Second, Jesus himself distributes the bread, just as he will at the Last Supper. (In the Synoptics, it is the disciples who do the distributing.) Third, the Greek word for "fragments," *klasma,* is the same word used in the *Didache,* our earliest manual of church practice, for the eucharistic bread remaining after the meal. And fourth, Jesus told the disciples to gather up the fragments, foreshadowing a practice of conserving leftover bread.

The multiplication of fish as well as bread is interesting. In Numbers 11, Moses worried about where to get meat for the Israelites, who were complaining that they had only manna to eat in the wilderness. He said it would require all the fish of the sea to feed them. John may have been saying to Jewish Christians, "Here is one greater than Moses."

The people reacted to the miracle by exclaiming that Jesus was the prophetic figure who would herald the new age of God. But as we shall see in the next reading, their understanding was very superficial.

O God, I am thankful for John's inclusion of the small boy in this wonderful story. It reminds me of the way you can use my poor gifts if I but yield them to you. Let me be as generous as the boy, that I may see miracles around me every day. In Jesus' name, amen.

Day 305   *John 6:15*

THE TEMPTATION IN THE WILDERNESS

*J*ohn's Gospel does not contain a full-blown narrative of the temptations of Christ such as the one we find in Luke 4:1-13. The portrait of Jesus in this Gospel is of a confident, self-assured Messiah almost above temptation. He is human enough to weep (11:35) and thirst (19:28). But he is also the eternal Word, and shows no signs of an inner struggle with the Tempter.

Yet this single verse (6:15) is a hint that John knew the tradition of the wilderness temptations, for it barely masks a temptation similar to the second one in Luke's account: the temptation to become a king without going through the horror of the cross.

The eloquence of John's statement lies in its terseness and simplicity. Jesus saw the mounting enthusiasm of the people for the miracle he had performed, and, not wishing to be a political king, withdrew to the mountain by himself. Some ancient manuscripts say that he actually *fled* to the mountains.

To understand the full irony of the verse, we must turn ahead to Jesus' trial before Pilate, in which Jesus is accused of making himself King of the Jews (18:33-37). To Pilate's question, "Are you the King of the Jews?" Jesus eventually responds, "My kingdom is not from this world" (18:33, 36). And later, when Jesus is crucified, Pilate defies "the Jews" by placing a sign on the cross that reads "Jesus of Nazareth, the King of the Jews" (19:19).

The true qualities of royalty in any person are unrelated to the approval of the crowds. They are inner qualities, qualities in the bone and marrow. Jesus showed his character by refusing to be swept into a position of earthly power by people who did not understand his real mission among them.

O God, in whose deep silences all truths become clear, teach me to depend less on my own wisdom and more on yours. You have ordained that poverty may be riches, weakness strength, and loneliness the ground of true companionship. Through Jesus Christ, our Lord, amen.

Day 306   *John 6:16-21*

CROSSING THE SEA

*A*t first sight, John's account of the storm at sea and Jesus' walking on the water appears disappointingly plain and undramatic when compared to Matthew 14:22-27 and Mark 6:45-51. It seems shorn of all the exciting details, as if John had no interest in it and merely wanted to get it over with. But reflection may convince us otherwise.

First, we need to recall the setting of the story, sandwiched between the feeding miracle (6:1-15) and an important discourse on the bread of life (6:25-59). All of this occurred, we were told in verse 4, at Passover time. So it all has an obvious relationship to Jewish memories being rehearsed at Passover, about God's saving the Israelites by letting them cross the Red Sea and then feeding them manna in the wilderness.

John's abbreviated account of the stormy crossing, in other words, would have evoked for Jewish Christians powerful associations with the crossing of the Red Sea. For the new Israel, the church, it symbolized a moment of passage as important as the original crossing.

We remember, too, that Jesus' words to the disciples, "It is I; do not be afraid" (v. 20), are formulistic. That is, the translation of the Greek also meant "I am" or "I am who I am," the same words used by God in Exodus 3:14 to identify the divine presence to Moses. As we have noted before, John's Gospel uses this self-identifying formula for Christ a number of times; and whenever we encounter it, we may be sure that there is deep theological significance.

Finally, there is the curious note that once Jesus had entered the boat with the disciples, "the boat reached the land toward which they were going" (v. 21). Is this a mere fairy-tale touch—zip! and they were at their destination? Or does it have a more esoteric meaning? Perhaps it means that Jesus' followers needed to wait no longer for the fulfillment of God's promises to Israel, for the Messiah was already among them!

PRAYER

Dear God, there are such spiritual depths in this small passage that I feel like the disciples, floundering in the waves. Let Christ come to me amid the threatening waters and join me in my frail vessel, that I may not be afraid but may rejoice as the early Christians did, with singing and everlasting joy. Amen.

Day 307   *John 6:22-40*

A SERMON ABOUT BREAD

*W*hat a sight the people's crossing of the sea must have been—thousands of them going to look for Jesus! But Jesus was impatient with them because they had fastened upon the sign (his feeding them) and not what it meant in terms of the arrival of God's realm. They were looking for a perpetual lunch counter!

Don't spend yourselves for the food that perishes, said Jesus. Seek instead the food that will give you eternal life.

"What must we do to perform the works of God?" the people asked (v. 28). They were trying to be like their ancestors in the wilderness, wanting to know what they must do or how they must behave in order to keep God's manna coming their way.

It was God who gave their ancestors the bread in the wilderness, said Jesus, not Moses. And it was God who was trying to give them the true bread from heaven now. Apparently the people finally understood what he was saying, and asked, "Sir, give us this bread always" (v. 34).

In response to their humble supplication, Jesus spoke the words in verses 35-40, one of the great "I am" speeches of the Fourth Gospel. "I am the bread of life," he said (v. 35). And then, in effect: "Whoever comes to me will never be hungry or thirsty. And I will keep those persons and raise them up at the last day. It is my Father's will that whoever sees the Son and believes in him have eternal life, and be raised up to eternal life."

PRAYER
Lord, give me this bread, that I may neither hunger nor thirst. Help me to see beyond mere physical tokens to the food that is eternal. Let my praise be always for the gifts of the Spirit, more than gifts of the flesh. For they shall not perish or fail me, whatever happens. Amen.

THE MYSTERY OF THE BREAD

*A*s the last verse indicates, this exchange between Jesus and "the Jews" occurred in the synagogue at Capernaum, not among the simple folk by the sea. Word had reached some of the elders of the synagogue that Jesus had said to the people that he was the bread that came down from heaven. "Why, we know this man's background," they whispered among themselves. He is from Nazareth. How can he claim to have come down from heaven?"

Jesus scolded them for murmuring. He knew they couldn't understand, because God had not given them understanding. They would die, like their ancestors who had eaten manna in the wilderness. But those who came to the Son believing would have eternal life.

The comparison of bread and manna is similar to Jesus' discussion with the woman at the well in John 4. He told the woman that anyone drinking from Jacob's well would thirst again, but those drinking of the water he would give them would never thirst. Here he says that those who ate manna in the wilderness died, but those who eat the bread he gives will never die.

Unlike the common people by the seashore, "the Jews" stumble and take offense at Jesus' words. With all their cleverness, they cannot understand the mystery.

Let us remember again that John composed his Gospel especially for Jewish Christians who were exiled from the synagogues. We can imagine the effect this passage must have had on them. It portrays the leaders of the synagogues as being dull and unperceptive, unable to grasp the teachings accepted by the simple people at the seashore. The Eucharist was folly to the synagogue leaders because they did not see how a man born of human flesh could have come down from heaven. But the Christians understood and knew that they had eternal life by eating the "flesh" and drinking the "blood" of the Messiah.

PRAYER
What a wonderful gift it is, Lord, to see you in Communion, to know in some mysterious way that when I eat the bread and drink the cup I am feeding upon you. Nourish me today so that I may dwell with you forever. And let my life become food for others, for your name's sake. Amen.

SOME DISCIPLES GO AWAY

*T*he difficult teaching of verse 60 is the word of Jesus in verses 51-58 about eating his flesh and drinking his blood. The mystery of the sacramental body was anathema to Jews. Paul said the cross was a stumbling block to them (1 Cor. 1:23). They simply could not tolerate the idea of another human being's becoming a sacrificial lamb for them. Even some of Jesus' disciples complained about the saying (v. 61), as "the Jews" had in the earlier passage (v. 43). Jesus' question to them, "Does this offend you?" employs the verb from the same root as the noun Paul used in 1 Corinthians 1:23. They reacted as "the Jews" in the Gospel generally did.

The reference in verse 62 to the Ascension is tantamount to saying, "What if you were to see the one who will die and give his flesh as an eternal meal rising to be with the Father? Then would you realize the connection between this bread and spiritual reality?"

The disciples Jesus was addressing were obviously a larger group than the twelve. Luke 10:1 refers to "the seventy." Probably these were the ones referred to in this section of John. But after this confrontation about spiritual matters, many "turned back" and no longer followed—all of them, apparently, except the twelve.

John, in keeping with his heavenly image of Jesus, carefully points out that Jesus knew all along which disciples did not believe and which would eventually betray him. We were told in 2:25 that Jesus "knew what was in people." Perhaps this is why the question in verse 67 ("Do you wish to go away?") is worded in the Greek to imply a negative answer. Jesus knew the twelve would remain and that Judas would be the one to turn him over to the enemies.

PRAYER

What a sad picture, Lord, of the humanity you came to save. There is weakness and treachery in the best of us—even those who have been with you as disciples. The bright note is your own presence in our midst, manifested in the bread and wine of Communion. Forgive our shortcomings and feed us on your eternal self, that we may not fall away or betray you. Amen.

GOING TO JERUSALEM

The Gospel of John is more centered in Jerusalem than are the other Gospels. In the Synoptics, most of Jesus' ministry occurred in Galilee. Here, with more than two-thirds of his Gospel yet to go, John shifts our attention to the ministry in Jerusalem. The stage is already being set for Jesus' great conflict with the authorities and his crucifixion.

It seems odd that Jesus' brothers should bait him to go to Jerusalem for the Feast of Tabernacles and that he should at first refuse to go. His answer to them was that his time had not come. The Greek word for "time" here, *kairos,* means "fullness of time," as opposed to *chronos,* which means time in the mere linear sense. But later, after the brothers had gone, Jesus apparently decided that his *kairos,* or special hour, had come, and he went secretly to the city. This agrees with Mark 9:30-31, which reports that Jesus didn't want anyone to know he was going to Jerusalem and that he used the time on the journey to explain to the disciples that he would be killed there.

"The Jews" were expecting him at the feast. Probably they were already at work attempting to turn the populace against him. The word used in verse 12, "there was considerable complaining about him," may also be translated "muttering" or "murmuring," suggesting a gossip campaign.

The phrase "for fear of the Jews" in verse 13 sets the tone for the confrontations to follow. These particular Jews—obviously the authorities in Jerusalem—are seen as both treacherous and powerful. They are emissaries of the darkness and are naturally opposed to the light of the world. A grand conflict is inevitable.

PRAYER

O Lord, even your own brothers in the flesh did not understand you. What a dark and ignorant place the world can be! How blind we often are to one another and to the truth! I pray for a light in the darkness, for even a glimmer to follow in my own personal dealings. Let me not fail to understand those close to me, for in serving them I am able to serve you, and in loving them I show my love to you. Amen.

THE GREATEST RABBI OF ALL

*T*he people were amazed at the depth and perception of Jesus' teaching. Most rabbis merely repeated the teachings of other rabbis. But not Jesus. There was a freshness, an incisiveness, an authority about his manner that was lacking in others. "My teaching is not mine," he explained, "but his who sent me" (v. 16).

Jesus raised the issue of the plot to kill him. No plot had been made public, but he knew of its existence the way he knew other things—because he is the eternal Word. It all went back to the healing of the crippled man on the sabbath (5:2-18). "I did one thing," he said, in effect, "and it shocked you all."

Jesus used a rabbinical argument to justify the healing. A male child was supposed to be circumcised the eighth day after birth. If the child was born on the sabbath, the rite was permitted on the following sabbath (which could be counted as day eight). If circumcision was permitted, which was deemed good for the whole body, then why wasn't the healing of the whole body, which obviously did more for the person affected? Be sensible, he said in verse 24.

The people were confused. Jesus seemed so wise, so right, that it was hard not to believe he was the Messiah. Yet they knew his family and where he came from. So how could he possibly be the anointed one of God? "You think you know me," Jesus was saying, "but you obviously don't know God, who sent me."

It was an effective point, and it carried the argument back to the center of the matter: Jesus knew God, and his enemies did not. Many people believed him. But the authorities only intensified their efforts to arrest him. Only the fact that his hour had not yet come deterred them; God would not give them the power they needed until the time was right.

PRAYER

I know how the authorities felt, O God. I, too, have trouble with the fact that Jesus came from Nazareth and had a family like my own. But that is because my spirit, like theirs, is too earthbound and prosaic. When I am in prayer and am no longer hindered by human rationality, I know he is the Christ and that I am part of your new order. Grant that the mood of my praying may more and more dominate the rest of my life, that I may live for the new order every hour and with every ounce of my being. For his name's sake, amen.

THE BAPTISM OF THE SPIRIT

*O*ne of the central images of the Feast of Tabernacles, which cele-brated the wilderness wanderings, was water. One of the many Scripture readings used in the synagogues during the feast was Zechariah 14:8-9, which spoke of the day when living waters would flow out of Jerusalem. During each morning of the feast there was a dramatic procession from the Temple down to the fountain of Gihon, where a priest filled a golden pitcher with water, and back to the Temple, where he circled the altar and poured the water into a silver funnel, which returned it to the earth.

It was probably at this moment on the final day of the feast that Jesus stood up and cried out, "Let anyone who is thirsty come to me, and let the one who believes in me drink. As the scripture has said, 'Out of the believer's heart shall flow rivers of living water' " (vv. 37-38). We can imagine the impact of such an announcement, especially at a time when opinions about Jesus were divided and everyone was talking about him.

When the police who had been sent to arrest Jesus returned to the chief priests and Pharisees without him, their leaders demanded to know why. "Never has anyone spoken like this!" they said (v. 46). They, like all the common people, were deeply impressed.

The leaders were angry. But one of their number spoke courageously in favor of justice. It was Nicodemus, the ruler who had come to Jesus by night (John 3:1-21). Jesus had spoken to him about baptism by "water and the Spirit." Did Nicodemus recognize a connection between that nocturnal conversation and Jesus' announcement at the feast about "rivers of living water"? Nicodemus's point was a telling one: Their very law provided for hearing a man before judging him (cf. Exod. 23:1; Deut. 1:16-17). But the others were beyond reason. As tools of darkness, they were intent on putting out the light.

PRAYER

Lord, what a glorious scene this must have been, when you stood up at the feast and announced the "rivers of living water"! How prone I am to choke with thirst, when you are ready to provide your Spirit in measureless abundance. Help me this day to live with the image of the rivers and to come to you repeatedly for my baptism of joy. Amen.

THE WOMAN TAKEN IN ADULTERY

*M*any modern translations omit this passage or confine it to a footnote, for it is absent from the most reliable ancient manuscripts. Some manuscripts place it in Luke, following 21:38, instead of John. But through the centuries it has become a beloved part of this Gospel, told again and again to illustrate the tender forgiveness of Christ.

Jesus came early in the morning to the Temple. The woman who was brought to him and accused of adultery had probably just been caught. Leviticus 20:10 commanded that a man and woman taken in adultery should both be put to death. The man does not appear in the story; possibly he eluded capture. The woman was either married or engaged, for intercourse with a single, unengaged woman was not considered adultery.

The scribes and Pharisees obviously hoped to entrap Jesus with the problem. If he said to set the woman free, he would be flouting a commandment of Moses; if he said she should be stoned, he would be in trouble with the Romans, who had rescinded the right of the Jews to carry out their own death penalty. It was a dilemma like that of Mark 12:13-17, where Jesus was asked whether it was lawful to pay taxes to Caesar.

We will always wonder what Jesus wrote on the ground with his finger. Perhaps it was his way of thinking. At any rate, his answer, when he gave it, was ingenious. It demonstrated that judging others is a reflexive act; we are condemned by the same standards we hold up for them.

There is one very good argument for the story's inclusion in John's Gospel, apart from the fact that it was found in some ancient manuscripts. That is the fact that it beautifully exemplifies the theme of wisdom, which many scholars have pointed out is basic to our understanding of the prologue and its hymn to the eternal Word. The decision of Jesus was much like that of the legendary King Solomon in 1 Kings 3:16-28, when two women claimed the same child. The people in Solomon's court stood in awe of him when he gave his answer to that problem. And many of us feel the same way about Jesus after observing how he handled a thorny question thrust upon him.

PRAYER

Teach me, O Lord, to number my own sins before counting the sins of others. Then let me wait upon your presence until I have received the judgment given to this woman. And I shall praise you for your great mercy, which is from everlasting to everlasting. Amen.

Day 314   *John 8:12-30*

THE LIGHT ON HIGH

*A*s there was a ritual during the Feast of Tabernacles for water, so there was one for light, commemorating the pillar of fire by which God guided the Israelites at night in the wilderness. It centered on lighting enormous candles in the outer part of the Temple. The candles were actually great golden bowls of oil with wicks made from the belts of the priests. When lit, the burnished bowls illumined the entire city of Jerusalem.

It may well have been in the context of such a ceremonial lighting that Jesus announced, "I am the light of the world. Whoever follows me will never walk in darkness but will have the light of life" (v. 12).

Once more we have an "I am" saying—one of the great messianic declarations of the Fourth Gospel. And once more it promises believers an entirely new quality of life.

The Pharisees characteristically challenged the assertion, saying that Jesus was his only witness. That was enough, said Jesus, because he of all men knew who he was and how he stood with the Father. The Pharisees, he said, judged according to the flesh, but he judged according to the spirit. (This may account for placing the story of the woman taken in adultery next to this passage.) As if to prove his point about them, the Pharisees misunderstood what he meant about going away; they thought he was talking of killing himself.

"Who are you?" they asked him. "I am who I have told you from the beginning," he said, in effect—the one sent by the Father. "When you have lifted up the Son of Man, then you will realize that I am he" (v. 28). There is the great *I am* again. The Revised English Bible translates this "you will know that I am what I am," which preserves the flavor of God's word to Moses, "I AM WHO I AM," and "Thus you shall say to the Israelites, 'I AM has sent me to you' " (Exod. 3:14).

We see why the author of the Fourth Gospel equates Jesus' being lifted up with his being exalted or glorified, for after his death people would realize that he was who he had said he was from the beginning of his ministry—namely, the Son of the Father, the I AM himself. Then there would be no question about his authority or the testimony he gave. People would know he was "the light of the world."

Meanwhile, the Son's chief comfort was this: "The one who sent me is with me; he has not left me alone" (v. 29).

PRAYER

I know, O God, what Jesus meant. I cannot bow before the cross without realizing his identification with you. There is a power and a mystery there that energizes my life with faith. Mediate your presence to me through that image and help me always to follow him who was crucified and raised from the dead. In his great name, amen.

Day 315   *John 8:31-59*

ONE GREATER THAN ABRAHAM

*T*his is a strange passage, because "the Jews" seem to be two different groups. At first they appear to be those who have believed on Jesus and are following him and thus by extension they are also the Christian Jews of John's audience. But at some point they change into the Jews who are Jesus' enemies and want to argue with him.

Much of the argument turns on the old issue of tradition: the Jews do not think Jesus represents the fulfillment of Jewish expectancies. At one point (v. 48) they even accuse him of being a Samaritan and having a demon because he speaks of not seeing death. Does Jesus think he is greater than their father Abraham, who died?

Abraham rejoiced at seeing his day, says Jesus. We assume this means that Abraham looked forward in faith to the fulfillment of God's promises for Israel.

The Jews taunt him. He is less than fifty years old, and speaks of seeing Abraham? "Very truly," says Jesus, "I tell you, before Abraham was, I am" (v. 58).

Here is the *I am* again—Jesus is the eternal *I am*. There is extreme majesty in the announcement, as if to say, "Fifty years? A trifle. Before Abraham was born, I already existed."

At this the Jews take up stones to throw at him. This probably does not imply a decision to execute him on the spot; the Jews did not have the power to impose the death penalty. Instead, it suggests the irateness of their spirits. Jesus has provoked them beyond their limits, and in exasperation they pick up stones to throw at him.

But, as Jesus slipped into Jerusalem secretly at the beginning of the feast, now he hides himself, possibly behind piles of stone or building materials being used to finish the Temple, and slips away. If any of the people he has been addressing have been his followers, there is no longer any question about where their sympathies lie. He leaves the Temple alone.

PRAYER

O God, all of this arguing is cloying to my spirit. Why are some people so inclined to quibble and misunderstand? Give me a loving and receptive spirit, that I may receive Christ without question or doubt. For he has revealed you in ways that I should never have known without him. Amen.

Day 316   *John 9:1-12*

THE LIGHT OF THE WORLD AND THE MAN BORN BLIND

*W*hen they first encountered this blind man, the disciples asked a typical question: Whose sin made the man blind, his own or his parents'? Disregarding such a question as inconsequential—people are always more significant than philosophical disputes—Jesus replied that the important thing was to do God's work for the man while there was still time. "Night is coming," he said, "when no one can work" (v. 4). Woven through Jesus' speech at this time were references to his crucifixion, when evil and darkness would seem to overcome the light.

So Jesus spat on the ground, made a bit of mud, and anointed the man's eyes with it. (In Mark 8:22-26 there is a similar account in which Jesus used spittle to heal a blind man.) Then he told the man to go and wash in the pool of Siloam. Why did the Messiah, who was able to heal the sick even at long distance (4:46-54), bother with this primitive method of healing?

Since Jesus' interview with Nicodemus in chapter 3, there have been references in the Gospel to "water and the Spirit." Washing in the pool of Siloam almost certainly had baptismal significance in the eyes of first-century readers. In fact, the early church adopted this passage as part of the educational preparation of persons approaching baptism. Depictions of the story appear several times in catacomb art, always in connection with Christian baptism. The French scholar F.-M. Braun has discovered that during the years when the early church followed the practice of scrutinizing candidates three different times before admitting them to baptism, this chapter was read on the day of the final scrutiny.

The early church also made a connection between baptism and light. Candles were lit and handed to persons who had just been baptized, as a symbol of their enlightenment in Christ. And baptismal liturgies always contained numerous references to light and illumination.

The man who had been blind from birth, then, was made to see, and he became an example to all of those seeking sight through faith in the Messiah. Obediently, the man went to the pool and washed as he was told. And others were astounded at the change in him. They argued among themselves (v. 9) about whether he was even the same man they had always known!

PRAYER

O God, I wonder if my faith and baptism have made this much difference in how I live and am perceived by others. Do I behave as one who has seen a great light shining in the darkness? Open my eyes daily to the splendor of the Messiah, that I may not dwell with a shadowed spirit. In his bright name, amen.

Day 317   *John 9:13-41*

THE BLINDNESS OF THE SIGHTED

*I*f some people only worked as hard to do good as they do to make trouble, the world would be a much happier place. But the Pharisees, bent on making trouble, wrangled with the formerly blind man and his parents over the nature of his blindness and that of his healer. Give glory to God for your healing, they said; we know that this man Jesus is a sinner. But the man's wit was quick, and he saw their game. What were they so insistent about, he wanted to know; did they want to become Jesus' disciples?

Angered, they accused him of being a follower of Jesus. They themselves, they proudly declared, were disciples of Moses. They knew God had spoken to Moses, but they didn't even know where Jesus had come from. The man twitted them. They didn't know where Jesus was from, but he had done the most wonderful work ever spoken of! If they had any sense at all, they would know Jesus had to be from God. Otherwise he could do nothing.

The Pharisees were irritated beyond control. "You were born entirely in sins," they said, "and are you trying to teach us?" (v. 34). This may have been a reference to the man's congenital blindness; they concluded that his sin had produced the condition. "And they drove him out" (v. 34).

Driving him out probably meant expulsion from the synagogue. Thus this passage would have spoken eloquently to the Christian Jews of John's time who were facing expulsion from the synagogues unless they recanted their Christian faith. John's intention in narrating the entire story may well have been to encourage the followers of Jesus, who had been baptized (gone to the pool of Siloam) and received their sight (their Christian enlightenment) not to deny their faith under threat of excommunication from Jewish places of worship.

The final scene between the man and Jesus summarizes the situation. The man who had been blind from birth could now see. What he saw clearly was that Jesus was the Son of Man, the long-awaited Messiah. And the Pharisees, who made such a point of being able to see life clearly and discriminately, were really blind to the most important thing in the world: the lordship of Jesus.

PRAYER

It frightens me, O God, to have a reputation for seeing. For it is in my contentment with this reputation that I am in most danger of not seeing—of being shortsighted, prejudiced, and wrong in my judgments. Teach me to rise each day and, recalling my darkness, humbly seek the light of Christ in my life. He alone has seen you and knows the meaning of everything. Amen.

Day 318   *John 10:1-21*

THE BEAUTIFUL SHEPHERD

*A*ileen Guilding, in her book *The Fourth Gospel and Jewish Worship*, points out that Ezekiel 34, which contains a passionate indictment of false shepherds, regularly served as one of the readings for the Feast of Dedication, mentioned in John 10:22. Therefore, just as ceremonials at the Feast of Tabernacles provided the background for Jesus' announcements in chapter 7 ("Let anyone who is thirsty come to me") and chapter 8 ("I am the light of the world"), so also this reading may well have prompted his discourse on shepherding.

The text in Ezekiel represents God as berating the selfish, thieving shepherds, and then saying that the divine presence will take away their function and assume it. This is essentially what Jesus was doing when he announced, "I am the good shepherd. The good shepherd lays down his life for the sheep" (v. 11). Jesus was the shepherd Ezekiel had promised, who would truly care for the sheep of Israel.

The references to the sheep gate in verses 7 and 9 are a bit confusing, because they introduce a different metaphor. But the intent is the same, for they have to do with the protection of the sheep. There was real intimacy, Jesus suggested, between him and his followers—the sheep knew his voice and trusted him.

Verse 16 has long taxed the imagination of commentators: "I have other sheep that do not belong to this fold. I must bring them also. . . . So there will be one flock, one shepherd." Given the audience of Christian Jews to whom John was writing, these words may well have meant that Jesus had followers in many places, not only among Jews in the synagogues, and that he would eventually bring them all together into a single flock.

The emphasis on the smitten shepherd is strong because Jesus was approaching the hour of his death. But John is the Gospel of life, not death, and even though the shepherd will be slain for the sheep, he will prove triumphant over death.

PRAYER

O splendid Shepherd, who laid down your life for me, I want to follow you wherever you lead. With you, even barren places become lush pasture lands, and the valley of the shadow of death becomes a field of everlasting flowers! Amen.

Day 319   *John 10:22-42*

THE CONSECRATED ONE

The Feast of Dedication (Hanukkah) celebrated the victory of Judas Maccabeus over the Syrians. In 167–164 B.C., the Syrians erected an idol on the altar of the Temple, constituting what the Jews called "an abomination of desolation" (Dan. 9:27). When the Maccabeans defeated the Syrians, a new altar was built and the Temple was rededicated. The memory of this important occasion was relived annually in the Feast of Dedication.

Against this background, it is interesting that Jesus, confronting "the Jews," referred to himself as the one "whom the Father has sanctified and sent into the world" (v. 36). The word for "sanctified" is the same one used for consecrating an altar or a temple. Jesus, at a time when Jewish minds turned to the consecration of holy places, offered himself as the holy person dedicated by God.

"The Jews" kept taunting Jesus to tell them if he was the Messiah so they could accuse him of blasphemy. When he finally said "The Father and I are one" (v. 30), it was enough. They picked up stones, ready to stone him just as they had been ready when he said he existed before Abraham (8:59).

Jesus stayed the barrage of stones by engaging them in a rabbinical argument. He cited Psalm 82:6, in which God, in a paganlike council of gods, denounced the other deities present for their injustice and said that, while they might be gods, they were going to die as human beings. If God called even minor deities "gods," Jesus was arguing, why should "the Jews" think he was blaspheming—he whom the Father had set apart and sent into the world—when he said he was the Son of God? If his works were not the Father's works, then they should not believe him; but if the works were what the Father would do, then they should understand that he was who he said he was.

"The Jews" tried to arrest Jesus, we are told, but he escaped again as on previous occasions, because his hour had not come. He went into Transjordan, to the area where John the Baptist had baptized, and for a while enjoyed the acceptance of the simple people of the land.

PRAYER

O God, I want to be a simple person. Remove all my pretension and unnecessary complexity. Let me meditate on you until all of my life is focused and plain. And then let others see you through me, shining through the aperture of my faith. For the sake of your heavenly realm, amen.

THE RESURRECTION AND THE LIFE

*T*his chapter is pivotal to the entire Gospel of John. The raising of a dead man was the most important sign Jesus could give of his authority as the Son of God. John wished to emphasize three things: Jesus' love for his friends; the absolute deadness of Lazarus; and the immediacy of life in Christ.

Jesus' love for his friends. All the biblical references indicate that there was a close personal bond between Jesus and Mary, Martha, and Lazarus. John, anticipating the next chapter of his Gospel (12:1-3), identified Mary as the one who anointed Jesus' feet with precious ointment. It was natural, when Lazarus became very ill, for the two sisters to send for Jesus. The proof of his love for them was his willingness to return to Bethany, only a short distance from Jerusalem, so soon after he had been forced to leave. But he had said that the good shepherd lays down his life for the sheep, and these people were among his sheep.

The absolute deadness of Lazarus. In none of Jesus' other raising miracles was so much care taken to demonstrate the full reality of death's presence. When Jesus heard that Lazarus was ill, he purposely tarried until Lazarus was not only dead but in the tomb for four days. Other touches confirm the presence of death: the stone rolled against the tomb, the mourners, the bandages on the corpse, and Martha's warning that there would be an odor in the tomb. This was no case of merely reviving a fainting man. Lazarus was firmly in the grip of death.

The immediacy of life in Christ. This was the major point of the entire story, as of the Gospel itself. Jesus did not respond immediately to the sisters' plea for help because he wished to provide the greatest sign of his power and purpose as the Messiah. Martha showed great confidence in him as the Christ, but seemed not to understand the enormity of his power. "I am the resurrection and the life," said Jesus—the climactic *I am* announcement! "Those who believe in me, even though they die, will live, and everyone who lives and believes in me will never die" (vv. 25-26). Going to the tomb, he cried out, "Lazarus, come out!" (v. 43). And the dead man came out, trailing the wrappings of death like ribbons from a birthday party!

PRAYER

My rational mind is shocked by this story, O Christ. It is like nothing I experience in daily life; yet its very outrageousness convinces me of its truth, and of the fact that I *should* experience it in daily life. Help me to know you so intimately through prayer and meditation that even my rationality shall come to understand and glorify you, for you are the Lord of both life and death. Amen.

Day 321   *John 11:45-57*

A MISUSE OF AUTHORITY

*I*n John's Gospel, people judge themselves according to their reactions to Jesus. Here is a primary example of this. The raising of Lazarus was Jesus' greatest sign of his union with the Father. Yet the members of the Sanhedrin, the council of Jewish elders, instead of accepting Jesus' messiahship, intensified their efforts to accomplish his death.

Like any group of "responsible citizens," they cloaked their designs in civic respectability. They were worried about what the Romans would do if Jesus continued to perform miracles and recruit followers. The Romans might become nervous, it was argued, and destroy the Temple, or they might even lay waste the entire nation. We can almost hear their voices as they discussed their "duties" under the present state of emergency.

In the end, the words of the high priest summed up the council's will: Jesus must die in order to avert a national disaster. But what was to be a judgment on Jesus turned out to be a judgment on the council members themselves. How many times, in how many places, have people in authority committed a similar transgression of justice because some individual or group of individuals constituted a threat or an affront to their positions or self-interest? Even parents are prone to misuse authority in this way, as a means of bolstering the self and its desires.

As his opposition intensified, Jesus continued to be careful, waiting for the hour when he would give his life for his sheep. John says he went to a town called Ephraim, near the wilderness, a place so remote that scholars today argue over which small village it may have been. There he stayed with the disciples until the Feast of Passover. And in Jerusalem, suspense was building among the people. The word was out that the Sanhedrin was set to arrest Jesus. Would he dare to come to the feast?

Day 322   *John 12:1-8*

A PROPHETIC ANOINTMENT

*T*his beautiful story is similar to those in Mark 14:3-9 and Luke 7:36-38. John alone mentions the names of Mary, Martha, and Lazarus, and identifies Judas as the disciple unhappy with Mary's wastefulness. Her act was indeed generous, if not wasteful. Nard, the ointment, was an extract from the roots and spikes of the nard plant, grown in northern India. It was extremely expensive, and was used sparingly in various perfumes, medicines, incenses, and burial lotions. The flask of nard Mary used probably cost about a year's wages for an ordinary worker. Judas, as the keeper of the group's treasury, was understandably dismayed.

Jesus' comment in verse 7 that the anointing was for his burial indicates the prophetic nature of Mary's act. He would soon die for his beloved sheep. That it was a prophetic gesture would explain why Mary anointed his feet instead of his head, as in Mark's Gospel. Perfume was normally put on the head to give a pleasant aroma to the person wearing it; but it was also put on the feet of a corpse to offset the odor of decay.

Some have been troubled by Jesus' apparent nonchalance about the poor in verse 8. Joachim Jeremias, however, has noted that rabbis distinguished between two kinds of good works: those pertaining to mercy (including the burial of the dead) and those pertaining to justice (including alms for the poor). Actions related to mercy were always considered more important than those related to justice. Thus Jesus was confirming an acceptable standard of piety, not a single action that happened to benefit him.

One important factor in Mary's behavior must not be overlooked, and that is the raising of her brother, Lazarus, as narrated in chapter 11. Mary could well part with the valuable perfume she had been saving for her own burial because she no longer felt the need of it. Jesus had raised her brother from the dead and declared that he was the resurrection and the life. In a wonderful display of faith, she was "wasting" the precious ointment reserved for her funeral preparations, confident that the Messiah had made it unnecessary.

PRAYER

O God, I have always admired the spontaneity and generosity of Mary's act and wished that I could behave as she did. Now that I see her motivation—how her life was transformed in the face of the resurrection—perhaps I can be like her. Let me see what she saw, that I may be as she was. Through Jesus, the giver of eternal life, amen.

Day 323   *John 12:9-19*

THE FALSENESS OF THE CROWDS

*J*ohn's account of the triumphal entry is less colorful than the accounts of Matthew, Mark, and Luke, because in John's Gospel Jesus has been in Jerusalem many times before and there is not the sense of drama associated with this particular entry. Here the drama springs from the raising of Lazarus and the fact that crowds of people have heard about it and want to see him as well as Jesus. The chief priests and Pharisees are worried, and see that they must put both men to death in order to stop the Christian movement.

The words with which the crowds greeted Jesus were from Psalm 118—except for the phrase "the King of Israel," which is probably a reference to Zephaniah 3:14-20. This passage includes the line "The king of Israel, the LORD, is in your midst" (Zeph. 3:15), and speaks of a time when the lame will be cured and the outcasts gathered together.

Verse 15 is a prophecy from Zechariah 9:9 that Israel's king would come riding on the foal of an ass. The comment in verse 16 that the disciples understood the significance of this only later, after Jesus had been glorified, is representative of the early Christians' process of assimilating all that had happened; they recalled what had occurred and was said during Jesus' ministry and reflected on it in the light of Scripture.

Looking back on Jesus' entry into Jerusalem, John realized that many of those who cried "Hosanna!" were also among those who shouted "Crucify him!" They went out to greet Jesus not because they understood him to be the Son of God but because they heard he was a miracleworker. The Pharisees despaired, however, when they saw the crowds, thinking the whole world had gone after him. John saw the irony in this. Jesus' real hour of glory would be when he was lifted on a cross and the crowds had fallen away—not now, when they were running to greet him.

PRAYER

O Christ, I am so easily blinded by the world's values that I fail to understand what is eternal and true. Teach me to see the world as you saw it, through the eyes of God, that I may not waste my time and energy pursuing the things that will neither last nor matter. For your name's sake, amen.

Day 324   *John 12:20-36*

THE ARRIVAL OF JESUS' HOUR

*T*hroughout the Gospel there have been references to Jesus' "hour" (2:4; 7:30; 8:20) and his "time" (7:6, 8). Now the hour has finally come. Jesus is ready to enter the fatal confrontation with the authorities in Jerusalem and lay down his life for his sheep.

Perhaps the coming of the Greeks signaled the moment he had been waiting for. The suggestion is that Jesus was in hiding, as he had been on other recent occasions, and his disciples felt some uncertainty about whether to take the strangers to him. We are not told whether the Greeks ever did see Jesus. What John cared about was the fact that Jesus viewed their coming as an indication that his time had come to be lifted up.

Jesus' metaphor to the disciples about a grain of wheat falling into the ground and dying was an important lesson. "What good is saving your life?" he asked, in effect. "If you do that, you destroy it. It is only by living generously—by sowing your life unsparingly, as wheat is sown—that you enable the future to spring from your deeds!"

Jesus had come to this hour to die and be lifted up. It would have been pointless to flee, now that the hour had come. Instead he prayed, "Father, glorify your name" (v. 28). Some thought they heard thunder. Those with faith heard otherwise. They said a voice replied, "I have glorified it, and I will glorify it again" (v. 28).

As Jesus had told Nicodemus that the Son of Man must be lifted up like the serpent in the wilderness (3:14), so now he repeated the necessity of his being lifted up in crucifixion (v. 32). The crowd, as usual, was uncomprehending. How could the Son of Man be lifted up? Surely the real Messiah would be above such a natural death.

Jesus' answer was simple: Walk in the light while you can and become children of the light. John had said in the prologue to the Gospel that the eternal light was shining in the darkness, and the darkness would not overcome it (1:4-5). In a little while, the light would seem to waver and go out.

PRAYER

O God, it takes a lot of living to understand what Jesus meant about dying. In selfishness, I try to preserve my life, but the minute I do that I lose something. Teach me to live generously, loving the world as you have loved it. Then I shall not fear dying, or that I am leaving anything behind, for it will all be invested in you, who have never suffered any good thing to be lost. Amen.

Day 325   *John 12:37-50*

A TIME FOR SUMMING UP

*T*he prophet Isaiah had a life-changing vision of God in all the divine sublimity, "high and lifted up," with seraphim flying around the holy throne. Apparently John understood his own experience with Christ in similar terms. Like Isaiah, he saw something almost beyond description: the incarnation of the eternal Word. Yet people had behaved as if Jesus were no more than a wandering minstrel. Their eyes beheld the glory of the Son of God, but they did not see him for who he was.

Some members of the Sanhedrin, John knew, believed Jesus was the Son of God. Nicodemus (3:1-14) was probably one of them. But they were afraid of being ejected from the synagogue if they confessed what they believed. They cared more for their reputations among men than for their reputation with God (v. 43). Worrying about what others think, John knew, could be spiritually fatal.

The Pharisees' fear of being put out of the synagogues must have struck home to John's target audience, the Christian Jews, who had a similar fear.

Perhaps it was for these people that Jesus is pictured in verses 44-50 as giving a kind of summary of what he has taught to this point in the Gospel. Those who believed in him were really believing in the One who sent him.

He was the light of the world, and those who followed him would not walk in darkness. He did not judge people, but people judged themselves by how they responded to him. And nothing he said was really his own word, but was given to him by the Father.

The hardest part, for John, was to understand how people could see and hear what they had seen and heard, and still not believe. Only Isaiah's words could explain it to him.

PRAYER

Lord, I, too, am guilty of seeing and hearing and not believing. Your signs and testimonies in my life have been amazing and have caused me to say again and again that I believe. Yet I live my life as if this were not so—as if I had seen and heard nothing. Forgive me and draw me once more to the center of your presence. Renew an excited spirit within me, and this time help me not to forget so quickly. For the sake of your new order, amen.

Day 326   *John 13:1-20*

SENT BY THE MASTER

*T*his passage has traditionally been interpreted as a wonderful lesson in humility; and indeed it is. But it is also richly suggestive in other directions as well.

First, it raises interesting thoughts about the date of the Last Supper. The other Gospels indicate that Jesus' final meal with the disciples was a Passover meal. But John here clearly says that it was "before the festival of the Passover" (v. 1). Later, John alludes to the day of crucifixion as the day of preparation for Passover (19:14). Pilate handed Jesus over to the Jews for crucifixion at noon that day—the very hour when the priests were slaying the Passover lambs. When we remember that John the Baptist announced, on seeing Jesus, "Here is the Lamb of God who takes away the sin of the world!" (1:29), we see that John shifted the time of Passover in his story so that Jesus became the true paschal Lamb, slain at the official time for slaughtering lambs for the Passover meal.

Then there is the significance of the footwashing. Five days earlier, Mary had anointed Jesus' feet in preparation for his death and burial (12:1-8). Perhaps Jesus was washing his disciples' feet as a sign of their eventual martyrdom for the gospel.

Finally, there is the relationship of the washing to the betrayer. Jesus said to the disciples, "You are clean, though not all of you" (v. 10). John said this was to indicate that Jesus knew one of them was going to betray him. If footwashing was indeed a preparation for martyrdom for the Gospel, then Judas would not have been clean, even if his feet had been washed, for he would never preach the gospel.

The proof that the footwashing pertained to the disciples' coming deaths and not merely to humility is contained in verses 12-20, where Jesus says that the disciples should be servants as he is a servant—that is, suffering servants. "I tell you this now," he says, "before it occurs, so that when it does occur, you may believe that I am he" (v. 19). Here again is the divine signature, the *I am* without a modifier. And Jesus concludes by saying that whoever receives one of those he sends receives him and the Father. In other words, the entire business of the footwashing has had to do with sending the disciples out to preach and subsequently to die for the gospel, as he himself was about to die.

PRAYER

Lord, prepare me to pay the price for the gospel that you yourself were willing to pay. Let me exclaim with Simon Peter, "Lord, not my feet only but also my hands and my head!" Let me give heart and soul and life for the gospel's sake, and I shall be happy beyond words. For yours are the power and glory forever. Amen.

Day 327   *John 13:21-30*

THE DRAMA OF BETRAYAL

*J*esus and the disciples probably dined in Roman fashion, reclining with their heads close to the table. The disciple "whom Jesus loved"—probably young John, who later wrote this Gospel—lay close to Jesus' breast. Because he was so close, Peter prompted him to ask which of them was going to betray the Master. "Lord, who is it?" asked John. "It is the one to whom I give this piece of bread," said Jesus, "when I have dipped it in the dish" (vv. 25-26).

Some interpreters have read into this a reference to Communion, especially the form of Communion known as intinction, in which the bread is dipped into the wine and the two are served together. The scene would thus connect with Paul's warning in 1 Corinthians 11:27-29 that anyone who eats the bread or drinks the cup unworthily eats and drinks judgment on himself.

Judas may still have been uncertain about whether to betray his Master. (Verse 27 says that Satan entered into him only *after* he took the morsel.) John seems to want us to know that God and the Messiah were directing events, not Satan. Jesus said to Judas, "Do quickly what you are going to do," as if prompting him to go through with it (v. 27).

There is an ominous note in the words "And it was night." Jesus had come as the light of the world and was opposed by the darkness (1:4-5). Near the end of his public ministry, he had warned that the night was coming (9:4). Now Judas had gone out into the darkness. Soon the darkness would appear to overcome the light.

PRAYER

O God, my heart has always cried for Judas. Why should one be given to darkness and another to light? What is there in me that I deserve your favor and another doesn't? Help me to be more worthy, that I may not betray the trust you have given me. Through Jesus, who suffers from all betrayal, amen.

Day 328   *John 13:31-38*

JESUS' FAREWELL SPEECH

*T*he farewell speech was a well-defined genre of Old Testament literature. It can be seen in the stories of Jacob (Genesis 47–49), Moses (the book of Deuteronomy), Joshua (Joshua 22–24), and David (1 Chronicles 28–29). It usually included an announcement of the speaker's departure, comfort for those remaining, a review of the speaker's life and achievements, a reminder to keep God's commandments, a call for unity and love among those left behind, a promise that the speaker's spirit would be close to those remaining, and a prayer for them.

Jesus' long discourse at the Last Supper in this Gospel fits all the standards for such a farewell speech. He called his disciples "little children" (v. 33), as a man might speak to those he was leaving behind at death.

"A new commandment," he called his directive that the disciples love one another. Was it really new? Certainly the Old Testament often spoke

322

of the importance of love. And when Jesus was asked to name the most important commandment (Matt. 22:34-40; Mark 12:28-31) his response included Leviticus 19:18, that one is to love one's neighbor as oneself. Perhaps the "newness" in this case lay in the motivational clause attached to the commandment: "Just as I have loved you." Jesus had described himself as the good shepherd who lays down his life for the sheep (10:11). Now, as he was about to die, he called for the disciples to love one another with the same faithfulness he was showing to them. People would know the disciples were followers of Jesus if they loved one another, for love was the distinguishing mark of his relationship to all of them.

Peter wanted to know where Jesus was going. He could not believe that the one who had raised Lazarus from the grave should be speaking of his own death. Apparently he began to understand, however, for he swore he would lay down his life for Jesus. It was a case of the sheep's being willing to die for the shepherd. But only the Shepherd's will was as good as his word. Peter would deny his relationship to Jesus three times before morning, and Jesus would give his life for the sheep on the following day.

PRAYER

Dear God, I am gripped by Jesus' linking the love commandment to what he has done for me. How can I not love others, given such a reminder? Yet I do not; I forget what he has done, and, like Peter, deny him without thinking. Remind me, and keep me this day before the cross. For his love's sake, amen.

Day 329   *John 14:1-14*

WORDS OF ENCOURAGEMENT

*T*he disciples were predictably distressed at Jesus' announcement of his departure. But his "comfortable teachings," many of them reminders of things he had said in his ministry, were drawn together as words of encouragement. Don't be upset, he told them; there are rooms for all of you in my Father's house.

The Greek word for "rooms" or "dwelling places" was customarily used for rest stops or temporary dwellings, not permanent homes. Early Church Fathers took this to signify a continuance of growth after death. The picture of moving from level to level in understanding is endorsed by the so-called "life after life" experiences many people report, in which they were greeted by a guide in the afterlife who would conduct them to deeper understanding of their new environment.

"Lord, we do not know where you are going," said Thomas. "How can we know the way?" (v. 5). Jesus responded with another *I am* saying, this time combining them with great predicate modifiers: "I am the way, and the truth, and the life" (v. 6). The eternal *I am* was all of these things; they need not worry as long as they remained in him.

But what did Jesus mean by saying "No one comes to the Father except through me" (v. 6)? Was this a declaration of exclusivism, that there is no salvation outside the Christian faith? Jesus and the Father were one, he had insisted all along; therefore, to come to the Father was to come to him as well. Philip felt an epiphany coming on. "Lord, show us the Father," he said, "and we will be satisfied" (v. 8). That is, it will be all we could ask. Didn't they understand? asked Jesus. They had already seen the Father— in him. The works he had done were the Father's works. He was the extension of the Father. That was the point of everything in the entire Gospel.

And there was more: The works Jesus had done, the disciples would now do. They had had their feet washed and were commissioned to go out and be servants in Jesus' place. The power of God would flow through them as it had flowed through him. Anything they asked in his name would be done.

It wasn't that there was magic in signing prayers in Jesus' name, but that there was power in the reality to which it attested. It spoke then—and still speaks—of our being in communion with the One whose name is employed, so that we signify by speaking his name that we are extensions of his work in the world. And there is nothing in the world, as the raising of Lazarus demonstrated, that can resist the power of the Son and the Father!

PRAYER

Dear God, I am prone to wish power for my own sake and to pray in Jesus' name without really dwelling in his Spirit. What a dangerous thing it is to pray in his name if I really mean it. Then I am like a toy sailboat swept out to sea on a bottomless tide! Help me to pray the phrase and mean it—whatever the cost. Amen.

CHILDREN OF THE COVENANT

I give you a new commandment," said Jesus, "that you love one another" (13:34). Now he says, "If you love me, you will keep my commandments" (v. 15). Both verses suggest that we are dealing in this passage with a new covenant situation. In the Old Testament the Jews identified themselves with God by keeping the commandments; Jesus expects his followers to identify with him the same way.

Covenant-keeping followers will be given a special "Spirit of truth" as a counselor and guide, and the Spirit will dwell in them. Jesus calls the Spirit "another Advocate," suggesting that he himself has been the first. This Advocate will help them to understand all that has happened. They will not be alone—will not be "orphaned." Earlier, Jesus called them "little children"; now he promises not to forsake them as children with no leadership or provision.

What does it mean that Jesus will come to them? Is this the *parousia,* or Second Coming? Possibly, but not as the Synoptic Gospels interpret the Second Coming. John is more inclined to think of Jesus' return as his spiritual reappearance to the disciples after his resurrection. Soon the world will not see him, but the disciples will see him (v. 19). Then they will know that he is in the Father (v. 20), and he will show himself to them (v. 21). Not only that, but both Jesus and the Father will come and make their home with the disciples (v. 23).

The word for "home" in verse 23 is the same word used in verse 2, "In my Father's house there are many dwelling places" (or "homes"). The idea is circular, to express the eternal truth of the new covenant. God will dwell with the children of the realm, and they will dwell with God. And the disciples will understand all these things later, after the resurrection has occurred.

PRAYER

O God, these matters are hard to understand unless one has felt them. Enable me to feel them more deeply and certainly from day to day, and to lead others to experience them as well, that we may dwell together with you in perfect unity. Through him who gave his life that we might know you as you are, amen.

THE GREAT BEQUEST

*T*his passage concludes the first section of Jesus' farewell speech, and Jesus emphasizes his departure. Again he speaks of the Advocate, this time using the full phrase "the Holy Spirit." The Spirit's work will be to continue teaching the disciples and to help them remember all of Jesus' words and understand them in the light of what transpires.

Jesus then makes his final bequest to the disciples—his peace. An itinerant rabbi with no worldly possessions, he gives a blessing of eternal consequence. It is not peace as the world understands it—a mere absence of conflict—but peace in the old Hebrew sense of *shalom,* as the fullness of life. And peace, along with grace, would become a part of the standard Christian greeting after Jesus' death and resurrection.

When Jesus says that the Father to whom he returns is greater than he, it is not a statement about unequal powers within the Trinity. Jesus simply means that he is returning to the One who sent him, who, in the sense of being the originating parent, always takes precedence.

Evil will appear to be in control of things, Jesus warns them. But it is only an illusion. Jesus is submitting to death, not at Satan's command, but at the Father's. This way the world can learn the meaning of true obedience and love.

Finally Jesus bids the disciples to rise and go out with him, terminating this part of the discourse. Some interpreters suggest that the second part (chaps. 15–16) occurs on the way to Gethsemane and that the image of the vine and the branches in 15:1-11 was occasioned by their passing either some vines or a pile of dead branches pruned from the vines. Others believe that the entire discourse took place in the upper room and the command to rise and go out was merely a displaced instruction. Either way, the sentence marks a clear division in the final discourse.

PRAYER

In the storms of life, O Christ, give me your peace, and I shall be content. Nothing matters as much as your presence. Teach me to be still and know you, that I may no longer fear the wind and the waves. For you are the Lord of all. Amen.

THE VINE AND THE BRANCHES

*H*ere is another *I am* passage, with Jesus this time using the grapevine as an image of his life and work. We recall that his images often reflected the failure of Israel and his own supplanting of old traditions— he was "living water" to replace Jacob's well, "the bread of life" to replace manna in the wilderness, "the light of the world" to replace the candles at the Temple, and the good shepherd to replace the hireling shepherds. By calling himself "the true vine" Jesus was reflecting again on the failure of national religion in Israel.

There are many references in the Old Testament to Israel as a vineyard (Isa. 5:1-7; 27:2-6; Jer. 5:10; 12:10-11) or as a vine (Ps. 80:8-11; Ezek. 17:1-10). Most of these references are negative; they deal with Israel's breaking of its covenant with God and God's consequent destruction of the vineyard or the vine. Jesus, by contrast with the unfaithful nation, was the genuine stock of the vineyard, the one for whom God cared and who would bear fruit for the great vinedresser.

Therefore, it was important that the disciples remain in him and not seek their life in another vine or vineyard. This was a clear word to Christian Jews facing expulsion from the synagogues. Only by keeping their attachment to Jesus would they have life.

There is even an ominous note for those who remain in Jesus but bear no fruit. They, too, will be cut away and destroyed, so that they do not inhibit the better branches from bearing fruit.

The image of the vine and the branches fits beautifully with the entire theme of unity in the farewell discourse. Over and over, Jesus stressed the importance of remaining in him as he remained in the Father, and drawing on his love as he drew on the Father's. If the disciples only continued in him, they would have Jesus' joy in them—the creative excitement of knowing they were at the center of God's will for human life—and their joy would be full.

PRAYER

Lord, help me to remain in you and follow your commandment to love others as you have loved me, that I may shout with joy at what I see and know. For yours is the life forever and ever. Amen.

THE GREATEST MOTIVATION OF ALL

I do not call you servants any longer," said Jesus, "because the servant does not know what the master is doing; but I have called you friends [the Greek word used means "beloved" or "loved ones"] because I have made known to you everything that I have heard from my Father" (v. 15).

What a touching scene this is—a man about to die, giving his farewell discourse, and saying to his servants, the ones who have tended to the basic needs of his life, "You are no longer my servants; you are my dearly prized friends, my loved ones"! What a sense of unity it implies. And what consequences it would have in the disciples' lives!

We hear a lot today about motivation. Firms search for ways to motivate employees. Teachers try to motivate students. Advertising agencies wish to motivate consumers. But here is the greatest example of motivation in the world.

Jesus was the incarnate Wisdom of God, the eternal Son, the King of Glory. Yet he loved his disciples with such intense passion that he laid down his life for them and called them his dearly beloved friends. "You didn't choose to follow me," he said, in effect, "but I chose you, because I knew you would be fruitful for the Father. Now, continue in my love by walking in the way I have shown you, and love one another in the way you see me loving you, and the Father will care for all your needs in my name."

Is it any wonder that the disciples went to the ends of the earth, suffered in prisons, or died on crosses for him? Who wouldn't have done the same?

PRAYER

In the stillness, O Christ, I know that you have loved me as you did your first disciples. The words you said to them are spoken to me as well. How can I love you, Lord? Let me withhold nothing of myself, but give you everything. For you have given all for me. Amen.

THE WORLD'S HATRED FOR THE DISCIPLES

If Jesus had testified to the disciples of his love for them, he had also to warn them of the world's hatred for them. The hatred would stem from the fact that they bore his name and were identified with the works he did. After all, he had many times revealed himself as the *I am* of God—the one whose presence makes all earthly institutions appear shabby by comparison. And those who had anything to uphold or protect in those institutions would be innately opposed to him, as the darkness is opposed to the light.

"The Jews" would hate the Christians because Christ threatened their authority in religious matters. The Romans would hate them because they worshiped Jesus instead of Caesar. Jesus said he was hated to fulfill the word of Psalms 35:19 and 69:4 about those who "hated me without a cause." From a spiritual perspective, neither "the Jews" nor the Romans had just cause to hate him. But the perfidious thing about hate is always its baselessness and ridiculousness. To understand everything, said Voltaire, is to forgive everything. Had "the Jews" and Romans only understood, they would have loved instead of hated.

The Advocate, said Jesus, would help to teach the disciples about these things and would bear witness to him. There would be times when they would need that witness, lest they think they had followed a madman and bargained poorly with their souls.

As we have noted all along, the Fourth Gospel was written primarily to encourage Christian Jews being put out of synagogues. In 16:1-14, Jesus said that the main purpose of his farewell speech was to prevent their falling away from the faith. He knew they would be expelled from the synagogues. Worse, the time would come when some Jews would even seek their deaths as worship or service to God. But they were to remain in him, as branches in the true vine, and he and the Father would care for them and give them eternal life.

PRAYER

Lord, I have seldom felt persecuted for my faith. Does this mean that my faith has not been radical enough to provoke the fear and envy of others? Help me to ponder this question today and face its implications in my daily life. For your name's sake, amen.

THE ROLE OF THE SPIRIT

*I*t was not necessary, as long as Jesus was with the disciples, that he tell them all the things he put into his farewell speech. Before leaving them, however, he wished them to be conscious of these matters. Did hearing them make the disciples sad? It shouldn't. Jesus' going to the Father would be to their advantage. He would send the other counselor of whom he had spoken, and that counselor would convict the world of its sin, injustice, and wrongdoing.

The idea is that the Spirit would set everything in a new perspective, so that many would understand that Jesus was not a self-willed impostor but the true Son of God. They would know that they sinned in not believing in Jesus; that they were unrighteous, because the Son of righteousness was killed and left in their midst; and that they were under judgment, because the Prince of this world, their ruler, had been judged.

The Spirit would also reveal many things to the disciples that they could not presently bear—either because there was too much for them to remember or because the sayings would tax their understanding. The Spirit's revelations would come as they needed them. The statement that "he will not speak on his own, but will speak whatever he hears" (v. 13) probably refers to the divine council; the Spirit repeats to the disciples what the Spirit has heard in the presence of the Father and the Son. "He will declare to you the things that are to come" (v. 13) does not mean that the Spirit predicts the future but that the Spirit interprets whatever happens. The verb translated "declare" means "to reannounce" or "to republish," as if the Spirit's function is to remind the disciples of what has already been declared and help them to see its relationship to everything occurring in the present. The Spirit will glorify Jesus by bringing to mind everything belonging to the Son.

PRAYER

Teach me, O Spirit, to listen to you about Jesus and the world. Help me to understand—to feel deeply—the things that matter about his incarnation and what it means to the world, that I may be your servant in all things. Through him who walked the land and sailed the sea, amen.

THE JOY BEYOND THE PAIN

A little while, and you will no longer see me, and again a little while, and you will see me" (v. 16). What did Jesus mean by these words? The disciples were rightly puzzled. Looking back, we can easily see what was meant by the first statement; it referred to Jesus' impending death. But did the second statement refer to his reappearance after the resurrection, to a second coming at some future time, or to the disciples' reunion with Jesus in the afterlife?

Jesus' analogy in verses 21-22, of the woman who goes through anguish in giving birth and then forgets the anguish in her joy for the child, almost certainly interprets the words as applying to the post-resurrection appearances to the disciples. They would suffer great pain at the time of the crucifixion, but it would be forgotten in their ecstasy at seeing him afterward.

"So you have pain now; but I will see you again, and your hearts will rejoice, and no one can take your joy from you" (v. 22).

Again, Jesus spoke to the disciples of asking "in my name." They had not done this before, he said; in the future, they should do it, and see how full their joy was. He was not giving them the key to self-indulgence, so they could ask indiscriminately for whatever they wished. His words must be interpreted in the light of the entire discourse and its emphasis on unity—on being in him and in the Father. A person in that intimate spiritual relationship does not desire things for the self. He or she wishes what the Father and Son wish: the healing of cripples, sight for the blind, the raising of the dead, the love of all people for one another. "Ask these things in my name," Jesus was saying to the disciples, "and you will have what you ask, and your joy will overflow."

PRAYER

Lord, I know your words were not meant for the disciples alone, but for all followers. I want to be part of the unity you described, so that my desires are transformed by your love and your truth. Help me to will the things you will, and to will them so devotedly that I may see them come to pass. For your name's sake, amen.

A NEW STAGE OF RELATIONSHIP

I have said these things to you in figures of speech," said Jesus (v. 25). What did he mean? Perhaps he was thinking of all the metaphors and analogies with which he had taught—the grain of wheat falling in the ground, the vine and the branches, the mother giving birth to a child. Now he was speaking plainly about his death, and soon he could speak more plainly about the Father.

He would no longer have to pray for the disciples. Secure in the Son's love and the Father's as well, they would be able to pray for what they needed.

Jesus had come from the Father to do the Father's work, and he was going back to the Father now that the work was done. The disciples seemed to understand. "Now we know that you know all things, and do not need to have anyone question you; by this we believe that you came from God" (v. 30). What did they mean by saying he didn't need anyone to question him? It may refer to the way the disciples and others constantly questioned Jesus in order that he could give them the truth; now, as Spirit, he would impart truth in another way, directly and without need of a rabbinical structure.

Again Jesus warned the disciples that they would have difficult times and would be scattered like sheep without a shepherd. But God would not leave them alone. However desolate things might seem—especially when Jesus was on the cross—God would be there. The world might hate them and give them enormous difficulty, but Jesus himself would continue to give them peace and joy, for he had overcome the world.

The tense of the last verb suggests that his overcoming did not even await the resurrection. His "hour" had come, and God was glorifying him through everything that transpired—even his trial and death!

PRAYER

Lord, I am grateful for the figures of speech that have taught me how to see you. It is wonderful to picture you as light and bread, shepherd and true vine. Yet the most thrilling moments of all are those when I annihilate all thought and feel you warm and strong as a presence without images or figures at all. Then I know you as the disciples did, and I understand your triumph over the world. Give me such a moment now, Lord, for your name's sake. Amen.

JESUS' GREAT PASTORAL PRAYER

_J_ ohn, unlike the Synoptic Gospels, includes no prayer of Jesus in Gethsemane, that, if it was the Father's will, the cup might pass from him. The Jesus of the Fourth Gospel is far more triumphant than the Jesus of the Synoptics. He does not agonize over the cross. Instead, he sees the cross as his hour of glory, when he will return to the Father. God has given him "authority over all people" (v. 2); he is already the cosmic Christ. Because there is no prayer in Gethsemane, then, John shares with us this long pastoral prayer—the prayer of the Good Shepherd for his sheep—which is structurally a part of the farewell speech begun in chapter 13.

The prayer is divided into three sections. First, Jesus addresses the Father and speaks of the hour of his glory (vv. 1-5). Then he prays for the disciples (vv. 6-19). Finally he prays for all who are to become followers in the years ahead (vv. 20-26). The prayer thus resembles one offered by Aaron, the high priest, in Leviticus 16:11-17. Aaron first prayed for himself, then for his priestly family, and finally for the whole people. John may well have been conscious of these parallels when he set down the prayer of Jesus, for, as Aaron was the great high priest of the old covenant, Jesus was the great high priest of the new!

Jesus begins the prayer by addressing the Father and asking for his glorification. Glory is a quality of Godhood. It emanates from God just as the energy of our solar system emanates from the sun. As the Son of God, Jesus had shared in that glory before coming into the world. Now, returning to the Father, he asks to share in it once more.

Seeing the Son's glory enables people to have eternal life; it is the way they know God. The cross is important. But John saw that what lies beyond the cross, the glory of the resurrected Messiah, is of most abiding importance to the Christian. The center of our worship is no longer the humble Jesus of Galilee. It is the exalted Christ of the resurrection.

PRAYER

Lord, as the moon possesses no glory of its own but reflects the brilliance of the burning sun, so help me in my darkness to receive the glory of your presence and reflect it to those who dwell in a land of shadows; for yours are the power and the glory forever. Amen.

THE PRAYER FOR THE DISCIPLES

*I*n some ways, this section of Jesus' great pastoral prayer seems to have been uttered not before Jesus' death but after his resurrection—indeed, many years later. Jesus speaks of the disciples' having kept God's word (v. 6) and having been hated by the world (v. 14). At the time of the prayer's setting, between the Last Supper and the visit to Gethsemane, these things can hardly have come to pass. In fact, Jesus has only moments earlier (15:18-27) warned the disciples that they will be hated, and has promised them the Holy Spirit for encouragement. We can only suppose that John, with the liberty of a creative editor, has written the prayer not only as it applied to the disciples when Jesus prayed it but also as it came to apply to them and other disciples years after Jesus' return to the Father.

"I have made your name known," Jesus prays to God (v. 6). What does he mean? Is he referring to the Aramaic word *Abba*, the familiar word for "father" or "daddy"? Or, more likely, is he thinking of his frequent use of the divine *I am* that we encounter throughout the Gospel? If it is the latter, he not only gave the great name but coupled it with several images that revealed the holy personality. *I am* was the bread of life (6:35), the light of the world (8:12), the door of the sheep (10:7), the good shepherd (10:14), the resurrection and the life (11:25), the true vine (15:1), the way, the truth, and the life (14:6). He made the crippled spring up (5:2-9), the blind see (9:1-12), and the dead live (11:1-44). Surely the disciples were overwhelmed by Jesus' revelation of the "name" of God. It is no wonder that they believed he was sent from the Father.

Now, as he returns to the Father, Jesus prays for the disciples and asks that they may be anointed in the truth as he has been. "As you have sent me into the world," he says, "so I have sent them into the world" (v. 18). That is, they are now being entrusted with the same mission the Messiah came on—to preach the Word, heal the sick, open the eyes of the blind, and generally manifest the Father's life and power.

PRAYER

What a name you have revealed to us, O Lord. It is a name of music and poetry, a name of life and love and joy, a name surpassing every name. Help me to live daily in its great mystery, until my life is fully converted to your way and I am yours for ever and ever. Amen.

A PRAYER FOR FUTURE BELIEVERS

*J*esus' great pastoral prayer finally includes all of those who would come to believe in him through the ministry of the disciples. It is essentially the prayer offered for the disciples themselves—that they may all be one with him and the Father.

We can imagine how encouraging this prayer was to the Jewish Christians being put out of their synagogues and separated from the Jewish communities. They must have read the words again and again, drawing hope and joy from the thought of being in Christ.

In verse 24, Jesus expresses a desire for both his present and future followers to be with him in the life after the resurrection, so they can behold the glory he had with the Father before the creation of the world. As believers, they already know something of this glory. But in the life beyond death they will be in the presence of eternal Wisdom in all its breathtaking glory, with no barriers to their understanding.

Phillips Brooks once spoke of the division between this life and the next as a curtain. Sometimes, he said, we see the curtain tremble, especially if a loved one has recently gone beyond. It is enough to remind us of the life on the other side. But when we die, we pass beyond the curtain, and nothing will then inhibit us from seeing and knowing all things.

Jesus was anxious for his followers to join him beyond the curtain. Then they would see all that they had believed and hoped, given form in the heavenly world. The "name" Jesus had revealed to them—that of the great *I am*—would be fulfilled in the unspeakable presence to which it alluded. The love with which they had been loved would see them safely home to the bosom of the Father, who would then be all in all.

PRAYER

I can live my life more fully, dear God, knowing that its ultimate destiny is to dwell with you forever. Let my words and deeds remind others of this knowledge, that they, too, may come to know you and live in your love. For the sake of your heavenly realm, amen.

JESUS TAKEN CAPTIVE

*T*he Kidron valley was formed by a little brook called "winter-flowing Kidron," because it was dry until the rains of February and March caused it to flow. At Passover time it was probably stained red by the blood of the Passover lambs slain by the priests at the Temple. As Jesus was accustomed to crossing the valley to pray in the garden of olives, Judas knew where to find him, and led the detachment of soldiers, chief priests, and elders to capture him.

John's is the only Gospel that reports the presence of Roman soldiers. In the other Gospels, it is the priests and elders and their police who come for Jesus. Perhaps John wished to emphasize the universal aspect of Jesus' enemies—Jesus had spoken with the disciples about being hated by "the world" (15:18)—and so included the Romans.

The soldiers and police came with "lanterns and torches and weapons" (v. 3). John probably liked this touch in his narrative, for it emphasized again the darkness out of which they came to Jesus, who was the light of the world. What happened when they met was astounding. They said they sought Jesus of Nazareth, and Jesus replied, "I am he" (v. 5). When he said this, they stepped back and fell to the ground. Again it is the great *I am*. At the announcement of who Jesus was, they were all struck to the ground.

John made a point of Jesus' securing the release of his disciples, saying he did not lose a single one of those whom God had given him. The same point has been made often in the Gospel—in 6:39; 10:38; in 17:12; and now here. This accent on the security of those in Jesus was surely for the benefit of Jewish Christians having to choose between Christ and the synagogue. The synagogue was willing to turn them out, but Jesus would never lose those whom God had given him.

Peter drew a sword and struck the slave of the high priest, cutting off part of his ear. But again Jesus was in command, ordering Peter to sheathe his sword. His hour had come, and he was ready to drink the cup his Father had given him. In the other Gospels he prayed for the cup to pass. Here he seems eager for the cross to come, that he may join the Father. His moment of triumph is at hand.

Lord, this was a dramatic encounter, when you faced your enemies and did not use your great power to overcome them. Teach me your calmness of soul before those who would be my enemies, that I may not be disturbed by the evil of the world. For you are my strength and my redeemer. Amen.

Day 342   *John 18:13-18*

THE INFIDELITY OF PETER

*B*ound by the soldiers and police, Jesus was taken to the home of Caiaphas, the high priest, where the focus is turned temporarily not on Jesus but on Peter, who in the garden had offered resistance to Jesus' arrest. There is also a mystery disciple with Peter, about whose identity interpreters have speculated.

Some think it was the beloved disciple John, who consistently hesitated to mention his own name in the Gospel. If it wasn't he, then why didn't he identify the disciple? He knew the other details, including the name of the obscure slave whose ear Peter cut off in the garden. Surely he would have known the disciple.

Others suggest that the unnamed disciple was Nicodemus, who was apparently a cryptodisciple and would have had easy access to Caiaphas's house. But again, why would John have failed to name him? He tells in the following chapter how Nicodemus came with spices to anoint Jesus' body.

The third possibility is that the unknown disciple was Judas. He was certainly known to the high priest, having negotiated with him for the betrayal of Jesus, and would almost surely have followed with the soldiers and police he had led to the garden.

The Gospel, however, is not concerned with answering our curiosity about this disciple. Its entire focus here is on Peter and his act of infidelity. No story in the annals of discipleship was more important to the distraught Jewish Christians than this one. If Peter could vacillate so greatly in a matter of hours, from singlehandedly attacking the soldiers to denying that he was a follower of Jesus, then the falling away of other Christians was an understandable act of human frailty. And if Peter could be restored to fellowship—even to leadership—then there was always hope for those who had denied Christ in the synagogues, that they could be forgiven and rejoined to the fledgling Christian community.

Lord, this is my hope, too. How often I deny you in my self-centeredness, my forgetfulness of others, and my doubts and fears. I am not worthy to be called your follower. Yet you forgive me and anoint me again with your Spirit and send me forth to do your bidding. Let me not fail you today, I pray, but live honestly and openly for you. For the sake of my friends and family, amen.

Day 343   *John 18:19-24*

JESUS BEFORE ANNAS

*T*here is some confusion in this passage about who the high priest was. Verse 13 said that Jesus was taken to Annas, the father-in-law of Caiaphas, who was high priest that year. Verse 19 says the high priest (Caiaphas?) questioned Jesus. And verse 24 says that Annas, not Caiaphas, sent Jesus bound to Caiaphas the high priest.

Actually, Annas was the head of a priestly dynasty and had five sons, all of whom became high priests in their time. And because Annas was so crafty and powerful, he continued to be known as high priest even when his sons were in office. So it was probably the old man himself who was up in the middle of the night, questioning Jesus about his teaching.

It all emphasizes the nature of the conflict revolving around the Son of God. Jesus was pitted against the most entrenched powers of the Jewish world, including this family of politically oriented priests. He had dealt openly with everyone, as he told Annas. But he was up against men who were devious and full of chicanery, plotting in secret and using their skills and experience to hold on to their worldly empires.

. The Temple police were obviously unaccustomed to hearing men brought before the old man speak to him boldly and self-confidently, as Jesus did. So they struck Jesus and commanded him to show more respect. But their force could not curb the spirit of the Son of God, who demanded to be taken to trial if he had done wrong. Old Annas, probably feeling deeply frustrated, could do no more, so he sent Jesus to his son Caiaphas, the official high priest for the year. Caiaphas would have to deal with the Galilean.

PRAYER

Lord, it is sad to me that religious leaders can be part of the web of evil and darkness in the world. I suppose any of us can, even without intending to. Teach me to live in such daily humility before you that I may never offend you while thinking I am performing my duty. For yours is a name above every name, both in heaven and on earth. Amen.

Day 344   *John 18:25-27*

AFRAID IN THE COURTYARD

*F*or the second time John mentions that Peter was warming himself at the charcoal fire in the courtyard of the high priest (vv. 18, 25). Jerusalem is one-half mile above sea level, and the spring nights are often quite chilly. The confrontation between Annas and Jesus may have required an hour or more, for Annas probably spent time conferring with his associates about what should be done with the Nazarene. Peter, having nothing to do but wait in the courtyard, undoubtedly grew cold and moved to the fireside.

We can imagine what was going through his head. Jesus had been marched off as a captive. The longer he was gone, the more frightened Peter became. Was Jesus less powerful than they had believed? Why didn't he strike his enemies a mortal blow and walk out of the high priest's house? The constant movement of soldiers and police must have been unnerving.

The girl who watched the gate had asked Peter if he was a disciple of Jesus, and he denied it (v. 17). Now, when others standing about the fire thought they recognized him, he denied it again. Then one of the servants of the high priest, studying Peter's face in the firelight, decided Peter must be the man who had attacked his cousin in the garden. Once more Peter denied his association with Jesus, and instantly he heard a cock crowing.

Peter's mind must have flashed back at once to the conversation at supper, when he said he would lay down his life for Jesus. "Will you lay down your life for me?" Jesus had asked. "Very truly, I tell you, before the cock crows, you will have denied me three times" (13:37-38).

Sometime between his burst of bravado in the garden and the crowing of the cock—as early as 3:00 A.M. in Jerusalem—Peter had lost his courage. With Jesus by his side, nothing could daunt him, not even a cohort of legionnaires. But alone in a courtyard, with a fire casting shadows on strange faces, it was a different matter. Something went out of him, and he was afraid.

PRAYER

I know the feeling, Lord; it happens to me. When I have been faithful at prayer and feel your presence, I am ready for anything. My pulse races to do your will. But when I have been unfaithful and feel as if I'm on my own, it is another story. Help me today to be faithful, that no shadows may frighten me. For your name's sake, amen.

Day 345   *John 18:28-32*

A FATEFUL MEETING

*H*ere we meet Pontius Pilate, who was the Roman governor of Judea from A.D. 26–36. Jewish authors of the period spoke disparagingly of him, though that was possibly to be expected. On the whole he appears rather colorless. His primary base was in Antioch, but he had doubtless come to Jerusalem to oversee the garrison during the Passover festivities.

There is some evidence that the Romans did not allow the Sanhedrin to impose the death penalty, and it is thought that this is why the chief priests and elders took Jesus to Pilate and accused Jesus of sedition, so that the Romans would give the order to execute him. It is possible that some crimes were still punishable by Jewish stoning, but the priests and elders probably wanted Jesus killed by crucifixion, which carried a holy curse upon it and would put him in disfavor with the people.

Always punctilious in their religious observances, the Jews took Jesus only as far as Pilate's door. Had they entered the house of a Gentile, where leaven was present, they would have become unclean and could not have participated in the Passover celebration. This was always their way; they tithed their little herb gardens of mint and cumin while failing to observe the more important matters of the law, such as loving God and their neighbors.

When Pilate asked for their charges against Jesus, their answer was contemptuous and unspecific. So he ordered them to take Jesus back and try him themselves. He had no stomach for getting involved in local conflicts unless he had to.

340

O God, I am often unaware, as Pilate was, of the most fateful meetings in my life. I never know when some casual conversation or minor relationship will become the turning point of my entire existence. Guide me into real awareness, that I may not miss the important connections you prepare for me, but may be ever ready to meet them with wisdom and joy. Through Jesus Christ my Lord, amen.

Day 346   *John 18:33-38a*

WHAT IS TRUTH?

*T*he main theological question of Jesus' trial was the nature of his kingship. "The Jews" had apparently told Pilate that Jesus designated himself King of the Jews. This was probably an insurrectionist title, calculated to brand Jesus as a popular revolutionary who wished to overthrow the Romans and reestablish Jewish rule over Israel.

"Are you the King of the Jews?" asked Pilate (v. 33). Jesus wanted to know if Pilate had asked for himself or mouthed the words of others. Pilate's response indicates a certain helplessness. After all, he was not Jewish, and he probably found the Jewish ways strange. "Your own nation and the chief priests have handed you over to me," he said. "What have you done?" (v. 35).

Jesus explained that his kingship was not of this world; if it had been, his followers would have fought for him. His mentioning the word *kingship* was enough for Pilate. Jesus must think he was some kind of king, even if he wasn't king of the Jews.

"You say that I am a king," said Jesus. "For this I was born, and for this I came into the world, to testify to the truth" (v. 37).

Ah, truth. Pilate was a Roman and had surely had some rudimentary training in philosophy. "What is truth?" he mused (v. 38). Facing this extraordinary man whom the authorities wished to execute, he probably wondered where the truth really lay. But despairing of knowing the real truth, he decided to settle for the part of the truth he understood—political expediency. It had generally served him well in the past. How could he know that he was about to become infamous for failing to recognize the man who stood before him?

How often, Lord, have I stood in Pilate's shoes, wondering what to do? And how many times have I erred as he did, guessing at the truth and failing to do it? Let me wait before you now until wisdom becomes courage and I learn to act out the truth, not merely discern what it is. For you are the way, the truth, and the life. Amen.

Day 347   *John 18:38b-40*

JESUS OR BARABBAS

*I*nnocent—this was Pilate's verdict. World traveler, hardened soldier, seasoned administrator, he was a wary man. How many times had he faced men before—corrupt officials, offending soldiers, habitual criminals? He had seen enough to know men, and he knew Jesus was not the kind of criminal he was accused of being. So Pilate announced to the waiting authorities and police outside the praetorium that he found no guilt in Jesus.

But the Jews had a custom that the procurator should release one prisoner to them at Passover. Matthew, Mark, and Luke all indicate that it was the governor's custom. Only John speaks of it as a custom of the Jews. Perhaps Pilate had made it an annual custom as a gesture of good will, and thus referred to it as *their* custom.

"The Jews" shouted down the idea of releasing Jesus. "Not this man," they cried, "but Barabbas!"

John calls Barabbas a robber or bandit. Jewish literature of the time frequently used this word to describe insurrectionist guerrillas who roamed the countryside making daring raids and sometimes killing people. Mark and Luke both identify Barabbas as a murderer, and Matthew says he was a notorious prisoner. John shows surprisingly little interest in Barabbas; for him the drama is clearly centered on Jesus and Pilate.

Could Pilate conceivably have believed that "the Jews" would ask for the release of Jesus, when they had brought Jesus to him with the express purpose of having him condemned and executed? Some have advanced the thesis that Pilate tried to release Jesus in order to avoid giving up Barabbas, who may have been a popular figure in Jerusalem. As we shall see, however, Pilate was apparently convinced of Jesus' innocence. And more than that, he seems to have taken an unusual interest in the most extraordinary prisoner he ever faced. "The Jews" may have charged Jesus with posing as a king; but Pilate, who knew about kings, recognized something royal in the man's demeanor.

PRAYER

O God, Pilate said he found no crime in Jesus, yet did not use his authority to set Jesus free. Why do so many of us lack the courage to do what we know is right? Help me to live today so that what I believe is enacted in my deeds, that you may be glorified and I may rejoice in my own integrity. Amen.

Day 348   *John 19:1-5*

BEHOLD THE MAN!

Scourging was the worst form of Roman beating. Inflicted with a whip into which were embedded bits of stone and metal, it was reserved for capital offenders.

The cruelty of the soldiers was not uncommon. Stationed far from home, among people often hostile to them, they released pent-up anger on unfortunate prisoners. Jesus' charge was that he was a king. On him, they could even vent their hatred of the nobility. "Hail, King of the Jews!" they cried as they danced around him, slapping him in the face (v. 3).

After the beating and mockery of Jesus, which he had surely observed, Pilate emerged again before the praetorium and told "the Jews," "Look, I am bringing him out to you to let you know that I find no case against him" (v. 4). Pilate had already announced Jesus' innocence (18:38); moreover, the scourging was normally the prelude to execution. Had Pilate decided to have Jesus crucified, then changed his mind during the scourging? Perhaps Jesus' behavior during the beating and mocking convinced him that he could not go through with the execution.

"Here is the man!" said Pilate as the beaten figure in purple and a crown of thorns was pushed out in their midst (v. 5).

What did Pilate mean by these words? Did he say them proudly, defiantly, as in "See what a man you are dealing with!" Or did he say it with pathos in his voice, as if to imply, "Look, he is only a broken man; why do you wish to crucify him?"

Whatever Pilate's intention in the utterance, there can be little doubt as to John's thought in including it in the Passion narrative. Throughout the Gospel he has taken pains to demonstrate the humanity of the eternal

Word. Jesus has thirsted, wept, loved, and now suffered. "Behold the *man.*" Not an angel or a spirit, but a man. John is not losing the chance to remind us that God has been in our midst in human flesh, loving us person to person!

PRAYER

O Christ, I am ashamed of the pain and indignities you suffered—you of all people. But I realize you still suffer whenever any of your little ones are subjected to pain or indignities. Make me more aware of where this is happening today and give me a chance to help you there. For you are the King of my life. Amen.

Day 349   *John 19:6-11*

THE LIMITED POWER OF PILATE

*P*ilate, it is clear, wanted to set Jesus free. But the Jewish authorities were persistent. "Crucify him! Crucify him!" they shouted. Angry, Pilate told them to do it themselves; he found no fault in Jesus.

They could not do it, of course, which was why they had brought Jesus to Pilate. So now they shifted ground. If they could not get Jesus condemned as a political revolutionary, they would accuse him of blasphemy. "We have a law," they said, probably referring to Leviticus 24:16, "and according to that law he ought to die because he has claimed to be the Son of God" (v. 7).

Pilate, we are told, was "more afraid than ever" (v. 8). Why? We have not heard before that he was afraid. What was he afraid of? That he could no longer save Jesus? That a revolt of the Jews was imminent? That he was going to bungle everything and get in trouble? Again he took Jesus aside to question him. "Where are you from?" he asked (v. 9). Was he hoping to shift jurisdiction over Jesus to someone else? (Luke says that Pilate sent Jesus to Herod for judgment, as Herod was tetrarch of Galilee.) John may have been more interested in his providing an opportunity for reminding us that Jesus was really from the Father, not some earthly location.

Jesus' silence fulfills the prophecy in Isaiah 53:7, which said that the suffering servant of God would be mute like a sheep before its shearers. And it emphasizes Jesus' regal control over the exchange with the Roman governor. You wouldn't have any power over me, Jesus told him, if it hadn't been given to you from God. Yours is a limited power, a proscribed power. Only God, the One sending me, has power over me. The only power you have is the power God lets you have. Whatever happens, therefore, is not really your fault; it is "the Jews' " fault. I let them take me in the garden because it was my time to do so. They are really the ones challenging the power of God.

PRAYER

I sympathize with Pilate, O God. He was dealing with matters he could not comprehend. Much of my life seems to be lived the same way, dealing with things beyond my understanding or control. Be merciful to me, a sinner, and let me live with love and courage. For your name's sake, amen.

Day 350   *John 19:12-16*

THE END OF THE TRIAL

*P*ilate had considered the charge that Jesus was a political enemy and dismissed it. He had investigated the possibility that Jesus was a religious criminal and decided he was not. Once more, he went outside to "the Jews" and attempted to persuade them to let him release Jesus. But "the Jews" were crafty and were bent on Jesus' destruction. If Pilate would do nothing about their report that Jesus was setting himself up as a king, they would go over his head. He was no friend of Caesar's, they said, and they would report as much to Rome.

Pilate surely blanched at this. If officially accused to Caesar, he would be the subject of an investigation. There was no telling what errors or corruption in his prefecture would come to light. At the very least, a cloud of suspicion would be thrown over him for all time. Future appointments would be jeopardized. Even his present authority might be withdrawn.

This argument finally crumbled Pilate. He could withstand his clever adversaries no more. Peter had denied his Lord three times. Pilate had tried three times to save him. Now Pilate could—or would—do no more.

Jesus was brought outside onto the *lithostrotos,* the place of wide paving stones. Pilate seated himself on the judgment bench, from which official sentences were decreed. John is careful to note the hour—it was twelve noon. Mark 15:25 sets the time of crucifixion at 9:00 A.M. But John is interested in the symbolism of a noontime crucifixion on the day before Passover—the very hour when the priests in the Temple began to slay the thousands of lambs required for the Passover meal!

"Here is your King!" said Pilate at the hour of the slaughtering (v. 14). Is there an echo of John the Baptist's voice in 1:29, "Here is the Lamb of God who takes away the sin of the world!"? Both statements begin with the Greek word *ide*, "behold" or "here is." But "the Jews" were not having the Lamb for their King. "We have no king but the emperor," they said (v. 15). A damning admission for a group of Jews!

PRAYER

O Lamb of God, who takes away the sins of the world, be my King, now and forever. Amen.

Day 351   *John 19:17-22*

PILATE HAS THE LAST WORD

*A*ll the Gospels are remarkably taciturn about the execution of Jesus. Perhaps the writers could not bear to describe it. Or perhaps they revered it too much to expound upon it. But there are interesting details in this brief passage.

The Synoptics all report that Simon of Cyrene was compelled to assist Jesus with his cross. John says Jesus bore his own cross. Perhaps John saw it as theologically important to depict Jesus bearing his own cross—he was the regal Son of God.

The crucifixion occurred at "The Place of the Skull." *Golgotha* was the Hebrew word for "skull," and *calvaria* the Latin word. Either it was a skull-shaped hill, or a skull had once marked it as a forbidden site. Ancient Christian legends suggest that it may have been the burial place of Adam and that the blood of Jesus, the second Adam, was spilled on the skull of the first one.

The dominant note of the passage is the information that it was Pilate who had an inscription placed on the cross. All the Gospels refer to the inscription, but only John connects it with Pilate. It was written in three primary languages, emphasizing Christ's universality, and was apparently the plaque bearing a criminal's accusation, commonly carried ahead of the man or hung by a cord about his neck.

This information forms a fitting climax to the drama of Pilate's struggle for the release of Jesus. Failing to persuade "the Jews" to accept the release, he printed the words of accusation on a public placard. "The Jews" objected that what he printed was inaccurate—Jesus only *said* he was King of the Jews. "What I have written I have written," said Pilate (v. 22).

It was almost a confession of faith on Pilate's part. Perhaps he did not fully understand the significance of the title; he was a foreigner and probably not a religious man. But something about Jesus compelled Pilate's respect and wonder. For him, Jesus *was* the King of the Jews, even though his throne was a cross.

PRAYER

O Lord, how did Pilate live with what he saw that day? I am grieved merely to read about it. Grant that I may never stray from the tragic scene, except to experience the joy of your resurrection. For you are the Risen One with nail prints in your hands. Amen.

Day 352   *John 19:23-25a*

THE TUNIC OF JESUS

*J*ohn alone has told us that the soldiers who crucified Jesus were a quaternion—a band of four. It is possible that a quaternion was assigned to each man being crucified.

When the soldiers had put Jesus on the cross, they exercised their privilege of dividing his belongings among themselves. Probably one received his *tallith,* or robe; one his cincture, or girdle; one his head covering, something like the modern *kafia*; and the fourth, his sandals.

The seamlessness of the robe or tunic did not indicate that it was particularly expensive. It was merely in keeping with a law in Leviticus 19:19 that forbade wearing a garment woven of two kinds of material. Tunics and robes that had not been pieced together were common, for this showed at a glance that the law was honored.

The soldiers cast lots for the tunic to avoid cutting it up. John saw this as fulfilling a prophecy in Psalm 22:18 about a man's enemies dividing his possessions among them. Psalm 22, incidentally, is the one beginning, "My God, my God, why have you forsaken me?" cited by Mark 15:34 as one of Jesus' words from the cross. John would not have quoted this verse of the psalm because of his emphasis on the constant unity of the Son with the Father.

Jesus was apparently left naked on the cross, as most men wore either a tunic or a breechcloth beneath their clothing, but not both. He died, therefore, as he had come into the world—without property or clothing.

PRAYER

O Lord, you were the victim of such humiliation, yet turned it into glory and triumph. Help me to love you so much that I will not worry about my own defeats in the world, but will rejoice in the light of your victory. For yours is the kingdom forever. Amen.

Day 353   *John 19:25b-27*

THE TRUE HOLY FAMILY

*T*he preceding scene (vv. 23-25*a*) revealed four soldiers. This one has four women—Jesus' mother, his aunt, and the two other Marys. According to one scholar who has studied the matter thoroughly, the families of those crucified were usually permitted to remain by the side of their dying relatives. We know from the Synoptics that Jesus traveled in the company of a number of women, as well as his disciples, and that his mother was often in the group.

Looking down from the cross, Jesus saw his mother among the women standing there. At a slight distance stood also the beloved disciple John. "Woman," Jesus said, using the word he had addressed her with at the wedding in Cana (2:4), "here is your son" (v. 26). To John, he said, "Here is your mother" (v. 27). It was a transaction similar to ancient contract scenes in which a dying man made provision for a wife or children or parents being left behind. Perhaps Jesus, who had known what kind of death he must die, had made the arrangements earlier, and now in the final hour of his consciousness was sealing what had been decided.

The Gospel of John has no birth narrative for Jesus, and so contributes nothing to the story of the holy family as found in Matthew and Luke. But it has this touching scenario in which Mary, the mother of Jesus, is given into the care of the disciple John. In other words, it gives us the picture of another kind of holy family—one built on the mutual love and commitment of the members.

In this sense, the picture prefigures the nature of all Christian fellowship. Those of us who are one with Jesus and God are also one with each other. Jesus has commanded us to love one another (15:17). We are to care not only for Jesus but for all those who are of his family as well.

PRAYER

What a tender picture, O God, of the life in your Son. How different it is from life in the world, where we dwell in isolation and loneliness. Grant that I may truly care for others in the fellowship and share whatever I have with them, for your Son's sake. Amen.

Day 354   *John 19:28-30*

IT IS FINISHED

*J*ohn says that Jesus said "I am thirsty" in order to fulfill the Scripture (probably Ps. 69:21), "They gave me poison for food,/ and for my thirst they gave me vinegar to drink." But probably more important to John's theology was the fact that the incarnate Lord of Glory exhibited his true humanity by asking for a drink. Here was no Docetic Christ. He was a human being in the fullest sense.

The word *hyssop* has caused commentators some concern. The hyssop bush was not uncommon, but its stalk was not very strong and seems an unlikely kind of stick to have used to extend a sponge soaked in wine. Some scholars, therefore, suggest that there may have been a scribal error in copying the word and that it was originally *hyssos,* a javelin or spear. But John may well have intended the word *hyssop* because the hyssop plant was used at the time of the exodus to sprinkle the blood of the paschal lamb on the door posts of Israelite families (Exod. 12:22). Jesus was the Lamb of God, taking away the sins of the world (1:29). It would have been extraordinarily fitting for a hyssop plant to have come in contact with his suffering body in the final moments of the crucifixion.

Having received the vinegary wine, fulfilling the Scripture, Jesus said, "It is finished," bowed his head, and gave up his spirit (v. 30). If John had been present at the cross during Jesus' most agonizing moments, when he said "My God, my God, why have you forsaken me?" (Matt. 27:46; Mark 15:34), or if he knew the tradition of the saying, he omitted it from his narrative. Similarly, he did not mention Jesus' crying with a loud voice, "Father, into your hands I commend my spirit!" (Luke 23:46). His Jesus simply bowed his head in a quiet manner and gave up the spirit.

John had emphasized all along the unity of the Son and the Father. This was the hour of the Son's glory. He did not vent his agony or in any way voice misgivings about what was transpiring. For this cause he had come into the world.

PRAYER

Lamb of mercy, I wait reverently before this image of your crucifixion and listen as you say, "I thirst." Would, Lord, I could give you everything for which you thirst: an end to human suffering, a universal community of love, the joy of your whole creation. At least let me give you no cheap wine, but the very best I have. For your name's sake, amen.

Day 355   *John 19:31-37*

THE WOUNDED SIDE

The Romans were usually in no hurry to remove bodies from crosses. Sometimes they took days. But Passover was coming, and Pilate didn't want any more trouble from these bothersome people who had threatened to report him to Rome, so he sent the delegation they requested.

Breaking an executed man's legs was not an unusual practice. It was accomplished with a large mallet. But Jesus' legs were not broken, because the soldiers saw that he was already dead. True to John's portrait of him, he remained in control of his own death, dying before the soldiers came. One of the soldiers did, however, plunge a spear into his side. At once, John says, blood and water came out.

Doctors have spoken of the impossibility of a flow of blood and water from the side of a dead man, as blood does not generally flow after the heart stops beating. But John was obviously concerned here with theological imagery. Jesus stood at the Feast of Tabernacles and alluded to "rivers of living waters" flowing from the faithful person (7:38). And water was rich in associations: the water from the rock struck by Moses (Num. 20:10-11); the water of life; the water of baptism. Jesus had told the woman at the well that anyone drinking the water he would give would never thirst (4:13-14). And the imagery of blood is fully as strong as that of water in Hebrew lore: the blood of the Passover lambs; the blood of covenants; the blood containing the spirit of life.

John no doubt saw sacramental meaning in the flow of blood and water—something beyond mere physical possibility. Perhaps the Early Church Fathers had the best attitude. They regarded the event as a miracle and saw verse 35, about the witness (surely John himself), as proof of this. An ordinary event, they reasoned, would not have required the special testimony of a witness.

PRAYER

O Jesus, born to die but alive forevermore, help me to turn my eyes upon you. "Let the water and the blood, from thy wounded side that flowed, be of sin the double cure, save from wrath and make me pure." Amen.

Day 356   *John 19:38-42*

THE SECRET DISCIPLES

*H*ow encouraging this passage must have been to Jewish Christians afraid to confess Jesus in the synagogues! At last, two members of the Sanhedrin, the council that had sought Jesus' death, came forward to claim his body and display their allegiance to him. Mark 15:43 and Luke 23:50 both identify Joseph as a member of the council, and we know from John's report of the meeting between Nicodemus and Jesus (3:1-14) that Nicodemus was, too.

Jesus had said in 12:32, speaking of his death on the cross, "I, when I am lifted up, will draw all people to myself." Was this part of what he meant—that even the secret followers among the rulers of Israel would come out of hiding and own their discipleship?

Matthew 27:60 says the place of burial was in Joseph's own new tomb. As Mary had used her burial ointment to anoint Jesus (John 12:1-8), Joseph was surrendering his own resting place. The body was washed, covered in the mixture of myrrh and aloes, and wrapped in linen cloths. The amount of myrrh and aloes was very great—enough, in fact, to indicate that Nicodemus regarded Jesus as a person of royal status. The fact that the tomb was in a garden also betokens the royal nature of the burial; kings and rulers were usually buried in such surroundings, while common people were buried in ordinary burial grounds. It was only fitting, after the emphasis on Jesus' kingship throughout the trial and crucifixion, that he be interred in a royal manner.

To comprehend the daring of Joseph and Nicodemus in preparing the body and burying it, we need to remember the Jewish associations of death and defilement. Touching the dead made any person unclean for seven days (Num. 19:11). This meant that the two men could not eat the Passover meal the evening of Christ's death. Their families and friends would know they had been defiled. There was no way of keeping their devotion secret any longer.

We can only suppose they had discovered something that made their risk worthwhile—that the one who died on the cross was the real Passover Lamb, who takes away the sins of the world!

PRAYER

Lord, give me a simple faith, that I may feel at all times the mystery of your presence and serve you as the King of my life. For your mercy's sake, amen.

Day 357   *John 20:1-10*

THE EMPTY TOMB

*T*his passage is so vibrant with meaning and mystery that it is difficult for a Christian to read it without trembling. For two chapters we have been reading about the capture, trial, and execution of Jesus. The material was heavy, sorrowful, dirgelike. Now the pace quickens and the material lightens. Suddenly people are running and speaking breathlessly. There is excitement, hope, the dawning of belief.

Forty-eight hours earlier, Mary of Magdala (a small town near Capernaum, in Galilee) had stood with Jesus' mother near the cross. Now she was coming to mourn his death—to weep and wail in Israelite fashion. Her discovery and report sent Peter and John racing to the tomb. John, younger and more athletic, arrived first. Peering in, he saw the grave cloths lying on the stone shelf that ran around three sides of the tomb. Peter, not stopping to think about defilement from contact with the dead, plunged inside. In the shadowy halflight he saw not only the linen cloths but also the head covering, which, instead of lying with the linen cloths, was rolled up and lying by itself.

If robbers had stolen the body, they would not have troubled to unwrap the spiced grave clothes and lay the head covering neatly aside. The disciples were clearly dealing with something greater than a body theft.

The report is that both disciples came to believe when they saw the evidence of the empty tomb. That they did not know the Scripture pertaining to the resurrection may strike us as very unusual. But we should remember that John has consistently emphasized Jesus' reunion with the

Father, not his resurrection as such. Repeatedly, in the farewell speech of chapters 14–17, Jesus spoke of going back to the Father, not of shortly returning to the disciples.

It was natural, therefore, that the two disciples, on making the astounding discovery of Jesus' resurrection, returned to their homes. (Apparently they were not living at the same address in Jerusalem.) Their heads were filled with the wonder of what they had seen, but they did not anticipate seeing Jesus again before they, too, went to be with the Father. They were probably quite content with the evidence that Jesus had triumphed over death.

PRAYER

Lord, my heart beats faster and faster as I contemplate this marvelous Scripture. How simply and beautifully it describes the wonder of that remarkable scene! I can enter the amazement of it as if I were there. Thank you for this vivid memory from the two disciples and what it has meant to believers through the ages. Let it remain strong and active in my mind, transforming the way I view the world and my role in it. You have overcome everything—even my lethargy! Amen.

Day 358   *John 20:11-18*

THE APPEARANCE TO MARY MAGDALENE

*T*his is surely one of the most tender scenes in the entire Bible. Mary, her eyes clouded by tears, looked inside the tomb and saw two angels sitting on the stone shelf. Apparently she believed someone had taken the body away, for that is what she said when the angels asked why she was weeping. Jesus asked a second time why she was weeping. Confused, thinking he was the keeper of the garden, she responded again that she was looking for the body. But when Jesus spoke her name—"Mary"—she knew instantly it was her Lord.

"Rabbouni!" she exclaimed (v. 16). It was the Hebrew word for teacher or master, but in a special form of the word, indicating an affectionate relationship. Perhaps we could translate it "Dear Master."

It has always interested readers that Mary recognized Jesus the moment he spoke her name. The passage suggests the intimate relationship that always exists between Jesus and the individual believer. And it echoes something Jesus had said in the Good Shepherd passage: "He calls his own sheep by name and leads them out. . . . And the sheep follow him because they know his voice" (10:3-4).

When Mary tried to embrace Jesus, he told her not to hold him because he had not yet ascended to the Father. This may appear contradictory to verse 27, where Jesus tells Thomas to feel the wounds in his hands and side. But John was only giving us vignettes of appearances to suggest that Jesus was triumphant over the grave. John's real interest was still in Jesus' returning to the Father. The manner of his appearances to the various disciples was probably of little consequence. Everything was told to verify the one overriding claim of the Gospel: that the Word that had become flesh had overcome the world and been reunited with the Father.

Mary, like a faithful witness, went back and reported to the disciples what she had seen and heard. This time she did not use the word *Rabbouni.* She said: "I have seen the Lord!" (v. 18).

PRAYER

Like Mary, Lord, I want the reality of sacred moments to linger forever, so that it transcends all other realities. But, like Mary, I cannot hold you; the world is too much with me. Only in prayer and meditation can I experience the union with you and the Father that overcomes the world. Therefore, help me to pray as constantly as possible, even when I have to be doing other things. For there is nothing like being in your presence, which even the tomb could not contain. Amen.

Day 359   *John 20:19-23*

THE RECOMMISSIONING OF THE DISCIPLES

*T*he disciples, we are told, were in fear of "the Jews." Perhaps they thought that now that the sabbath was over the authorities would round up Jesus' associates—or that they would be blamed for the disappearance of the body! We can imagine their excitement as they talked about the experiences of that first Lord's Day. And suddenly, as they talked, Jesus appeared in their midst.

"Shalom halekem," he said, "Peace be with you" (v. 19). It was the formula spoken by God to Gideon in Judges 6:23 when Gideon was frightened at seeing the Lord's angel. Only now it bore the added meaning given by Jesus in his farewell speech when he said to be at peace because he had overcome the world (16:33).

After showing the disciples his hands and side—emphasizing the brokenness of the body now raised up before them—Jesus repeated the words "Peace be with you" (v. 21). They were to understand that God's peace keeps even one whose body is mutilated in the divine service. And this time Jesus added the Johannine form of the Great Commission: "As the Father has sent me, so I send you" (v. 21). Having said this, he breathed on them, imparting the Holy Spirit to them. The Spirit would empower them to carry out his commission in the world, including the condemnation and forgiveness of sin.

One of the fascinating things about this brief passage is the number of references it bears to the form of early Christian worship, so that we could almost take it as a prototype of a worship service. First, the meeting took place on the first day of the week, as Christian worship did. Second, it occurred behind closed doors (early Christians often met in hiding). Third, the followers of Jesus were probably talking about their earlier experiences of Jesus. Fourth, Jesus manifested himself to them, as Christians believed he would in the Eucharist ("Our Lord, come" was the standard eucharistic prayer). Fifth, Jesus said, "Peace be with you," the formulaic greeting used in the Eucharist from earliest times. Sixth, the followers received the gift of the Spirit. And, seventh, they were empowered to represent Jesus in their dealings with others.

PRAYER

Lord, the Scripture says the disciples were glad when they saw you. I, too, am glad when I feel your presence. Come, I pray, behind the closed doors of my life and breathe your Spirit upon me, that I may feel empowered to represent you in the world. For your peace is all the armor I require. Amen.

Day 360   *John 20:24-29*

THE GREAT CONFESSION

We can imagine how awful Thomas must have felt to have missed out on Jesus' appearance to the disciples the first time. But he was not left out for good. A week later they were gathered in the same place, and this time Thomas was with them. The similarities to the first occurrence, and the fact that they were both on Sunday, suggests that this was another worship service, the second such occasion for the fledgling church.

Again, when Jesus appeared, he said, "Peace be with you" (v. 26). Then he offered himself to Thomas for Thomas's handling. And once more early Christians were bound to see eucharistic allusions in what transpired. Jesus' hands, his body, were the bread. The wounded side, from which water and blood had flowed (19:34), represented the wine. The injunction to have faith would be especially relevant to persons approaching the sacred table.

Thomas's response to the invitation of Jesus was precisely the one desired of every follower: "My Lord and my God!" (v. 28). It was the highest word of personal confession spoken in the entire Gospel. Jesus had been called Lamb of God, Teacher, Lord, and King of Israel. He had called himself the bread of life; the light of the world; the resurrection and the life; the gate of the sheep; the good shepherd; the way, the truth, and the life; and the true vine. But Thomas's confession topped them all. It was the climax of understanding toward which the whole Gospel had been moving. And it is the insight to which every follower should rise each time he or she participates in Christian worship: "My Lord and my God!"

"Have you believed because you have seen me?" asked Jesus. "Blessed are those who have not seen and yet have come to believe" (v. 29). In the Eucharist, we all see by faith. We have not really seen, as Thomas did—not literally, with our eyes. But we have seen with our hearts, and that was finally how Thomas had to see, too.

PRAYER

My Lord and my God: It is a staggering confession, and I feel the weight of it as I make it. It changes the center of my life. I am no longer there, but you are. Come, Lord Jesus, and take full possession of me, for you are the one who died and is alive, and I want no life outside of yours. Amen.

Day 361 *John 20:30-31*

LIFE IN HIS NAME

*T*hese verses are actually a formulaic conclusion to the first twenty chapters of the Gospel, suggesting the probability that the Gospel originally ended here and an editor subsequently added chapter 21. This does not mean that chapter 21 is not John's, but only that it was appended later to the original version of the Gospel.

"Jesus did many other signs in the presence of his disciples," the ending says (v. 30). It is thrilling to think that what was written in the Gospels was only a portion of what Jesus did and said during his ministry. Imagine! There were probably dozens of major healings and dramatic encounters—perhaps hundreds—that did not get into the pages of the Gospels. The authors selected only the stories and sayings needed to present a true picture of Jesus' power and personality.

The "signs" included in his Gospel, says John, were put there so that the reader "may come to believe that Jesus is the Messiah, the Son of God, and . . . have life in his name" (v. 31). In this case, the verb translated "to believe" should be translated "keep believing" or "continue to believe." That is, "these are written so that you may continue to believe that Jesus is the Christ, the Son of God. . . . "

This would agree with our contention that the entire Gospel was written primarily to encourage Jewish Christians to continue in the faith, even if expelled from their synagogues, not to make new Christians. It would also help to explain why John presents a more exalted image of Jesus than the other Gospels; it was purposely intensified to appeal to persons who already had a basic introduction to the faith but needed a more "spiritual" narrative to deepen their perceptions of Christ and his faithfulness as the shepherd of the Christian flock.

PRAYER

Lord, when I think of how many wonderful signs have been done in your name, both during your ministry and since you breathed your Spirit into the disciples, my mind is boggled! They continue to be done throughout the world every hour! Give me eyes to see and ears to hear, that I may always have life in your name. For you are the Christ, the Son of God. Amen.

Day 362   *John 21:1-11*

AN AMAZING CATCH

*I*f this story was added after the Gospel was essentially finished, the question is why. The answer may lie in the symbolism of the sea and the fish, and their relation to the universal mission of the church. The story may well be a long, enacted parable about the work of the disciples and the early church.

It is interesting that only seven of the disciples went fishing. Seven in Jewish numerology was a universal number. It was believed there were seventy Gentile nations—seven (for universal) times ten (for wholeness or completeness).

The disciples fished at night—a natural time for fishermen who brought their catches to market in the early morning. But we must remember the light and dark symbolism in the Fourth Gospel. These men were fishing in the dark—that is, under their own power. Christ appeared to them as the day was breaking. They were successful in the light.

"Children, you have no fish, have you?" asked Jesus (v. 5). The Greek word used for "children" is *paidia,* which means "small boys" or "lads." It is the plural of the word used in 6:9 for the small boy brought to Jesus with the loaves and fishes, suggesting, perhaps, a link between the two multiplication stories.

The miraculous nature of the event is underlined by the fact that the great catch occurred essentially in the same spot where the disciples had been fishing and catching nothing. Jesus was Lord of the sea—and of the fish as well. And young John, the disciple, recognized Jesus through the sign of the fish. "It is the Lord!" he exclaimed (v. 7).

Jerome, one of the earliest commentators on the Gospel, said that Greek zoologists recorded 153 varieties of fish in the seas. If that was a generally known fact, then the number probably was a promise for the church's evangelism, which would win converts from every nation on earth. And the fact that the nets did not break (as contrasted with Luke 5:6, in which a miraculous draft of fish did break the nets) is also interesting, especially in the light of Jesus' promise in John 17:11-12 that none of those given to him by the Father would be lost.

The passage was clearly about the work of the early church as it set out to evangelize the world. Without Christ, the disciples would have been powerless. With him, they brought in great numbers of people. And, because of the unity of converts with the Son and the Father, true believers were never lost.

PRAYER

Thank you, Lord, for this graphic picture of the ministry of the early church. Help me to ponder it in considering the mission of the church today—and to take my place at the nets. You are the Lord, and we listen to your voice. Amen.

BREAKFAST BY THE SEA

*H*aving made his point about the missionary enterprise of the early church (vv. 2-11), John now turns to the manner in which the early church would be sustained, showing us this beautiful picture of Jesus feeding his disciples. It is the only story we have, in any of the Gospels, of a breakfast meal.

The wording of verse 13, "Jesus came and took the bread and gave it to them, and did the same with the fish," is particularly suggestive of the serving of the Eucharist. That the meal consisted of bread and fish, and not bread and wine, is not a strong impediment to this interpretation, for early Christian art (in the catacombs, for instance) often pictured fish as part of the Communion meal.

The fact that all of the disciples "knew it was the Lord" is further support for the eucharistic reference. In Luke 24:30-31, it was in the breaking of bread that the two disciples from Emmaus recognized the risen Lord. There was probably a general connection in the minds of early Christians between eating the Eucharist and discerning the presence of Christ.

This was the third time, says John, that Jesus revealed himself to the disciples after the resurrection. The other two occasions were on Lord's Days or Sundays. The stress on this time's being the third may well mean that it, too, occurred on a Lord's Day, further underlining the eucharistic reference of the passage.

The Gospel may have provided us, in the two upper room visits of Jesus, each on the first day of the week, and in this breakfast visit by the sea, with a normative picture of worship life in the early Christian community. From the first Sunday after the crucifixion—that is, Easter Day itself—the Christians did not fail to meet, break bread together, and experience the presence of Christ in their midst!

PRAYER

O Lord, known in the breaking of bread and drinking the cup, I am grateful for these powerful reminders of your suffering and for the promise that whenever we share them in your name you will be there, ministering to us as before. Grant that Christians everywhere may give more reverence to this sacred occasion and that, sensing your presence, we may return doubly faithful to our mission in the world. Amen.

A TOUCHING INTERROGATION

*W*e have observed many times through the Gospel that it was especially directed at converts who were tempted to fall away from the faith. At the same time, it attempted to encourage those who had apostatized to return to the fold. No example was more powerful in this encouragement than Simon Peter's, for Peter had flagrantly denied Jesus not once but three times, and then had returned to favor and become the leader of the church in Jerusalem. Here in verses 15-19 we have one of the most tender and most beloved pictures of Peter's restoration and recommissioning by Jesus.

Three times Peter had denied his Lord; three times his Lord questioned him. Scholars have shown that repeating questions and vows three times was often done in ancient times to indicate the contractual status of a verbal exchange.

The first time Jesus questioned Peter, saying, "Simon son of John, do you love me more than these?" (v. 15). We cannot be certain what "these" referred to. Some think it meant the fishing boats and nets—the symbols of Simon's occupation. Others believe it meant the disciples—did Peter love Jesus more than they did?

How could Peter prove that he loved Jesus? He had already denied his Lord after promising to die for him. Now the only appeal was to Jesus' intimate knowledge of him. "Lord, you know everything; you know that I love you" (v. 17). Surely Jesus knew what was in Peter's heart and understood how faithful he would be now that Jesus was alive forevermore!

Jesus' replies that Peter should feed and care for his little ones, on the other hand, were his way of accepting Peter's love and giving him responsibility at the same time. It was tantamount to saying, "Yes, I know you love me, and you shall show it through my flock, which I entrust to you."

But Jesus is utterly realistic, and concludes the conversation by alluding to how it will be as Peter assumes responsibility and eventually faces death for his faith as Jesus did. Caring for the sheep leads to martyrdom for them. And at last Jesus says, "Follow me" (v. 19), words he had doubtless spoken to Peter in the beginning of Peter's discipleship, but which now carried an even more transcendent meaning.

PRAYER

Lord, this is a model commissioning service. Peter is tested, he answers that he loves you, you tell him to care for your sheep, and you predict his death in the ministry. Help me to love you so much that I, too, will be ready to die in your service. You are the Good Shepherd, and you have laid down your life for me. Amen.

WHAT ABOUT THE OTHER PERSON?

*H*ow easy it is to understand Peter's interest in what John would be doing while he was following Jesus and dying for the faith. We are forever trying to condition our service to Christ on what others are or are not doing for the heavenly realm. We give or withhold gifts on the basis of what others are giving. We go or refuse to go on the basis of whether they are going. We would do well to mark the words Jesus addressed to Peter: "What is that to you? Follow me!" (v. 22).

Once more we need to remember the effect of the Gospel on Jewish Christians facing expulsion from their synagogues for the faith. How would they have interpreted this passage? Surely they would have heard in it the warning we have heard—to follow Christ faithfully without making the behavior of others the model for our own actions. Some Christians who read the text were actually facing death for Christ. They were not to hesitate because others were not put in the same situation. Their devotion was to Christ, not to some kind of moral consensus.

"Suppose," Jesus said, in effect, "I said to John, 'You stay right here until I return for you.' Would that make any difference in what I have asked you to do? No. I have told you to follow me. You have said you love me. Now follow me!"

This is as close as the Gospel of John comes to talking about the Second Coming of Christ. Its emphasis is on the constant union of believers with Jesus and the Father, not on a visible return of Jesus to earth. That is the point of the appearance narratives in the Fourth Gospel: Jesus comes to his followers as they worship and eat the eucharistic meal. They are not to pine for the end of the world and a new age. A new age dawned with the coming of Jesus and the imparting of his Spirit. Eternal life is a possession of all who believe in his name.

PRAYER

Guilty, Lord. I am guilty of having waited to see what others would do for you. What if you had waited for someone else to love me and die for me? Forgive me as you forgave Peter, and use me in whatever way you wish, for your name's sake. Amen.

THE FINAL WORD

$\mathcal{W}$e come at last to the second, final conclusion of the Gospel. "This is the disciple who is testifying to these things and has written them," it says, "and we know that his testimony is true" (v. 24). The "we" suggests that at least this passage, if not the entire twenty-first chapter, was written by an editor. His reference to John is in the third person: "his testimony is true."

Perhaps this writer was one of John's disciples, and, in ruminating on the stories of Jesus he had heard John tell, he decided that the ones in chapter 21 should be added to the Gospel originally written or dictated by John himself. Therefore, he appended the narratives of the fishing expedition, the meal at the seashore, the commissioning of Peter, and Peter's asking what John was to do. And then, in verse 25, he imitated John's original conclusion in 20:30-31.

Again we are told that Jesus did countless wonders—too many to put in any book. But what wonders we have seen in this book! Water turned to wine, blind men given sight, lame persons made to walk, a dead man raised. The risen Christ appearing to his disciples, displaying his wounds, and causing a skeptic like Thomas to cry out, "My Lord and my God!" What more could anyone ask?

The author had been confronted by the problem of Jewish Christians' deserting the faith because of new rules excluding them from the synagogues. He wanted to remind them of the essentials of the faith, and to do so in such a compelling manner that they reaffirmed their belief in Jesus as the Messiah. So he showed them what it meant that God, the eternal Word, had become flesh and dwelt among us. The old religion was totally inadequate beside him. He was the bread of life; a fountain of living water; the way, the truth, and the life; the good shepherd; the doorway of the sheep; the true vine; the resurrection and the life. He was one with the Father, and he wanted to keep all the Father had given him in perfect unity with them. To this end, he had sent his Advocate, his Spirit, among them to teach and guide them after he had his hour of glory and returned to be with the Father. How could anyone leave the Christian faith after being reminded of all this?

We live in a tough world, too, where people daily desert the faith. Therefore, the Gospel is as meaningful to us as it was to its original readers. And it is to be hoped that we, like Thomas, will come through our doubts to fall down before Christ and exclaim, "My Lord and my God!" If we do, we will fulfill the promise of Jesus in 20:29: "Blessed are those who have not seen and yet have come to believe."

PRAYER

How wonderful, Lord, was the witness of John! He has made me see and feel and understand things I could never have known without him. Grant that I, in turn, may be the kind of witness he was, and share your life-giving presence with my world. For you are the resurrection and the life, and there is no other one like you, or will ever be. Amen.